RACIAL CROSSINGS

Damon Ieremia Salesa is an Associate Professor of Pacific Studies at the University of Auckland.

Racial Crossings

Race, Intermarriage, and the Victorian British Empire

DAMON IEREMIA SALESA

OXFORD
UNIVERSITY PRESS

Great Clarendon Street, Oxford, OX2 6DP,
United Kingdom

Oxford University Press is a department of the University of Oxford.
It furthers the University's objective of excellence in research, scholarship,
and education by publishing worldwide.

Oxford is a registered trade mark of Oxford University Press
in the UK and in certain other countries

First published 2011
First published in paperback 2013

British Library Cataloguing in Publication Data

Data available

Library of Congress Cataloging in Publication Data

Data available

ISBN 978–0–19–960415–9 (hbk)
ISBN 978–0–19–967374–2 (pbk)

Acknowledgements

The past should always humble us. Certainly writing this book, and studying these pasts, has humbled me. Knowing the lives that came before and speaking of them is a great burden and a great responsibility: it has also been a great privilege. Kia māhaki: I know this, and I have tried to conduct myself properly. For my failings I ask forbearance.

The present has humbled me no less. The generosity and knowledge of others has been given more freely and generously than I deserve, and the payment for this now seems meager. But it is all I have, and so I give it.

This book began as a thesis at Oxford University, and those debts remain large. Megan Vaughan kindly picked up a stray student and saw me through to the end. Other faculty were equally generous: William Beinart, Judith Brown, John Darwin, and especially Nancy Leys Stepan, who provided much needed early guidance. But Oxford was a fortunate place for me because of the company of other wonderful students of empire: Jo Duffy, Andrew Fairweather-Tall, Anselm Hagedorn, Merata Kawharu, Melanie Newton, Jeremy Osborn, Simon Potter, Paul Tapsell, Oloya Tebere, and Ruth Watson. I know I have heavy intellectual and personal debts to Mark Hickford, Zoë Laidlaw, Helen Tilley, and Damen Ward: it is written here, and I hope that they can see it in this book.

I was my good fortune to have landed at the University of Michigan, Ann Arbor, a haven for innovative and critical scholarship of empires, race and history. My thanks to everyone—faculty and students—who has shared knowledge and time with me. Special thanks to Paulina Alberto, Matt Briones, Kathleen Canning, Rita Chin, Josh Cole, Jay Cook, Matt Countryman, Phil Deloria, Greg Dowd, Geoff Eley, Julie Ellison, Dena Goodman, Jesse Hoffnung-Garskoff, Kali Israel, Sue Juster, Mary Kelley, Val Kivelson, Matt Lassiter, Barbara Metcalfe, Farina Mir, Ian Moyer, Leslie Pincus, Sonya Rose, Ann Stoler, Tom Trautmann, and Penny Von Eschen. I owe much to my Michigan Asian/Pacific Islander American Studies colleagues: Tina Delisle, Scott Kurashige, Emily Lawsin, Susan Najita, Sarita See, Amy Ku'uleialoha Stillman and, especially, Vince Diaz. The Great Ocean is a way away, but we still see it.

At other institutions Tony Ballantyne, Antoinette Burton, Catherine Hall, Chris Hilliard, Maya Jasanoff, Miranda Johnson, Paul Kramer, Philippa Levine, Alan Ward, and especially Nick Thomas all gave much needed assistance and time. In New Zealand, friends, mentors, and teachers continue to give of their knowledge, time and support: especially Dame Judith Binney, David Colquhoun, and the staff of the Alexander Turnbull Library, Raewyn Dalziel, Derek Dow, Linda Bryder, Huni Fifita, Brett Graham, Hugh Laracy, Malama Meleisea, Matt Melvin, Hazel Petrie, Barry Rigby, I'uogafa Tuagalu, Charlie Tu'u, and Al Wendt.

This book argues for the grounded and family natures of politics and ideas in the 1800s, but it has taught me no less about these things in my own life and work. To my parents, Tusanilefaia'ao Ieremia and Yvonne Joy, to my wife Jenny, my daughters Mahalia and Esmae, and my siblings Shane Akerei, Situfu Jordan, Fialogo Toaiva, and Leilani Esmae Sieni, I owe more than everything. Fa'afetai tele lava! Malo 'aupito! My debts to all of my family—Aiolupo, Aoina, Bratton, Latu, Salesa, and Toalepaiali'i— are marked on, and between, each line. Ralf Bratton, Toalepai Si'ueva, Rev. Salesa Eteuati, Lilomaiava Pau, Sala Aoina, Iko Toalepaiali'i, Jeanette Skippy Patuwai, all saw this begin, but not end. You are remembered.

The histories presented here do not belong to me, even as I belong to them. Stumbling in the 'smoke of events', I have struggled to honour these ancestors, to treat them each with respect and dignity, to see them clearly, and to see them critically. In this I see my own failings, but I hope they are of ability, not aroha/alofa, or commitment. I have tried to be tika. Our ancestors did not always agree, and neither will we. I find encouragement in these words of Tawhiao:

> Ko tahi te kohao o te ngira e kuhuna e au te miro ma, te miro pango, te miro whero.

Ia manuia!

Contents

Key Māori Terms and Concepts

Long vowels are not marked in quotations unless indicated in the original text.

Aroha	Love, compassion
Hapū	Clan
Hāwhe kāehe	'Half-caste(s)': a transliteration of the English, if not a direct equivalent
Iwi	Largest scale descent group, 'tribe'
Kāinga	Community, village, settlement, residence
Kāwanatanga	'Governorship', a critical term in the *te Reo* text of the Treaty of Waitangi
Kīngitanga	The King Movement, centred on the Waikato and with beginnings in the 1850s (see Chapter 5)
Mana	Power, prestige, authority, control, 'psychic force', spiritual power, charisma. For a fuller discussion of the divine dimensions at work, see Māori Marsden, 'God, Man and Universe: a Maori View', in Michael King, (ed.), *Te Ao Hurihuri: Aspects of Maoritanga* (Auckland, 1992)
Māori / Tangata Māori	Ordinary person, indigenous person to New Zealand (see Introduction)
Pā	A fortified settlement, fortress, typically with earthworks and palisades
Pākehā	Foreigner, stranger, white person (see Introduction)
Pākehā Māori	Foreigner, stranger, or white person living as a part of indigenous families and communities
Rangatira	'Chief', a leader, a person of *mana*
Rangatiratanga	'Chieftainship': a critical term in the *te Reo* text of the Treaty of Waitangi
Takawaenga	Mediator, go-between, intermediary (see Conclusion)
Tangata Whenua	People/person of the Land, used here interchangeably with 'indigenous person' (see Introduction)
te Reo	The Language: the Maori language, the shared language of Tangata Whenua which has several dialects
Tiriti o Waitangi	The text of the Treaty of Waitangi in te Reo/Maori language (1840)
Whakapapa	Genealogy, lineage, 'the principle of descent' (see Chapter 3)

Whānau	Family, in a way that accords with the Pākehā and anthropological sense of 'extended family'
Whanaunga	Relative, kin, relation
Whanaungatanga	Family relationships, kinship, sense of family connection

Introduction: The Problem of Racial Crossing

It is surprising how often, after closer investigation, the Victorians seem not as 'Victorian' as we imagine. As good an example of this as any is the 'crossing' of races—different races associating, liaising, reproducing, marrying or consorting. Almost intuitively we might expect that in this most imperial of ages, its most imperial of people, the British, would be set against such things. Despite expectations that everywhere there would be efforts to punish race crossing, to condemn it, to exorcise and legislate against it, this was rarely the case. After the abolition of slavery (1834), one will find few laws that do this in the British Empire. With the exception of a few, largely unsuccessful, attempts to regulate concubinage amongst colonial officials, there were few attempts to outlaw interracial marriages between the abolition of slavery and the rise of apartheid in South Africa (which was by that time a self-governing dominion). And most of these efforts, such as those in South Australia, were specific, local and often temporary.

This is not to say that the British and their colonies were unconcerned with racial crossing. On the contrary, throughout the nineteenth century race crossing was considered a serious and recurrent problem—it was just not a simple one. In various parts of the Empire these years were filled with black and yellow 'perils', all kinds of fears and controversies, as well as a kaleidoscope of fixations, books, studies and discussions that were driven by one or another kind of racial crossing. These were not matters that could be easily banished by blunt laws, simple declarations, or spuriously engineered ideas, nor could they be controlled or ordered by policy or official fiat. Interest in racial crossing did not always manifest blatantly, and was as often chronic as it was acute, insinuated into policy and other techniques of governmental and social management. The complexity of all that came to overlay and underpin the practices, discourses and experiences of race crossing is richly revealing of British, imperial and colonial histories.

Though capable of being described or classified, the relevance, forms and meanings of race crossing differed from one locale to another. In many colonies, and in Britain, many people understood that race crossing, in some sense, had a centrality to important developments—even if what that centrality was, or meant, was contested. Yet racial crossings were not intrinsically troublesome to colonialism. To be sure, it was common for racial crossings to be seen as challenges, threats or difficulties. But in many instances racial crossings were seen as solutions or benefits, strategies *of* colonialism not challenges *to* it, improvements rather than difficulties or quandaries. At different moments in different places, racial crossing meant widely variant, even contradictory things.

As a result there was not a singular or universal predicament of race crossing, no reiterating history of development, no unified terminology, nor a common set of circumstances. Though many scholars wrote as if there was such a singularity (some historians still do), and sought to construct some equivalencies between different situations of racial crossings, or define some theoretical constant, any specific historical investigation seems only to put this to rest. The differences are too important or too large, the political, social and cultural landscapes—and, of course, the individuals—too different. Even the vocabulary of these situations was nuanced and particular. Mixed marriages in the nineteenth-century Cape Colony, for instance, were not simply John Smith and Pocahontas moved, revisited, updated and multiplied. Intimacy between different people of different races was always, in some way, idiosyncratic. This makes it even more important to understand why these disparate matters were lumped together, seen as comparable, and understood in relation to each other. Why would it be expected that a 'half-caste Maori' was in some sense similar or comparable to a Canadian Metis? How, and why, were these variant practices and histories of racial crossing in the Empire fashioned as a coherent problem?

The problem of racial crossing was never restricted to any one easily bounded location, colony or nation, nor one set of actors, events or developments. It was multitudinous and distributed: racial crossing was evidently a problem not only in the colonies, but in domestic British discourses. Metropolitan discourses commonly arrived at the topic on very different trajectories to those produced from colonial encounters. Whether attempting to explain human variety, interrogating questions of species difference, or pursuing projects as different as Reform and Salvation, for much of the nineteenth century race crossing was a surprisingly common domestic theme. It was a mainstay of writing about the colonies and Empire, as well as in the circles of ethnologists, anthropologists, theologians, physicians and natural historians. But concern with racial crossings drew attention not only from intellectuals and scholars explicitly concerned with themes of race, nor just imperial officials, but different kinds of observers, writers and 'participants'. Economists, historians, geologists, classicists—as we might call them now—all had their investments in questions of race and what happened when these races met. At any rate the interest of very different people in the subject, with such different reasons and reasoning, points to a compelling and recurrent concern: an interest in racial crossing with resonance and consequence that invites further study.

By the 1830s, racial crossing was becoming established as a widely evident concern. However, in the decades following, a conjuncture of discursive changes, colonial practices and colonial experiences helped fashion this loosely related set of concerns into a more bundled problem. This was in part precipitated by earlier developments, not least (though certainly not only) those in 'scientific' discourses beginning around the turn of the nineteenth century. In these domains various definitions of race had begun to push at the boundaries of central understandings, in particular challenging notions of 'species'. At the time, hybrid animals—those produced through crosses of different species—were generally thought to be uniformly sterile. A range of influential scholars, from John Ray to Comte de Buffon had long seized upon this infertility to prove the distinction between species.[1] The typical example of this was the crossing of the horse and donkey, which resulted in the mule or hinny, neither of which could usually produce offspring. This was generally interpreted as a special endowment to maintain the order of nature, and by the first part of the nineteenth century the hybrid creature was established as a way of identifying and defining species difference. The natural order was invested with political, religious and other significances, so the difference was, as we will see, never solely about the subject at hand.

For much of the eighteenth century the crossing of human races and the mixing of species were not then seen as analogous or similar, and 'hybridity' was not a term directly applied to people. This shift was a slow one, led in large part by writers such as Henry Home, Lord Kames, and the Jamaican planter Edward Long, who began in the 1770s publicly to argue that the human species was not single in origin and character, but multiple.[2] Though not the first or only ones to make this suggestion, they

---

[1] John Ray, *The Wisdom of God Manifested in the Works of the Creation* (London, 1691), p. 219; Comte de Buffon, *Barr's Buffon: Buffon's Natural History*, (ed.) James Smith Barr, 10 vols., (London, 1810).

[2] Henry Home, Lord Kames, *Sketches of the History of Man*, 4 vols., enlarged edn., (London, 1779); Edward Long, *The History of Jamaica*, 3 vols., (London, 1774).

were amongst the most important proponents of a view that appeared to challenge the fundamentals of the biblical account of human origin and early human history.[3] By the middle of the nineteenth century this new belief, 'polygenism' as it was called, was still controversial but was in much wider circulation and many elements were being entertained, often in unlikely places. There was little doubt that in Britain the biblical ortho- doxy, or 'monogenism', continued as the majority and orthodox view; one 1848 work weighed over one hundred and fifty 'learned and eminent men' against seventeen polygenists.[4] Yet the significance of polygenist thought had become clear: not only had it posed new questions, and offered very different, unorthodox answers, it had reinvigorated the study of human origins and differences. If, as polygenists argued, human races were as different as species, racial intermixture paralleled the crossing of animal species—it was unnatural, degenerate and unsustainable. This new challenge focused attention on racial crossings, which were now a proving ground for debates about humans, species, races and the natural and divine. The outcome and success of racial crossings could clarify the character of differences between races: were these differences graduated and essentially minor—within the family of man? Or were these racial differ- ences fundamental and enduring—differences of origin, and of species? Though formal polygenists remained relatively scarce, and it was a position that remained in many respects disreputable, there was no doubt that the debate reoriented and intensified scrutiny of racial crossings.

The contours of these elite intellectual and scholarly racial discourses were critical, but they were only one, comparatively orderly, set of a congeries of discourses. This elite story was once unfamiliar, but the rejuvenation of the historiography of race has made it less so. The works of Nancy Stepan, Stephen Jay Gould and George Stocking Jr guided much of this renewed interest in these questions.[5] This narrative now pervades the recent historiography of empire, although the work of these scholars was directed towards intellectual and disciplinary history, not that of empire. As a result the focus was, unsurprisingly, mostly on metropoli- tan locations and developments, and by and large on metropolitan elites. Even in Stocking's work, which engaged the contemporary rise of anthro- pology and British Empire, the Empire figures mostly as a field of

[3] Genesis 9: 19. See George W. Stocking, Jr, *Race, Culture and Evolution: Essays in the History of Anthropology* (New York, 1968).

[4] Thomas Smyth, *The Unity of the Human Races proved to be the Doctrine of Scripture, Reason and Science* (Edinburgh, 1851), pp. 58–64.

[5] George W. Stocking, *Victorian Anthropology* (London, 1987); id., *Race Culture and Evolution*; Nancy Stepan, *The Idea of Race in Science: Great Britain 1800–1960* (London, 1982); Stephen Jay Gould, *The Mismeasure of Man* (New York, 1981).

collection, while processing this 'data' takes place centrally amongst a small group of experts. This is an approach that can be broadened to include the workings and discourses of government, the networks of discourse and people that spread across the Empire, even those that these discourses increasingly claimed. Moreover, as historians such as Roger Cooter and Adrian Desmond have shown, there were critical sites and agents of discourses that were outside these elites, as amongst the 'masses' were vibrant intellectual, scientific and publishing markets.[6] So although the 'experts' undoubtedly had important roles to play in the shaping of racial discourses, as well as in shaping the Empire and its categories of rule, these processes involved far broader constituencies, which included and crossed different classes, and involved multiple places across the Empire, at times even incorporating those who were colonized.

To better comprehend the variegated and distributed qualities of racial and colonial discourses, it is useful to be open to the diversity of those concerned with it. The recent surge in works concerned with race and its history, and the continuing influence of some early works of historiography, has had the effect of producing what might informally be called a 'canon' of nineteenth century racial texts. This accords prominence to marginal works (such as Robert Knox's *Races of Man*) and has sidelined or overlooked vitally important works (like those by Thomas Arnold, Herman Merivale, or those by key geologists or political radicals).[7] It has also privileged published and non-official texts, to the great detriment of private correspondence and other writings, especially the writings of officials. Race, and more specifically the problem of racial crossing, was promiscuous, and could be found in more diverse locations than such a 'canon' acknowledges. John Morgan, a missionary and schoolteacher; Wiremu Patara Te Tuhi, editor of the Māori King's newspaper; Alexander Walker, a British radical writer and medical doctor; Montague Hawtrey, an English vicar; Maria Aminta Maning, a 'half-caste' woman; Thomas Arnold, historian and schoolteacher; George Grey, colonial governor—

---

[6] Roger Cooter, *The Cultural Meaning of Popular Science Phrenology and the Organization of Consent in Nineteenth-Century Britain* (Cambridge, 1984); Adrian Desmond, *The Politics of Evolution* (Chicago, 1989).

[7] Robert Knox, *The Races of Man* (London, 1850); Thomas Arnold, *The Effects of Distant Colonization on the Parent State; a Prize Essay Recited in the Theatre at Oxford, June 7, 1815* (Oxford, 1815); id., *An Inaugural Lecture on the Study of Modern History* (Oxford, 1841); Herman Merivale, *Introduction to a Course of Lectures on Colonization and Colonies* (London, 1839); Charles Lyell, *Principles of Geology: or, the Modern Changes of the Earth and its Inhabitants, Considered as Illustrative of Geology*, 3 vols., 6th edn., (London, 1840); Alexander Walker, *Intermarriage; or the Mode in which, and the Causes why, Beauty, Health and Intellect Result from Certain Unions, and Deformity, Disease and Insanity, from Others*, 2nd edn., (London, 1841); Patrick Matthew, *Emigration Fields* (Edinburgh, 1839).

these are just a few of those who took seriously the problem of racial crossing. Their impact was uneven, often localized or particular, but it was also frequently important and sometimes pivotal. Historians now generally take seriously the lower classes and the colonized as historical actors, but (for variant reasons) often consider them less seriously as thinkers and makers of discourse. Much as Chris Hilliard has revealed a 'literary history from below' and Adrian Desmond a 'radical science', there is a history of race 'from below', and from different sides, and inside out.[8] Such histories are certainly uneven, and may not always be visible, relevant or strong: but they at least trouble assumptions about elites as makers and others as receptacles of discourse—a belief that maps suspiciously close to the thoughts and assumptions of Victorian governing elites themselves.

The complexity of the problem of racial crossing makes even the choice of terminology difficult. Here the attempt is to encompass the problem through the use of the term racial 'crossing', which was an inclusive 'umbrella' term. Commonly used at the time, it is preferred for a couple of reasons: first, it was never associated with one or other 'schools' of thought or particular arguments or assertions (such as terms like 'hybridity' or 'mongrelization'); and second, and perhaps most importantly, because it was often used at the time, much as it is used here, as a kind of general descriptor—synonymous with 'mixture' and 'intermixture' which were also often used at the time. 'Crossing' encompasses a larger field of understanding than some similar terms, such as 'intermarriage', which implies a particular kind of institutionalized conjugal relationship, even though it was commonly used in situations where 'marriage' as such had not occurred or was seemingly not possible—as between plants.

Differences in the vocabulary of race crossing indexed how the problem connected various locations. Many terms were born of foreign or colonial roots. 'Eurasian' was a word of choice in India, and this is also where the ubiquitous 'half-caste' seems to have originated. 'Mulatto' derived from the Spanish word for mule; 'quadroon' and 'octoroon' came from Spanish America via the Caribbean; Métis and Métissage from French. These words had been inherited or trafficked into the British colonies, which in addition produced its own varieties, from Euronesian to Anglo-Indian or Eurasian, from 'Coloured-Persons', 'Half breeds' to 'Mixed race' and even 'European' or 'local European', some of which were in local usage, others of which circulated more widely.[9] Newer technical vocabularies

---

[8] Desmond, *The Politics of Evolution*; Chris Hilliard, *To Exercise Our Talents: The Democratization of Writing in Britain* (Cambridge, 2006).
[9] For a contemporary discussion see Thomas Hodgkin's critique of these terms and the problems of terminology, Wellcome Institute Library, London, Hodgkin Papers, WMS/

(such as 'racial hybrids' and 'racial hybridity') were consequently circulating in a complex, changing and spatially variegated lexicon. There were so many terms available, and they could quickly change. The famous ethnologist James Cowles Prichard was certain that people could not be hybrids and refused to label them as such; yet only two years after his death in 1848 his closest follower Robert Gordon Latham had begun using the term 'hybridism'.[10] These terms, concepts and languages were variable and relatively unstable, and could change dramatically, and relatively quickly, whether from place to place, or over the years.

Particular locations where race crossing was of obvious importance attracted special attention. By the 1860s many of these populations in the British Empire had become fixtures in narratives on racial crossing, whether the 'Cape Coloureds', the Métis of Canada, the Eurasians of India, the half-castes in New Zealand, or the smallest and perhaps most fetishized population, the descendants of the *Bounty* mutineers discovered on Pitcairn Island. These fixations often proved very durable, and most histories of racial crossing have stemmed from precisely such local contexts where a well-marked local population of racially mixed people has been historically prominent.[11] These kinds of works have usually picked one particular location, and written of it within traditions of national or regional historiography. The best of these works provide subtle, nuanced and informed analysis, rich in detail and instructive in the humbling extent of the British Empire. But the tendency of such works to approach their subjects more or less as isolates means imperial, transnational or transcolonial developments are often ignored, minimized or packaged in ways that make them uniform and stagnant rather than as integrated in networks of exchange or connection.

These 'local' histories of racial crossing (though the 'local' is often expansive) have increasingly converged with the work of a variety of postcolonial and feminist scholars. In the past two decades postcolonial critics, theorists and historians have been particularly drawn to 'hybridity' and other forms of racial, cultural and social mixing, for a variety of reasons, and perhaps not least due to a present they understand as hybrid. This has led to a new life, and a new salience for all kinds of concern in

PP/HO/D/D232, Thomas Hodgkin, 'On the Progress of Ethnology', fos. 51–2; for a later, ironic turn, see Cedric Dover, *Half-Caste* (London, 1937).

[10] Though to describe only what he called 'extreme intermixture'; Robert Gordon Latham, *The Natural History of the Varieties of Man* (London, 1850), pp. 555–7.

[11] For example D.N. Sprague, *Canada and the Métis, 1869–1885* (Waterloo, 1988); Robert Ross, *Adam Kok's Griquas: A Study in the Development of Stratification in South Africa* (Cambridge, 1976); Gad J. Heuman, *Between Black and White: Race, Politics, and the Free Coloureds in Jamaica, 1792–1865* (Westport, 1981).

racial crossing, and in particular for the language of racial and cultural hybridity. Race mixing, racial crossing, interracialism, interracial intimacy have all joined hybridity as subjects, not only in the nineteenth century, but in the twentieth and twenty-first. The best of this work has proven trenchant, and has changed many of the questions central to their subjects. However, as Robert J.C. Young has shown, there are some serious problems with this project, not least in its re-employment of much of the nineteenth-century racist vocabulary.[12] The intersections between feminist and postcolonial historians has proven particularly fruitful, where rigorous historical and archival research has been married with new questions and analyses of power, ones that have not only been interested in how racial crossing can unmask the production and opera- tions of colonialism and race, but in domestic spaces and formations— the intimate relations of households and families where racial crossings were lived and experienced.[13] These works successfully manage different dimensions: holding local and imperial, transnational and transcolonial simultaneously in view.

Evidently, the myriad connections and mobilities that constituted the British Empire ensured the problem of racial crossing was never simply a local problem. Recent conceptions of the British Empire, drawing on a complicated and contradictory genealogy, have evolved to pay these mobilities greater attention. Catherine Hall, in tandem with the work of others such as Ann Stoler and Fred Cooper, has led the questioning of prevalent understandings of centre/periphery, calling for their 'demoli- tion'.[14] The recent work of Hall, as well as those of historians such as Tony Ballantyne, Antoinette Burton, Philippa Levine, Thomas Holt,

---

[12] Robert J.C. Young, *Colonial Desire: Hybridity in Theory, Culture and Race* (London, 1995); also Avtar Brah and Annie Coombes, (eds.), *Hybridity and its Discontents* (London, 2000).

[13] Katherine Ellinghaus, *Taking Assimilation to Heart: Marriages of White Women and Indigenous Men in the United States and Australia, 1887–1937* (Lincoln, 2006); Sylvia Van Kirk, *'Many Tender Ties': Women in Fur-Trade Society in Western Canada, 1670–1870* (Winnipeg, 1981); Adele Perry, *On the Edge of Empire: Gender, Race, and the Making of British Columbia 1849–1871* (Toronto, 2001); Henry Reynolds, *Nowhere People: How International Race Thinking Shaped Australia's Identity* (Camberwell, 2005); C.J. Hawes, *Poor Relations: The Making of a Eurasian Community in British India 1773–1833* (Rich- mond, 1996); Kuntala Lahiri Dutt, *In Search of a Homeland: Anglo-Indians and McClukie- gunge* (Calcutta, 1990), pp. 27–35; Kenneth Ballhatchet, *Race, Sex and Class Under the Raj: Imperial Attitudes and their Critics, 1793–1905* (London, 1980); Indrani Chatterjee, 'Colouring Subalternity: Slaves, Concubines and Social Orphans in Early Colonial India', *Subaltern Studies*, X (1999), pp. 49–97.

[14] Catherine Hall, *White, Male, and Middle Class: Explorations in Feminism and History* (Cambridge, 1992), p. 25. Frederick Cooper and Ann Laura Stoler, 'Between Metropole and Colony: Rethinking a Research Agenda', in Frederick Cooper and Ann Laura Stoler, (eds.), *Tensions of Empire: Colonial Cultures in a Bourgeois World* (Berkeley, 1997), p. 15.

Alan Lester and Zoë Laidlaw, have refined this, and demonstrated the ways in which it is useful for understanding the nineteenth-century British Empire as a collection of networks or circuits or webs.[15] These studies elucidate how the government and comprehension of empire was networked, not only with official circuits of personnel, policy, law and correspondence, but also with extra-official ones that were commercial and religious, scholarly and professional, personal and familial. This is an understanding that this book shares and draws upon. These networks were cultural artefacts, historically situated and spatially and socially variegated. They did not indiscriminately connect: in Britain, for instance, what was drawn into these imperial circuits is what John Darwin has suggested were 'domestic bridgeheads'—colonies, you might say, of imperial interest in Britain.[16] 'Imperial networks', as Laidlaw reminds us, 'connected people first, and places second.'[17] But if networks connected people, what activated these networks and invested them with meaning was discourse.

Nineteenth-century imperial networks changed dramatically, but fundamentally differ from those of the present. They were anchored in their own specific geographies, technologies and temporalities. It may be true that today, as Antonio Negri and Michael Hardt observe, 'we see networks everywhere we look', and that the 'network has become a common form that tends to define our ways of understanding the world and acting in it.'[18] 'Network' is best used carefully, particularly as a critical metaphor, but what Negri and Hardt missed is that in the context of empire is no simple anachronism. It is worth noting that the rise of the use of the word 'network' in its 'social network' sense was entangled with empire: the *Oxford English Dictionary*'s first recorded use in this way (1884) is in a biography of Charles Gordon.[19] Equally, the centrality of networks

Also, Nicholas Dirks, 'Introduction', in his, (ed.), *Colonialism and Culture* (Ann Arbor, 1992), pp. 1–25.

[15] Tony Ballantyne, *Orientalism and Race: Aryanism in the British Empire* (Houndmills, 2002); Antoinette Burton, *At the Heart of the Empire: Indians and the Colonial Empire in Late-Victorian Britain* (Berkeley, 1998); Philippa Levine, *Prostitution, Race, and Politics* (London, 2003); Thomas Holt, *The Problem of Freedom: Race, Labor, and Politics in Jamaica and Britain, 1832–1938* (Baltimore, 1992); Alan Lester, *Imperial Networks: Creating Identities in Nineteenth-Century South Africa and Britain* (London, 2001); Zoë Laidlaw, *Colonial Connections, 1815–45: Patronage, the Information Revolution and Colonial Government* (Manchester, 2005).

[16] John Darwin, 'Imperialism and the Victorians: the Dynamics of Territorial Expansion', *English Historical Review*, 112 (1997), pp. 614–42.

[17] Laidlaw, *Colonial Connections*, p. 35.

[18] Michael Hardt and Antonio Negri, *Multitude: War and Democracy in the Age of Empire* (New York, 2004), p. 142.

[19] Archibald Forbes, *Chinese Gordon: A Succinct Record of His Life* (London, 1884), p. 140.

reiterates the ancestry of the British Empire to our own world, as well as the enduring relevance and efficacy of networks as a 'form of organization' of material, people and knowledge. Moreover, though these historical actors came to use the word 'network' only later, they shared similar understandings about 'connections' (as Laidlaw highlights), 'circles', 'ties' and 'relations', both spoken and unspoken. This should not overstate the ubiquity and eminence of networks, which for all the connectivity they inscribed, were defined as much by their disconnections and unevenness, their ruptures, absences and limitations. The problem of racial crossing dramatizes these discursive movements, so connections can be plumbed, and disconnections appreciated. At times racial crossings, intersections and disconnections also illuminate other, even competing—often indigenous or subjugated—forms. These forms sometimes opposed colonial and imperial networks, sometimes were juxtaposed with them, other times intersected them.

It is worth stressing the materiality of these discourses, which were physically located, occurring in actual places and not divorced from social practices. Discourses were not ethereal or disembodied, but occurred in actual places, whether in parliaments, the Colonial Office, missions and scientific societies, or in newspapers, journals, to the readerships that publishing and writing constructed. As James Epstein has reminded us, 'the production of meaning is never independent of the pragmatics of social space.'[20] Such a caution can be found in the fate of a multi-volume set of *Milner's Church History* that early missionaries took to New Zealand. Missionaries brought the volumes as spiritual sustenance, but the pages ended up in the hands of a local indigenous leader who used the pages to prime his people's firearms.[21] Evidently books were not intangible vessels for transferring discourse, but were subject to the usual strictures of life, within the rhythms of ordinary existence. Indeed, these discursive encounters can be likened to the meeting of people, and regarded as—to use the phrase of Greg Dening and D.J. Mulvaney—'encounters in place'.[22] Appreciating the 'encounters in place' which animated particular discourses reveals how they were contestable, sensitive to locality and time, creative and specific. Discourses were connected by and circulated through networks, but these networks did not do so freely and promiscuously, but constrained and arranged them, circulating them in certain

[20] James Epstein, *In Practice: Studies in the Language and Culture of Popular Politics in Modern Britain* (Stanford, 2003), p. 109.

[21] Marianne Williams, journal, 12 January 1824: Caroline Fitzgerald (ed.), *Letters from the Bay of Islands: The Story of Marianne Williams* (Phoenix Mill, 2004), pp. 79–80.

[22] D.J. Mulvaney, *Encounters in Place: Outsiders and Aboriginal Australians 1606–1985* (St Lucia, 1989); Greg Dening, *Performances* (Chicago, Chicago).

ways, and depositing them into certain places. Nor did they work evenly upon people, whose differences informed the ways in which these discursive encounters played out.

Appreciating these 'encounters in place' emphasizes the powerful importance of the many locations, both colonial and metropolitan, where discourse was articulated. Explicitly political places, such as Parliament, councils and courts, are instructive in the kinds of class, gender and racial differences that organized not only the consumption of, but participation and access to, particular discourses. This was as apparent in colonial societies as in metropolitan ones. Schools, newspapers, missions, bureaucracies, and the many other critical sites for colonial discourse, reflected a similar discipline. But spaces of articulation were also ones of contest and challenge. The excluded jostled for entry into these spaces, or co-opted their forms; they argued, ignored and refused. Women demanded to hear, and then be heard, at the Ethnological Society of London. In New Zealand, indigenous people petitioned government, occupied the pulpit, wrote letters to newspapers, even travelled to England for audiences with Victoria. But colonial circuits and discourses were never the only ones extant; there were many other discursive sites and networks. Rarely were they entirely separate. Those who sought to disrupt or enter places of colonial discourse met with varying degrees of success and efficacy. Colonial agents persistently strategized to dissemble or control indigenous networks, discourses and places of assembly, with similarly mixed results.

Colonial and imperial archives epitomize the struggles over discourse, place and power that structured the problem of racial crossing. The official archives, for instance, were places profoundly closed to those they sought to colonize. The appearance of such people in the archive was heavily controlled and regulated, was encoded in colonial taxonomies, and circulated through official networks and discourses. As both bodies of discourse and physical entities, colonial archives exerted enormous control over who might be archived and how: the illiterate, women, the lower classes, the 'unconnected' and the colonized, in particular, found themselves put into discourse, and they could not enter on their own terms. Others, too, even amongst metropolitan and colonial elites, were also subject to the careful regulation of archives: most requests for information and knowledge were denied, and access was strategically distributed as a means of power, patronage or privilege. Correspondence had to work its way through narrowly prescribed archival channels (all correspondence from the colonies had to be 'officially received' through colonial governors, for instance). These exclusions concentrated rather than circumscribed the power that the colonial archive exerted. The archives were conduits that guided and framed policy, organized and directed action, defined and disciplined space and people, authorized, legitimated and made illicit. 'Colonial conquest', as Nicholas Dirks has written, 'was about the production of an archive of (and for) colonial rule.'[23] Archives were not inert, mere records or remains of the past, but active in conditioning the present—as well as the histories that followed. These colonial archives held race as a fundamental principle, whether in organizing correspondence, framing statistics or apportioning jurisdiction.

Race added a dimension that allowed the specific and peculiar experiences of certain people and groups of people to transcend their immediate realms. Race was an archival principle, but it was more than that: a comparative dimension that made the Empire easier to archive, signify, consume, integrate and administer. In one telling example, a parliamentary committee folded the peoples of Southern Africa, North America, New Zealand, Australia and the Islands of the Pacific into the racial category of 'aborigine'.[24] This, as with other racial categorizations, produced commensurabilities that made certain administrative techniques and forms of knowledge transferable and mobile—in this case asserting the uniform fragility of these 'aborigines', and their need for 'protection', which had the prerequisite of colonial rule.[25] From otherwise disparate, complex, messy and peculiar situations one could now discover, or be directed towards, commensurabilities and common elements. These processes of commensurability enabled a quality of empire that Benedict Anderson and, following him, Cooper and Stoler have called 'modular'.[26]

The modular qualities of empires are particularly evident in imperial 'problems'—cohesive preoccupations that were widely shared. Across the British Empire the 'protection' of certain races was obviously one of these 'problems'; 'freedom' was another. Thomas Holt has provided a powerful account of the imperial and colonial concern with slavery and its attempts to end it.[27] Rather than seeing freedom as a localized development of 'abolition' or free labour, or as an abstraction promulgated at the imperial scale, or even as a singular moment of crisis, Holt recognizes freedom as a

[23] Nicholas Dirks, *Castes of Mind: Colonialism and the Making of Modern India* (Princeton, 2001), p. 107.
[24] Most accessibly, Aborigines Protection Society, *Report of the Parliamentary Select Committee, on Aboriginal Tribes, (British Settlements); Reprinted with Comments* (London, 1837).
[25] On the complicated origins of this Committee and Report see Zoë Laidlaw, '"Aunt Anna's Report": The Buxton Women and the Aborigines Select Committee, 1835–37', *Journal of Commonwealth and Imperial History*, 32:2 (2004), pp. 1–28.
[26] Benedict Anderson, *Imagined Communities: Reflections on the Origin and Spread of Nationalism*, 2nd edn., (London, 2001), e.g. p. 4; Cooper and Stoler, 'Between Metropole and Colony: Rethinking a Research Agenda', pp. 13–14.
[27] Holt, *The Problem of Freedom*.

problem that was widespread, enduring, multifarious, concrete and which worked out in multiple locations. The problem of freedom was, as he puts it, 'at once a problem in the social and economic reconstruction of the lives of freed people, a problem in British intellectual and political history, and a problem in race relations, colonialism and imperialism.'[28] Philippa Levine has shown, with similar cogency, how prostitution was a similarly imperial problem.[29] The problem of prostitution went far beyond sexual transactions: through the 'vector' of venereal disease, prostitution was to have profound and confounding effects, as women and other races were made targets of sexual and social regulation, not least through a series of Contagious Diseases Acts. These Acts proved highly contentious, and occasioned considerable social and political trouble, pushing 'the imperial government to the brink . . . on several occasions.'[30] Framing these concerns as problems appreciates their strong nodal qualities, their capacity to draw together or articulate (in Stuart Hall's sense) different discourses, people, networks and concerns.[31] These imperial problems were 'lumps'.[32]

Racial crossing remained an abiding problem through much of the nineteenth and well into the twentieth century. Part of this was due to the enduring conjuncture where racial crossing remained a cornerstone of the colonial management of races, a preoccupation of a number of discourses, and a lodestone in the thought and study of human variety. These convergent interests in racial crossing brought intellectual and scholarly concern into recurrent conversation with practice, power, and discourses of government. And although the students of racial crossings were inclined to overestimate its significance, there was no question that the problem was one of continuing importance that transected the different communities of interest. 'Are the causes which have overthrown the greatest of nations not to be resolved by the laws regulating the intermixture of the races of man', the anthropologist James Hunt asked in 1864. 'Does not the success of our colonisation depend on the deductions of our science?'[33]

*****

Recent attention given to the distribution and economy of colonial discourses, and not just their content, has reoriented received understandings of

---

[28] Holt, *The Problem of Freedom*, p. xxi.
[29] Levine, *Prostitution, Race and Politics.*   [30] Ibid., p. 328.
[31] Stuart Hall, 'Race, Articulation, and Societies Structured in Dominance', in *Sociological Theories: Racism and Colonialism* (Paris, 1980), pp. 305–345.
[32] Frederick Cooper, *Colonialism in Question: Theory, Knowledge, History* (Berkeley, 2005).
[33] James Hunt, 'The President's Address', *Journal of the Anthropological Society (JAS)*, 2 (1864), p. xciii.

empire and colonialism. A variety of historians have shown this by turning to locations where particular problems are unusually evident, intense or important. Holt and Catherine Hall turned to Jamaica to study the problems, respectively, of freedom and whiteness, Timothy Keegan analysed the development of a 'racial order' using South Africa, and Adele Perry used a focus on British Columbia to explore the problem of (amongst other things) frontier masculinity.[34] It is in this mode that this study turns to New Zealand. Most colonial locales had some engagement with the wider problem of racial crossing, but for New Zealand it was of particular importance. For one thing New Zealand was a privileged colony, a colony of settlement that was unusually well connected and well publicized. Not only was it the first major colony formally acquired during Queen Victoria's reign, but to many British politicians, businessmen, officials and settlers, New Zealand promised to be the 'Britain of the South', holding peculiar prospects for replicating the social and economic conditions of England. Certain features seemed to set it apart. It was a colony of settlement, but without convicts or a pre-existent settler population (such as the Boers or French-Canadians), initially partly driven by a joint-stock company, with a temperate climate, at the end of the longest emigration route in the world. The indigenous peoples already living in New Zealand were customarily seen as unusually advanced for 'aborigines', with great potential. Some asserted New Zealand as a chance for the redemption of empire and its ideals or practices, others as a place to make atonement, others still as a place for experimentation or great profit. Each of these understandings (as even this short list suggests) was referential—whether back to metropolitan Britain, or to other colonies on which New Zealand was supposed to improve or with which it could be contrasted. Discussions about, and policies of, racial crossing—evident in New Zealand from its very beginnings—were to prove durable and critical.

In New Zealand the problem of race crossing was to prove extraordinarily important to the wider practices of colonization, particularly through what became termed 'racial amalgamation'. This is a term familiar to students of New Zealand's nineteenth-century history, though it has been widely misunderstood. Its familiarity comes from Alan Ward's seminal work, *A Show of Justice: Racial 'Amalgamation' in Nineteenth-Century New Zealand*, which first posed the idea that certain forms of race crossing were central to New Zealand's nineteenth-century history. 'Racial amalgamation', as Ward established, was the central strategy of colonial government policy regarding

[34] Catherine Hall, *Civilizing Subjects: Metropole and Colony in the English Imagination, 1830–1867* (Oxford, 2002); id., *White, Male, and Middle Class*; Holt, *The Problem of Freedom*; Timothy J. Keegan, *Colonial South Africa and the Origins of the Racial Order* (Charlottesville, 1996); Perry, *On the Edge of Empire*.

indigenous people and groups in the nineteenth century. His work (first published in 1973) seemed to set the scene for subsequent studies of race crossing and native policy more generally, but almost none followed.[35] Ward's primary focus was the political dimension of 'racial amalgamation', but he was well aware that it also connoted what might now be called a 'biological' amalgamation (something some historians misunderstood).[36] Racial amalgamation, as this book further explores, was not simply an earlier incarnation of 'assimilation'. Ward observed that racial amalgamation was not only informed government policy and practice, but was directed at interpersonal, affective and sexual relations, although he wrote of them only briefly. This insight was then largely neglected until new postcolonial and feminist historians began to turn towards domestic and intimate domains with new energy.[37] Although Ward's study of racial amalgamation preceded the recent upsurge in studies of colonialism, race, sexuality and gender, when read alongside these it seems remarkably prescient.

The scarcity of attention given to racial crossing was not due to such concerns lying outside the traditional interests of New Zealand historians. Colonialism, in one way or another, has remained a prevailing theme in the historiography, 'race' has been the subject of a number of monographs and articles, and women, marriage and the family all found considerable historical attention at various points, for a variety of reasons.[38] But, as with other specific national or colonial histories, one of the results of adopting too narrow a frame was to truncate or disconnect subjects that needed to be understood in articulation. Keith Sorrenson, a pioneer and doyen of the

---

[35] Alan Ward, *A Show of Justice: Racial 'Amalgamation' in Nineteenth Century New Zealand*, revised edn., (Auckland, 1995 [1973]). Ward began, but did not finish, an investigation into half-castes; Alan Ward, personal communication.

[36] For example, Keith Sinclair, 'The Aborigines Protection Society and New Zealand: A Study in Nineteenth Century Opinion', Masters thesis, University of New Zealand, 1946, p. 72; K.R. Howe, *Race Relations, Australia and New Zealand: A Comparative Survey* (Wellington, 1977), p. 22.

[37] M.P.K. Sorrenson, 'Maori and Pakeha', in Geoffrey W. Rice, (ed.), *The Oxford History of New Zealand*, 2nd edn., (Auckland, 1992), pp. 152, 154, 162–5; M.P.K. Sorrenson, 'How to Civilize Savages: Some "Answers" From Nineteenth-Century New Zealand', *NZJH*, 9 (1975), pp. 97–110; Malcolm Nicolson, 'Medicine and racial politics: changing images of the New Zealand Maori in the nineteenth century', in David Arnold, (ed.), *Imperial Medicine and Indigenous Societies* (Manchester, 1988), pp. 66–104.

[38] Ian Wards, *The Shadow of the Land: a Study of British Policy and Racial Conflict in New Zealand 1832–1852* (Wellington, 1968); A.H. McLintock, *Crown Colony Government in New Zealand* (Wellington, 1958); John Stenhouse, '"A Disappearing Race Before We Came Here": Dr Alfred Kingcome Newman, the Dying Maori and Victorian Scientific Racism', *NZJH*, 30 (1996), pp. 123–140; Angela Ballara, *Proud to be White? A Survey of Pakeha Prejudice in New Zealand* (Auckland, 1986); David Pearson, *A Dream Deferred: the Origins of Ethnic Conflict in New Zealand* (Wellington, 1990).

historical study of race in this period, is an interesting example of this. Sorrenson made the most significant contributions in the later half of the twentieth century, writing several important articles and producing two monographs that establish the basic contours of racial ideas and scholarship amongst New Zealand-based intellectuals. These, however, focus on the twentieth and late-nineteenth centuries and isolate local developments from other transcolonial, transnational and international ones.[39] In his subsequent work Tony Ballantyne showed how this isolation was not one that characterized these racial scholars, and their own thinking about race—not least through 'Aryanism'—was ordinarily keyed into imperial and transcolonial dimensions. Even when New Zealand-based scholars appeared to be working most in local registers, larger webs of discourse shaped their understanding.[40] This meant that even in the apparently distant and remote colony of New Zealand, colonials found not just another native race, nor just 'Māori', but 'Aryan Māori'. New Zealand history was never as disconnected, nor as provincial, as it has sometimes been taken to be.

To be sure, most of the literature that has taken up questions of racial intermarriage and other kinds of interracial intimacy have tended to stress the uniqueness or exceptionality of New Zealand. In these works New Zealand has been figured as a place of unusual beneficence and toleration for interracial relationships. The literature itself, however, is not large. Disproportionately the historiography is concentrated in biographical studies and in regional histories, something that seems to have been long true in Canada and South Africa, as well as other places. The apparently transgressive nature of these interracial relations—though, as is argued here, they were not as transgressive as has been assumed—means that the subject is also amenable to certain sensational or titillating modes of historiography.[41] In more traditional genres of history the New Zealand field has also seen small studies of intermarriage by Graham Butterworth and, more importantly, by Atholl Anderson.[42] Yet, in the past few decades of historiography, in which New Zealand has claimed the attention of a large number of historians, there have been very few

---

[39] Sorrenson, 'How to Civilize Savages'; M.P.K. Sorrenson, *Maori Origins and Migrations: the Genesis of some Pakeha Myths and Legends* (Auckland, 1979); M.P.K. Sorrenson, *Manifest Duty: the Polynesian Society over 100 Years* (Auckland, 1982).

[40] Ballantyne, *Orientalism and Race*, chs. 1, 3, 5.

[41] See, for instance, Trevor Bentley, *Captured by Maori: White Female Captives, Sex and Racism on the Nineteenth-century Frontier* (Auckland, 2004); Richard Wolfe, *Hell-Hole of the Pacific* (Auckland, 2005).

[42] Atholl Anderson, *Race Against Time: the Early Maori-Pakeha Families and the Development of the Mixed-Race Population in Southern New Zealand* (Dunedin, 1991); id., *The Welcome of Strangers: an Ethnohistory of Southern Maori A.D. 1650–1850* (Dunedin, 1998).

attempts to seriously grapple with racial crossings in a larger, more inclusive, and critical frame.[43]

The most ambitious attempt to frame race crossing within the context of a national or colonial history has been by James Belich. His brief address on the subject of racial intermarriage in New Zealand is one of the most intriguing passages in his recent, innovative, general history.[44] Belich has consistently tried to engage critically with race, and his work has been consistently provocative, although his approach differs fundamentally with that adopted here. In his most important work Belich argued that race was a 'bias', and that texts in which race is present can at times be sifted through and that race can be 'subtracted out'.[45] This view, which sees race not as constitutive, but as a kind of distortion, does not interrogate the fundamental racial and colonial categories nor seek to explain how they work instrumentally through colonialism. Though the larger arguments laid out here are, for the most part, compatible with Belich's work, this book makes a fundamentally different argument and adopts a different approach—that race was elemental: that New Zealand was a 'racialized state', one associated with a nineteenth-century British Empire increasingly organized and ruled through discourses and practices of race. The elemental and productive characteristics of race were what invested racial amalgamation, and other aspects of the problem of racial crossing, with both centrality and significance in New Zealand and beyond.

New Zealand has come to claim a kind of racial exceptionality that is still current, and which has its roots in the period with which this book is concerned. This unusual historiographical valuation of race relations in New Zealand is worth emphasizing. Historians, and not only partisan New Zealand ones, have long been convinced that 'race relations' in New Zealand were superior to elsewhere. As New Zealand's most famous historian, Keith Sinclair, put it, New Zealand's race relations were 'better' than in South Dakota, South Africa or South Australia.[46] Imperial historians, such as Victor Kiernan and Robin Winks, have followed a similar line. Winks, for instance, argues that of all the colonies of settlement, 'the harshest race relations developed in Australia, the least harsh in New Zealand'.[47] It is

---

[43] Most notably, Kate Riddell, 'A "Marriage" of the Races? Aspects of Intermarriage, Ideology and Reproduction on the New Zealand Frontier', M.A. thesis, Victoria University of Wellington, 1996.

[44] Belich, *Making Peoples*, pp. 251–7.

[45] Ibid., p. 22.

[46] Keith Sinclair, 'Why are Race Relations in New Zealand Better than in South Africa, South Australia or South Dakota?', *NZJH*, 2 (1971), pp. 121–7.

[47] Robin Winks, 'A System of Commands: The Infrastructure of Race Contact', in Gordon Martel, (ed.), *Studies in British Imperial History: Essays in Honour of A.P. Thornton*

difficult to know, apart from the mathematics of body counting, how to measure 'race relations'; yet it is revealing that an important element in most of these histories is the focus given to intermarriage.[48] Interracial intermarriage is commonly used in these and other accounts as a kind of index of 'good' race relations, one on which New Zealand gets nearly full points. (This has a striking similarity with Brazil's twentieth-century reputation as a place where race relations were also preternaturally 'good'—and for which the putative place of racial crossing is equally fundamental.[49]) These kinds of assessments of race relations were also always comparative claims, addressing other places and other histories. Most importantly, these kinds of interpretations had widespread and enduring public popularity, even after the surprisingly late retreat of academic historians from such positions (a retreat significantly enabled by Alan Ward's work, and the wider political efforts of Māori people in the 1960s and 1970s). Behind the approving assessments and even those of its critics, lay the same remarkably durable idea that a favourable disposition towards intermarriage was indicative of a softer, more humane colonial encounter. As is argued below, this was an idea already common in nineteenth-century Britain, where many argued that Britain (and Britons) emerged out of an intermarriage of the different races of England, Scotland and Wales, in a 'marriage' epitomized in Sir Walter Scott's historical novels: voluntary, racially and politically uplifting.[50] This assumption is not just questionable, but is in many respects an artefact of these histories. 'Racial amalgamation', as is argued below, like other attempts to advance certain kinds of interracial marriages and intimacies often marked not a 'good' colonialism but an unusually intensive, potent and ambitious species. Interracial affective ties and marriage, when effectively combined with law, policy and other forms of statecraft, could prove to be strikingly invasive, expansive and virulent colonial strategies.

Still, until very recently, racial intermarriage and other kinds of racial crossings in New Zealand had received little serious historical attention. In the light of recent and contemporary New Zealand experiences, where 'racial crossings' were, and are, commonplace, this seems difficult to

(Houndmills, 1986), p. 19. Also see Armitage, Andrew, *Comparing the Policy of Aboriginal Assimilation: Australia, Canada and New Zealand* (Vancouver, 1995).

[48] Victor Kiernan, *The Lords of Human Kind: European Attitudes to the Outside World in the Imperial Age* (London, 1969), pp. 262–4.

[49] See Thomas Skidmore, *Black Into White: Race and Nationality in Brazilian Thought* (New York, 1974) and Mark Alan Healey, 'Powers of Misrecognition: Bourdieu and Wacquant on Race in Brazil', *Nepantla: Views From the South*, 4 (2003), pp. 391–402.

[50] See Chapter 4.

reconcile.[51] Yet historians have, if apparently belatedly, begun to turn increasingly towards these topics. It seems, however, that this interest owes almost as much to international and postcolonial scholarly developments as to local or national origins. Particularly important, again, has been the work of feminist and gender historians who have been closely attuned and responsive to the revaluation and exploration of marriage, family and children. By engaging the 'domestic' seriously, and investigating the private realms and 'intimate domains' of colonial New Zealand, these historians have recognized these as places of vital state and political activity, often with histories that are outside or contrary to received historical narratives.[52] This has brought the work of gender or feminist historians especially close to racial crossings when the focus has been on particular individuals, where historians have described experiences patently incompatible with prevailing analyses that suggested stark, masculine, opposed and fixed colonial milieux. Patricia Grimshaw's work on Heni Pore, Jesse Munro's on Suzanne Aubert and, most notably, Judith Binney's biography of Te Kooti are key examples of this.[53] In each of these pieces the central individuals are shown to be living in complicated and variegated social, political and cultural surroundings—usually outside the main colonial settlements and townships—where the limitations of monolithic categories of race, gender or class are clear.

Angela Wanhalla has written an especially important study of the community of Maitapapa, on the Taieri plains in Otago, part of the deep south of New Zealand.[54] This small community had a much higher rate of intermarriage than most—whether those belonging to the same indigenous group (Kai Tahu), or others in the territory of New Zealand. By far the most important work of its kind, Wanhalla's study is richly local, with a command of the particulars of individuals and their kin relations that troubles simple understandings of New Zealand colonialism. Her history has clear ramifications for wider histories of Kai Tahu, as well as

---

[51] Paul Callister, Robert Didham and Deborah Potter, 'Ethnic Intermarriage in New Zealand', Statistics New Zealand Working Paper, 2005.

[52] A representative volume would be Barbara Brookes, Charlotte Macdonald and Margaret Tennant (eds.), *Women in History 2* (Wellington, 1992).

[53] Judith Binney, *Redemption Songs: A Life of Te Kooti Arikirangi Te Turuki* (Auckland, 1995); Patricia Grimshaw, 'Interracial Marriages and Colonial Regimes in Victoria and Aotearoa/New Zealand', *Frontiers*, 23:3 (2002), pp. 12–28; Jesse Munro, *The Story of Suzanne Aubert* (Auckland, 1996).

[54] Angela C. Wanhalla, 'Transgressing Boundaries: A History of the Mixed Descent Families of Maitapapa, Taieri, 1830–1940', PhD thesis, University of Canterbury, 2004; id., 'Marrying "In": the Geography of Intermarriage on the Taieri, 1830s–1920s', in Tony Ballantyne and Judith A. Bennett, (eds.), *Landscape/Community: Perspectives from New Zealand History* (Dunedin, 2005), pp. 72–94.

for colonial and national histories, though with some specification. Due to patterns of recurrent intermarriage, as well as a number of regional and colonial developments, the people of Maitapapa eventually dispersed—'a story of cultural disintegration and loss', though they and their descendants retained an enduring sense of community and kinship. Wanhalla compellingly advances a central argument that the figure of the 'half-caste' was a dangerous one for the colonial state and many colonial institutions, a figure that threatened categories of people and property.

No less important than Wanhalla's work is Judith Binney's recent essay on some aspects of race crossing. One of New Zealand's leading historians, Binney draws upon a career of research to highlight the complicated and often transgressive histories of certain racially mixed individuals. She demonstrates how they were problematic for indigenous and settler communities as well as colonial government. Binney's expertise in the regional histories of the Bay of Islands and the east coast of the North Island enabled her to map some revealing connections of kinship, social circles and interests between a number of different mixed families. There was not, as Binney initially imagined, a mixed 'subculture', but these connections amounted to 'an identifiable network of inter-connected families', mixed families that were associated with the colonial establishment.[55] The work of both Wanhalla and Binney is especially instructive in their focus on the *whānau* (extended family) in its 'mixed' incarnations, detailing its centrality to lived experiences of racial crossing. This study hopes to work with these studies by further exploring the entanglement of *whānau* and other domestic and intimate formations with colonial practices and statecraft, as well as the many attempts to comprehend racial crossing and integrate it with various kinds of knowledge. It also tries to square the challenges that half-castes presented to colonialism with the challenges that colonialism presented to half-castes and others. The two, it is clear, were part of the same problem of racial crossing. The putative instability of racial crossings made many racially crossed people and relations troublesome for colonialism; yet this instability was produced or appropriated by the colonial state and its agents, and could prove potentially as dangerous for indigenous communities.

---

[55] Judith Binney, '"In-Between" Lives: Studies from Within a Colonial Society', in Tony Ballantyne and Brian Moloughney, (eds.), *Disputed Histories: Imagining New Zealand's Pasts* (Dunedin, 2006), pp. 93–117. Other relevant recent works include Manying Ip, *Being Māori-Chinese: Mixed Identities* (Auckland, 2008); Senka Bozic-Vrbancic, *Tarara: Croats and Māori in New Zealand* (Dunedin, 2008); Patricia Grimshaw, 'Interracial Marriages and Colonial Regimes in Victoria and Aotearoa/New Zealand', *Frontiers*, 23:3 (2002), pp. 12–28.

Few things capture how racial crossing was at once apparently simple and yet deeply complex than the fundamental racial terms upon which much was hung; when treated historically, they morph from being concrete and straightforward to complicated and unstable. 'Native', an indispensible term throughout much of the British Empire, and a category of rule in New Zealand, was as much an artefact of government as an instrument. One of an array of available terms, it was by no means a monochrome or uncontested category, neither within specific colonial and British circles, nor by those who were being made into 'natives'. Australia and Canada, for instance, fellow colonies of British settlement whose histories were often closely connected with New Zealand's, had overlapping but significantly different terminologies. In New Zealand the most favoured terms were originally 'aborigine' and 'savage', but 'barbarian', 'heathen', 'Indian' and 'New Zealander' (until at least the 1850s this was interchangeable with 'native') were also in use. This eventually gave way to 'native' as the term of choice. Canada and Australia shared much of this language, but settled on different sets of favoured terms. Evidently, the raising of one particular term over another was no simple devolution of imperial categories. The categorization of New Zealand's 'natives' was consequently at once local and imperial, a creative reinvention of a circulating language that facilitated 'coming to terms' with both the magnitudes of empire and the particularities of a new colony. These colonial categories were racial, but they were never only racial, which explains why the heightened concern in race crossing was not marginal or esoteric but percolated with power, and why the study of 'racial' discourse alone cannot fully account for these categories and their histories.

These developments remain important because these received terms and concepts have a residual power that continues to shape the work of historians and public understandings of the past. In New Zealand this is disguised, as the word 'native' is now mostly unused.[56] But 'native' did not disappear so much as it was reconfigured, replaced almost seamlessly in official discourse by 'Māori'. After 1947, when the Department of Native Affairs became the Department of Māori Affairs, 'Māori' was essentially substituted for 'native' in official discourse. This particular change was not the result of any underlying shift in governmental practice or discourse. Nor was it due to a discovery that 'native' was a disparaging term (which was apparent decades earlier). Rather, the change was occasioned by the political necessity of a government dependent for its

---

[56] Though see Vicente Diaz and J. Kehaulani Kauanui, 'Native Pacific Cultural Studies on the Edge', *Contemporary Pacific*, 13:2 (2001), pp. 315–41.

electoral majority on four 'native' members, men long aware that the term
was pejorative. The appropriation of 'Māori' as a formal replacement for
'native' was consequently an expediency that was, in key ways, something
like the semantic equivalent of a palace revolution—and would remain so
until more substantial political changes reoriented official discourses in the
1970s and 1980s.[57] Yet despite this shifting and complicated history, the
term and category of 'Māori' has usually been treated as transhistorical or
ahistorical. It is also treated, too often, as transcultural, confusing shared
usage of the same term by different people with shared *understandings*.
This makes it harder to appreciate the largely autonomous usages of
'Māori' by indigenous people and groups, and to make the kinds of
distinction that can refine historical analysis in useful and enlightening
ways. It is certainly the case, as James Tully has recognized in legal
contexts, that language can constrain or distort understandings and
claims; while at the same time presenting the only 'normative vocabulary' available for indigenous groups.[58] Part of the urgent work of
historians, then, is to contextualize, historicize and denaturalize the
basic racial and colonial categories of New Zealand. This process
might at times seem strange to many New Zealand readers precisely
because of the enduring power of these categories. Indeed, it is telling
that in the pages of young critical historians, one can still find assertions
that New Zealand did not have any 'rigid race definition ... in contrast
to Canada, the Caribbean, India and especially South Africa.'[59] This is
an adjunct to the view that New Zealand's race relations were exceptional and to some degree benevolent. It is at odds with the arguments
pursued below, which outline the ways that racial discourses were
fundamental to colonialism in New Zealand, as elsewhere, and how
these categories were connected to others in the British Empire and
have proven remarkably stable and resilient. Much of New Zealand's
colonial history was characterized by attempts to institute a bi-racial
code, attempts that were, in some areas, remarkably successful.

To make this argument more distinct, here the word 'Māori' is used
more narrowly, especially with regard to the nineteenth century. Angela
Ballara has concisely pointed to the historical grounds for this:

> In a sense it was true that there was no 'Māori' social organization or history
> until after significant pan-Māori movements began their reaction to Europe-
> an settlement. The word 'māori' meant ordinary, common as against exotic,

[57] For example Aroha Harris, *Hikoi: Forty Years of Māori Protest* (Wellington, 2004).
[58] James Tully, *Strange Multiplicity: Constitutionalism in an Age of Diversity* (Cambridge, 1995), p. 39.
[59] Riddell, 'A "Marriage" of the Races', p. 7.

or fresh, as in ordinary drinking water. It was applied by Europeans to Māori people only after Māori had begun to use the term to distinguish their own normality as a people from the exotic or alien newcomers.[60]

This is exactly the point. To use the term to describe indigenous groups and society prior to these pan-tribal developments and especially prior to the widespread use of the word itself—which begins in the 1850s—is both analytically confusing and anachronistic. Indigenous groups did share a common language—*te reo*—but between the different indigenous groups were marked differences, in dialect, organization, custom, histories and politics. In the nineteenth century the primary political and social unit of these different indigenous societies was a shared one—the *hapu*, a descent group up to several hundred people in size. *Hapu* were flexible and dynamic, membership was multiple and mobile, but the conglomeration of *hapu* were not a 'race' nor any such equivalent. Nor were these patchworks of peoples and practices a single 'culture'. Shared language and protocols, rules and customs (*tikanga*) did not make them one, and Ballara has even likened the differences between some different indigenous groups to ethnic differences.[61]

Indigenous understandings of Māori collectivity and subjectivity need to be distinguished from colonial practices and discourses that routinely used the same terms, though with different understandings and to different effect. Māori is a contested term, with its usages in variegated indigenous discourses often very different to how it has been used officially or colonially, where it commonly substituted for 'native'. That contestation needs not only to be recognized, but to be seriously entertained. At issue is not just connotation or meaning, but ways of classifying: construing 'natives' as a uniform group, a 'race' who were known or knowable, individuals who were fungible, a legible population that was interchangeable and subject. Indigenous understandings of how people related to each other, how they were connected, and how they could be and should be ordered and understood, contrasted fundamentally with colonial taxonomic practices, and still do.[62]

The analytical distinction between indigenous peoples and groups on the one hand and the colonial categories and discourses devised to contain

---

[60] Angela Ballara, *Iwi: The Dynamics of Māori Tribal Organization from c.1769–1945* (Wellington, 1998), p. 42.
[61] Ibid., pp. 127–8; she is referring to differences between *iwi*.
[62] Lachy Paterson, '*Kiri Ma, Kiri Mangu*: The Terminology of Race and Civilisation in the Mid-Nineteenth-Century Māori-Language Newspapers', in Jenifer Curnow, Ngapare Hopa and Jane McRae, (eds.), *Rere Atu, Taku Manu* (Auckland, 2002), pp. 78–93.

them on the other needs to be clarified. As with some authors I have chosen to do this by employing 'Tangata Whenua', People of the Land, and what I take to be a near equivalent in English, 'indigenous people'.[63] This draws a clearer distinction between the people, their own discourses and experiences as Tangata Whenua—a description commonly used at the time of themselves—and the colonial discourses and categories charged with cataloguing them and putting them into discourse—which were comprehended under 'native', its many kindred terms and, later, the official and unofficial colonial appropriations of the term 'Māori'. Tangata Whenua recognizes the specificity of each of the groups it identifies, their primacy, and above all their connection to particular places and histories, though it is not without its own complications.

This terminological difficulty around 'native' and 'Māori' was specific to New Zealand, but in important ways it was not unique. Indeed, such problems were articulated with other, including larger and recurrent, problems of enacting and stabilizing colonial administration, jurisdiction and order. As Ann Stoler has argued, colonial regimes were commonly part of '"taxonomic states," whose administrations were charged with defining and interpreting what constituted racial membership, citizenship, political subversion, and the scope of the state's jurisdiction over morality.'[64] This did not mean, of course, that these states met their charge very well, but it did mean that these problems of taxonomy were enduring priorities, no less in the 1870s when this study ends, than in the 1830s, when it begins—if in different ways. These taxonomic procedures alone ensured that racial crossings were pivotal to colonial statecraft, whether in the strategy of racial amalgamation as envisioned in New Zealand or as proposed in the Canadas (outlined in Chapter 1), or as formulated by imperial experts. What these categories sought usefully to organize and arrange was messy, diverse, changing and multifarious. 'Categories of difference are protean', as Sander Gilman has observed, 'but they appear as absolutes.'[65] These kinds of taxonomies were tasked with making people 'legible', as James Scott has put it, though this legibility usually required the continued application of power to sustain it.[66] But such

<hr />

[63] For example, Andrew Vercoe, *Educating Jake: Pathways to Empowerment* (Auckland, 1998), p. 68, cf. Paterson, *'Kiri Ma, Kiri Mangu'*, pp. 81–2; J.G.A. Pocock, *The Discovery of Islands: Essays in British History* (Cambridge, 2005), pp. 199–225.

[64] Anne Stoler, *Carnal Knowledge and Imperial Power: Race and the Intimate in Colonial Rule* (Berkeley, 2002), p. 206.

[65] Sander L. Gilman, *Difference and Pathology: Stereotypes of Sexuality, Race, and Madness* (Ithaca, 1985), p. 25.

[66] James Scott, *Seeing Like a State: How Certain Schemes to Improve the Human Condition Have Failed* (New Haven, 1998), pp. 11–83; cf. Nicholas Thomas, *Colonialism's Culture: Anthropology, Travel and Government* (Cambridge, 1994), p. 79.

combinations of power, knowledge and order were often manifest in the most mundane ways, which was precisely why race could be so pervasive, and yet seem natural and indispensible: in this period, not least in the new colony of New Zealand, the ways in which race became a 'virtual reality' (as Paul Gilroy has put it) can often be charted.[67]

Treating the parameters of the problem of racial crossing broadly requires holding multiple fields and grains of analysis in view. An opportune moment for this is the development of 'systematic colonization' as idea and as intended practice, the subject of Chapter 1. This came to fixate on an idea of incorporating different populations or races—'racial amalgamation'—and this initially surprising turn can only be understood with reference to multiple contemporary developments, from evangelicalism, the abolition of slavery, the attempted union of Upper and Lower Canada, domestic reform in Britain, and desires to re-energize, perfect and make profitable the process of colonization. In New Zealand colonialism came to claim jurisdiction over, but did not inaugurate, relations between indigenous societies and outsiders. By 1840 and the formal annexation of New Zealand, all kinds of relationships with foreigners and colonizers were vigorously established, almost entirely under the aegis of indigenous leadership. These relations, the subject of Chapter 2, bore some similarity to other 'frontier' milieux, and their intimacies and domestic relations challenged the ambitious new colonial administration in many ways. But despite the richness and productivity of these 'interracial' relations, their position on the margins or outside the ambit of colonial rule meant they were commonly seen not as opportunities but as a kind of 'pandemonium', as one official put it. The attempts of colonial government, systematic colonizers and missionaries to transform this pandemonium into a colonization they considered proper, one that was more amenable to their own taxonomies and practices of administration is the focus of Chapter 3. Central to this transformation was not an opposition to racial crossing, but rather a different, narrow and more regulated vision of 'racial amalgamation'. That this was shared by multiple, often opposing colonial interests is perhaps counter-intuitive, but in its contexts becomes unsurprising. Chapter 4 shows how the ferment over the problem of racial crossing, which spanned these decades, dramatizes certain kinds of commonality, ones not well understood by a focus solely on the theatrics between radically opposing wings in various racial debates. Attending to the diversity of 'encounters in place' over racial crossing better specifies the

[67] Paul Gilroy, *Against Race: Imagining Political Culture Beyond the Color Line* (Cambridge, MA, 2000), p. 11. A powerful example of this is Tim Keegan's study, *The Origins of the Racial Order*.

political and social dimensions of the problem and its interlocuters, while foregrounding the distribution and economy of these conversations. This makes apparent that it was common to maintain that *properly* managed and administered racial crossings could be beneficial and helpful to race relations and colonial rule. The final chapter explores how such views, and such practices, fared in the face of intense crisis. This crisis, which played out on an imperial scale, was a protracted and damaging war waged between colonial and imperial forces and large parts of New Zealand's indigenous population (1860–72). This occurred at a time when New Zealand had become something of a poster child in Britain for racial amalgamation and benevolent empire. At stake was the capacity and nature of colonial rule and indigenous independence; yet the war was also understood by some to be not just political, but racial, a 'war of races' where the problem of racial crossing remained integral. Could the policy of racial amalgamation be sustained? Was racial amalgamation part of the problem or part of the solution? These questions brought the problem of racial crossing to the fore in new, if familiar and recurrent ways. But the specifics of war, particularly in 1863 and 1864, loaded new freight, as racially mixed marriages, families and people were fingered by these problems in unexpected ways.

1

Amalgamating Races: The 'New System' of Colonization and Racial Management

The settlement of New Zealand came at an unsettled time. As Boyd Hilton has argued, the first part of the nineteenth century 'really *was* an "age of crisis"—politically, socially, and intellectually'. The deep-seated fear of revolution amongst governments and elites adjoined various other problems, such as free trade, currency, poor relief and, of course, reform.[1] In the Empire there was crisis too, if in different ways—from the end of transportation, the Frontier Wars in the Cape Colony to the French Canadian 'rebellion' in 1837–38. The 1830s were a particularly uncertain time, with critical developments domestically and imperially, and from these contexts emerged the substantial imperial interest in New Zealand.

From even before it was a colony, this interest in New Zealand had taken a distinctive turn. Proponents of colonization, from a broad spectrum of political backgrounds, had begun to formulate strategies of 'racial amalgamation'. These strategies informed the colonization of New Zealand, especially the governing of 'natives' and land, articulating a racial and political vision of a single, 'racially amalgamated', colony. This was a particular form of regulated racial crossing, one to be guided and controlled by a colonial government. As a strategy it stemmed from a variety of sources, not only (or even primarily) from a 'humanitarianism' held to be influential in the 1830s and 1840s. Racial amalgamation had much more varied origins, and shared a common impulse that was widely evident elsewhere, both in Britain and the Empire, utilizing processes of inclusion as ways of classifying and managing populations unequally.

---

[1] Boyd Hilton, 'Politics of Anatomy and an Anatomy of Politics, *c.*1825–50', in Collini *et al.*, (eds.), *British Intellectual History: History, Religion, and Culture*, p. 183.

NEW ZEALAND AND SYSTEMATIC COLONIZATION

The organization that eventually became the New Zealand Company was one of several bodies which promoted 'systematic colonization'. Systematic colonization was a body of thought which planned overseas settlements in a way that would either run at a profit or at least without financial aid from government. These were intended to be stable societies reproducing British conditions by ensuring that land was utilized appropriately and that sufficient cheap labour was available. Systematic colonization offered a solution to the population pressure some perceived as weighing on Britain, it utilized some of the latest findings of political economy (then a leading branch of study), and it was a way of reforming not only colonization, but of building a reformed colonial society.[2] The first of these settlements was South Australia, founded by the South Australia Company, which had been enabled by an 1834 Act and which first left Britain in March 1836.[3] In the following years New Zealand became popular amongst systematic colonizers, and several organizations made plans to systematically colonize New Zealand, with each taking its own peculiar form. Strikingly, *all* the major systematic colonizers interested in New Zealand proposed policies that included variants of racial amalgamation.

Historians have written extensively about the New Zealand Company.[4] Begun in 1837 as the 'New Zealand Association', it became the 'New Zealand Colonization Company' in August 1838, before evolving into the New Zealand Company in March 1839. The Company contained considerable personal and financial resources, and was equipped with a large collection of notables and patrons. The original directorate included peers (Lord Durham and Lord Petre), clergy (Rev. Samuel Hinds), MPs (Francis Baring, Sir William Molesworth, Henry George Ward) and businessmen (such as Charles Enderby). It was initially mostly Whigs, with a few radicals, or radical sympathizers; and virtually all might broadly be described as reformers. The radicals were 'philosophic radicals', the kind of person that mothers (especially Tory mothers) warned their sons

[2] See particularly, Donald Winch, *Classical Political Economy and Colonies* (London, 1965).
[3] Which also proved a failure, a project taken over by the Colonial Office in 1842. Douglas Pike, *Paradise of Dissent: South Australia, 1829–1857* (London, 1957).
[4] See, most recently, Philip Temple, *A Sort of Conscience: The Wakefields* (Auckland, 2002); Patricia Burns, *Fatal Success: a History of the New Zealand Company* (Auckland, 1989); Adams, *Fatal Necessity*.

about.[5] They gained the ears and eyes of leading Whigs, including Lord Melbourne and his lieutenant Lord Howick.[6] The New Zealand Company's political clout, as well as their access to resources and capital, made them pre-eminent amongst the several private colonizing ventures concerned with New Zealand. The Company induced government into protracted discussions about acquiring and then, after 1840, maintaining New Zealand as a colony.[7] Between 1836 and 1844 there were no less than four parliamentary committees connected with New Zealand.

The central features of 'systematic' or 'scientific' colonization, or the 'New System' as the Company called it, are widely known. At the heart of its operation were two main principles. These were '1st, the sale of lands, at an uniform and sufficient price; and 2dly, [*sic*] the employment of a large portion of the purchase-money as an Emigration Fund.'[8] The correct operation of the system was to be ensured by the monopoly of the Company on the sale of land, and the setting of a 'sufficient price'. This, it was supposed, would concentrate the intended settlement, stopping it from spreading out by preventing easy access to land. Emigrants who came out without capital would be forced to sell their labour, consequently guaranteeing capitalists a supply of labour and a good return, and creating a harmonious society with a balance between labour and capital. The sale of lands would keep the Company in funds, so they could then regulate emigration, taking out selected emigrants as required, subsidizing them if necessary. Quite quickly the New System would, in theory, produce a microcosm of the mother country, complete with upper, middle and working classes (though without the poor).

Leading members or supporters of the Company saw themselves as 'Colonial Reformers', consciously aligning themselves with the reforms then underway in Britain.[9] This was common at the time, as many radicals turned to the colonies seeing them as an extension of social problems in Britain, or as potential solutions to these problems.[10] They were against aristocratic rule, and favoured colonial self-government but, as their

---

[5] Mrs Hawtrey to Montague J.G. Hawtrey, [June or early July 1838], in Florence Molesworth Hawtrey, *The History of the Hawtrey Family* (London, 1903), II, p. 140.
  [6] Durham University Library (DUL), GRE/B80/2A, Howick to Major John Campbell, 1 November 1837; ibid., Campbell to Howick, 18 October 1837.
  [7] There were even three parliamentary committees in six years: GBPP 1837–38, xxi (680); GBPP 1840, vii (582); GBPP 1844, xiii (556).
  [8] John Ward, *Information Relative to New Zealand, Compiled for the Use of Colonists* (London, 1840), p. 129.
  [9] Charles Buller, *Responsible Government for Colonies* (London, 1840), p. 20; Charles Buller, *Systematic Colonization* (London, 1843), pp. 39–40.
  [10] William Thomas, *Philosophic Radicals: Nine Studies in Theory and Practice, 1817– 1841* (Oxford, 1979), p. 372.

theorizing showed, they were reformers not revolutionaries. The society they wished to produce was to be a colonial reconstruction of Britain, one that was class-based, and though there would be mobility between the classes, this would be achieved through labour, and would have clear limits. A clear function of the Company proposal was to protect the value of capital as it migrated from Britain to New Zealand. If you went out as a gentleman, the system would not only allow you to travel, but to arrive, first-class. Paying an expensive price for land was the cost of ensuring that only the wealthy would buy land.

Land was the central focus of this theory and—it had not escaped the theorists—the New Zealand 'aborigines' (as they typically called them) were living on the lands in question. This was where 'racial amalgamation' was crucial. The entire system of colonization formulated by the New Zealand Company was based upon acquiring huge tracts of land at nominal prices. In the language of the Company and the times, these were 'waste lands'.[11] A waste land was an uncultivated or unowned or wild piece of land, a wilderness. Such lands had been widely perceived in North America, and again and more recently in South Australia. In South Australia, smaller native populations and an extensive land mass coupled with the British approach of treating it as *terra nullius*—a land without people—allowed the conclusion to be drawn that such lands lay waiting for British colonization. There the aborigines were seen as hunter gatherers, and it was decided they were not people who owned the lands they hunted over. In New Zealand the prospect was different, as it was believed that natives were more sedentary, agricultural, and had quite densely settled many parts of the islands, particularly in the north. There was little doubt, in any of the travellers' accounts on which the Company's descriptions of New Zealand were based, that New Zealand 'aborigines' had some notion of possession of their lands.[12] Even if the 'aborigines' sold up willingly and cheaply, this still left them as a population that had to be dealt with. 'Racial amalgamation' was the part of the system that dealt not only with the 'aborigines', but underwrote the acquisition of lands, and the systematization of relations between 'aborigines' and 'settlers'.

In theory racial amalgamation was extraordinarily simple. After all purchases the Company would set aside a proportion of lands as native reserves, as had been done in other colonies such as North America. These would be a new kind of reserve, the Company trumpeted, not vast tracts as in the Americas, but smaller ones which were to be intermixed among the

---

[11] For example, the 1836 Commons' Select Committee on Colonial Waste Lands and Emigration.
[12] See Adams, *Fatal Necessity*; Hickford, 'Making "Territorial Rights of the Natives"'.

lands of the colonists. One-tenth of the lands in the new settlements would be reserved for the 'aborigines', and there would be no separation between aborigines and settlers as had happened elsewhere. The model of racial amalgamation would be etched on the landscape, speeding the process of civilization and amalgamation, providing everyday opportunities for social and sexual intercourse. Racial amalgamation would, it was supposed, civilize natives by making civilization accessible; it would enrich them by making the smaller pieces of land more valuable; it would bring natives into a smaller and settled space where government could be more easily exercised. The whole scheme was still premised on the willing sale of land to the Company, but who could not see that to sell land would make economic sense? Ten acres in the planned townships would be worth more than a hundred in the back blocks. Or so the argument ran. In the hermetically sealed world of the Company's theories, 'aborigines' operated with the economic logic of settlers.

There is no question that in the Company's original formulations racial amalgamation was *racial*. This was apparent in the Company's initial publication, especially in an appendix proposing 'exceptional laws in favour of the natives of New Zealand'. Here racial amalgamation was substantiated not only as a land policy, but as one between races. The 'natives' were to be taken under the paternal care of the Company, who would put in place 'exceptional laws' until the natives could assume a real equality with the settlers. The Company would not only purchase and reserve lands for all the natives, but ensure that native chiefs retained their rank, by making special grants of land to them. This native hierarchy would be further endorsed by 'a principle of social alliances' between native and settler families. The native system of rank was to be grafted onto the British system of class. It was all systematic:

> The same power which man thus exercises over the productions of the earth, is equally to be exercised over the various races of his kind. . . we cannot find an instance of any race that ever attained to a high state of culture, or as a nation emerged from barbarism, except by the ingrafting of a gentler scion upon the wilder stem.[13]

From the control of land would come the control not only of capital, labour, and thus class (and gender), but also race.

The Company's first publication, over 400 pages long, was anonymously co-authored by Edward Gibbon Wakefield, John Ward and Montague Hawtrey. Wakefield is generally supposed to have been the 'genius'. An

[13] [Hawtrey], 'Exceptional Laws', in [Ward and Wakefield], *The British Colonization of New Zealand*, p. 420.

'expert' on systematic colonization, he was proclaimed as 'the Discoverer of the New System'.[14] He was also notorious, having been jailed for kidnapping an underage heiress and forcing her to marry him. Many contemporaries did not trust him: he 'feigned friendship and cordiality', one thought, others that he spoke 'low coarse and unmanly insinuations', and had an 'utter contempt for truth'.[15] But although the leading light, Wakefield was by no means the sole author of Company policy. Ward was the Company secretary, who had published in the leading Whig journal, the *Edinburgh Review*, 'on subjects of jurisprudence, Civic Economy, and Colonization' and was well acquainted with Wakefield's ideas on colonization.[16] Hawtrey was an Anglican pastor, who was Wakefield's neighbour.[17] His interest in New Zealand was neither professional nor commercial, but an 'impulse of a stronger nature'.[18] This strange trio of a philosophic radical charlatan, a Whig secretary and a Tory vicar gave birth to the Company's initial formulations of racial amalgamation.

Hawtrey extended their first rumblings to a book-length treatment of racial amalgamation and native policy. *An Earnest Address to New Zealand Colonists* laid bare the Company's ideas, in all their splendour and *naïveté*.[19] But if some of its trappings were unusual, underpinning them was a common belief: the separation of races would ensure permanent inequality. Only amalgamation could facilitate equality of rights, and only full, racial amalgamation could make amalgamation work (English law was 'law suited for a people of one race'). As Hawtrey observed:

> We can hardly expect that at any future period the country will be inhabited by two races equally civilized and happy, and enjoying the same social and political privileges, but perfectly distinct from each other in blood and complexion. We may support the natives in a position of advantage for some years to come... but if we wish to see the country inhabited by a powerful, happy, and well-ordered people, we must look forward to the amalgamation of the two races into one.... the New Zealanders possess those

---

[14] Ward, *Information Relative to New Zealand*, p. 143.

[15] DUL, GRE/B/B126/11, Stephen to Howick, 16 June 1845; CO 209/3, White to Wakefield, 4 January 1838, fo. 204; GRE/C3/1A, Howick, diary, 16 December 1833.

[16] CO 208/185, Minutes, 2 May 1839, Wakefield's testimonial, fo. 101.

[17] Montague J.G. Hawtrey, *Justice to New Zealand, Honour to England* (London, 1861), p. 9; Hawtrey to Russell, undated, printed in *New Zealand Journal*, no. 31, 24 March 1841, p. 76.

[18] Mrs Hawtrey to Montague J.G. Hawtrey, [June or early July 1838], in Florence Molesworth Hawtrey, *The History of the Hawtrey Family* (London, 1903), II, p. 140. Both Hawtrey and his father, John, were involved in Company affairs; CO 208/185, Memorandum, 13 December 1837, fo. 118; ibid., minutes, 29 April 1839, fo. 134.

[19] Montague Hawtrey, *An Earnest Address to New Zealand Colonists, with Reference to their Intercourse with the Native Inhabitants* (London, 1840).

mental and physical qualities which would qualify them for matrimonial alliance with Europeans, and give the hope of a fine and intelligent progeny.

Hawtrey knew that amalgamation was not the work of days, and was not so naive to think that all would be sympathetic. But he took hope from the example of Pocahontas and John Rolfe, the numbers of half-castes already supposed to be living in New Zealand, and the prospect that 'the daughters of the native chiefs will be among the most richly endowed heiresses of the country.'[20]

Amongst systematic colonizers the racial amalgamation of the New Zealand Company was not unique. This is apparent when the plans that other organizations made for New Zealand are considered. By 1839 there were already several such organizations, though most were soon to fade into obscurity, and some never emerged from it to begin with. On the whole they were formed during the scramble of 1838–39, once it seemed clear that New Zealand would be annexed. At least two others detailed policies of racial amalgamation, but neither ever left Britain.

The 'New Zealand Society of Christian Civilization' was formed after the Company (then still the Association) had failed in an attempt to gain a government charter for their colonizing efforts. This failure ruptured alliances within their directorate. In response a group broke away and made their own submissions to the Colonial Office. George Lyall and (Colonel) Robert Torrens led the efforts of the New Zealand Society to gain a government charter. The Society made several proposals and Torrens, a political economist, theorist of systematic colonization, South Australian Commissioner and an MP, was likeliest the main shaping force. The Society proposed to cross not only British and native persons, but also their forms of government, into a racially crossed leadership. For example, leading the settlement would be a racially amalgamated council of Aldermen and 'Areekee' (as in *ariki*, leading chief). Rank would be privileged over race, with an amalgamated hierarchy spanning any racial divide. Settler leaders (the Aldermen) would acquire the rank and privilege of Chiefs of New Zealand, as would those who married into the upper ranks of either race. ('Inhabitants of the native race, marrying Wives of the European race, and inhabitants of the European race, marrying the Daughters of Native Chiefs, shall acquire the rank and privileges of Chiefs.'[21]) Here it was apparent that whiteness (and white womanhood particularly) itself conferred a kind of rank, so that a 'native' marrying a white woman

---

[20] The quotations are from ibid., pp. 78, 94, 99.

[21] CO 209/3, Robert Torrens, 'The New Zealand Society of Christian Civilization', fos. 299–312.

was definitely thought to be marrying 'up'. Yet, undoubtedly serious as this deeply flawed proposal was, it ultimately failed to attract sufficient support from investors, officials, lobbyists and would-be colonists.[22]

The 'Scots New Zealand Land Company', another organization that also proposed racial amalgamation, was entirely different from the New Zealand Company or Torrens' Society. The Scots Company was not a profit-driven concern like most others, but was proposed as a loosely organized cooperative of '*working capitalists*', pooling their money together to send families out a few at a time.[23] An organization that historians have ignored, the Company hoped by colonizing New Zealand to improve the lot of the working classes, to strengthen the British nation, and to further advance humanity (including the native New Zealanders) generally. In the small literature the Scots Company produced, it was clear that it used a different language to that of most other systematic colonizers. Theirs was not a language of price, labour and capital, but of nature and agriculture. The Scots Company's politics were properly 'radical'. Unlike the New Zealand Company it hoped not to replicate British society in New Zealand, with its protection of the property and privileges of the better classes; instead the Scots Company saw colonization as a chance to remake society, and offer the working man a better chance—'if necessary, to turn the world upside down.'[24]

The driving force of the Scots Company was Patrick Matthew, an intriguing figure who is now best known for anticipating Darwin's theory of evolution by natural selection.[25] An Edinburgh educated fruit-farmer and tree-grower, Matthew was a gentleman with radical views, a local representative to the London Chartist Convention of 1839. He opposed commercial control of emigration and colonization, and regarded the New Zealand Company's ideas as 'moonshine'.[26] A consciously scientific writer, Matthew theorized about the benefits of racial intermarriage. The New Zealand Company's strategy of a racial

---

[22] The plan was heavily criticized by missionaries: Minutes, 26 March, 16 April, 1839. CMS G/C1, v.17, pp. 572–3, 589–90.

[23] [Patrick Matthew], *Prospectus of the Scots New Zealand Land Company* (Edinburgh, 1839), pp. 9, 20. Original emphasis. Though it was to be joint-stock as well; Patrick Matthew, *Emigration Fields: North America, the Cape, Australia, and New Zealand* (Edinburgh, 1839), pp. 235–7. There is a copy of this in CO 209/4, fos. 670–89. Matthew is not named as author, but was Chairman of the Company, and the writer quotes heavily from *Emigration Fields*; there is little doubt that Matthew was the author.

[24] Patrick Matthew, *Emigration Fields*, p. 74.

[25] See W.J. Dempster, *Patrick Matthew and Natural Selection* (Edinburgh, 1983); K.D. Wells, 'The Historical Context of Natural Selection: The Case of Patrick Matthew', *Journal of the History of Biology*, 6 (1973), pp. 225–58. Adrian Desmond, *The Politics of Evolution: Morphology, Medicine, and Reform in Radical London* (London, 1989), p. 425.

[26] Patrick Matthew, *Emigration Fields*, pp. 139, 98; [Matthew], *Prospectus*, p. 8, 9–11n.

amalgamation by intermixing native reserves with the lands of British colonists was one of the few points with which Matthew agreed. Yet Matthew's conception differed in significant ways; in New Zealand, he wrote, a

> firm and friendly union between the British and New Zealanders would soon raise these islands... to a pitch of prosperity, which would render them supreme in the Pacific; and the amalgamation of the two races (British and New Zealand), the one the foremost in civilized life, and the other in savage life, or natural stamina, like engrafting the finest varieties of fruits upon the purest crab, may be expected to produce a people superior in physical and moral energy to all others.[27]

Like the skilled horticulturalist he was, Matthew planned to produce better results through careful, though this time racial, engrafting. Impressed by the New Zealand climate, Matthew considered New Zealand the most eminent 'emigration field'. In the tropics he regarded race crossing as expedient; in the temperate colony of New Zealand he thought that it was desirable, and should be planned. Because Matthew believed in what he called 'the circumstance-adaptive law', which meant that people were adapted to their 'climate', a cross between the British and New Zealand races would confer this adaptation, enabling successful colonization.[28] Such adaptation was essential, because for Matthew it was the race more suited to the climate, not the morally superior or most civilized, that would eventually triumph. The amalgamation of Britons and New Zealand natives would do away with this problem, while also producing a new, vigorous race. Like the New Zealand Company, Matthew was assured by the knowledge that '[t]he amalgamated race is springing up in Sydney, where a number of British masters of vessels who trade in those seas, keep New Zealand wives.'[29]

Though both the Scots Company and the New Zealand Company used the same trope—the grafting of one plant onto another—to describe their plans for racial amalgamation, their purposes were clearly a world apart. The Scots Company was hitched to the political concerns of the Chartists, and these were soon to stumble (though the Scots Company failed more directly because of its lack of finance and political backing). The New Zealand Company, and the New Zealand Society of Christian Civilization with it, was associated more with the politics of reform, which trimmed of their hard edges and much of their substance,

---

[27] Matthew, *Emigration Fields*, pp. 134–5.
[28] Matthew, *Naval Timber and Aboriculture*, p. 108; Matthew, *Emigration Fields*, pp. 3, 80, 83, 100.
[29] Ibid., p. 135n.

would at least have a modicum of success. Here it is crucial to observe that racial amalgamation could appeal to a broad political constituency: not only Whigs and 'philosophic radicals', but Chartists as well as Tory vicars.

Within the expanding universe of interest in New Zealand colonization the only real alternative to racial amalgamation on offer belonged not to conservatives or opponents of 'aboriginal rights', but to the missionary societies, the Wesleyan Missionary Society and the Anglican Church Missionary Society. From the outset the mission societies were firmly against systematic colonization in New Zealand. Their main argument was the familiar one, that Europeans were too rapacious, that if they came to New Zealand they would sooner or later, and probably sooner, wipe out the aborigines.[30] This had been endorsed by the 1837 'Aborigines Report'.[31] But the missionary societies were still opposing colonization long after, unbeknownst to them, the Colonial Office had decided that the annexation of New Zealand was a 'fatal necessity'.[32] Eventually they proposed their own colonization scheme, but it was too little too late, a loosely thought out (and to Lord Glenelg, obviously self-interested) theocracy.[33] The mission societies had vigorously denounced the systematic colonizers, and especial vitriol was saved for the policy of racial amalgamation, and Hawtrey's amalgamationist appendix. The secretary of the Wesleyan Missionary Society, John Beecham, wrote of this:

> If this plan is the highest effort, the most perfect result of the practical wisdom of the [New Zealand] Association, slender indeed are their claims to public confidence. It is a reverie in which the classical student might benevolently and safely indulge on the banks of the Isis or the Cam; but calculated to fill all sober minds with alarm when they find it proposed by a public company. . . .[34]

Beecham did not doubt the author's good intentions (and he guessed accurately Hawtrey's Cambridge background in classics), but he mocked the details of the plan, in which he saw facile debts to Sir Walter Scott, and suspicious use of 'transplanting'.[35] The mission societies were set against the idea of racial amalgamation, suggesting that 'natives' needed to be kept apart from settlers, and the further apart the better. Natives, they argued,

---

[30] Dandeson Coates, *The Present State of the New Zealand Question Considered in a Letter to J.P. Plumtree* (London, 1838).

[31] GBPP 1837, vii (425): 'Report From the Select Committee on Aborigines (British Settlements)'.

[32] DUL, Grey papers, GRE/B115/1: Lord Melbourne to Howick, 26 June 1837.

[33] CO 209/3, fo. 168: marginal note on Coates to Glenelg, 23 July 1838.

[34] John Beecham, *Colonization: Being Remarks on Colonization in General, with an Examination of the Proposals of the Association Which has been Formed for Colonizing New Zealand*, 4th edn., (London, 1838), p. 41.

[35] Beecham, *Colonization*, pp. 36–40.

needed to be Christian and thoroughly civilized before they could be 'mixed up with well-regulated society.'[36] But here the missionaries had made a serious misjudgement; already, as the next chapter will show, there were hundreds of British and other foreigners living or passing through New Zealand. New Zealand was not, and could not be, insulated from the world, and the Colonial Office realized this. Though suspicious of the systematic colonizers, the language and policy of racial amalgamation was insinuating elsewhere. In official circles, which intersected those of the New Zealand Company, racial amalgamation began to seem more appropriate than racial separation.

RACIALLY AMALGAMATING THE CANADAS

Racial amalgamation was not as original or unique as the promoters of systematic colonization in New Zealand professed. When certain other developments in the Empire are brought into the frame, racial amalgamation as imagined for New Zealand seems less exceptional. The language of racial amalgamation was surprisingly promiscuous, and points to multiple incarnations of racial amalgamation both as a 'bio-political' strategy, and a racialized explanation. The reiteration of racial amalgamation as a strategy in different locations illuminates connections and circulations both between particular people and of certain discourses, not least those that problematized racial crossings. A remarkable example of this was evident in a very different but closely contemporary situation, in Canada.

By late 1838 in Canada some long-standing concerns had come to a head. In Lower Canada there was a struggle between the Executive (which was British) and the Assembly (which was predominantly French). By November 1837 the situation had worsened into 'rebellion'.[37] The local and imperial government were at a loss; their answer was to send the Earl of Durham on a special mission as Canadian governor. Having been involved with the Reform Act of 1832, Durham was already well known in England, if somewhat wrongly, as 'Radical Jack'.[38] He was also the head of the New Zealand Company, and he took Wakefield and Charles Buller, also from the Company, with him to Canada. Given the shady prospects for their New Zealand colonization when they departed, *The Times* saw Durham's mission to Canada 'as a temporary *solatium* for the non-realization of their

---

[36] Beecham, *Colonization*, p. 13.
[37] Peter Burroughs, *The Canadian Crisis and British Colonial Policy, 1828–1841* (London, 1972).
[38] Thomas, *The Philosophic Radicals*, pp. 351–69.

Polynesian hopes.'[39] But Durham, Wakefield and Buller, the most prominent of the Colonial Reformers, saw it as another chance at colonial reform.

The most public outcome of Durham's brief sojourn in Canada was the
'Durham Report', published in 1839.[40] The Colonial Reformers hailed it as
the founding document of colonial self-government; Buller called it 'the text
book of colonial reform'.[41] It was dismissed by others as without accuracy,
practicality or originality; one critic called it 'a tissue of misrepresentations',
already 'refuted in every important particular'.[42] The historian Ged Martin
has shown how the impact of the Durham Report on subsequent colonial
events has been overestimated, yet even in Martin's work it is clear that the
Report found a significance, and a readership, highly unusual for an official
paper on colonial matters.[43] The two main measures recommended by
Durham were the union of Upper and Lower Canada, and the granting of a
degree of self-government. Self-government was overlooked, but in 1841 an
act of union for Upper and Lower Canada was enacted. This effectively gave
anglophone settlers a political majority over their francophone counterparts,
who had previously been the majority in Lower Canada. The idea of
Canadian political union was by no means new. It had been suggested to
cabinet in 1822, and in 1839 Lord Brougham thought it 'as old as the
hills'.[44] Edmund Burke had argued against such an amalgamation in 1791,
and others now assumed his mantle. But the proposal in the Report was not
simply for a governmental or 'political' union, but for a union of 'races'.

In the Report the French Canadians were depicted as 'natives', a different
and inferior race, in many ways not unlike the New Zealanders. The use of
'race' was not merely an accident of language.[45] The Report urged that this
was 'not a struggle of principles, but of races'—'a contest of races'.[46] The
'superior political and practical intelligence of the English' was contrasted
with the 'hopeless inferiority' of the 'French Canadian race'.[47] The French

[39] *The Times*, 19 October 1838.
[40] C.P. Lucas, (ed.), *Lord Durham's Report on the Affairs of British North America*, 3 vols.,
(Oxford, 1912). The Report was originally published with despatches and appendices in
GBPP 1839, xxxii.
[41] Charles Buller, 'Sketch of Lord Durham's Mission to Canada in 1838', in Lucas,
(ed.), *Durham Report*, 3, p. 375.
[42] J. Pakington, *Hansard*, 3rd series, 1841, liv, col. 716.
[43] Ged Martin, *The Durham Report and British Policy: a Critical Essay* (Cambridge,
1972); John Manning Ward, *Colonial Self-Government: the British Experience 1759–1856*
(London, 1976), pp. 38–81.
[44] E.L. Woodward, *The Age of Reform 1815–1870* (Oxford, 1938), p. 365.
[45] Durham was not the sole, and perhaps not even the main, author. It is likely that
there was unacknowledged input from Buller, and probably Wakefield and Turton. See
Chester New, *Lord Durham: a Biography of John George Lambton, First Earl of Durham*
(Oxford, 1929), appendix one.
[46] Lucas, (ed.), *The Durham Report*, 2, pp. 16, 27.
[47] Ibid., 2, pp. 292–4, 46. This was the view, also, of some historians: see Burroughs,
The Canadian Crisis, pp. 94–6.

Canadians were a 'stationary' population, 'a people with no history, and no literature', the remains of an 'ancient colonization'.[48] To a minor extent, class might mitigate race (a few French Canadians among the 'higher classes' had 'adopted some English customs and feelings'), but the Report described the differences between the two races as stark.[49]

Many evils stemmed from racial segregation, the Report argued. There were far too few 'intermarriages' between the French and British races, and those who tried to conciliate between the two 'opposite races' were treated as 'renegades from their race'. Only those in the lower classes, 'the ruder order of people', continued to form 'domestic connexions'.[50] (This, as will be seen below, echoed a common theme in depictions of interracial marriage.) The Report could see no good in 'perpetuating that very separation of the races', this 'state of feeling... among each of the contending parties, or rather races'. It proposed that legislative union would 'at once decisively settle the question of races' and 'form a great and powerful people'.[51] Such an amalgamation would 'elevate' the French from their inferiority by 'obliter-ating the nationality of the French Canadians'.[52] The French would be amalgamated politically, in order to become a minority to British settlers in any representative assembly; they would be amalgamated socially, so that schools, language and customs would not set them apart; and, lastly, they would be amalgamated 'racially', so that any distinctions of origin, of 'race' and 'nationality' would, as in Durham's words, be 'obliterated'. The Catholic and primarily agricultural French Canadians would be reformed, in a manner that disappointed the more deeply radical, who had hoped for substantial changes in Canadian governance.[53]

The Report was making a complex and wide-sweeping argument couched not just in a language of politics, but of race.[54] Some scholars have either overlooked the racial argument or, like Janet Azjenstat, sug-gested that Durham did not regard race as a matter of 'origin or genetic inheritance'. This not only misunderstands the complex of ideas which were subsumed in race (discussed more fully in Chapter 4) but the evidence of the Report itself, which described the Canadian struggle as a 'feud of origin'.[55] It was in the omnivorous, bio-cultural contemporary sense that the Report used race—an aggregate of 'physical, moral, and political' qualities—and such a racial view of Canadian affairs was

[48] Lucas, (ed.), *The Durham Report*, 2, pp. 46, 294, 291.
[49] Ibid., 2, pp. 30, 44.   [50] Ibid., 2, pp. 43, 19, 20, 44, 43.
[51] Ibid., 2, pp. 63, 260, 309.
[52] Lucas, (ed.), *The Durham Report*, 2, pp. 292, 287–9.
[53] Thomas, *The Philosophic Radicals*, p. 403.
[54] Lucas, (ed.), *The Durham Report*, 2, pp. 288, 79.
[55] Janet Azjenstat, *The Political Thought of Lord Durham* (Kingston, 1987), p. 109n. She quotes this passage of the Report herself, p. 4.

common.[56] Witness J.T. Leader, the radical MP, in his Commons' speech on the Canadian situation:

> It was only recently that a gentleman had been arguing with him [Leader] that the beavers were the first possessors of North America: they were driven out by the Indians, who had too much intelligence and skill for them. The Indians were supplanted by the French, and now came the Anglo-Saxons, and the French Canadians, being the weaker, must submit; it was a law of nature. That might be very true; but it would be a disgrace... to help the strong to crush the weak.[57]

So it was that even those who opposed union agreed with a 'racial' interpretation. The Irish MP Daniel O'Connell, for instance, regarded the French as 'the native population', and criticized amalgamation as a despicable attempt to 'annihilate them as a separate race' (an attempt in which he saw echoes of Irish policies).[58] Sir John Pakington, a severe critic of both union and the Report, felt that the 'only part of the report which was to be relied on was... that portion of it which spoke of the feelings of the two races in Canada.'[59] Like others he saw in the Report a strange and improvident logic, first highlighting the differences between the races and their antagonisms, and then arguing that they should be mixed into a single, united political, racial and social community. Nonetheless the Whigs mostly supported political amalgamation, with Lord John Russell, future Colonial Secretary, leading the way.[60]

In the parliamentary debate over Canadian union, Charles Buller described the French Canadians as having been 'enslaved and degraded' by the old French monarchical ways. He argued that a union or amalgamation that placed the French 'on an equality with the rest of the population' was the only way they could be 'civilised and free'.[61] Buller's rhetoric of slavery, civilization and freedom was surely no accident. Only a few years before the slaves in the British colonies had been emancipated, and the power of its language remained. Buller was suggesting that there was, in the condition of the French Canadians, actually something that could be paralleled with emancipation. A new set of relations had to be defined, not only with government but with the 'market'. The backward French Canadian farmers needed to be freed, not from slavery but from the *ancien*

[56] James Browne, 'Africa', in Macvey Napier, (ed.), *Encyclopaedia Brittanica*, 7th edn., (Edinburgh, 1842), 4, p. 162.
[57] J.T. Leader, *Hansard*, 3rd series, 1839, xlviii, col. 1205.
[58] Ibid., col. 1198.
[59] J. Pakington, *Hansard*, 3rd series, 1840, liv, col. 716.
[60] *Hansard*, 3rd series, 1839, xlvii, cols. 1254–75.
[61] Buller, *Hansard*, 3rd series, 1839, xlvii, col. 1202.

régime, with its primarily agricultural and supposedly 'priest-ridden' ways. As with emancipation, union would incorporate through supposed terms of 'equality' while ensuring that differentiations and inequities were renewed, maintained or established.

When Lord Glenelg oversaw the final shaping of emancipation (he was also Colonial Secretary during the Canadian 'rebellion', which was partly why he was removed), he and other colonial officials had to give meaning to 'freedom', by defining its limitations and privileges. This meant the removal of restrictions in laws, tax and the elective franchise, as well as in access to public institutions such as schools, militia and churches.[62] But freedom was far from absolute, as Thomas Holt has observed. For ex-slaves freedom was a revelation, but it was not a revolution. Indeed, their freedom, although built on the pretence of equality, had been explicitly framed to ensure continuity between slavery and post-emancipation.[63] For slaves the abolishing of slavery meant incorporation in a new conception of a colonial polity and the furnishing, ostensibly, of equal rights before it. Yet as subsequent events in the post-abolition British Empire were to make clear, though slaves became legally free of their former masters, they had been made subject to the market and 'an economic system based on inequality', inequalities distributed through differentiations.[64] These differentiations were racial, but not only racial, and were intensely marked: indeed, it was a symptom of abolition that racial distinctions gathered a new intensity in this era of 'freedom'. Other modes were required to sustain inequality in times of putative equality.

The similarities between the union of the Canadas, racial amalgamation and Jamaican freedom are striking. In each the constitution or re-constitution of the colonial polity incorporated and differentiated at the same time, and in each taxonomies of race were intrinsic to these developments. Elsewhere, too, there were parallel processes, such as in New South Wales, where convicts were neither slaves nor citizens; and in South Australia, where it was initially intended to establish new relations between the aborigines and the colonial polity.[65] That this was happening as Britain itself was undergoing domestic

---

[62] Holt, *The Problem of Freedom*, p. 72; PP 1837–8, xxxix, (154–I), p. 9–11: Glenelg to West Indian governors, 6 November 1837; also CO 854/2, circular, 6 November 1837, fos. 78–80.

[63] Henry Taylor, *Autobiography of Henry Taylor*, 2 vols., (London, 1874), 1, pp. 157–63: Henry Taylor, minute, 14 January 1839.

[64] Holt, *The Problem of Freedom*, p. 6.

[65] Jan Kociumbas, *The Oxford History of Australia: Volume 2, 1770–1860, Possessions* (Melbourne, 1992), pp. 150–177; Pike, *Paradise of Dissent*. Buller was also acting as an agent for the Australian Patriotic Association (who sought emancipation in New South Wales). Zoë Laidlaw, personal communication.

reform was not coincidental. As the Colonial Reformers showed, both conceptually and in their network of personnel, these matters were closely connected—in figures like Lords Durham, Howick and Glenelg, and the fingers of men such as Wakefield and Buller. (In domestic reform the significance of empire seemed to multiply.[66]) The discursive connections were laid plain in racial amalgamation: such policies followed the same rationality, were couched in closely similar language, whether the Durham Report or the writings of systematic colonizers. Racial amalgamation demonstrated the ways that race was a political problem and politics was a racial one. Racial amalgamation, far from being unique or special to New Zealand, was a specific incarnation in a concatenation of analogous political and discursive projects, ranging through much of the Empire and Britain. That such developments were underway is less striking if their connection to a moment when an Imperial Liberalism was not only identifiable and coherent, but also increasingly ascendant. Seen in this light racial amalgamation seems far less a flight of fancy or a contrarian, but a solution that was kindred with many others, perhaps even modular solution. As in Canada, in New Zealand racial amalgamation was a strategy for dealing with the problem of different races with different politics by means of crossing, of union. This strategy was not built on the denial or disavowal of difference, or even transcendant sense of equality, but rather on the careful recognition and fostering of differences. The incorporation of different races consequently underwrote the expansion and strengthening of the polity, a polity that could, as a result, enunciate equality while fabricating a racial taxonomy through which to operate unequally. Though the short-term results were cast in the striking form of interracial association and marriage, in the longer term other races were to be subject to a managed disappearance: where the cost of 'elevating' the colonized race, as the Durham Report had put it, was 'obliterating' it.[67]

THE NEW ZEALAND COMPANY AND THE FAILURE OF RACIAL AMALGAMATION

On 10 July 1850 the New Zealand Company resigned its charter. But the 'New Zealand Bubble' had already been long burst. Almost five years beforehand Wakefield had admitted that the Company was 'defunct' as a colonizing venture. At any rate this was even then obvious:

---

[66] Miles Taylor, 'Empire and Parliamentary Reform: The 1832 Reform Act Revisited', in Arthur Burns and Joanna Innes, (eds.), *Rethinking the Age of Reform: Britain 1780–1850* (Cambridge, 2003), pp. 295–311.

[67] Lucas, (ed.), *The Durham Report*, 2, pp. 292, 287–9.

the Company had only about £10,000 worth of land in New Zealand yet owed its shareholders around £400,000.[68] The New System was in tatters, and among the many wrecks was racial amalgamation. After all the 'puff' the Company had generated, the actualities of New Zealand had hit hard.

Partly because the Company's rhetoric is not always taken seriously, the failure of racial amalgamation is not well studied. The Company's historical reputation is ruined, echoing the views of it held by many of its investors and other contemporaries.[69] *The Times* denounced the Company as 'a system of monstrous plunder' and 'absolute swindling', one intent on reaping enormous profits at the cost of 'dupes in this country who are infatuated enough to be guiled by them.'[70] Few recent historians have been sympathetic to the high principles the Company once claimed.[71] Many of its plans failed. The Company regarded 'natives' with a posturing paternalism, considering them largely devoid of any (adult) agency, and the way it treated them was generally below even these standards. Yet, ironically, the Company played a vital role in the development of understandings and policy regarding 'natives'; it initiated discussions about native policy in New Zealand from which later policy was partially derived and, crucially, defined some terms in which this policy was couched. The Company was also particularly successful in generating interest in New Zealand as a potential colony, and the propaganda with which they flooded the British market was to remain in circulation for decades.

The Company's policy of racial amalgamation had one concrete dimension, the system of native reserves—which would amalgamate owners by amalgamating their lands. 'Tithes' would be set aside for the natives, and the settlers would be their civilizing neighbours. The rest of the amalgamationist approach was entrusted to a belief that they were taking out settlers of a better class than was customary, and the reassurance that such matters were gradual, and would take time. It was quite clear from the instructions to the leader of the first expedition, Edward Gibbon's brother, William Wakefield, that the main objectives were to accumulate land and

---

[68] DUL, Grey Papers, GRE/B79/11/41, Buller to Earl Grey, 3 August 1846, enclosure by Wakefield. The enclosed accounts showed that, on paper, they were £296,863 in debt, as of 6 April 1846.
[69] The best coverage is given by Burns, *Fatal Success*; and Adams, *Fatal Necessity*.
[70] *The Times*, editorial, 27 July 1840.
[71] See Erik Olssen, 'Mr Wakefield as an Experiment in Post-Enlightenment Experimental Practice', *NZJH*, 31 (1997), pp. 212–15.

intelligence.[72] The expedition took out 'a scientific man' and a surgeon, but the basic matter of land purchasing took precedence.[73]

The New Zealand Company's preliminary expedition went out in May 1839, followed soon after by ships filled with emigrants. The intention was to get to New Zealand before the Crown, purchasing lands before the Crown could intervene. There was nothing much that was 'systematic' about the circumstances of the first voyage, nor about the beginnings of Company settlement, as the first emigrants found to their horror. For the first emigrants the 'settlement' at Port Nicholson (now Wellington) was a small collection of wooden huts; food was short, and the promised land was nowhere to be seen. There were large indigenous communities living nearby, and to British senses the land was just as strange. It was spring/ early summer in Britain, yet the settlers in New Zealand were coming into winter. Perhaps they thought the world had turned upside down, which in a way it had.

Tangata Whenua did not indiscriminately sell their best land, and most of the first Company purchases were rushed, poorly managed affairs.[74] There was confusion over what 'sale' meant, and there were incompetent dealings, with some that were deliberately fraudulent. There were problems with language, and the initial expedition went out without a surveyor, an obvious oversight. The arrival of New Zealand's 'lieutenant governor' in early 1840 and his extension of British sovereignty over the islands made things, from the Company perspective, even worse. From that point on (with only a few exceptions) land had to be acquired through the government, which made it much more expensive, and evaporated any hopes of a Company monopoly. Before they could 'amalgamate' land, the Company had first to purchase it, and this was proving difficult. The Company had also managed the rare colonial feat of almost balancing the sexes.[75] This meant that if intermarriage were to happen, the pool of available settlers was small (a point some observers had noted beforehand).[76]

There was a quantum leap between a paper 'aborigine' and actual Tangata Whenua. Few emigrants expected to find the preponderance of resources so heavily on the side of 'natives' when they arrived. It was they that controlled the land, dictated the terms of trade for virtually all items,

[72] New Zealand Company, *Twelfth Report*, pp. 1f–15f: William Wakefield, 'Instructions'.
[73] CO 208/185, New Zealand Company minutes, 17 April 1839, 22 April 1839, fos. 131, 132.
[74] Jellicoe, *The New Zealand Company's Native Reserves*.
[75] *Report of the Directors of the New Zealand Company*, 4 (1841); G.T. Bloomfield, *New Zealand, a Handbook of Historical Statistics* (Boston, 1984), pp. 40–3.
[76] GBPP 1840, vii (582), p. 146: 'Select Committee...Respecting the Colonization of New Zealand'.

as well as if and when encounters could take place. Company officials began to realize that it was unlikely that local people would live where the Company preferred.[77] There were other problems too. It was also apparent not all emigrants would entertain kindly feelings towards the 'aborigines'. Such a different way of living few of them had imagined, and none had previously seen. While their descriptions settled on the emblematic— the tattooed faces, the different language, dress, houses and food—the colonists found most of what was different disconcerting. This was worsened by the ill-preparation of the Company. Hungry and desperate settlers were more easily jealous of the well-provided-for and land-rich locals.

The arrival of the governor and his declaration of British sovereignty underlined that the Company had no authority. The Company even lacked authority over its own settlers. On the other hand, this meant the Company was also free of any real responsibility. Ultimately, a Company document announced, 'the welfare of the native-born subjects of her Majesty in New Zealand, has devolved entirely and exclusively on her Majesty's Government.'[78] The Company could thereafter comfortably, if disingenuously, jibe that it could have done better had it been given the chance.

The Company made initial attempts to implement its amalgamationist native reserves system. Edmund Halswell, yet to see New Zealand, was appointed as Commissioner for Native Reserves. At £300 per annum it was more than a nominal appointment.[79] He was ordered to reserve lands for natives that were interspersed among the lands of colonists, and to respect the superior position of chiefs. If his appointment was a sign of some commitment, his instructions showed ambivalence. Halswell arrived in New Zealand in early 1841, by which time the Company had begun reserving lands for natives. He was even given official status by the governor, being made a regional 'protector of aborigines'.[80] This was a codification of the continuities between the Company and the colonial government.

Tangata Whenua would not move on to their allotted reserves as the Company desired. Some individuals might, but never communities as a whole.[81] The decision was then made to lease the native reserves, and put

[77] CO 209/17, Richard Hanson, report to the APS, May 1842, fos. 352–60.
[78] *Report of the Directors of the New Zealand Company*, 12 (1844), p. 78g: Halswell's Instructions, 10 October 1840. Endorsed by the 1840 select committee; PP 1840, vii (582), p. ix–x.
[79] CO 208/180, Minutes, Directors, 2 July 1840, fo. 162; *New Zealand Journal*, 24 May 1845, p. 125.
[80] Jellicoe, *The New Zealand Company's Native Reserves*, pp. 17–32.
[81] Dieffenbach, *Travels in New Zealand*, 2, pp. 145–7.

Halswell in control of the funds. This was a major departure from Hawtrey's plan of settling colonists and natives in close proximity, but was still consistent with some of Halswell's instructions. The money earned from the reserves was to be the major civilizing influence, not the natives' neighbours.[82] Halswell remained outwardly optimistic. 'From what I already know of these people, and the daily experience I acquire', he wrote, 'I have little doubt of being able to accomplish what the Company desire for their improvement.'[83] This confidence seemed less justifiable after a year in the job, as Halswell was squabbling with lessees and the colonial government.[84] By April 1842 Halswell's position was superseded by a trust to control native reserves made up of the new Bishop of New Zealand, the Chief Justice and the governor.[85] In a little over two years the main Company initiative to amalgamate natives had been severely curtailed, and transmuted into something quite different that was now beyond their control.

The entire Company system was in deep trouble. There may have been over 6,000 Company emigrants in the first two years, but from the end of 1841 until mid-1844 only another 3,000 joined them.[86] The colonial government had overturned several of the Company's larger land claims, and the Company was in financial distress, from which the Colonial Office was reluctant to relieve them. The years 1843 and 1844 were particularly grim. In 1843, near the Company settlement of Nelson, a posse of Company settlers and officials had attempted to assert rights of 'purchase' over a piece of land that was still possessed by Ngāti Toa. The incident, 'The Wairau Affray', had ended with four Ngāti Toa and twenty-two of the colonial posse dead, a tragedy that was a public relations disaster for the Company and proved a personal one for Wakefield, as his brother Arthur was amongst the dead. Elsewhere the Company's luck was no better. Even a parliamentary committee that the Company engineered back in Britain seemed to have little positive effect; with the Company in deep trouble, members and investors abandoned them.

In 1845 a Company document reaffirmed that racial amalgamation was a Company aim. This paper urged that 'the Imperial Government. . .

[82] Agreement, New Zealand Company and Russell, 18 November 1840, s.13.

[83] *New Zealand Journal*, 14 May 1842, p. 113: Halswell's Report, 11 November 1841.

[84] Viscount Howick, Speech, 18 June 1845, *A Corrected Report of the Debate in the House of Commons, 17th, 18th and 19th June, on the State of New Zealand and the Case of the New Zealand Company* (London, 1845), p. 147.

[85] *Report of the Directors of the New Zealand Company*, 12 (1844), pp. 108–9g: Willoughby Shortland to Swainson, 26 July 1842.

[86] PP 1844, xiii (556), p. 694: 'Report from the Select Committee Appointed to Enquire into. . . New Zealand'.

adopt [measures] with the purpose of substituting amalgamation for extermination'.[87] It emphasized the importance of settler attitudes; that government goodwill towards natives was not enough. The 'essential means' for successful amalgamation was, the Company argued, dependent on an 'earnest adoption of the principle of amalgamation' by settlers.[88] But by this time the Company's position was no longer one of any authority. They were primarily critics and lobbyists, as only the colonial government could enact even the most minor native policy.

From 1846 the Company began to propose a different model of race relations. In this new model they resigned themselves to restricting English laws only to colonial settlements, and to leaving the natives as they believed they were, a distinct race. Amalgamation, they decided, would take place more gradually, as 'natives' themselves came to desire it. The British settlements would be completely distinct from natives, and consist only of 'such portions of Territory as the Governor may feel himself capable of effectually holding subject to British Authority'.[89] The natives were to be left to their 'Exceptional Districts or Outside Territory', and all English people would be kept from residing there without licence.[90] The Exceptional Districts were to be 'beyond the pale of English law', 'Native usages alone [were] to be recognized; no Judge or other European Civil Officer [was] to be maintained there'.[91] Natives who resided inside the settlements would be amalgamated, but beyond the settlements all things European ended. Such settlements, it was supposed, would attract natives and tame them through their own desires and acquisitiveness; European settlements would render apparent the superiority of the European life.

This proposal pushed the achievement of racial amalgamation even further into the distance; but it also countenanced the kind of system that the Company had long criticized. Their stance had been radically different only a year earlier. 'It is impossible to reconcile the Missionary System with that of the Company', Charles Buller had written then. 'In every respect they go on opposite principles.' As he explained, the missionaries wanted to prevent colonization,

[87] National Archive of New Zealand (NANZ), New Zealand Company (NZC) 31/32, [E.G. Wakefield], 'Relations with the Natives', fo. 34.

[88] Ibid., fos. 34–5.

[89] Earl Grey Papers, GRE/B147/15: Report of Special Committee of the New Zealand Company, 24 August 1846, enclosure C.

[90] CO 208/188, fo. 451: Minutes of Special Committee, 25 August 1846.

[91] CO 208/301, fos. 273–96: Harrington, 'The New Zealand Company', 17 August 1846; Earl Grey Papers, GRE/B147/15: Report of Special Committee of the New Zealand Company, 24 August 1846, enclosure C.

to preserve the nationality of the New Zealanders; to keep them apart from European contact; and to maintain their exclusive property in the whole soil of the Islands. Our system, on the contrary, was to treat the soil as unappropriated whereever it was not in some way occupied; to vindicate to the Crown the ownership of all the unoccupied expanse; turn to account those peculiar facilities which the Aboriginal Race of New Zealand appear to possess, for intermixture and amalgamation with the European population. These two systems are essentially antagonist.[92]

The Missionary System, which the Company reconfigured in its proposal of 'Exceptional Districts', was substantially a recognition of the way things were. Tangata Whenua remained staunchly independent and had the weight of numbers and the force of arms. The Company had finally realized that although it might have a chance of reorganizing settlers, the 'aborigines' were not to be susceptible to the same arguments or inducements. Its system could not deal with the actualities and exigencies of New Zealand. The arrival of a colonial government put paid to Company hopes of a monopoly over purchasing lands and settlement, and meant they could not assume authority over settlers, lands or 'natives'. But the system could cope even less well with Tangata Whenua who were real, live agents and did not conform to the simple economic rationality of Company theories. These 'natives' would dispose of their land as they chose, and even when they chose to sell would not necessarily sell it cheaply; they did not move onto reserves at Company whim, and showed no willingness to become an indigenous working class. Nor did they ask for, nor need, Company endorsement to keep their status as chiefs.

THE COMPANY'S RACIAL AMALGAMATION REPOSSESSED

Even in 1847 the Company maintained its theory offered a 'good system'.[93] The incoming Colonial Secretary, Earl Grey, was forcefully told by a Company supporter that New Zealand was the most favourable place for a systematic colonization. 'If you do not succeed in resuming the colonization of N.Z. that will itself be a bar to your colonizing any other part of the world.' The 'spectre of the N.Z. Co.', he continued, 'destroyed in what was after all the best effort at colonization during the last 100 years, will scare every capitalist in the country from venturing in any similar

[92] CO 208/188, fos. 295–6: Buller to Stanley, 14/15 April 1845.
[93] Grey Papers, GRE/B79/11/37: Buller to Earl Grey, 3 August 1847.

enterprise.'[94] Such a description was brazen exaggeration, but not without any cause: New Zealand had been extremely widely publicized, and had drawn its influential support because it was held to be a model of reformed colonization. The 'best effort' had dismally failed. Earl Grey realized, sadly, 'that I can do nothing to promote "systematic coloniza[tio]n". There is not a farthing to be had from the T[reasury] & without some money very little seems possible.'[95]

The Company had proven its strengths were political: it was extremely able at lobbying and generating publicity. For over a decade it had been embroiled with government, with its men of influence keeping up what Wakefield called a 'New Zealand war': politicking and pressuring for government sanction, aid and, ultimately, rescue.[96] One critic of the Company was stunned by their 'unsparing use of every species of puff, direct or indirect, public dinners, fetes, advertisements of colonial cadet-ships, party periodicals... and pamphlets'.[97] Its colonizing attempts were deeply flawed and troubled, but the Company had not ceased; they had cornered most of the public discourse about New Zealand, its only real challengers in this field being the mission societies, whose favourable descriptions of New Zealand and its people served, unintentionally, as endorsements. Much of the literature regarding New Zealand that was available in Britain in the 1840s and 1850s bore the Company's stamp in one way or another.

A lasting result of this was that the Company had ensured that New Zealand was seen as a perfect place for colonization. By 1840 the supposed 'great natural superiority of this fine region' was already a commonplace.[98] New Zealand's climate was universally depicted as temperate and inviting, from the vulgarized notions found in children's books to more specialized literatures. New Zealand, one systematic colonizer stated, had a much better climate and soil than the Canadas or Australia—and this at a time when 'climate' was widely considered 'the most powerful' of the agents of bodily change.[99] The New Zealand Company's scientist (also a doctor) observed that 'no country is better suited for a colony of the Anglo-Saxon

[94] Ibid., GRE/B79/11: Buller to Earl Grey, 15 March 1847.
[95] Ibid., GRE/B79/11: Earl Grey to Buller, 2 February 1847; Morrell, *British Colonial Policy*, p. 473.
[96] BL, Add.Ms 35261, Wakefield Letters: Edward Gibbon Wakefield to Charles Torlesse, [undated], fo. 71.
[97] Theosophilius Heale, *New Zealand and the New Zealand Company* (London, 1842), p. 9; Earl Grey Papers, GRE/B126/11: Stephen to Howick, [?] February 1845.
[98] *Tait's Edinburgh Magazine* (1839), p. 611; 'New Zealand', *Dublin Review*, IX (1840), pp. 211–13; S.M.D. Martin, *New Zealand, in a Series of Letters* (London, 1845), p. 238.
[99] GBPP 1837–1838, xxi (680), p. 126: 'Select Committee Report on New Zealand'.

race than New Zealand'.[100] Such views of the New Zealand climate were supplemented by claims to its having geographical and physical advantages. She was the 'Great Britain of the Southern Hemisphere', with the ideal geographical position, climate, waters and natural productions.[101] In New Zealand, some said, the British race would be even healthier than back in Britain, the children would be 'ruddy and robust'.[102]

The Company had also ensured that New Zealand was seen as having the best 'natives'. Though in the eighteenth-century accounts of James Cook and Marion Du Fresne New Zealand natives were depicted as fierce, warlike and savage, negatively contrasted with their Tahitian relatives, by the 1840s the Company had successfully rehabilitated them. Typically, the New Zealanders were regarded as 'vastly superior' to other natives, and 'if properly dealt with, appear more likely to amalgamate with the white settler.'[103] Company literature had ensured that the native race was described positively. They were good-looking, intelligent, somehow closer to Europeans in descent or complexion.[104] They were eminently civilizable, and could be placed at a relatively advanced stage of human progress. The native race had a system of rank, they were settled on particular pieces of land which they understood themselves to own, they cultivated the soil, and they were sometimes (but not always) considered to treat their women well. If they were savage and warlike, and many British seamen had already lost their lives to them, this at least showed them to be bristling with martial vigour. By promoting the climate, land and natives of New Zealand as eminently suitable for colonization (and doing so with considerable success), the Company had depicted all the necessary ingredients for a supposed successful racial amalgamation.

This was by no means entirely or even mostly cynical; amongst Company personnel there was genuine belief in the strategy of racial amalgamation and the conceptions that underlay it. Wakefield himself wrote enthusiastically of racial amalgamation both in public and private. In a letter to his sister he described Hawtrey's essay on racial amalgamation

[100] Ernest Dieffenbach, *Travels in New Zealand; with Contributions to the Geography, Geology, Botany, and Natural History of that Colony*, 2 vols., (London, 1843), I, p. 183.
[101] The depiction of New Zealand as a future Great Britain of the South was already, by 1842, passé. CO 209/3, CMS Petition, [January 1838], p. 162.
[102] R.G. Jameson, *New Zealand, South Australia and New South Wales* (London, 1842), p. 256; John Dunmore Lang, *New Zealand in 1839: or Four Letters to the Right Honourable Earl Durham* (London, 1839), pp. 53–4.
[103] 'Traits of the New Zealander', *Chambers's Edinburgh Journal*, n.s. IV (1845), p. 87.
[104] GBPP 1837–1838, xxi (680), pp. 46, 61: 'Report'.

as 'the beautiful appendix'.[105] His father, Edward, even after one son
had been killed in New Zealand, continued to 'believe that the native
New Zealander will in the course of a generation or two amalgamate and
sink into civilis[atio]n and Christian habits. But not if kept as a distinct
race... The only way to preserve them, is not to separate them as a distinct
race'.[106] Hawtrey tried doggedly to have his ideas on reserves and amalgamation taken up, even after the Company's early failures. From his
home in England (he had changed his mind about going out), he raised
the issue directly with the Colonial Office. He argued that the reserve
system and guaranteeing the chiefs their 'security of station' was the best
native policy.[107] Hawtrey insisted that the old system of separate reserves
was misconceived, though he no longer opposed the leasing out of the
native reserves to colonists.

The reportage from New Zealand was equally positive about racial
amalgamation. Though it was not always clear what was being signified by
racial amalgamation, it was considered to be advancing, and was widely
praised.[108] The Company's draughtsman supposed 'in half a century
the interests of the two races will be one; and that the extermination of the
aborigines will only take place in the amalgamation with the Europeans.'[109]
New Zealanders, another Company supporter wrote, would 'civilize easily',
and had already showed their willingness to adopt European customs,
industries and habits. Their 'physical superiority' was most striking:

> The women are for the most part comely, and many very beautiful. Moreover
> they are gentle in their manners, and much attached to the men with whom
> they connect themselves. Several of the Europeans have taken New Zealand
> wives, and there is every probability of an extensive amalgamation. Of course
> occasional union will take place between Europeans and the women of all
> native tribes with whom they have intercourse, but amalgamation properly
> speaking has never taken place any where but in New Zealand, Tahiti, Hawaii,
> and other islands of the Pacific. In short the character of the New Zealanders
> forbids the idea of extermination. They may ultimately be lost by amalgamation
> with Europeans, but that is a process which is not only brought about without
> suffering, but is productive of the happiest consequences.[110]

[105] BL, Add.Ms 35261, Wakefield Letters, Edward Gibbon Wakefield to Catherine
Torlesse, 12 October 1837, fo. 12. Also, NZC 31/32, [E.G. Wakefield], 'Relations with the
Natives', fo. 34.
[106] RHL, Mss.N.Z.s.1, Edward Wakefield to James Backhouse, 17 July 1844, fos. 2–3.
[107] *Report of the Directors of the New Zealand Company*, 12 (1844), pp. 69g–70g:
Hawtrey to Lord Stanley, 30 March 1842.
[108] 'Glimpses of New Zealand', *Chambers's Edinburgh Journal*, n.s. iv (1845), p. 55;
John Walton, *Twelve Months' Residence in New Zealand* (Glasgow, 1839), p. 33.
[109] Charles Heaphy, *Narrative of a Residence in Various Parts of New Zealand* (London,
1842), p. 66.
[110] 'New Zealand', *Dublin Review*, ix (1840), p. 213.

Nor was it only Company propaganda which continued to see racial amalgamation in a positive light. A prominent German professor, Carl Ritter, thought intermarriages would result in 'progressive affinity', and 'the introduction of a race of hybrid children'. (This was, it seems, the first use of the word 'hybrid' to refer to mixed race New Zealanders.) At the very least, he supposed, this was 'a posterity by no means ungraceful, which will at least not fall back to cannibalism.'[111]

The Company's 'scientific man', Dr Ernst Dieffenbach, was the most detailed and significant of commentators. By 1842 he was back in England, publishing what were to become standard works on New Zealand, and touring various scientific societies.[112] Although an equivocal supporter of the Company's version of racial amalgamation, he was a great proponent more generally. Dieffenbach was uniformly positive in his descriptions of the 'native population', and often commented on the progress of race crossing specifically. His work lent gravitas to Company 'puff'. Throughout his travels in New Zealand Dieffenbach had been struck by such crossings already in progress. In the South Island particularly, he found places where the 'intermixture... between Europeans and natives is complete.' There were large numbers of 'half-caste' children, who were 'of a healthy constitution, and of good character'. He was deeply impressed by such children, who were 'all uncommonly well formed... [and] speak both the Mauri [*sic*] language and the English.'[113] From these 'mixed marriages' resulted 'one of the finest half-castes that exists, and I would add, also an improvement on the race'.[114] He imagined that there would soon be 'an entire mixture'.[115] The fortunes of racial amalgamation, it was clear, would not be reducible to the political and commercial fortunes of the New Zealand Company.

The continuing relevance of racial amalgamation was evidently not because it had been proved either sound or effective. The Company's ideas about racial amalgamation were vague, cavalier, rough and impractical; Wakefield happily left 'all *the filling up* of an extensive project to others', in this case, Hawtrey. 'In fact', he wrote, 'I have not time to attend to details'.[116] In such 'details' the effectiveness of the Company's racial

[111] Carl Ritter, *The Colonization of New Zealand* (London, 1842), p. 19.
[112] J.C. Prichard, *Researches into the Physical History of Mankind*, 3rd edn., (London, 1836–47), 5 [1847], pp. 129–33.
[113] *New Zealand Journal*, 7 August 1841, pp. 202–3; also see ibid., 18 September 1841, p. 239.
[114] Dieffenbach, *Travels in New Zealand*, 2, p. 41.
[115] Ernest Dieffenbach, *New Zealand and its Native Population* (London, 1841), pp. 27–8.
[116] BL, Add.Ms 35261, Wakefield Letters, Edward Gibbon Wakefield to Edward Wakefield, 22 October 1841, fo. 58.

amalgamation rested; but the enduring appeal of racial amalgamation more broadly clearly did not. Plainly, the persistence of racial amalgamation stemmed from reasons other than a sensible and measured Company formulation, or any proven success. Racial amalgamation had a life far beyond that of the Company largely because it corresponded with other developments apparent throughout Britain and its empire. Paralleling 'solutions' to problems as seemingly diverse as Canadian union and West Indian freedom, racial amalgamation was a kind of 'reform for aborigines'. Each of these different 'problems' and their 'solutions' were entangled not only through the political rationalities (especially that becoming familiar as Liberalism) but through overlapping networks of people, such as Durham, Glenelg, Buller and Wakefield. Moreover, in keeping with the contemporary practice of 'reform' racial amalgamation appeared to cede more than it actually did. Equality was the flag around which racial amalgamation gathered, but it was an aspiration, both distant and conditional. As racial amalgamation's proponents (and their successors) were to claim, racial amalgamation could make colonization humane: and yet many of the immediate steps of colonization, whether violence, assertion of colonial power or the fetish of racial differences, seemed remarkably familiar.

2

'Pandemonium on Earth'? Intimacy and Encounter in Pre-Colonial New Zealand

Foreign and indigenous bodies had long been encountering each other in New Zealand. By the time New Zealand was remade as a British colony, in 1840, there had been close to a century of such encounters. Even by 1840 the archipelago had seen significant demographic alteration. A population that might have been 100,000–160,000 when the *Endeavour* visited in 1769 was, probably, 70,000–90,000 in 1840, mostly due to the ravages of disease.[1] The population of resident Europeans or other foreigners had been zero in 1769, but by 1839 was probably around 1,200, with hundreds more constituting a 'changing population' linked to the cycling in and out of ships and crews.[2] By the mid-1830s New Zealand had a new innovated space, a port town with thousands of indigenous residents and hundreds of foreigners, and had forged a new 'extensive intercourse' between the archipelago and Sydney.[3] There were hundreds of foreigners residing in indigenous communities, and a score of smaller, often seasonal, communities that foreigners had solely or jointly founded.

From Sydney or London the archipelago seemed to be disordered and disorganized. Empire had occasioned most of these early encounters, but they remained beyond its effective jurisdictions. Attempts to control British subjects or other foreigners residing in New Zealand through the flexing of empire were unsuccessful. Various attempts were tried: extending the jurisdiction of New South Wales courts, appointing (toothless) officials, conducting punitive expeditions. The actualities of these encounters, however, were only too evident. Those foreigners who lived in the archipelago

---

[1] Ian Pool, *Te Iwi Maori: A New Zealand Population Past, Present and Projected* (Auckland, 1991), p. 57; Anne almond, *Between Worlds: Early Exchanges Between Maori and Europeans, 1773–1815* (Auckland, 1997), p. 265.

[2] William Wade, *A Journey in the Northern Island of New Zealand* (Hobart, 1842), p. 184; *Church Missionary Record*, December 1839, x, p. 288.

[3] *Historical Records of Australia*, xvi, p. 511: Goderich to Bourke, 2 May 1833.

were subject to the prevailing political and social powers, which with a few exceptions were the local indigenous communities and leaders. The writ of empire ran only as far as Tangata Whenua and unruly foreigners let it.

The decades before 1840 present an uneven and complicated web of narratives. Interspersed in these narratives, just as they were interspersed in these communities, were foreign bodies. These individuals were predominantly arranged into an indigenous order, but it was an order not fully legible in imperial terms. Indigenous rule was either disavowed by officials or considered to be failed or failing. But the political relationships that were extended over these foreign bodies were not the only ones. Different kinds of relationship—those of exchange, of labour, and particularly of intimacy—also worked to connect or incorporate foreigners with indigenous societies.

Intimate relations, whether those of affect or domesticity, the spiritual or the carnal, wove foreigners into the orbits of indigenous life. These produced, as they did elsewhere, 'tender ties'—integrative renditions of intimacy that were construed by foreign onlookers as racial crossings.[4] In New Zealand these intimate relations were common, indeed prevailing, foreign experiences. The central inquiry of this chapter addresses how these kinds of intimate encounters were recognized, how they were circulated and understood by foreign and colonial interlocuters as the crossings of different races. The stories corralled in this chapter consequently track how an archipelago of encounters and individuals who could not be disciplined or even easily or coherently described, could be supposedly reduced to a single colony, and made subject to a simplified and stabilized (if not stable) racial taxonomy.

INTIMATE ENCOUNTERS

European and American voyagers came to New Zealand for various reasons: exploration, to be missionaries, to whale offshore or inshore, to relax or repair; for seal skins, flax, victuals, salted pork, or timber. Some simply came to escape where they had left, whether the convict settlement at Sydney or the ship they came on. Before 1840 as many as 2,000 ships had visited the archipelago, most of which were ocean whaling ships. One important history has described these encounters as being between 'Two Worlds'.[5] This does not quite communicate the particularity and localism

---

[4] See also Sylvia Van Kirk, *'Many Tender Ties': Women in Fur-Trade Society in Western Canada, 1670–1870* (Winnipeg, 1980); Stoler (ed.), *Haunted By Empire*.

[5] Anne Salmond, *Two Worlds: First Meetings Between Maori and Europeans, 1642–1772* (Auckland, 1991).

that was involved. It was not a generalized Europe and New Zealand that came into 'contact'. It is people, rather than cultures, which meet, and for reasons as simple as this, as well as ones more complex, the early encounters were enormously varied. This was not so much a meeting of two worlds, but rather of many.

Tangata Whenua soon described these foreigners as 'Pākehā'. The common history that Pākehā shared was not of geography or 'race', but of ships: they were the *tangata kaipuke*—the Ship People.[6] It was not the land masses of Europe, Australia and America that came to New Zealand, but fragments brought by their floating outposts. Sailing encompassed a way of life, and to some extent each ship had its own culture, its own hierarchy, its own formations of power and authority. A ship was a 'floating city' and a 'fatherland...so well organized, so imposing'.[7] Curious fragments, weeks, if not months, from 'home', the early ships which visited New Zealand were fatherlands in another sense: male societies, where women were rare and exotic mixtures of different races were common. Ships, especially whaling ships, were amongst the most heterogeneous societies in the world. 'The mixture of people to be found amongst the South Seamen is extraordinary', marvelled one traveller, and possibly it was these kinds of shipboard race relations, more than those of Europe or America, which seamen took ashore.[8]

Regular visits by Pākehā began when whaling ships started 'fishing' New Zealand's offshore waters from the early 1790s after intermittent visits since 1769. Also in the 1790s gangs came ashore in search of seals. Trade of some sort was engaged in by virtually all the ships that visited, mostly for ships' victuals, with fresh water and vegetables, pigs and fish being the most common. Extensive trade in more lucrative New Zealand items waxed and waned; voyagers saw the potential of New Zealand trees as spars as early as the 1790s, and soon after discovered New Zealand flax as a source of linen (a trade begun in the 1790s and peaking around 1831).[9] Other commodities were also tried, and curiosities, salted pork, and the gum of the Kauri tree (used for its resin) were among them. The eclectic set of voyages which brought Pākehā encompassed such a variety

[6] Also variously called *tangata ke* (different or strange people), *tangata pora* (*pora* being another word for vessel), or *takata pora* (a dialectal variation, primarily Kai Tahu).
[7] Dumont D'Urville, *New Zealand 1826–1827*, (trans.) Olive Wright, (Wellington, 1950), p. 98.
[8] J.C. Byrne, *Twelve Years' Wanderings in the British Colonies from 1835 to 1847*, (London, 1848), p. 67.
[9] Felix Maynard, *The Whalers*, (ed.) Alexandre Dumas, (trans.) F.W. Reed, (London, 1937), p. 146.

of motivations and trajectories that individual encounters were always particular.

The relationships wrought by these voyages were uneven. Partly this was because vessels favoured particular anchorages, and these varied seasonally and according to economic activity. Some districts became well known as anchorages before the turn of the century, such as Tamatea or Dusky Sound, others grew popular only as time wore on and voyagers grew more confident, such as Hokianga. Settlement was equally uneven, and the places chosen were often exigent. Sailors would run ashore wherever they could, whenever they so desired. The site the first missionaries chose in 1814 owed to a chief who promised his patronage. Shore whaling stations were where bay whaling was best; and the seal gangs followed the seals from one rookery, until depleted, to the next. Accidents of geography, resources and political relations shaped the topography of encounter. The archipelago had been fixed on Pākehā maps and imaginations; well before 1820, New Zealand was a stop on international seaways.

Pākehā brought opportunities, but also enormous potential for disruption and trouble. As well as new things and new people, new relationships were all potentially threatening to established political and social orders. It was a matter of the first importance to local communities, and particularly local leaders, that Pākehā, and exchanges with them, be controlled. Initially trade and violence were two exchanges that Tangata Whenua and Pākehā utilized, while relying on customary sources of order such as the leadership of chiefs or shipboard discipline. But as visits were prolonged, and as Pākehā became residents and not just visitors, different relations proliferated.

The most significant of these new relations were intimate. These were regularly, but not only, carnal, and included other affective relations, including friendships, patronage and the spiritual. Intimacy within Tangata Whenua was located within a universe that was gendered and hierarchical, but with kinship and a multi-dimensional existence that traversed these differences. As Anne Salmond has described it, indigenous existence

> was ordered by networks of kinship and alliance. The old cosmological chants recounted the emergence of the world in a language of whakapapa, or genealogical engagement. In everyday life, these links emerged as nets of relationships between people and places, animated by reciprocal exchanges.[10]

The principle of reciprocal exchange, *utu* (payment, satisfaction, balance), a currency of this exchange, *mana* (spiritual power, divinity, energy, authority), as well as the complex of practices, beliefs and institutions

---

[10] Salmond, *Between Worlds*, p. 509.

relating to *tapu* (sacred) and its opposite, *noa*, were principal forces.[11]
Tapu, for instance, could be found in most aspects of life, and could on
occasion be lost or endangered, not least by inappropriate intimacies. Even
the most simple and inert item was enmeshed in a complicated systems
of meaning. Encounters between Pākehā and Tangata Whenua were
moments when imperial circuitry and 'nets of relationships' amongst
Tangata Whenua coincided.

Tangata Whenua had quickly established relations of exchange with
Pākehā, and these relations had been construed as 'trade'. The 'natives'
proved to be, one Pākehā thought, very savvy traders: 'It would take three
Armenians to swindle him' (when it apparently took three Greeks to
swindle an Armenian).[12] Particular items were especially valued. One
Pākehā explained that in New Zealand fish-hooks had a value resembling
copper, axes and hoes to silver, while muskets and powder were as
gold.[13] There were thousands of muskets in New Zealand by the mid-
1820s, and the 'natives' were said to 'love firearms above anything else.'[14]
Yet the state of the New Zealand market could quickly alter, and from one
visit to the next ships often found very different items in demand. The
arrival of the musket was emblematic of how trade could be, initially, far
more important and widespread than Pākehā themselves. Things like
muskets and disease, two things Pākehā brought but did not control,
had widespread and fundamental effects.

Both Pākehā and indigenous people had, in a relatively short time,
made material exchange carnal. These encounters were intimacies that
helped discipline and control Pākehā, even if Pākehā familiarized them
as 'prostitution'. This was unsurprising as prostitution was integral to a
seaman's world; but these sexual relations were regularly different, with
longer-term relations not unlike 'marriages of convenience', or even, as
one writer later put it, the example of Pocahontas.[15] Of course, prostitution in British or other societies was complex, but that complexity was
different. In New Zealand, sexuality was in many ways unrecognizable to

[11] These translations should be considered only expedient; these are enormously significant concepts, and the meanings of them are still much debated.
[12] J.H.H. St John, *Pakeha Rambles Through Maori Lands* (Wellington, 1873), pp. 167–8;
also McNab, *The Old Whaling Days*, p. 488: Watkins, journal; Nicholas, *Narrative*, 2, p. 50;
John Savage, *Some Account of New Zealand* (London, 1807), p. 57; Wade, *A Journey*, p. 22.
[13] Elder (ed.), *Marsden's Lieutenants*, p. 173: Kendall to the secretary of the CMS,
14 August 1820.
[14] D'Urville, *New Zealand*, p. 220: M. Gaimard, diary. Also see Richard Davis,
Missionary Register (1827), p. 624.
[15] Hawtrey, *An Earnest Address to New Zealand Colonists*, p. 94. A whaleship, *Pocahontas*, was active in New Zealand waters.

seamen: there were no dowries nor banns, no prostitutes, pimps, brothels or churches. There were differences in status and rank seamen generally could not recognize, subtleties about the 'network of relationships' of which they were almost completely unaware. Still, with the innovation sprung of desire the seamen managed, and pragmatically they made their own sense.

Seamen whose main encounters with indigenous people were in trade—whether material or carnal—had only their own understandings of what was going on. Most ships were involved in sexual exchange, and in most cases some sort of 'payment' was central to many short-term sexual liaisons, but the significance of these was more various, different and potentially greater than the term 'prostitution' suggests.[16] Payment was often in the sense signified by *utu*, where the balance or satisfaction might lie with the larger group and not only with the individual. Journal keepers were generally reticent in documenting these encounters too closely, and often spoke in polite terms and euphemism. 'The ladies at [Cloudy] bay were very condescending, and took lodgings on board the ship, to the great satisfaction of the sailors', wrote one captain. 'They were very industrious in washing &c.'[17] The '&c' was generally done when ships were in harbours, at anchor. But even when vessels were coasting, or dropped anchor some distance offshore, Tangata Whenua would come in canoes to trade pigs for blankets, guns and powder.[18] It was not unusual for young 'maidens' to also be in these canoes.[19] At anchor the pattern seemed generally the same: the ship came into the harbour, '[t]he crew went on the spree.'[20]

The experiences of a French naval vessel in 1824 can perhaps stand for the experiences of many ships. Shortly after the vessel anchored twenty local women came on board, and were greeted by the sailors with 'a generous hospitality'.[21] The officers could scarcely have kept the women off the ship even if they had wanted, or at least so they claimed. 'These New Zealand women were not fussy', one crew member observed, and soon enough there was on board a 'general prostitution'.[22] The fornication itself was perhaps familiar, but some reflected that things were not quite as

[16] Though formalized prostitution can differ widely: Judith R. Walkowitz, *Prostitution and Victorian Society: Women, Class, and the State* (Cambridge, 1982); Luise White, *The Comforts of Home: Prostitution in Colonial Nairobi* (Chicago, 1990).
[17] W.B. Rhods, *The Whaling Journal of Captain W.B. Rhodes: Barque* Australian *of Sydney 1836–1838* (Christchurch, 1954), p. 17: 20–23 September 1836.
[18] D'Urville, *New Zealand 1826–1827*, p. 129.
[19] Rhodes, *Whaling Journal* , p. 81: 22 February 1838.
[20] *Extracts from . . . Duperrey*, p. 163: Jules Alphonse Rene Poret de Blosseville, journal.
[21] Ibid., p. 95: Charles Hector Jacquinot, journal, 3 April 1824.
[22] Ibid., pp. 136, 137: Rene Primevere Lesson, journal.

they might have expected. It seemed, for instance, that all the women were 'slaves'.[23] Strangely, at least to French eyes, some married women also came on board, but they made it clear that they were 'taboo' (*tapu*). Officers soon considered that a married woman was adulterous on pain of death.[24] One of the ship's medics connected the restriction of 'prostitution' to slave women to the prevalence of venereal disease (especially syphilis and gonorrhoea, whose introduction he blamed on the English).[25] It was apparent that this was not the 'prostitution' to which the seamen were accustomed and which they initially expected, and they seemed to have a wide experience in this area. None of the seamen were in doubt that the way these encounters were sexualized intimately related to indigenous life onshore.

It is not surprising that indigenous communities responded to the arrival of the Ship People in carnal ways. Their demands in this respect were obvious, and earnest, from the very first encounters. A lack of satisfaction in this respect could well have led to trouble and made Pākehā unmanageable, particularly when their readings of indigenous bodies were so sexually charged and fetishized 'naked' indigenous bodies. Nor were such usages unprecedented; as with politics elsewhere, indigenous politics was in some ways constituted through the intimate. One *whakataukī* (proverb) reminds that '*mo te wahine me te whenua e mate ai tangata*', 'for women and land people perish.' That few Pākehā at this time wanted land heightened the significance of women. The political nature of these carnal affairs was often explicit. In one instance a chief tried to throw overboard ship girls from a neighbouring *hapū*, maintaining it was his right to demand that the girls on board in his harbour were local.[26] In the most important example, this kind of dispute widened into a large-scale war, now known as the 'Girl's War' of March 1830. This was an inter-tribal engagement sparked by an English whaling captain who replaced his two young indigenous wives with another two. This became a dispute amongst the young women and their families and, as the women involved were women of importance and influence, women of *mana*, this was amplified into a chiefly dispute, and then a tribal one. The whaling captain, Brind, tried unsuccessfully to get Pākehā ships at anchor involved,

[23] Ibid., p. 99: Jacquinot, journal, 3 April 1824; others agreed, for example, PP 1837–1838, xxi (680), pp. 66–7: 'Report . . . into the Present State of the Islands of New Zealand', Joseph Montefiore, evidence.

[24] *Extracts from . . . Duperrey*, p. 99, 121, 138: Jacquinot, journal, 3 April 1824, Victor Charles Lolte, journal, Lesson, journal.

[25] Ibid., p. 161: Lesson, medical journal; also, ibid., p. 119: Lolte, journal.

[26] Richard A. Cruise, *Journal of a Ten Months' Residence in New Zealand* (London, 1823), pp. 264–5: 5 November 1820.

and further bloodshed was only avoided through a peace brokered by missionaries.[27]

But these encounters structured around exchange and the sexual were not always restricted to slaves. In the far north, recent military success had led to an increase in the number of 'slaves' (*kuki* or *taurekareka*). Yet others, many of whom were very young, were also involved. Such women, some Pākehā observers thought, went on board urged on by parents and relatives, in order to access muskets and powder.[28] From harbour to harbour there was considerable variation over what Tangata Whenua allowed.[29] Yet though sex before life-partnership was generally accepted by Tangata Whenua, indigenous standards were different, not lax. There were, for example, plenty of words of opprobrium in *te Reo* for promiscuous women.[30] There were definitely standards of sexual modesty, and protocol. Adultery (*pūremu*), especially if a chief was the offended party, could well be punished by death.[31] In some cases it is clear that women went on board for their own reasons. Missionaries had to comfort one chief who had two wives go on board and was inconsolable, and intent on taking his own life.[32] They also counselled another chief who refused to believe that his wife had acquired a nail by 'honest' means, and was equally upset.[33] The shape of Pākehā demand meant that women enabled preferred access to new forms of exchange, and with that came opportunities for transformation, either of their own personal position or of matters more broadly.

However, these fleeting encounters were only a part of the spectrum of relations. It was common, for instance, for ships to return to anchor at the same point. Often seamen, especially captains, would maintain or cultivate a relationship with a particular woman.[34] These were not the sexual

[27] Samuel Marsden, *The Letters and Journals of Samuel Marsden 1765–1838*, (ed.) John Rawson Elder, (Dunedin, 1932), pp. 457–60, 460–1, 468: Marsden, sixth New Zealand journal, 8 March 1830, 9 March 1830, 18 March 1830. The missionary version is not undisputed, but was widely followed at the time, e.g. [Robert Burford], *Description of a View of the Bay of Islands, New Zealand* (London, 1838), p. 8. Smith (*Maori Wars*, pp. 442–6) gives a brief account, which is largely restated by Crosby (*Musket Wars*, pp. 214–17).
[28] D'Urville, *New Zealand 1826–1827*, p. 225: M. Quoy, diary.
[29] Cruise, *Journal*, pp. 171–2: 30 June 1820.
[30] Bruce Biggs, *Maori Marriage: an Essay in Reconstruction* (Wellington, 1960), p. 19.
[31] J.A.M. Chouvert, *A Marist Missionary in New Zealand, 1843–1846*, (ed.) Jinty Rorke, (trans.) Patrick Barry, (Whakatane, 1985), pp. 33–4; St John, *Pakeha Rambles*, p. 50; Nicholas, *Narrative*, 1, pp. 183–5.
[32] Henry Williams, *The Early Journals of Henry Williams, Senior Missionary in New Zealand of the Church Missionary Society, 1826–40*, (ed.) Lawrence M. Rogers, (Christchurch, 1961), pp. 42, 117–18: 13 February 1827, 27 March 1828.
[33] *Missionary Register*, (1816), pp. 504–5: Marsden.
[34] Nicholas, *Narrative*, 1, pp. 210, 229.

transactions to be expected in a brothel: a women might be days or weeks on board.[35] It was mostly whalers in these relations, and the structures of their lives, especially the whaling season, influenced the form it took. The women were not always solely 'theirs', nor was it expected that the seamen would remain. A woman might receive a man even though they had been together only casually, and he had been away for months.[36]

Shorter-term relations were markedly different to those lasting relationships with local women. Through long-term relationships Pākehā were associated to a particular community (in a very real sense 'owned' by them), and were both tied to and in a sense 'controlled' by a woman. As mediators at such a time, this role could easily alter a woman's life. It was not a role for just anybody. If Pākehā were rare in the locality, such a precious thing was hardly likely to be entrusted to a woman of no importance. Pākehā such as these were often pampered, and found themselves, often more by their own good fortune than good management, well connected. 'Many of the Europeans on the island', wrote one New Zealand regular, 'have married into the most respectable native families, and live in the greatest comfort'.[37] But the boon, especially where and when Pākehā were precious (or if they were particularly competent), was also on the other side. As will later be explored, one Pākehā could attract others, and could facilitate and mediate their coming.

In New Zealand, as in many other comparable situations, these women were an essential part of the man's life, a means of accessing labour and resources, and a guarantee of their continued safety. 'In fact it is not safe to live in the Country without a Chiefs [*sic*] daughter as a protection', wrote one sojourner, 'as they are always backed by their Tribe . . . they become useful and much attached if used well, and will suffer incredible persecution for the man they live with.'[38] Presumably this affect was often mutual—men ran away from ships and stayed their lives to be with women they cared for; and a marriage with an important woman could even give a Pākehā a unique access to influence.[39] In one account an indigenous woman 'married' to a Pākehā seemed well aware of her own importance:

---

[35] Cruise, *Journal*, p. 168: 28 June, 28 November 1820.
[36] John Boultbee, *Journal of a Rambler: the Journal of John Boultbee*, (ed.) June Starke, (Auckland, 1986), pp. 57–8, 65, 85, 108.
[37] Dillon, 'Extract of a Letter', p. 5.
[38] Edward Markham, *New Zealand or Recollections of It*, (ed.) E.H. McCormick, (Wellington, 1963), p. 40: [21 February to 30 June 1834].
[39] GBPP 1837–1838, xxi (680), p. 86: 'Report . . . of New Zealand', Polack, evidence.

By and by you go to Otago to Waihora—to Toutu. You stay three weeks—you stay five weeks—you stay two moons—you come back—you say Hullo where's the cow? Gone. Where the bull? Gone! Where the goatee? Gone! Where the chikeni? Gone. The blankety gone the stockeni gone all all gone. You get the Mourie woman, by and by you go to Otago... you stay five weeks—you stay two moons—you come back you say—Hullo where's the cow? Me say 'All right' You say Where the Bull? all right. You say where the goati—me say all right—You say where the chickini? Me say all right. The blankets all right the stockini all right—all all right—are very good the Mourie woman.[40]

At best then, these relations conferred a mutual advantage. But not all Tangata Whenua approved of such practices, and many Pākehā did not. Well aware that these relationships provided wealth and security, one Pākehā onlooker still thought it 'questionable however if it was worth forfeiting so much, to gain so little'.[41] Such functional views were those of, or given to, outsiders; within these relations there were also dynamics of desire, love and affection so often secluded from historians. Yet the role that affect played in structuring these relations is concealed, not invisible.

Intimate relations worked as ways of extending and preserving social and political order. This it seemed to help achieve; a traditional means transformed for a new predicament. '*He taura taonga e motu, he taura tangata e kore e motu*', the *whakataukī* runs: 'Bonds made by treasures will break, [but] bonds made by people will not break.'[42] Indigenous communities in general, despite the effects of disease, newcomers and new things, remained orderly and powerful. 'We do not see the New Zealanders drinking, swearing, fighting and murdering one another', wrote an early missionary, 'as is the case among us.'[43] Tangata Whenua were strong consumers of muskets, but on the whole were not, at least until the later 1830s, very much interested in alcohol.[44] Favoured items such as blankets, muskets, powder, shot and tobacco ('almost every man and woman either chews or smokes, or both') had been made a part of everyday life.[45]

[40] Alexander Turnbull Library (ATL), qMS-0139-0140, J.W. Barnicoat, Journal 1841–1844, fo. 56. This was Makariri, who lived near the mouth of the Clutha river; her husband was George Willsher: Wakefield, *Adventure in New Zealand*, pp. 27, 36–7.
[41] Russell, *A Tour Through the Australian Colonies*, p. 283.
[42] [Te Matorohanga], S. Percy Smith, *Lore of the Whare Wananga, or Teachings of the Maori College on Religion, Cosmogeny, and History*, 2 vols., (New Plymouth), 2, p. 136; Ballara, *Iwi*, p. 138.
[43] CMS, *Proceedings*, (1823–4), p. 189: Samuel Marsden.
[44] Markham, *New Zealand*, pp. 45, 89n.14; Elder (ed.), *Marsden's Lieutenants*, p. 68: Kendall to CMS secretary, 26 July 1814; Robert McNab (ed.), *Historical Records of New Zealand (HRNZ)*, 2 vols., (Wellington, 1908), 1, p. 593: Commissioner Bigge's report.
[45] William Barett Marshall, *A Personal Narrative of Two Visits to New Zealand* (London, 1836), p. 119.

But such inclusions were judicious; indigenous technologies that were practically superior, such as fishing lines and nets (so good that Pākehā took to using them) were maintained.[46] The indigenous response to Pākehā was generally receptive, but it was always considerate: if Tangata Whenua were sometimes very hospitable, this was by no means always; women were always able to leave their husbands, and Pākehā who were arrogant, violent, rude or overbearing were handled judiciously.[47]

But there were by-products to these intimate configurations, the least desirable and most devastating of which was disease. In general diseases quickly had effect, but sexually transmitted diseases, in particular, were early interlopers. By the 1820s disease had already had repercussions on the health of many indigenous communities, and had already affected population numbers. 'That scourge, the venereal disease', wrote one missionary, 'we find everywhere we move—even infants are born with it.'[48] In an interlacing dynamic, ship girls were soon communicating disease back to the medium—ships' crews—that brought it.[49] But a world of intimacies gave rise to other things besides. Most starkly, perhaps, were those who descended from these encounters, literally, individuals that Pākehā would come to call 'half-castes'. But these encounters claimed, and began to establish, new territories and spaces.

NEW GROUND: SEALING AND BAY WHALING

By 1792 the first Pākehā sealing gang had come ashore in the south of New Zealand. In 1827 the first shore whaling station was established. Though these were very different economic activities, and were generally based in different locations, they had much in common. Both sealers and shore whalers brought their lives ashore from their ships, and stayed after their ships had gone. Neither were truly independent, so relied either on Tangata Whenua or supplies brought by their ships. For Tangata Whenua, both brought increased access to foreign people, goods and technologies, even if their own links to a distant world were not often sustained or reliable. Encounters between locals, sealers and shore whalers were often lasting and meaningful, and might leave all parties altered.

---

[46] GBPP 1837–1838, xxi (680), p. 25: 'Report...of New Zealand', John Watkins, evidence.
[47] Boultbee, *Journal*, p. 102; Williams, *Early Journals*, p. 147: 24 October 1828.
[48] Ibid., p. 428: 24 March 1835. This was in the Waikato, a long way from the main port of Kororāreka.
[49] D'Urville, *New Zealand 1826–1827*, p. 226.

Sealing and shore whaling often brought Tangata Whenua and Pākehā to live and work together in such ways that politics, economics and families became interdependent and interconnected.

Sealing gangs were working in New Zealand from the 1790s until a final collapse about 1826—a collapse to be expected given the numbers of skins sealers were taking. Sealers mostly came by way of Australia, though there were Americans, Irish, Australian aborigines and African Americans among them. One passing sailor came upon 'a number of suspicious characters [who] were in the neighbourhood a Sealing', and this epitomizes how they were not generally from the 'respectable' classes.[50] The focus of sealing would periodically shift, as one rookery was depleted and the gangs moved on to another. Seals were taken in their thousands, and the easy pickings found initially at places like Tamatea (Dusky Sound, in the southwest of the South Island) were depleted by 1803. The focus of sealing then moved to the southernmost region of New Zealand, the bottom of the South Island and the islands offshore, the largest of which was Rakiura, or Stewart Island. In this region sealing peaked about 1810, though there was something of a revival in 1823–1826. This area, known in *te Reo* as Murihiku, had good pickings of both seals and whales, and the small indigenous communities in this often difficult part of the world quickly felt the presence of strangers.[51] Yet because many sealing operations were located in inhospitable isolated areas, some sealers might be ashore months, and see only a handful of locals.[52] As the numbers of sealing gangs increased, and the numbers of seals decreased, sealers had to diversify into other areas of commerce, and this meant encounters with Tangata Whenua were more frequent and regular. Sealers began to live more often in indigenous communities, and a number of sealers stayed on. In a few cases the sealers joined with Tangata Whenua to found new communities. Perhaps the best example of these communities was the settlement founded by sealers and indigenous men and women on Codfish Island. Previously uninhabited, its indigenous name was Whenua Hou, aptly meaning New Land.[53] Though settlement did not last long, with all people gone by 1850, it was a unique community, one spun from

[50] Basil Howard, *Rakiura: A History of Stewart Island, New Zealand* (Wellington, 1940), p. 360: Thomas Shepherd, Journal of the *Rosanna*, (1826), 13 March 1826.
[51] Wanhalla, 'Transgressing Boundaries'; Atholl Anderson, *The Welcome of Strangers: An Ethnohistory of Southern Maori A.D. 1650–1850* (Dunedin, 1998), pp. 63–110.
[52] *HRNZ*, 1, p. 559: McDonald, [1821], evidence for Commissioner Bigge's inquiry.
[53] Robert McNab, *Murihiku, a History of the South Island of New Zealand from 1642 to 1835* (Wellington, 1909), p. 350; Linda Scott and Finlay Bayne, *Nathaniel Bates of Riverton: His Families and Descendants* ([Christchurch], 1994), pp. 39–52.

indigenous and Pākehā economics, practices and ideas, with the small community eking out a small living on a blustery island.[54]

The sealers left very few records. One of the few sealing journals, by John Boultbee, gives the impression of a tough, hard, dangerous life, with a gang working in a context of strong (if small) local communities and a loose network of scattered Pākehā. Boultbee was in New Zealand from 1825 to 1827, and he spent considerable time in indigenous villages, though he also spent periods of months away from them. Few sealers, it seems, spoke *te Reo* well, but this was not insuperable. Boultbee had at least one indigenous partner with whom it seems he had a child, but left them, 'tired of rambling', stowing away on a departing vessel. This was the fate of most sealers, yet a significant number either stayed on in indigenous communities for longer periods, or ran away to them. It was the sealers who began what one historian has termed the South Island's 'lasting mixing of the races'.[55]

Shore whaling was a much later arrival in New Zealand than sealing, but quickly developed to become important. Though the first station was set up only in 1827, within a decade and a half around fifty sites had been worked.[56] Individual proprietors became famous or infamous, such as John Guard and the Weller brothers, and the more resourceful businessmen among them soon had multiple stations under their guidance (Johnny Jones, for instance, had seven).[57] Small outposts generally in sheltered bays, the shore whaling stations were hardly impressive. In the stations the work of cutting the whale up, and trying-out its oil (by boiling the blubber) was done. Unlike ocean whaling, the whales were chased and caught near to shore, then rowed in and winched up to be processed. Even more than sealing, shore whaling was dangerous and difficult work. Killing whales with a harpoon and a lance from a small wooden boat could never be otherwise. The whale could sometimes be '*a very wicked fish*'.[58]

To Pākehā looking from outside, whaling stations often seemed disorderly and disgraceful. '[N]ever, perhaps, was there a community composed of such dangerous materials and so devoid of regular law.' The shore whalers were 'a mixture of runaway sailors and escaped convicts', but they

---

[54] Anderson, *The Welcome of Strangers*, pp. 68, 183, 190; J. Turnbull Thomson, 'Extract from a Journal', *JRGS*, xxviii (1858), p. 314.

[55] Claudia Orange, 'The Maori and the Crown (1769–1840)', (ed.) Keith Sinclair, *The Oxford Illustrated History of New Zealand*, 2nd edn., (Auckland, 1996), p. 25.

[56] McNab, *The Old Whaling Days*, pp. 274–8, 286, 297–8. Dieffenbach, Wakefield, passim.

[57] Wakefield, *Adventure in New Zealand*, pp. 33–4; McNab, *The Old Whaling Days*, pp. 98–111; Alfred Eccles and A.H. Reed, *John Jones of Otago: Whaler, Coloniser, Shipowner, Merchant* (Wellington, 1949).

[58] Russell, *A Tour Through the Australian Colonies*, p. 286. Original emphasis.

were more mixed than that, incorporating large numbers of Tangata Whenua.[59] One unsympathetic viewer thought the well-known station at Waikouaiti was

> like other whaling-stations . . . a picture of the most perfect neglect of any-
> thing like order or neatness. The huts in which the men live—rickety
> things—are stuck about in all directions. . . . There seemed, however, to be
> an abundance of poultry, as well as dogs and pigs; and another common
> feature of whaling-stations was also to be seen there in perfection, in the
> shape of a variety of dirty native women—half-dressed in tawdry European
> clothes, with a proportionate number of half-caste children.[60]

But only superficially did these communities lack order. Whaling stations might not have been neat, but as working societies they were lent a basic order by the whaling itself. There was occasionally trouble within the stations, but no more so than on board ships. Criticisms of the whaling stations' 'neglect' seemed directed more at the way they appeared to cross indigenous and Pākehā ways. They were communities crafted from ma-terials at hand, both indigenous and Pākehā. Diets were mixed, as were styles of housing and agriculture.[61] Here, not only had 'natives' become like Europeans, but Europeans had 'gone native', and the two crossed—'half-dressed' and 'half-caste'.

Unlike their ocean-going counterparts, the shore whalers could not simply sail away. This fundamental difference meant that in a general way, which was also not true of most sealing activity, shore whaling was thor-oughly entwined with indigenous life. In the summer, after the whale season was over, some shore whalers would act as traders, others would go to their wives' villages to cultivate.[62] This integration was apparent in other ways, as the stations were subject to indigenous politics. On a number of occasions whaling stations were 'looted'.[63] The station at Piraki, for example, was caught first between the raids of northern people against the locals, and then, not long after those ceased, between those of two factions of Kai Tahu.[64] On other occasions, the whaling stations themselves went to war, aiding Tangata Whenua, their patrons, to defend against other indigenous marauders.[65]

[59] Wakefield, *Adventure in New Zealand*, pp. 36, 35.
[60] Frederick Tuckett, in the *Nelson Examiner*, 20 July 1844.
[61] Morton details some of these aspects, *The Whale's Wake*, pp. 210–63.
[62] F.A. Anson (ed.), *The Piraki Log (E Pirangi ahau koe) or Diary of Captain Hempleman* (London, 1910), p. 121: 1 April 1841; Wakefield, *Adventure in New Zealand*, p. 35.
[63] Such as the Otago whaling station in 1834; McNab, *Murihiku*, pp. 414–15; McNab, *The Old Whaling Days*, pp. 103–4.
[64] Those led by Te Matenga Taiaroa and Hone Tuhawaiki.
[65] ATL , qMS-0942, James Heberley, 'Reminiscences', fos. 60–61.

The whalers seemed to lead relatively comfortable lives, 'each to possess a native wife or mistress, some of whom were of prepossessing appearance, and their children especially.'[66] Just as scores of indigenous women found partners at the station, many men found work there. Hundreds of 'half-caste' children, as some Pākehā were already calling them, were born in or around whaling stations. At one station, Te Awaiti, there were about twenty five 'half-caste children', 'all strikingly comely, and many of them quite fair, with light hair and rosy cheeks; active and hardy as the goats with which the settlement also swarmed.'[67] One traveller estimated that in some parts of New Zealand two-thirds of indigenous women who were not elderly were living with European men.[68] These women, the whalers' 'Whaheen' (*wahine*, woman), kept house, cleaned, cooked, tended children, animals and gardens, and mended clothes and people.[69] In such instances the dimensions of a sexual economy were apparent. Skills and labour combined with the political significance and influence of these women. A large number of shore whalers married women of *mana*, daughters of chiefs and leaders. In some cases, perhaps, settlement was even conditional upon these marriages.[70]

As a major industry, however, shore whaling like sealing was to be short-lived. There were still whaling stations well into the twentieth century, but by the 1840s many stations were struggling to fill their barrels with oil. Just as the sealers before them, whalers had to adjust to declining numbers of prey. They diversified into trade and agriculture, and ambitious leaders of stations, such as Johnny Jones or Captain Hempleman, even eyed the surrounding lands and thought of settlement. (One of the well-known Weller brothers, George, who ran several whaling stations, claimed 400,000 acres of land.[71]) Whales grew scarce, profits fewer, and many stations suffered from a 'complication of wants.'[72] But even after the general failure of both shore whaling and sealing, the transformations they had begun continued.

The 'New Ground' of settlements like Codfish Island or the whaling stations had at their centres new arrangements of intimacy. These secured not only companionship and access, but labour, life and property. Angela

[66] Thomas Morland Hocken (ed.), *Contributions to the Early History of New Zealand* (London, 1898), p. 209: Frederick Tuckett, diary, 19 April 1844.

[67] Wakefield, *Adventure in New Zealand*, p. 36; also, p. 32.

[68] Frederick Tuckett, diary, 22 May 1844, in Hocken, *Contributions*, p. 223.

[69] Anson (ed.), *The Piraki Log*, p. 139: 14 July 1842.

[70] John Logan Campbell, *Poenamo: Sketches of the Early Days of New Zealand* (London, 1881), p. 36. Wakefield, *Adventure in New Zealand*, p. 33; Morton, *Whale's Wake*, pp. 250–1.

[71] McNab, *The Old Whaling Days*, pp. 278–9.

[72] Anson (ed.), *The Piraki Log*, p. 134: 18 June 1842.

Wanhalla's study of Maitapapa, by far the most detailed, reveals how complicated and variegated the experiences of even a small community could be.[73] These developments were always particular to the local textures of place and kinship, integrated to and transforming—but never erasing—indigenous practices and beliefs. These new grounds were crossings, intersections managed not only through threats of violence or self-interested trade, but through affect—*taura tangata*—the ties of people, communal work and family.

DIFFERENT TERRAINS OF INTIMACY

Though there were 'wooden worlds' and new communities jointly built, these were just the fringes of an archipelago that remained overwhelmingly indigenous. Things were different again when Pākehā came ashore *alone*, and operated individually within indigenous communities. By 1800 this had begun, with Pākehā coming ashore for many reasons: to desert their ships, to escape prison sentences, to search for adventure, to make a profit, because of the lures of indigenous life. By 1840 there had been hundreds of these transient individuals, though by their nature they were difficult to count. At a single gathering of Tangata Whenua in 1834, twenty Pākehā were counted, and at any one time there might have been as many as 200 throughout New Zealand.[74] It is difficult to know exactly what to call these people, for they were called many things, including 'traders', 'ramblers', 'beachcombers', or 'Pākehā Māori'. 'Pākehā Māori', a term in use by the 1820s, is perhaps the best, but no term was universal. Most, if not quite all, were men. To the Pākehā they left behind, who carefully measured boundaries between 'civilized' and 'savage' life, between European and 'native' races, these men were transgressors. They were 'going native', 'taking up the mat'. They were, in a way well understood by those who disapproved of them, crossing races.

One European thought, disapprovingly, that as far as Pākehā Māori were concerned, 'The tale of one is that of all.'[75] This was a caricature, but not one without insight. Although Pākehā Māori came from varied backgrounds, and lived unique lives, they shared a common predicament. For them life was lived largely on indigenous terms, or at the very least on

---

[73] Wanhalla, 'Transgressing Boundaries'; Wanhalla, *In/Visible Sight*.
[74] Markham, *New Zealand*, p. 49: [5 March 1834].
[75] Byrne, *Twelve Years' Wanderings*, p. 68. See H.E. Maude, *Of Islands and Men: Essays in Pacific History* (Melbourne, 1968); I.C. Campbell, 'European Transculturalists in Polynesia, 1789–ca.1840', PhD dissertation, University of Adelaide, 1976.

indigenous sufferance. Relations between these men and Tangata Whenua had, then, to be symbiotic. A fortunate Pākehā Māori gained a stable and sheltered life, and fortunate indigenous patrons a means to all sorts of gains. A Pākehā Māori was a mediator, an opportunist, simply trying to do 'the best he can for himself amongst the natives.'[76] They spoke *te Reo*, they lived in *whare* (houses), ate an adapted indigenous diet, and were governed by a local politic.[77] It was not easy for these people, trying to come to terms with cultural, linguistic, social and political differences. Their lives were shaped by relativity, yet one informed by dependence and an often keenly felt lack of power, surrounded by people on which Pākehā Māori depended yet might still dislike: everyday superiors about whom they griped and sniped.[78] Behind them a precious few left accounts or memoirs of their experiences, and many more, having taken indigenous 'wives', left children.

Not all Pākehā Māori were 'white' men. One of the most 'successful' of Pākehā Māori was a Tahitian, Jem, who had studied for a time with missionaries in Sydney.[79] There were many other Polynesians, Indians and Australian aborigines, and also a handful of women, who lived as Pākehā Māori. Yet Pākehā Māori were not Tangata Whenua, and to a large degree their value lay in this difference. Life for most Pākehā Māori was precarious, and their safety and prosperity turned on communities and politics they often did not understand, let alone participate in: they were generally safe, finding life no more or less dangerous than life at sea, but it was not always easy. These were new conditions, those of another society, and there were many differences both great and small. Most accounts written by Pākehā Māori show that they had, in general, respect and regard for Tangata Whenua.[80] But it was rare for Pākehā Māori to stay for more than three or four years, and those who stayed in indigenous communities for longer periods were exceptional.

Pākehā had no intrinsic value (except, one cynic suggested, as food). They were generally valued for the access to goods and the skills they brought. The most famous account by a Pākehā Māori recalls in exaggerated fashion the typical worth of Pākehā. A trader might be worth twenty times his own weight in muskets, a 'second-rate *pakeha*' his own weight in

---

[76] Elder (ed.), *Marsden's Lieutenants*, p. 133: Kendall, journal, 21 January 1817 (of 'Mills').
[77] McNab, *Murihiku*, p. 328: Captain Edwardson, *Nouvelles Annales des Voyages*.
[78] Boultbee, *Journal*, p. 76; Markham, *New Zealand*, p. 39: [21 February to 30 June 1834].
[79] Nicholas, *Narrative*, 1, pp. 92–6.
[80] 'I have seen more friendship amongst [the Maori] than I have subsequently amongst the white people . . . of the boat I was in.' Boultbee, *Journal*, p. 76.

tomahawks, and a poor Pākehā his weight in fish-hooks. As for runaway convicts, who hid when other Pākehā were in the vicinity, *he aha te pai?* (what good was he?). As valuables, Pākehā were carefully managed by Tangata Whenua, 'honoured, cherished, caressed, protected and plucked. Plucked judiciously... so that the feathers might grow again.'[81] Pākehā would thus settle under chiefly patronage, and become 'the tribal pakeha'.[82] This patronage saved many a Pākehā Māori, and its withdrawal often obliged a Pākehā to leave, or cost him his life. The chief Whakataupuka, for example, kept his people from killing a group of eight Pākehā boat builders by giving them an infant child to sleep in their house.[83]

The life of a Pākehā Māori—'going native'—was regarded by most Europeans as scandalous. In their eyes you could not 'go native' respectably. If there were a dozen Pākehā involved in an inter-*hapū* war, it was to be expected they would all be described by missionaries as 'miscreant Europeans', no matter how bravely they might have fought or how honourably they may have behaved.[84] 'Nothing can be more lawless than the Europeans who are there [in New Zealand]', one witness told a British parliamentary committee. '[T]hey frequently lay aside the English Dress, and take up the native Mats, and have promiscuous Intercourse with the Native Women.'[85] The adjective was 'lawless', yet the practices were far from illegal. There was more at stake than was being professed. Pākehā were not behaving as 'Europeans' should. Before the 1840s there was scarcely a European 'society' in New Zealand, only the gentility cultivated by missionaries, 'respectable' ships' captains and naval officers. These 'respectable' folk were constructing their own sense of race symbolically. Pākehā Māori belonged to the same 'race' and 'nations' as these Europeans, yet their lives were not marked apart from 'natives'. Edward Markham, a Pākehā Māori, reflected upon this having watched a dozen Pākehā drink a keg of rum empty, fight until it was dark, and then continue to fight by torchlight. The day's events were common practice, but nonetheless Markham sensed the symbolics were wrong: 'I was certainly ashamed that Europeans could degrade themselves so before their New Zealand Boys.'[86]

Such moments make clear that European identifications of race were not solely based on physical markers such as skin colour and hair or other seemingly natural ones such as language. In such contexts Pākehā Māori

---

[81] Maning, *Old New Zealand*, pp. 19–20, 21; Nicholas, *Narrative*, 1, pp. 213–19.
[82] Thomas Gudgeon, *The Defenders of New Zealand* (Auckland, 1887), p. 597.
[83] Boultbee, *Journal*.
[84] CMS, *Proceedings*, (1837–8), p. 69.
[85] PP 1837–1838, xxi (680), p. 19: 'Report... into the Present State of the Islands of New Zealand', John Watkins, evidence.
[86] Markham, *New Zealand*, p. 40: [21 February to 30 June 1834].

proved deeply troublesome. Difference was embodied in actions and
things, from clothes to conduct. Missionaries, for instance, were never
anything other than fully dressed. Yet Tangata Whenua began wearing
clothes as a sign of their solidarity with Pākehā, because of their novelty, to
symbol their own differences (such as rank). Meanwhile many Pākehā
Māori put clothes aside, and 'took up the mat'. Tattooing was another
comparable example, as Tangata Whenua admitted a handful of Pākehā
Māori to the honour of *ta moko* (the full facial tattoo) to enable them in
battle, and to engrave on them a history and a sense of belonging. They
were marks that could not be erased, and as some of these Pākehā later
found out, this made them strangers when they returned to Britain or
Australia, where people hissed and jeered at them. 'Clothes' on a 'native',
and tattoos on a European, were marks out of place, and they made
meanings and distinctions ambivalent.

'Successful' Pākehā Māori all forged relationships of intimacy and affection with Tangata Whenua. These relationships, their entry into the inner-
most realms, lent their lives stability. It really was the *taura tangata* –the
human ties—that endured, not least in the families that they joined or
created. The wives and children who wove these strangers into networks of
place and kin accomplished the most critical work, which was little appreciated in Pākehā Māori writings. The political and cultural significance of
Pākehā Māori has been overestimated in a recent popular history,[87] but it is
obvious that in New Zealand they were important as mediators of change,
if not as instigators. They lived on their wits, their good luck, judgement
and skills, but they had not the sorts of power that other Pākehā would later
command. Few Pākehā Māori ever told Tangata Whenua what to do, and
most had to subject themselves to practices with which they disagreed. It
was affection and intimacy that made this bearable: 'I have seen more
friendship amongst [Tangata Whenua]', a Pākehā Māori wrote, 'than
I have subsequently amongst the white people.'[88]

By the 1830s the singular experiences of Pākehā Māori were not the
only Pākehā ones. Perhaps the majority were not living within indigenous
communities, nor in the innovated places gathered around sealing and
whaling, but in and around the port towns. The Bay of Islands was New
Zealand's leading anchorage, and inside the bay lay Kororāreka, one of
several places competing to be known as the 'hell of the Pacific'.[89] There

[87] Bentley, *Pakeha Maori.*
[88] Boutlbee, *Journal,* p. 76.
[89] Notably with Levuka (Fiji), Apia (Samoa), Papae'ete (Tahiti), and Honolulu (Ha-
waii). See Caroline Ralston, *Grass Huts and Warehouses: Pacific Beach Communities in the
Nineteenth Centuries* (Canberra, 1977).

were other smaller but important ports nearby, one further up the east coast at Whangaroa, and another across on the west coast at Hokianga, but it was the Bay of Islands, and particularly the Beach at Kororāreka, which was most important.[90] By the time the missionaries arrived at the Bay at the end of 1814 it was already an established place of resort for European, Australian and American vessels. In a sense the Bay of Islands was New Zealand's entrepôt, and the rest of the country its hinterland.[91] Many ships would only call there, and most would call there first. The Bay 'was not the occasional anchorage of a casual whaler, but was the principal rendezvous, 16,000 miles from home, of a thriving American industry'— an industry that had over 650 ships and supported some 15,000 workers.[92] In a busy year 100 or more ships might anchor in the Bay, which meant at any one time hundreds of sailors might be prowling the Beach.

'Respectable' Pākehā often observed that the most savage people in New Zealand were in fact Europeans. By 1835 there was an established divide between those who were 'riff-raff' and those who were 'respectable'.[93] The 'respectable' Pākehā had to symbolize their difference from those running amok by denigrating them, which they did with great energy. It was a place where 'natives' had been 'contaminated'; where they had used new skills and encounters to learn new vices, rather than to be civilized. 'It is impossible to place these [white] people in too low a light', wrote one captain; another that Kororāreka 'is chiefly inhabited by the lowest order of vagabonds, mostly runaway sailors and convicts, and is appropriately named "Blackguard Beach".'[94] The missionaries thought it 'A dreadful place—the very seat of Satan.'[95]

These were not empty observations. The demands of ships had shaped the local market, whether in the rearing of pigs, onions and potatoes, carnal opportunities or the nearly fifty grog shops to be found by the 1830s. It was difficult to keep order on board ships anchored in a bay full of temptation. Watches fell asleep and crew covertly went ashore, succumbing to lures. Coopers, blacksmiths, sawyers, boat builders and carpenters could easily make a living, and one captain complained that his carpenter wished to leave, having seen four others in the Bay of Islands 'settled on shore, with as many wives as they thought proper to keep, and

[90] Cowan, *The New Zealand Wars*, 1, p. 7.
[91] Alexander Spoehr, 'Port Town and Hinterland in the Pacific Islands', *American Anthropologist*, 62 (1960), pp. 586–92.
[92] Robert W. Kenny, 'Yankee Whalers at the Bay of Islands', *The American Neptune*, xii, (1952), pp. 31–2.
[93] Ralston, *Grass Huts and Warehouses*, p. 151.
[94] John B. Knights, Journal, Mss, quoted by Robert W. Kenny, 'Yankee Whalers', p. 29.
[95] Williams, *Early Journals*, p. 182: 26 June 1831.

under no control'.[96] Another captain complained that as soon as he signed
on some new sailors, others ran away, and it was not uncommon for
vessels to be too short of hands to sail. Discipline was difficult enough to
keep at sea, but more so when ships were at anchor. Sailors mutinied,
drank, quarrelled, and even tried to kill each other.[97]

But the disorder so denounced by respectable Pākehā was more apparent than real. Tangata Whenua were still very much in control, and
wielded an effective authority, even if some Pākehā thought it too loose.
The Bay had already been a strongly populated area prior to the Pākehā
onslaught. There were important *kainga* (communities) in the vicinity
prior to Pākehā frequenting it, and these visits encouraged more Tangata
Whenua to settle nearby. There was little question as to whom this bay
belonged. Though to some extent Kororāreka was an exception, traditional sanctions such as *tapu* were still in force, though they were judiciously
applied, with the occasional 'foreigner's exemption'.[98] The Pākehā population was not so easily managed, however, with as many as fifty European
families around northern bays in 1839.[99] However, the reach of indigenous society and leadership was normative, and even after 1840, when
British government had come to the region, the balance of power was still
in indigenous hands.

Nevertheless, even within the contexts of these towns, the visibility and
significance of intimate connections were apparent. The numbers of
European families in these areas were increasing, but the great majority
of resident Pākehā men had a 'native wife' and some 'fine children'.[100]
This was an arrangement common to those in townships, on 'new
ground', or living singularly as Pākehā Māori. The circumstances were
themselves critical: the concentration and proximity of these developments had ramifications. By 1839 there were so many half-caste children
in Kororāreka that a British resident organized a series of meetings in an
attempt to endow a school for such children.[101] Foreshadowing later
developments, the proposal stemmed from seeing these children as
being in some sort of danger. Though recognizing that the fathers were
likely to support their children's education, it was a stated purpose to
'rescue' these half-castes from 'Heathen ignorance and superstition', and

[96] Dillon, *Narrative*, I, p. 206.
[97] Rhodes, *Whaling Journal*, pp. 15–16, 49–50, 51: 5 September 1836, 13 April 1837,
2 May 1837.
[98] ATL, qMs-1980, 'Events in the Life of Phillip Tapsell', p. 99; Wade, *A Journey*,
pp. 52–3.
[99] CMS, *Proceedings*, (1839–40), x, p. 90: Henry Williams, 11 January 1839.
[100] Dillon, *Narrative*, I, pp. 190–3.
[101] This was James Busby, the 'British Resident', the only British official in town.

the 'contamination of their present associates'—presumably the very communities and relationships which had produced them.[102]

RESPECTABLE MEN

The first missionaries, from the Church of England's Church Missionary Society (CMS), established their station at Rangihoua in the Bay of Islands in 1814. By 1823 the Wesleyan Missionary Society (WMS) joined them, basing themselves in the Whangaroa Harbour, about fifty miles north of the Bay of Islands. The missionaries brought ambitions which set them apart from their countrymen; they came not simply to live alongside 'natives' and make their livings, but to change them. In other islands of the Pacific mass conversions had often taken place within months; in New Zealand there were no substantial numbers of converts before 1830, and not thousands until nearly 1840.[103] The missionaries remade their lives in New Zealand, holding services where they might, preaching in a foreign tongue, even on occasion worshipping 'on the beach'.[104]

The missionaries' first need was protection. Tangata Whenua were largely indifferent to the message of the missionaries at first, but never to their potential uses. 'They plainly tell us if we will not issue powder and muskets we must go away', bemoaned one missionary.[105] The first patron of the CMS, Ruatara, died soon after they had arrived, and his successor Hongi Hika monopolized their efforts, so much so that other indigenous groups demanded either equal access or their own missionaries.[106] Hongi, however, gave little attention to the missionaries' teachings, and reportedly saw the missionaries 'merely as a means of attracting European ships'.[107]

---

[102] [Victoria Institute], 'Prospectus of an Institution for the Maintenance and Education of Children, the Offspring of English Fathers by New-Zealand Mothers', broadsheet, printed at Paihia, 29 July 1839, ATL. See also Ruth Ross, *New Zealand's First Capital* (Wellington, 1946), p. 31; [H.S. Chapman], 'New Zealand', *Dublin Review*, ix (1840), p. 205.

[103] J.M.R. Owens, *Prophets in the Wilderness: the Wesleyan mission to New Zealand, 1819–27* (Auckland, 1974); Judith Binney, *Legacy of Guilt: a Life of Thomas Kendall* (Auckland, 1968); Niel Gunson, *Messengers of Grace: Evangelical Missionaries in the South Seas, 1797–1860* (Melbourne, 1978), John Garrett, *To Live Among the Stars: Christian Origins in Oceania* (Suva, 1982).

[104] Marsden, *Letters and Journals*, p. 151: Marsden, second New Zealand journal, 22 August 1819.

[105] John Butler, *Earliest New Zealand: the Journals and Correspondence of the Rev. John Butler*, (ed.) R.J. Barton, (Masterton, 1927), p. 78: journal, 13 March 1820.

[106] Marsden, *Letters and Journals*, pp. 204–7: second New Zealand journal, 19 October 1819.

[107] *Extracts from . . . Duperrey*, p. 144: Lesson, journal.

Initially the missionaries were isolated and powerless. 'Consider', begged one of the missionaries, 'the absolute control which the natives have over us directly and over property and proceedings indirectly'.[108] Several times missionaries had to leave or abandon their stations. The 'father' of the New Zealand CMS mission, Sydney-based Samuel Marsden, claimed to recall one Saturday evening where he was sitting 'meditating upon the 72nd Psalm' while outside his window a young woman was killed and offered as a sacrifice to an indigenous god.[109] This was a long way from Britain and the supervising committee, from whom it might take two years to hear a reply, and distant even from Sydney, where their superior was based. The superiors seemed never truly to understand what it was to be entirely dependent on those whose very souls they wished to transform.

In New Zealand, as elsewhere, the early missionaries were, by and large, journeymen. Their faith, not their education, nor necessarily even their skills, brought them to New Zealand. They were rope-makers and farmers, smiths and teachers as often as they were 'clergy'. The composition of the missionaries reflected the early emphasis placed on 'civilizing'. Until the numbers of converts increased, missionary influence derived in large part from their artisans. As marginal people at home, many missionaries knew that land in New Zealand was, as one put it, 'their only chance'; and the CMS missionaries were the largest purchasers of land in New Zealand before 1839.[110] The missionaries included 'swearers' and former Australian convicts. As one missionary (himself not free from aspersion) recounted, 'Thieves, drunkards, swearers, blasphemers, fornicators etc., are, and have been employed in the Society's service'.[111]

The missionaries tried to set themselves apart, from both the 'heathen' natives and the European 'riff-raff' who surrounded them. The missionaries generally reserved their missionary spirit for 'natives', and tried to keep away from whale ships and other Pākehā as much as possible, as their superiors advised.[112] After 1823 the CMS settlement was directly opposite Kororāreka, and two very different styles of Pākehā living went on within sight of each other, separated by a few miles of sea.[113] Missionaries sought to symbolize their difference, to themselves, as well as to Tangata Whenua

---

[108] Elder (ed.), *Marsden's Lieutenants*, p. 173: Kendall to the secretary of the CMS, 14 August 1820.
[109] Marsden, *Letters and Journals*, p. 489: fourth New Zealand journal, 26 April 1830.
[110] PP 1837–1838, xxi (680), p. 47: 'Report', John Flatt (CMS catechist), evidence.
[111] Elder (ed.), *Marsden's Lieutenants*, p. 178: Kendall to the secretary of the CMS, 14 August 1820.
[112] Elder (ed.), *Marsden's Lieutenants*, p. 206: Marsden to outgoing missionaries, 7 September 1823.
[113] *HRNZ*, 2, pp. 721–2: Marsden to CMS secretary, 27 March 1837; *Missionary Register*, (1838), p. 218.

and other Pākehā. They dressed 'properly', observed the sabbath, maintained careful and regular 'contact' with their superiors in Sydney and Britain, and often retired into the civilizing influence of the pen. They were people of peace, and of religion. But the standards they set they themselves struggled to achieve, and consistently the difference between themselves and other Europeans and 'natives' was compromised. The first group of CMS missionaries bickered intolerably; on one occasion the bickering turned into a brawl, with one missionary armed with a chisel (inflicting some cuts) and the other with a gun (getting off two unsuccessful shots).[114] Worse, the first missionary to live in New Zealand, Thomas Kendall, was for a time 'a minister living in fornication', cohabiting with a Tangata Whenua teen.[115] William Yate, another CMS missionary, was charged with mutually masturbating and having oral sex with indigenous males, and although charges were never proven, they were endorsed by affidavits.[116] Neither missionary was particularly sorrowful, and their brethren were left embarrassed, trying to explain the public doings of those who were supposed to set very different examples.[117]

Yet if there were two matters which did truly set the British missionaries apart from natives and other Pākehā, it was 'their' women, and their Book. 'The Bible, and that alone', wrote Kendall, 'can teach [natives] a better system of morality.'[118] The Word was the missionaries' treasure, both in the religious and literal sense. The first missionaries were bound to have problems, then, for as of yet they had no Bible. There was not even, at the time when missionaries first arrived, a uniform system of writing *te Reo*. The missionaries had virtually no materials with which to begin their studies and their orthography, and it was little wonder that for years language was seen as 'the great obstacle'.[119] The first portion of Scripture in *te Reo* was not printed until August 1827, and it was not until late 1833 that a substantial portion was available. It was only after a renewed emphasis on religious teaching rather than 'civilization', a reorganization and emphasis on schools, and the rendering of the Book into *te Reo*, as well as missionary success in mediating and peace-making, that missionary fortunes picked up. Tangata Whenua became avid readers and writers, and books soon became most treasured possessions. At last, by the 1830s, the missionaries had a unique and valuable commodity, a marker of their

[114] Elder (ed.), *Marsden's Lieutenants*, p. 246: Francis Hall to secretary of CMS.
[115] Elder (ed.), *Marsden's Lieutenants*, p. 189: Marsden to Kendall, 11 June 1822.
[116] Judh Binne, 'Whatever Happened to Poor Mr Yate? An Exercise in Voyeurism', *NZJH*, 9 (1975), pp. 111–25.
[117] Marsden, *Letters and Journals*, p. 351: fourth New Zealand journal, 19 August 1823.
[118] Elder (ed.), *Marsden's Lieutenants*, p. 141: Kendall to Marsden, 25 July 1817.
[119] Ibid., p. 142: King to Secretary of the CMS, 1 December 1818.

difference. 'Their cry was the same as in almost every place we staid [*sic*] at', wrote one missionary. 'Books, books, "E mate ana matou i te puka-puka kore," We are ill (or dead) for want of books.'[120]

But the presence of women was no less important, as this encapsulated how the intimate lives that missionaries lived and modelled would be different. For unlike most other Pākehā in New Zealand, amongst the missionaries were 'white' women, who were both practical means of civilizing (workers) as well as almost mystical symbols of civilization and domesticity. There had originally been some debate about whether missionaries should be married, particularly as New Zealand was not considered safe.[121] Others even suggested that missionaries might be more effective if they took native women as wives, an idea apparently not entertained by the missionaries themselves.[122] Yet in retrospect it seemed almost natural that missionary women should be there, as they offered a working example of domesticity, and also allowed a heightened contrast with indigenous conceptions of gender. Mrs Leigh's work amongst native women was described by one writer (prone to exaggeration) as 'a new era in the history of woman'.[123] Yet like literacy, missionary women were functional as well as symbolic; they were more than exemplars of purity, but protectors. Missionary men were surrounded by sexual 'danger', and the indigenous religion missionaries confronted was, to the missionary eye, dangerously sexual.[124] 'The Committee cannot but be sensible', wrote one Wesleyan missionary, 'that the Danger to which single men are exposed in this land from Temptation to Native Females is *Great*, but they can form but an imperfect idea of this, without they come and live amongst them themselves as single young men.'[125] They brought hierarchies of race and gender, and these, as Catherine Hall has suggested, lay 'at the heart of the missionary enterprise'.[126]

Consequently, missionaries were not merely observers of racial crossings but, in their own way, participants. Tangata Whenua were often 'polygamous', particularly *rangatira* (chiefs, leaders), and this practice was

[120] Wade, *A Journey*, p. 125.
[121] *Church Mission Society, Eighth Report*, p. 19. Cf. Marshall, *Two Visits to New Zealand*, pp. 52–4.
[122] Dillon, *Narrative*, 2, p. 334.
[123] Alexander Strachan, *Remarkable Incidents in the Life of the Rev. Samuel Leigh* (London, 1853), p. 189.
[124] Binney, *A Legacy of Guilt*, pp. 125–57; HRNZ, 1, pp. 563–4: Marsden to J. Butterworth, 21 July 1821; Belich, *Making Peoples*, p. 136.
[125] Nathaniel Turner, journal, 13 September 1825, cited in Owens, *Prophets in the Wilderness*, p. 74.
[126] Catherine Hall, *White, Male and Middle Class: Explorations in Feminism and History* (Cambridge, 1992), p. 234.

an obvious target for missionary opprobrium and attempts at reform. While warfare and cannibalism preoccupied missionary attempts at reform, the domestic lives of indigenous communities were also regularly targeted.[127] Missionaries made their attempts to reorder villages not only spiritually but physically, changing the ways houses were constructed and laid out; and what occurred within those houses was equally of concern. Tangata Whenua were told, regarding marriage, that 'it was much more proper that these affairs should be written on paper than to follow their native customs.'[128] As missionary efforts became more successful, these reforms directly affected Pākehā who lived alongside or within these communities, and the missionary assaults on domestic and sexual relations were perhaps the areas where these Pākehā were most vulnerable. 'The white men almost generally are living with native women', wrote the missionary William Watkin, 'and my coming here is looked upon rather suspiciously by them, for they know enough of [Christianity] to be aware that if it prevails they must marry the women or lose them.'[129]

As Watkin's comment suggested, the missionaries did not veto interracial marriages. What they found repugnant was what they called 'concubinage'—the unmarried cohabitation of a Pākehā man and an indigenous woman. (If both parties were 'native', being both 'heathens', it was not generally called concubinage.) As an attempted corrective of this, throughout the 1820s and 1830s missionaries married more than 100 mixed couples. The first of these, between the trader Philip Tapsell (Hans Peter Falk) and Maria Ringa in 1823, was controversial. The missionary who officiated was Kendall, who had gone ahead without the consent of his brethren. Ringa had first to be baptized, and some missionaries were not convinced that Ringa held genuine religious conviction.[130] The criticism was apparently justified, for Ringa ran away from Tapsell within days. But proof that such marriages were not opposed in principle came with Tapsell's second marriage, when he was married by Marsden himself, to a sister of an influential chief who was, in Marsden's words, 'clean in her person, well-dressed in European clothes'. She was also well domesticated, having lived with a missionary family, and even spoke English. Marsden could see no impropriety in marrying them, and the couple did not wish to live in sin. Their wedding, on 21 April 1830, was well attended by

[127] Wakefield, *Adventure in New Zealand*, p. 31.
[128] Williams, *Early Journals*, p. 108: 26 February 1828.
[129] Watkins, journal, reprinted in McNab, *The Old Whaling Days*, p. 488.
[130] See Binney, *Legacy of Guilt*, p. 111–112, n.48; Dillon, *Narrative*, II, p. 333. A copy of the marriage certificate can be found in Elder (ed.), *Marsden's Lieutenants*, facing p. 224.

missionaries and Tangata Whenua. Marsden was well satisfied with
the affair, writing in his journal: 'The more Christian customs and
manners prevail in New Zealand the more improvement the natives will
make in the arts of civilization, and I consider lawful marriage of the first
importance.'[131]

In their opinions of concubinage, and their limited approval of mixed
marriage, the New Zealand missionaries were consistent with their societies
at home and their brethren overseas. A visiting missionary looked upon
intermarriage approvingly, noting that many Europeans had 'formed connections with native women', some of which had 'afterwards been rendered
respectable and permanent by marriage'. He looked forward to 'New
Zealanders and Europeans ... coalesc[ing] into one Christian and virtuous
people in a comparatively short period of time'.[132] Back in Britain the
greatest fear amongst most clergy was the *illicit* sexual liaison, one not
recognized in the religious sense, not one that crossed 'racial' boundaries.
This was one of the most depraved things religious folk had noticed about
slavery, the immoral carnal relations it created. William Wilberforce was
aghast that a slave or mulatto woman might 'deem an illicit connection
with White man more respectable than a legal union with a Coloured
husband'.[133] Such opinions were directly available to the New Zealand
missionaries.[134] Wilberforce could call upon the authority of no less than
William Paley to prove the 'fact' that 'the criminal commerce of the sexes
corrupts and depraves the mind and moral character more than any single
species of vice whatsoever.'[135]

The missionaries were not always alone in their notions of respectability. Most often ships' officers and captains kept them company, and
occasionally there were devout sailors. By 1833, however, the first 'official'
had joined them. James Busby became the British 'Resident', taking up a
piece of land not far from the mission at Paihia. Busby had the job of
taming the British who resided in New Zealand, and extending British
influence. For these purposes he was essentially powerless, an 'isolated
individual, not having even the authority of a magistrate, encircled by
savages, and by a most troublesome class of his own inhabitants'.[136]

[131] Marsden, *Letters and Journals*, pp. 481, 487, 553n: fourth New Zealand journal,
4, 20 April 1827.
[132] Lang, *New Zealand in 1839*, p. 58.
[133] William Wilberforce, *An Appeal to the Religion, Justice, and Humanity of the Inhabitants of the British Isles, in Behalf of the Negro Slaves of the West Indies*, new edn.,
(London, 1823), p. 18.
[134] Also Wilberforce, 'Annual Address', *Missionary Register*, (1828), pp. 321–2.
[135] Paley is quoted by Wilberforce, *An Appeal to the Religion*, pp. 18–19.
[136] Robert Fitzroy, *A Narrative of the Voyage of the H.M.S. Beagle*, (ed.) David Stanbury,
(London, 1977), p. 319.

He was later joined by an American consul, James Clendon (an Englishman), in 1839.[137] That same year French Roman Catholic missionaries arrived. The converts to the Wesleyan and Anglican missions, who called themselves *mihinare* or missionaries, were soon facing the converts of the Catholics, who called themselves *epikopo*, from the Latin *epicospus*. With an understatement typical of these religious rivalries, the British missionaries published pamphlets warning of the *anatikaraite* (the anti-Christ). The Catholic missionaries returned the favour, with as much passion but fewer resources. The Catholics were readier to 'rough it', and placed less emphasis on 'civilizing'. It was 'better to go to heaven having worn the native dress, than to go to hell with European clothes', their instructions told them.[138] This gave many of their encounters a different quality. 'On my journeys', as another brother wrote, 'to advance the work of God, I live like the natives'.[139] The Marist missionaries did not come as recognizable 'domestic' units. There were no sisters with them initially, and they came as groups of men.

The claims of missionaries to respectability rested upon their understandings of virtue, the proper and the decent. In practice this was apparent in their gendered and regulated forms of sociability, their claim to manifest the godly, and a discipline over not just the public but the personal and the intimate. Conversion was not simply adherence to the Christian god, but adherence to the propriety of such practices and conduct. It was an announced missionary intention to remake indigenous configurations of intimacy, and to revalue indigenous understandings of the carnal—primarily but not only through the redefinition of conjugality. Unlike Pākehā Māori, or those strangers who clustered in towns or around whales and seals, for missionaries intimacy became not just a way of relating or connecting with indigenous people and communities, but a target for reform. A Christian marriage was, as Marsden put it, 'of the first importance'. But the missionaries found much of their own power through another sense of intimacy that did not simply conflict with indigenous ones but partially coincided. Like Tangata Whenua the missionaries believed in the power and reality of a hidden universe. Their claim to jurisdiction over indigenous lives and bodies drew from this intimacy which they held as transcendent. For Tangata Whenua it was a new god, for missionaries the true god. But it was the missionaries who

---

[137] *HRNZ*, 2, p. 604: Clendon to Secretary of State, 27 May 1839.
[138] Peter McKeefry (ed.), *Fishers of Men*, (Auckland, 1938), p. 15.
[139] Ibid., p. 71: J.B. Petitjean to Father Colin, [1841], 'What golden opportunities to practise poverty!', exclaimed one Marist priest. Ibid., p. 60: Michael Borjon to Father Colin, 21 January 1842.

claimed the communing with the supernatural, the all powerful—an intimacy that brought them not just to New Zealand but to their knees and, eventually, where many Tangata Whenua joined them.

CHILDREN OF THE BEACH

Few are surprised that the early encounters between indigenous people and Europeans produced conflict and violence. Some historians even consider there was comparatively little trouble, all things considered. It is tempting to think that intimate relations between Europeans and 'natives' mitigated or mediated the violence or conflict that might otherwise have happened. Certainly intimate relations were one way of incorporating newcomers into an established social fabric and stabilizing developments in places and times that were in considerable flux. But, importantly, because there were different conceptions of correct or licit forms of intimacy, these domains could themselves become terrains of conflict. Missionary interest in matters moral, carnal and conjugal, as well the nascent efforts of European denizens of Kororāreka to form a school to rescue 'half-castes', pointed to impulses that might contest these relations. Critically, these efforts foreshadowed the particular importance that 'half-castes' would come to occupy, both as emblems and products of racial crossing, as well as points of entry or leverage into indigenous 'intimate domains'.

Europeans in New Zealand were using the term 'half-caste' from the 1820s. It described all racially mixed children regardless of the supposed fractions of parentage or 'blood' they possessed (a usage that long continued). This term was always to be more a symbol of status than biology, applied selectively, for it was never completely apparent who was or was not racially crossed. 'Half-castes' were a category, like race, that was obviously manufactured, a fixity made of fluidity. The term itself connected observations and understanding to the larger problem of racial crossing, and these were to weigh upon actions and behaviours, even as they interacted with a local environment.

John Savage, a doctor travelling on board a vessel visiting New Zealand in 1806, was the first to write about a mixed child. For him the child was a curiosity, examined with a detached eye: 'the difference between this child and those of the unmixed native is very remarkable: the native child looks full in your face with a perfect confidence; this half-bred child is all bashfulness'. He thought 'it' had the same colour complexion as other native children, but lighter hair. He could, he remarked, see no reason why the mixed child would develop to be superior to the native.[140] His curiosity was shared by others, as in a later visit by HMS *Dromedary*.

> A fine little child, the son of a British sailor by a native woman, was observed in a canoe alongside, and its mother consented, after some hesitation, to permit it to come on board. She seemed quite fond of it, and was quite uneasy during its absence from her. It was nearly naked, but as fair as if it had been born in England; and it naturally excited so much interest in the ship, that it was returned to its parent with a very comfortable supply of clothing and several days' provisions.[141]

The *Dromedary*, later accused of being 'a floating castle of prostitution', also apparently left a few such children in its wake.[142] But it is interesting that even in these short observations, much of the concerns to be pursued in the next decades were at least partially present. Interest in half-castes was regarded as 'natural'; there were questions about the care of such children, their potential and future was considered, as were external marks of their difference, and the two 'sides' of their parentage were compared. Such questions were not unique to New Zealand, least of all the possibility that they might be inferior to both parents, as similar concerns to these had all manifested elsewhere.

Questions were raised about the apparent lack of similar children to be seen. As put by Richard Cruise, on board the *Dromedary*, there was so much sexual intercourse between Europeans and 'native' women, yet there seemed to be 'very limited offspring of this connection'—he saw only two of this 'cast'. To his mind this 'afforded reason to presume that infanticide exists here to a considerable extent.'[143] He had himself no evidence at all of such matters; but suspicions of infanticide were a cargo of racial crossing, in his instance probably informed by Australian discourse where it was often assumed that half-caste children were killed by their aboriginal mothers (with equally scarce evidence).[144] Infanticide was, also, yet another marker of savage society. Nearly 20 years later this was still a line of enquiry for a parliamentary select committee. Even in its most initial moments the recognition of 'half-castes' was couched in terms of danger and salvage, ones informed by other colonial locations.

Even from passing ships the identification of half-castes—driven by concern and curiosity—was coupled with impulses to intervene. Whether

---

[140] Savage, *Some Account of New Zealand*, p. 92.
[141] Cruise, *Journal*, pp. 109–10: 23 April 1820.
[142] John Williams, *The New Zealand Journal 1842–1844 of John B. Williams of Salem, Massachusetts* (Salem, 1956), p. 37: journal, 1842.
[143] Cruise, *Journal*, pp. 288–9.
[144] GBPP 1837–1838, xxi (680), p. 51: 'Report', Fitzroy, evidence.

it targeted them as a group or as individuals, there was the desire to 'save [the half-caste child] from the demoralising contagion of native habits'. To such observers these children were between a rock and a hard place; with savages for mothers and, typically, 'a profligate Englishman for his father'.[145] The comments of one onlooker, Frederick Tuckett, seem to encapsulate these views.

> It is much to be deplored, that [the children of Pākehā whalers] should grow up wholly uneducated, and left destitute in the event of the death of the father. Some provision might easily and justly be made for them, by securing to them in right of the mother, a home and sufficient land of good quality for their permanent maintenance ... If the British public, who contribute such large funds in aid of missions, would require in return, as a primary object, the formation of industrial schools, their labours would be far more useful, and need not be any the less pious.[146]

The 'rescuing' of half-castes, making some sort of provision for them, or, as with Tuckett's last suggestion, institutionalizing them, were to prove persistent themes. Besides the planned 'Victoria Institute' for half-castes, there were many other attempts. The missionaries baptized many half-castes, bringing them within the mission fold.[147] From even before there was government to instigate, half-castes had become potential objects of policy.

The careful curiosity and occasional interventions of Pākehā contrasted with the relations Tangata Whenua established with such children. The term *hawhe kaehe*, a transliteration of 'half-caste' which later became common in *te Reo*, was not in use at this stage. Indeed, there is not much evidence that these children were treated differently from other children borne by indigenous mothers. Indigenous conceptions of descent could cope with such developments. As Ballara explains, '[t]he point of attachment to any iwi or hapū can be through father or mother, grandfather or grandmother, on either paternal or maternal sides, and this is why Tangata Whenua were and are able to claim membership of many hapū and multiple iwi.'[148] This was why, although a Pākehā father could never completely be a part of a *hapū*, though he might be cherished and protected, his children were born members of *hapū* through their mother.[149]

[145] Marshall, *Two Visits to New Zealand*, p. 246.
[146] Hocken, *Early History of New Zealand*, p. 209: Frederick Tuckett, diary, 19 April 1844.
[147] Perhaps the earliest of these was Kendall after he 'fell', baptizing James Danger Price, son of a woman from Rangihoua and Henry Sinclair Price, a ship's first officer. Waimate Registers, cited in Judith Binney, *The Legacy of Guilt: A Life of Thomas Kendall* (Auckland, 1968), p. 124 n.29.
[148] Ballara, p. 149.
[149] Makereti Papakura, *The Old Time Maori*, p. 42 (Ballara, pp. 147–8).

Through genealogy, *whakapapa*, such children were not fractionalized into 'halves', but effectively seen as multiples, 'doubles', existing as descendants of many ancestors held in common with their kin. Even in the narrowest of kin groups this was true, as their family relationships were established by common ancestry through their mother. All supposedly 'mixed' children thus belonged in a *whānau* (clan or family in an 'extended sense') and were *whanaunga* (kin or relatives).[150] A mother's relatives rarely ostracized children with Pākehā fathers, for their relationship was clear, direct and recognized within the ordinary confines of indigenous relations. This was furthered by most of these children residing in the community of their mother, and consequently being integrated through the distribution of property, participation in communal and family life, and conformation with community laws and protocols. The standing of a family, however, might still be greatly influenced by the social significance of the Pākehā father, particularly if he was of established importance to the community.

In settled relationships in this early period, half-caste children might have mothers who were important women, and fathers who, although Pākehā, might as traders and mediators be men of some significance. Many prominent families of half-castes descended from such situations, with advantages in wealth and opportunity that were unusual in the archipelago. Through a father they might claim access to mission education and literacy, bilinguality, or even a trade. Through their mother, they had *whānau* (family in the extended sense) and *hapū*, might be part of the same economic unit, might be apportioned use or ownership of communal property. 'Half-caste', as a term and a category, grew out of a genealogy of European colonial engagements. As in other Polynesian societies, amongst Tangata Whenua the term 'half-caste' was not only not necessary but required both a change in underlying indigenous discourses about kinship or a substantial change in circumstances to make the term meaningful.[151] Later colonial attempts to intervene in indigenous intimate and family life would archive precisely this characteristic. The primary architecture used in *te Reo* to formulate kin relationships was *whakapapa*. It was possible to understand and live with these children, and their later lives as adults, without any reference to 'half-castes' or any equivalent concept.

But experiences were exceedingly diverse; there were also many children who followed fleeting exchanges, or who could claim less importance. These children might have a father who was unknown or departed or not valued, or a mother who might herself be marginal or of less significance.

[150] Ranginui Walker, *Ka Whawhai Tonu Matou: Struggle Without End* (Auckland, 1990), p. 64; also Ballara, *Iwi*.
[151] Salesa, 'Troublesome Half-castes', ch. 2.

Unsurprisingly, some disparaging nicknames for some of those who had a
Pākehā father have made it into the written record, and perhaps these
generally addressed those whose fathers were either not integrated into
indigenous communities or for whom there was little respect, such as *o te
parara* (out of the [whaler's] barrel), *utu pihikete* (paid for with biscuits),
and *hupaiana* (hoop iron).[152]

However, there are many other, very clear, indications that most—
almost all—'half-castes' found an accepted place in indigenous society. In
particular, it was common for indigenous leaders to set aside land for these
children. This was an endorsement of their belonging, reiterating that they
were Tangata Whenua, a pattern that was to become increasingly important as the children became adults. In 1844 Tuckett encountered some
half-caste land owners:

> There is a young man and his sister, the children of an Englishman deceased,
> by a Maori woman. They are grown up—the former about eighteen, very tall
> and good looking. They are the proprietors of a portion of land at Otago, in
> their mother's right, which is admitted by the other natives.[153]

This process was already well underway beforehand. By needs it had to be,
for 'half-castes' had to make their living like any of those they lived
amongst. Land was unquestionably being set aside for them as early as
the 1820s, and was likely to have been happening before. One 'half-caste'
remembered his uncle, the famous leader Pomare, telling him that a piece
of land 'is now yours as you were born here . . . he then took my Father and
showed him the boundary and gave him the deeds'.[154]

Culturally, 'half-castes' were diverse: some inhabited profoundly indigenous subjectivities, speaking only *te Reo*. Others, such as one of William
Cook's sons, 'could write [in English]; and spoke English very perfectly',
and wrote letters that strongly suggested they thought themselves different,
in important ways, from other members of their *hapū*.[155] Most commonly,
however, even those that Pākehā observers identified as 'half-castes', at this
time could only speak a little or no English. The majority of these children
lived either in the interstitial communities largely built by their mothers and
fathers—the port towns and whaling stations—or in their mother's *kainga*

---

[152] Teone Taare Tikao, (ed.) J. Herries Beattie, *Tikao Talks: Treasures from the Ancient
World of the Maori*, new edn., (Auckland, 1990), p. 155; J. Herries Beattie, *Traditional
Lifeways of the Southern Maori: The Otago University Ethnological Project, 1920*, (ed.) Atholl
Anderson, (Dunedin, 1994), p. 424; cf. Anderson, *Race Against Time*, p. 2.
[153] Hocken, *Early History of New Zealand*, p. 219: Tuckett, diary, 10 May 1844.
[154] NA, OLC 1/72, George Cook, evidence, 12 October 1857. Benjamin Morrell, *A
Narrative of Four Voyages* (New York, 1832), p. 364: 7 January 1830.
[155] Boultbee, *Journal*, p. 93.

that their fathers had entered. A few were to be as mobile as their footloose fathers, and one young half-caste girl, the granddaughter of the leading chief Te Pahi by his daughter Te Atahoe and the Pākehā Māori George Bruce, was left at an orphanage in Sydney in about 1810. Bruce and Te Atahoe had gone to Bengal, and Te Atahoe died on the return in Sydney.[156] Bruce wore the *moko* on his face, felt ostracized and embarrassed in Sydney, and apparently for this reason left his extremely young daughter behind.[157] One half-caste is hinted at as a result of Te Mahanga's visit to Britain in 1806, where he went out with some money he had been given and got a 'wife', who he reported was pregnant by the time he left.[158]

It would be possible to reconstruct the individual lives of a number of 'half-castes' who were born in these years before 1840. Many people who might be described as half-castes, and who later become prominent, were born in these years. This includes two future members of parliament, Wiremu Te Kakakura Parata and Wiremu Pere (baptized as William Halbert). Parata was the son of Captain Trapp, of the *Julian*, who had taken a wife from Fouveaux Strait.[159] Wi Pere, the son of the trader Thomas Halbert and Riria Mauaranui, his fourth wife, was one of a large family of 'half-castes' from Halbert's six marriages to indigenous women.[160] The Jenkins sisters, a dynasty of daughters from the whaler William Jenkins' relationship with Pairoke, were also of this time, later becoming well-known hoteliers near Wellington.[161] The Tapsell family, which was to be one of the most prominent families, also dated from this time, with Phillip Tapsell's three marriages to indigenous women.[162] However, the trouble with such an enterprise is that it assumes that the category of 'half-caste' was at that time somehow meaningful, stable or relevant. There is little evidence to suggest this was the case, and almost none to suggest that in these years those labelled 'half-castes' considered themselves thus. The discourses, relations of power and institutions that would later make half-caste meaningful and important, both as a subjectivity and as a subject position, were not yet in place.

From certain perspectives of empire half-castes embodied the complications of a New Zealand that had not only encountered, but was entangled

---

[156] Edward Robarts, *The Marquesan Journal of Edward Robarts 1797–1824*, (ed.) Greg Dening, (Canberra, 1974), pp. 182–9; D. Wayne Orchiston, 'George Bruce and the Maoris (1806–8)', *JPS*, 81 (1972), pp. 248–52.

[157] Salmond, *Between Worlds*, pp. 364–6.

[158] Savage, *Some Account of New Zealand*; Dillon, *Narrative*, I, pp. 201–3; Salmond, *Between Worlds*, pp. 331–48.

[159] McNab, *The Old Whaling Days*, pp. 202–3.

[160] See entries in *Dictionary of New Zealand Biography* (*DNZB*), 1.

[161] ATL, qMS-1900, 'The Story of Whaler Jenkins and Wharemauku'.

[162] ATL, qMs-1980, 'Events in the Life of Phillip Tapsell'.

with, new people and things. By the time of British annexation in early 1840, the divide between 'natives' and 'Europeans' which seemed 'natural' only 70 years before, was no longer quite so monochrome and straightforward. The limits of different populations and jurisdictions were in some cases indistinct, and missionaries, officials, seamen and, in many locations, Tangata Whenua had all been altered by dint of their encounters. Tangata Whenua might dress as Europeans and speak English; an Englishman might have forgotten much of his English and be tattooed. As a canoe approached a trading vessel—which might be manned by Polynesians, Australian aborigines or Native Americans—a Tahitian or a Bengali might emerge amongst Tangata Whenua as interpreter. The archipelago's indigenous people and their ways of life, already elusive and ineffable, had been further complicated and entangled with the arrival and activity of Pākehā.

One Pākehā writer spoke for many when he contemplated some of what he had seen in New Zealand. He called it 'Pandemonium on earth'.[163] It was a society which seemed 'immoral' and 'disorderly', and in Britain people solemnly discussed what they called 'the Emergency of New Zealand'.[164] But New Zealand was not without order, and only seemed so to those uncomfortable with a place ordered by people it could only recognize as 'natives'. A recent history has called this period 'Old New Zealand', describing it as 'the hybrid world' which continued in places until it was swamped by new tides of settlement in the 1870s.[165] This touches something characteristic of the period, but complicates it, for these were societies that were no more or less hybrid than the worlds that came before or followed. Indeed, as was to become evident in scholarly accounts fixated on the 'hybrid' (see Chapter 4), the notion of the hybrid helped crystallize the recognition of racial, and species', purity. The notion of the hybrid reified differences into separate monochromes that were then combined, rather than acknowledging pre-existing variation, complexity and entanglement. Perhaps more importantly, to make this world 'hybrid' understates the degree to which this world peculiarly, and predominantly, belonged to and was controlled by Tangata Whenua.

The inscription of New Zealand as a pandemonium, a place of disorder and savagery, profoundly shaped colonial developments. For one thing it helped lever the archipelago into the British Empire, depicting it as ungoverned, reading annexation as a 'fatal necessity'. These discourses also

---

[163] S.M.D. Martin, *New Zealand, in a Series of Letters* (London, 1845), p. 89. He was referring specifically to whaling communities and the mixing of Maori and Pakeha freely.
[164] PP 1837–1838, xxi (680), pp. 277–86, 312: 'Report . . . into the Present State of the Islands of New Zealand', William Garratt, evidence; John Beecham, evidence.
[165] Belich, *Making Peoples*, p. 129.

connected New Zealand with larger problems, including that of racial crossing, which reached across the Empire—whether through missionaries' sensibilities about conjugality or assumptions about infanticide. The pandemonium also identified a lack of order not just in governance and law but in intimate and personal realms, even perceptibly in the bodies of 'half-castes', as the effort to start New Zealand's first half-caste school showed. This diagnosis led to the prescription that a great variety of indigenous domains were greatly in need of intervention and government, of both temporal and spiritual kinds. The pandemonium held together both strategic and intimate interests: criticisms about 'promiscuous intercourse' in New Zealand, for instance, might refer to carnal traffic, the arms trade or that of human heads.[166] The Emergency of New Zealand called for urgent action by colonial and imperial interests to take it. This urgency continued to be preoccupied with racial crossing. 'Half-caste children', one observer remarked breathlessly, 'are always destroyed, unless preserved by paternal affection'. 'What remedy remains then for the preservation of the race, but the settlement of the whites among them, and their amalgamating in civilized life?'[167]

[166] *HRNZ*, 1, p. 588: Commissioner Bigge to Earl Bathurst, 27 February 1823.
[167] *New Zealand Journal*, 31 August 1844, p. 555.

3

The Experiment of Racial Amalgamation

By 1837 the supposed 'pandemonium' in New Zealand was, in the eyes of concerned British observers, no longer acceptable. For missionaries, some naval officers, officials in Australia and many interested people in Britain, it was an issue more of when, rather than if, New Zealand would become 'British'. The Colonial Secretary in 1837 was Lord Glenelg, and he had concluded that the 'only Question' regarding New Zealand was a choice between 'a Colonization, desultory, without Law, and fatal to the Natives, and a Colonization organized and salutary.'[1] These were the broad goals of colonization, a transformation from 'pandemonium' into 'a Colonization organized and salutary'. Multiple pressures, particularly from the mission societies, the systematic colonizers and the New South Wales government, all weighed in: by late 1839 a nascent colonial government was on its way to New Zealand.

In New Zealand's early colonial years 'European' settlement was concentrated in only a few places—'the six colonies of New Zealand'.[2] These six colonies aside (indeed, at times a few of these included) New Zealand remained in practice politically and economically dependent on the *ancien régime*, Tangata Whenua leadership and communities, in their differing local forms. In 1853 a local Ngāti Whatua leader was still describing the settler capital, Auckland, as 'the township on our land'.[3] At the beginning of 1840 there were only about 2,000 or so Pākehā. By 1844 there were around 12,500, and by 1852 there were around 27,500. By 1858 this number had doubled, and they numbered nearly 60,000.[4]

It became apparent to some Tangata Whenua that these Pākehā were not like those of previous years. They were *pakeha hou* as some called them, New Pākehā; Pākehā who, one leader lamented, 'did not seem to

---

[1] CO 209/2, fo. 410: Glenelg to Durham, 29 December 1837.
[2] William Fox, *The Six Colonies of New Zealand* (London, 1851).
[3] Te Kawau, in C.O. Davis (ed.), *Maori Mementoes* (Auckland, 1855), p. 65.
[4] G.T. Bloomfield, *New Zealand, a Handbook of Historical Statistics* (Boston, 1984) pp. 42–4.

know the chiefs from the slaves.'[5] They seemed to have little intention of spreading themselves among indigenous communities, or of living in conformity with indigenous social practices (unless compelled). Previously Pākehā children usually grew up in or around indigenous communities and spoke *te Reo*; but the children of the New Pākehā were distant from, and might even be afraid of, Tangata Whenua.[6] In previous years indigenous societies had handled small numbers of Pākehā with some aplomb, but were now confronted with numbers and concentrations that exceeded expectations. Though it proved to be limited, it was telling that within a few years these differences had reached a point of armed conflict.

The problems that colonial government faced were not always, or even often, so raw. Though conflict and force were important attributes of colonial governance, the problem of organizing and governing New Zealand was equally reliant on certain kinds of discursive or conceptual work. Most relevant here was the development and imposition of a racial taxonomy in the first few years of colonial government, a taxonomy through which government was long to continue to operate. This taxonomy was deeply implicated in understandings and policies of racial amalgamation, and it illuminates the ways in which racial amalgamation could countenance equality and inclusion while sheltering and facilitating differentiation and disparity. At a time when policy choices were understood to be at extremes—on the one hand there was complete separation of the settlers from natives, and on the other was unrestricted and undifferentiated 'equality'—racial amalgamation reconciled these two extremes. Through its various manifestations, it consistently strove neither to separate nor to indiscriminately merge, but to regularize and discipline relations between the races, to transform a supposed 'pandemonium' of indigenous rule and intimacies into a 'colonization organized and salutary'.

'THE EXPERIMENT OF AMALGAMATION' AND THE COLONIAL OFFICE

Many historians have focused their imperial researches on the Colonial Office.[7] Reformed in the 1830s, primarily by James Stephen, it is an

---

[5] Edward Jerningham Wakefield, *Adventure in New Zealand, from 1839 to 1844*, (ed.) Robert Stout, (Christchurch, 1908 [1845]), pp. 149, 221. (The leader was Te Puni).

[6] Constantine Dillon, *The Dillon Letters: the Letters of the Hon. Constantine Dillon, 1842–1853*, C.A. Sharp (ed.), (Wellington, 1954), p. 79: Dillon to Lady Dillon, 5 September 1848.

[7] Most importantly: John W. Cell, *British Colonial Administration in the Mid-Nineteenth Century: the Policy-Making Process* (New Haven, 1970); Paul Knaplund, *James Stephen and*

attractive object of study. But policy generally, and 'racial amalgamation' in particular, was a discourse of larger habitat. If the Colonial Office was a domestic face of colonial policy, the governors were in New Zealand, and each was only a part of extensive social, intellectual, bureaucratic and political milieux which jointly fashioned policy. The governors were overseen by the Colonial Office in London and, in turn, the head of the Colonial Office, the Secretary of State for the Colonies, was himself guided, acting as 'the channel, not the origin, of [any] decision.'[8] He had to liaise with the Board of Trade, the Admiralty, the War Office, the Law Officers, Treasury and Cabinet, as well as the members of the Office itself, and Parliament. The Office selected the governors and sometimes top-ranking officials, oversaw the colonies and managed domestic matters, but most executive and legislative power had to be devolved; the Empire could not be run from London. Colonial legislation might be rejected once it reached Britain, or governors might be recalled, but on the whole the Office was necessarily more concerned with the larger strategies of government. The outstanding character at the Office in these years, James Stephen, summed up the Office's approach to guiding its governors. Directions amounted 'to not much more than saying—Go and do the best you can to give effect to the views of the Gov[ernment] as explained in the accompanying Papers.'[9] It did no good, another official warned, to 'harass [governors] with fruitless attempts at guidance across perhaps half the circumference of the Globe.'[10]

In Britain, the colonies and colonial policy were mostly important in times of crisis or within certain 'bridgeheads'. Government during these years was generally through vulnerable coalitions of quite diverse interests, and they changed with relative frequency (five different cabinets 1834–1846, and five different colonial secretaries in the decade after Glenelg). Only the permanent staff of the Colonial Office lent continuity, and amongst these were influential characters, most famously Stephen ('Mr Mothercountry' his opponents called him).[11] The Office spoke with many rather than a single voice, and had to listen to many more. Whatever

the *British Colonial System 1813–1847* (Madison, 1953); W.P. Morrell, *British Colonial Policy in the Age of Peel and Russell* (London, 1966); W.P. Morrell, *British Colonial Policy in the Mid-Victorian Age: South Africa, New Zealand, West Indies* (Oxford, 1969).

[8] CO 325/47, [unpaginated]: James Stephen, 'Colonies and Colonial Policy', [undated]; also see Ronald Hyam, *Britain's Imperial Century, 1815–1914*, 2nd edn., (Basingstoke, 1993), ch. 1.

[9] CO 209/38, fo. 250: Stephen to Hope, 21 May 1845.

[10] CO 325/47, fo. 27: F. Elliot, 'A Few Remarks on the Causes of the Unpopularity of the Colonial Office'.

[11] Buller, *Responsible Government*, pp. 77–9.

views the Colonial Office had were always constrained and mediated by domestic politics, fiscal limits, individual idiosyncrasies, local exigencies and limited intelligence. The Colonial Office was heterogeneous, funnelling differences through process, with a bureaucratic rigour but not much of a 'system'. To give the Office coherence was to see 'a Bug-a-boo'.[12] As Stephen put it: 'the ambition of every Secretary of State and his operations will be bounded by the great ultimate object of getting off his mails.'[13]

One must see multiple, diverse and contingent origins in any policy, and racial amalgamation is no different. Partly an inheritance from the New Zealand Company, partly a 'middle way' in reformed colonization, it drew from many other sources besides. Yet in another sense its origins were plain. The first significant official use of the word itself, 'amalgamation', was in an 1844 parliamentary committee report. This recommended that 'every effort should be made to amalgamate the two races'. This report was blatantly derivative of the Company's native policy. The proposed native reserve system was that of the Company's, one which had them 'interspersed' among European settlers ('scattered, a few together, among the European population' amalgamation was more likely).[14] It was no surprise that the author of the report was the third Earl Grey (former Viscount Howick), longtime supporter of systematic colonization generally and of the Company in particular. Whenever possible the natives would be placed 'on a footing of perfect equality', and would even be employed in the civil service. Earl Grey would, in 1846, become Lord Russell's Colonial Secretary; these would be the halcyon days of racial amalgamation. But well before then amalgamation had migrated into the internal papers of the Colonial Office. In the 1845 draft instructions for the new governor of New Zealand, the parliamentary undersecretary George Hope had written of how it was

> imperative upon the Crown as a question of honour and justice no less than of policy—that subject to obligations imposed by that treaty [of Waitangi] it has been the wish of Her Majesty's Government, by every means in their power, to promote the amalgamation of the two races and the gradual subjection of the Aboriginal race to British laws and institutions.[15]

[12] CO 325/47, fo. 7: F. Elliot, 'A Few Remarks on the Causes of the Unpopularity of the Colonial Office'.
[13] Caroline Emelia Stephens, *The Right Honourable Sir James Stephen: Letters with Biographical Notes* (Gloucester, 1909), p. 42.
[14] PP 1844, xiii (556), pp. iii, xi: 'Report from the Select Committee Appointed to Enquire into . . . New Zealand'.
[15] CO 209/38, fo. 257: Hope, draft instructions, May 1845.

This passage did not survive to be in the final instructions given to Sir George Grey, but it was significant in at least two ways. One, it showed that Hope considered amalgamation as something distinct from the political process ('subjection'); and two, it signalled that racial amalgamation had migrated into the official arena.

The Office and the colonial service were no places for abstraction. 'Whoever would contribute any thing really serviceable', Stephen suggested, 'must constantly to stoop from the lofty regions of abstract philosophy and principle, to many minute and wearisome details.'[16] Any exploration of 'racial amalgamation' as colonial policy must follow a similar path; though the pages of the Colonial Office are generally dearth with 'philosophers'. But if there was a 'philosopher' of racial amalgamation at the Colonial Office, it was Herman Merivale. A professor of political economy at the University of Oxford (1840–1847), Merivale was Stephen's successor as permanent undersecretary (1847).[17] Merivale specialized in the political economy of colonies, and Stephen was a great admirer of his work.[18] This admiration, Merivale's long tenure as undersecretary and his competent work suggest that although he did not officially speak for the Office, his views were recognized as consonant and attractive, even before his arrival there.

For Merivale racial amalgamation was a saving grace. The great problem of 'aboriginal races' within the British Empire, it seemed to him (as to others), presented 'only three alternatives' to British government. The first was 'extermination': completely wiping out aboriginal populations in the British colonies, leaving them empty of people and free for settlers. The second was what he called 'civilization, complete or partial, by retaining [native races] as insulated bodies of men, carefully removed . . . from the injury of European contact': in short, the placing of aborigines on reservations, and using government to ensure that they remained separated (or protected) from settlers. The third and final alternative was the 'amalgamation' of colonists with aborigines. This was reminiscent of much of what the Company had earlier said, and Merivale's conclusion was also similar. Extermination, Merivale argued, was unconscionable, and simply could not be considered. The ongoing segregation of aborigines and settlers was 'impossible', only breeding a continued native dependency on colonists. In Merivale's eyes 'there remains only the third alternative, that of amalgamation; and this I am most anxious to impress upon your minds'.[19]

---

[16] CO 325/47, [unpaginated]: James Stephen, 'Colonies and Colonial Policy'.
[17] See *DNB*, xxxvii, pp. 280–1; Cell, *British Colonial Administration*, pp. 16–18.
[18] Earl Grey Papers, GRE/B115/4A: Earl Grey to Merivale, 23 October 1847.
[19] Herman Merivale, *Lectures on Colonization and Colonies*, 2 vols., (London, 1841–1842), 2, p. 179.

Merivale's was amongst the clearest and most forthright formulations of racial amalgamation. His advocacy of racial amalgamation was coupled with an unusually clear definition that is worth quoting at length.

> By amalgamation, I mean the union of natives with settlers in the same community, as master and servant, as fellow-labourers, as fellow-citizens, and, if possible, as connected by intermarriage. And I mean by it, not that eventual and distant process . . . but I mean an immediate and an individual process—immediate, if not in act, at least in contemplation. . . . I am chiefly anxious to point out to you, that, however improbable the success of any particular project of amalgamation may seem, amalgamation, by some means or other, is the only possible Euthanasia of savage communities. . . . And we have this advantage at least, that we are on untrodden ground. The experiment of amalgamation . . . cannot be said to have been hitherto tried by any government.[20]

The dimensions of Merivale's racial amalgamation were unusually explicit, as was his contention that it was new and experimental. For Merivale it was the only sensible, humane and practical course. Yet, perhaps most significantly, Merivale was under no illusion that this 'humanity' would lead to an endpoint not entirely unlike racial amalgamation's alternatives. The terminus of racial amalgamation, at least as far as aboriginal races were concerned, was a kind of tender obliteration, by means of racial crossing and civilization; or, as Merivale put it, a 'Euthanasia of savage communities'.

The problem of race crossing was central to the shaping of Merivale's conception of racial amalgamation. Racial amalgamation was proposed as a way of managing or even harnessing the problems that were acute at racial crossings, and Merivale went as far as to add an appendix on the desirability of racial intermarriage. For him intermarriages (and perhaps even just 'durable connexions') were a way of correcting the 'mutual revulsion' that stemmed from 'prejudices of colour'. Some feared that 'the multiplication of "half castes"' threatened the extinction of pure bloods, but Merivale regarded this as a boon. Mixed race people were improved, and Merivale cited 'strong testimony to the superior energy and high organization of many of these half-blood races.' He drew on several treatises to underwrite his argument that mixed races were characterized by 'prolificness and the energetic'. These were general views, but Merivale gave them specific application. Well before he was at the Colonial Office he noted that native New Zealanders were 'semi-civilized' 'cultivators of the soil', who unlike the American Indians invited rather than repelled European society. For Merivale New Zealand thus seemed a particularly

---

[20] Ibid., 2, pp. 180–81.

suitable place for the 'experiment' of amalgamation, and the indigenous
New Zealanders were 'altogether more promising subjects for experiment.'[21]

The Colonial Office in the 1830s and 1840s has often been characterized as 'humanitarian'. This is a diffuse and not always helpful description,
but perhaps nowhere is it more accurate than concerning the spectre of
'aboriginal extinction' or 'extermination'. The catalogue of disastrous
effects that European expansion had wreaked on so many different people
around the world was well known.[22] It was 'impossible to cast the eye over
the map of the globe, and to discover so much as a single spot', Lord John
Russell lamented, where civilized men had not wrought destruction
upon savages.[23] Any number of popular, often religious, pamphlets and
books mused on the topic. The abolitionist Thomas Fowell Buxton and
his family engineered and managed a parliamentary select committee
(1835–1837) which drew both heat and light to the matter of 'aborigines'.
Moreover, by 1840 none at the Colonial Office would have disagreed with
Merivale that this state of affairs was unacceptable. This moral viewpoint
was further complicated because the reasons for this depopulation were
deeply contested. People blamed disease, warfare, even the weight of
'savagery' for the decline; many turned to Thomas Malthus. There was
no consensus on the precise agent of decline: was it simply unavoidable,
the course of history? Some, such as Stephen, thought it wrong but
believed that nothing could be done. Others, such as his colleague Vernon
Smith, believed that wise policy and disciplined settlement might reverse
the decline.[24]

Buxton's Aborigines Committee helped crystallize a notion of 'aborigines', fashioning them into a recognizable imperial problem.[25] This
conception brought all the indigenous people of southern Africa, the
Americas, Australia, New Zealand and the Pacific Islands under the
heading 'aborigine'. Further, it established that the aborigines (almost by
definition) were endangered, both in their property and their lives. The
committee sparked a small but significant interest, best seen in the
Aborigines Protection Society, founded in 1837. Officials, too, began to
understand 'aborigines' as a pan-colonial issue, much as one would then

[21] Ibid., 2, pp. 201, 219–20, 125, 157, 200.
[22] See Patrick Brantlinger, *Dark Vanishings: Discourse on the Extinction of Primitive
Races, 1800–1930* (Ithaca, 2003).
[23] CO 380/122, fos. 71–76: Russell to Hobson, 9 December 1840.
[24] CO 209/8, fo. 446: Stephen to Vernon Smith, minute, 28 December 1840; CO 380/
122, fo. 151: Vernon Smith to Russell, 5 November 1840.
[25] PP 1837, vii (425): 'Report From the Select Committee on Aborigines (British
Settlements)'.

talk of 'slaves'.[26] While slaves needed to be freed, though, the chief predicament of aborigines (also called 'natives') was that they needed to be 'protected'.

Yet to focus only on fears about aboriginal depopulation, as some historians have done, is to neglect crucial elements of 'humanitarianism'. Although disease was often named as a cause, extinction was generally seen as an outcome of a wider process—a competition for resources and their control. It was common to see in this a natural antagonism between races, a 'war of races'.[27] This was a Malthusian war of settlement, reproduction and 'checks'. Sheep took on native forest, imported grasses took on native grasses; European children seemed to outlast and outnumber native ones, displaying the war's racial aspects. These questions of population and political economy were, as Boyd Hilton has shown, deeply inflected at this time by soteriological ('salvationist') religious beliefs. This imbued economics and politics with a sense of 'atonement', mediating the severity of Malthusian views.[28] But the 'war of races' was still seen as harsh. The Colonial Office, for instance, feared the damage, the poor publicity and fiscal cost of actual conflict, but the notion of a threatening 'war of races' was pervasive. Much more than armed conflict was implied in the 'war of races', and this war was the 'calamity' of the colonial predicament. 'The common calamity of all our colonies', wrote James Stephen, 'is that they are composed of different, and often hostile races'. To him racial war was almost a natural state, one only to be avoided by careful policy and government; this was one reason he was reluctant to devolve authority to the settlers, for fear that 'we should place the weaker though more numerous race, helplessly at the power of the stronger minority.'[29] Aboriginal depopulation was thus proof not only of the primacy of the 'war of races', but that the settlers would, as a matter of course, win.

It is only in these contexts that some of the proposals made by the Colonial Office make any sense. For example, Stephen recommended arming and training indigenous people in New Zealand, so that they might withstand the settler onslaught, a proposal entertained for other colonies too.[30] Lord John Russell agreed with him, and instructed the first

[26] *Historical Records of Australia*, series 1, xx, (Sydney, 1924), p. 774: Russell to Gipps, 25 August 1840.
[27] CO 325/47, [unpaginated]: James Stephen, 'Colonies and Colonial Policy'.
[28] Hilton, *The Age of Atonement*.
[29] CO 209/51, fos. 275–8: Grey to Earl Grey, 25 March 1847; CO 209/4, fo. 329: Stephen to Labouchere, minute, 1 March 1839; CO 380/122, fo. 75: Russell to Hobson, 9 December 1840; CO 325/47, James Stephen, 'Colonies and Colonial Policy', [unpaginated].
[30] *Historical Records of Victoria*, (Melbourne, 1983), 2B, p. 757: Stephen to Vernon Smith, minute, 10 December 1839.

New Zealand governor to arm the New Zealanders in order to make them
'ferocious' to colonists. Once he arrived in New Zealand Hobson quickly
realized the natives were quite ferocious enough, yet Stephen remained

> convinced that the only way to protect Aborigines, or indeed, any other race
> of men is to make them formidable. If we could train these People to act as
> Militia or an Armed Police, we should do them more good than by enlisting
> a thousand Protectors for their defence.[31]

Those in the Office thought themselves above it, but they identified
an innate or natural 'jealousy' between races.[32] How could the Office
act against 'the contempt and aversion with which the European race
everywhere regard the Black races'?[33] Matters seemed to bear the Office
out. In South Australia, the government had to go as far as issuing a
'proclamation that the Aborigines are "Human Beings Partaking of Our
Common Nature"'.[34] Whatever their disinterests, the Office gentlemen
were still conscious and proud of their 'Anglo-Saxon Race', and had few
doubts as to the ultimate fate of any aborigines who might oppose them.[35]

With extinction as one imagined result, and the separation of feuding
races as the other, it was little wonder that the Colonial Office might agree
with Merivale (and the New Zealand Company) that racial amalgamation
was attractive. Moreover, it was consonant with 'protection', the broad
platform of the Office's policies. But in general they realized that protection was less a solution than an ongoing relationship. Officials had doubts
about their ability to continue 'protecting' aborigines as increasing numbers of settlers demanded more land and resources. Racial amalgamation,
even if at a distant future, promised at least some kind of resolution to the
problem at hand. In the interim governors were repeatedly told to 'protect'
the aborigines of New Zealand.[36] This agreed entirely with Buxton's
Aborigines report and, sure enough, Hobson established an official 'Protector of Aborigines' soon after he reached New Zealand in 1840. Six years
later, committee member William Gladstone was Colonial Secretary:
'I conceive it to be an undoubted maxim', he wrote, 'that the Crown
should stand in all matters between the colonists and the natives'.[37] This
maxim was to be held by most officials. This put them in a position not

[31] CO 209/8, fo.[?]: Minute, Stephen, 28 October 1840.
[32] CO 209/37, fo. 75: William Spain, 'Report', 31 March 1845.
[33] CO 209/35, fo. 47: Stephen, minute, 26 February 1846.
[34] *Historical Records of Victoria*, 2B, p. 757: Vernon Smith, minute, 11 December 1839.
[35] CO 209/4, fo. 329: Stephen to Labouchere, minute, 1 March 1839.
[36] PP 1841, xvii (311), p. 32: charter, enclosed in Russell to Hobson, 9 December 1840;
also ibid., p. 52: Russell to Hobson, 28 January 1841.
[37] PP 1846, xxx (337), p. 153: Gladstone to Grey, 31 January 1846.

only to keep the races apart and from war, but control and discipline the moments, places and relationships in which they came together. This was a tidy and maintainable view from the metropole, but in New Zealand it begged crucial questions, not least where did one race end and the other begin?

TWO RACES, TWO FORMS OF AUTHORITY

Even though Britain had apparently assumed 'control' of New Zealand, the first two decades of British government saw most Tangata Whenua remain independent. The Treaty of Waitangi (signed February to August 1840) had been a basis of the colony's foundation. It was understood by British officials to be a treaty of cession, which in English it was. But negotiations were primarily in *te Reo*, it was the *te Reo* text that was signed, and the *Tiriti o Waitangi* was substantially different. In the *Tiriti* chiefs (*rangatira*) were guaranteed their chieftainship ('*tino rangatiratanga*') and ceded only governorship ('*kāwanatanga*'), not sovereignty as in the English text. Moreover, not all chiefs signed, and it was never ratified.[38] As Judith Binney and James Belich have shown, after 1840 there remained two different forms of authority in New Zealand: an indigenous leadership and a new British colonial administration, substantially the forms recognized in the *Tiriti*.[39] Such questions of authority were entwined with race as colonial government—*kāwanatanga*—sought to comprehend, assert and remake its domains racially.

The formulation and mapping of racial taxonomies became an essential operation of colonial government. These were not, however, straightforward tasks. *Kāwanatanga* was curtailed by the continued power of *rangatiratanga*, the independence of the majority of indigenous people and communities. It was also confronted with a variety of people and communities that were importantly different, and which criss-crossed any divisions that might be supposed 'natural', particularly, but not only, in intimate ways. The limits of these two forms of authority were not clear;

---

[38] Alan Ward, *An Unsettled History: Treaty Claims in New Zealand Today* (Wellington, 1999); Giselle Byrnes, *The Waitangi Tribunal and New Zealand History* (Melbourne, 2004); Michael Belgrave, *Historical Frictions: Maori Claims and Reinvented Histories* (Auckland, 2005); Claudia Orange, *The Treaty of Waitangi* (Wellington, 1987).

[39] Judith Binney, 'Two Communities', in Judith Bassett, Judith Binney and Erik Olssen, (eds.), *The People and the Land/Te Tangata me te Whenua: an Illustrated History of New Zealand 1820–1920* (Wellington, 1990); Belich, 'The Governors and the Maori', in Sinclair, (ed.), *Oxford Illustrated History of New Zealand*, pp. 75–98; Belich, *The New Zealand Wars*, pp. 78–9.

the 'boundaries of rule' (to use Stoler's phrase) were not unambiguous.[40] Nor were the racial taxonomies simply recognitions or catalogues of pre-existing differences. The predicament of colonial government was, on the one hand, resolving human variety and connections into manageable taxonomic units, while also pursuing, through these and other means, the extension and solidification of colonial authority into indigenous domains.

Throughout the 1840s and 1850s these two forms of authority coexisted. In most of the country, *rangatiratanga* was in the ascendancy. As Governor Grey wrote in 1846, 'I doubt if there is any portion of the British possessions in which the administration of justice [meaning British justice] is so feeble, indeed, I might say so impracticable.'[41] He knew well, as did his predecessors and successors, that outside the main colonial settlements government was largely irrelevant. What had taken the New Zealand Company years to acknowledge, governors openly admitted: 'without some material alteration in the relations at present', Fitzroy wrote, 'it will be found impracticable to maintain the supremacy of British authority beyond a limited extent of country'.[42] The natives viewed the government and its officers with something approaching contempt, Fitzroy complained, and 'the simple fact of the case is, that the authority of the Government is disregarded'.[43] An Attorney General could do little but be laconic: 'so numerous are those Tribes and many of them so distant that were we disposed to [assert colonial law over them] we have not the power.'[44]

Any number of incidents daily brought home indigenous independence. Te Kawau, one of the patrons of Auckland, led some of his Ngāti Whātua kin to the Auckland gaol to extract a relation. This was the capital's gaol, literally at the heart of government, yet officials could only stand by and watch. In an emergency meeting of the Executive Council, the members decided it was a matter best left until the government had adequate force or power; in truth they had no decision to make, for they had no other option.[45] Te Kawau was losing his patience with Pākehā: 'the love of the many', he wrote, 'is growing cold'.[46]

---

[40] Stoler, 'Rethinking Colonial Categories: European Communities and the Boundaries of Rule', p. 148.
[41] CO 211/2, fo. 143: Grey's opening address, Legislative Council, 5 October 1846.
[42] PP 1846, xxx (337), p. 134: Fitzroy to Stanley, 17 September 1845.
[43] CO 209/38, fo. 17: Grey to Stanley, 22 November 1845.
[44] CO 211/1, fo. 44: Executive Council minutes, 28 December 1842.
[45] CO 211/1, fos. 152–61: Executive Council minutes, 21 February 1844.
[46] CO 211/1, fo. 159: Te Kawau to Clarke, 21 February 1844, in Executive Council minutes, 21 February 1844. (Recalling, it would seem, Matthew 24: 12).

In 1844, on the outskirts of Auckland, an enormous *hākari* (feast) symbolized this power and wealth. The centrepiece was a shelter four hundred yards long, where around 11,000 baskets of potatoes, 9,000 fish, 100 pigs, 1,000 blankets, as well as quantities of wheat, rice, sugar and tobacco were displayed before being shared out. (This at a time when the colonial government was virtually bankrupt.) *Hapū* had come from the Waikato, and colonial observers were amazed at the orderly nature of proceedings; despite the thousands present there was no crime or trouble of any sort. The food and goods were then parcelled out:

> at a given signal each tribe seized the food portioned out for it, and sixteen hundred men armed with guns and tomahawks danced the war dance. The soldiers in Auckland sunk into nothing before this host; and settlers, for the first time, admitted that they lived in New Zealand on sufferance.[47]

The governor was in attendance as an invited guest, and no doubt also found this demonstration instructive.

However, there was a key difference between *rangatiratanga* and *kāwanatanga*. *Rangatiratanga* was a form, rather than a body, of authority. It was dispersed and resided in individual, or collections of, *rangatira* (chiefs). *Kāwanatanga*, on the other hand, symbolized by the governor (*kāwana*), his laws and the Royal seals, was actually a single polity—if largely, as yet, in name only. The unity of *kāwanatanga* was a contrast to the localization of *rangatiratanga*. This was not so striking in the early 1840s, when many *hapū* or alliances were larger and more powerful than settlers and government. But as numbers increased, and soldier numbers were bolstered, this became more significant. Indeed, *kāwanatanga*, or at least its actions, partially precipitated the unprecedented: a broad-based alliance of different *hapū*, around 1858. This Kīngitanga (King movement), a major concern of Chapter 5, became the Crown's greatest opponent.

But neither *rangatiratanga* nor *kāwanatanga* had a natural 'constituency'. On the one hand, those that the government were calling 'natives' were neither uniform nor unitary. They generally lived in small kin groups or clans, *hapū*, normally numbering in the hundreds, and this was the most common and effective political unit. *Hapū* were local, diverse, drew from multiple memberships and could be antagonistic. As one indigenous leader warned a governor: 'do not suppose we ['Maori'] are one people'.[48] *Hapū* was the political and social actuality. On the other hand, while it seemed the majority of 'Europeans' were more unitary than 'natives', particularly

[47] Thomson, *The Story of New Zealand*, p. 90.
[48] CO 209/42, fo. 305: Puaha to Grey, 3 March 1846.

through their common origin and relations with government, this too was only superficial. Regional differences in the colony segmented the settler communities. Communications were poor and distances were large: news from Auckland might reach Wellington by way of Sydney.[49] Government was weak and limited and settlers were often uncooperative. In the 1840s New Zealand Company settlers often preferred Company officials to the government. Spatially, there was a significant minority of settlers who lived in or near indigenous communities, far from colonial settlements. Men and women were treated in starkly different ways, and colonial New Zealand was heavily invested in distinguishing between classes, even perceiving its own group of 'poor whites'—what one official called a 'lawless multitude'.[50] For many, colonial government was often irrelevant, confined as it was mostly to colonial settlements, and extending not at all into large parts of New Zealand. Individual and groups of 'Europeans' frayed the settler fabric.

Both *rangatiratanga* and *kāwanatanga* had problems with this lack of 'natural' or established constituencies; it was not always clear whose authority should be recognized or asserted. *Rangatira* and their communities frequently expected to retain authority and control over 'their' Pākehā, the ones who resided on land leased, given or 'sold' to them by members of a *hapū*. Most Tangata Whenua continued to treat Pākehā much as they had before 1840. Pākehā living amongst or next door to Tangata Whenua were consequently still subject to customary law and ordinary practices. Intimate relations continued to incorporate Pākehā into indigenous realms, but this was particular and personal, and did not involve the 'New Pākehā'. But something not unlike Te Kawau's actions, though in reverse, began to happen. 'Tribal' Pākehā began to turn to colonial authority for redress and 'protection'. Customary ways of gaining satisfaction for wrongs, which had been accepted (even if unhappily) before 1840 or in areas where *rangatiratanga* predominated, were no longer uniformly respected.[51] Where once a Pākehā would accept being ritually plundered (*taua muru*, a customary method of recompense), now colonists might complain (and might be listened to).

For the colonial government as for indigenous authorities, the question of authority was agonized. The Treaty of Waitangi had, apparently, made all Tangata Whenua into British subjects. But this was purely nominal. Early policy acknowledged them as subjects, but gave government discretion to

---

[49] Dillon, *The Dillon Letters*, p. 78: Constantine Dillon to Lady Dillon, 5 September 1848.
[50] CO 209/8, fo. 482: Vernon Smith, minute, 20 November 1840.
[51] CO 211/1, fo. 41: Executive Council minutes, 27 December 1842; Wade, *A Journey in the Northern Island*, pp. 52–3.

allow some indigenous customs to continue. Without coercive powers or institutions, this was only so much government talk.[52] The first Protector of Aborigines, George Clarke, knew that the 'natives' 'did not in the slightest way acquiesce in the right of the Government to interfere in quarrels purely native but only [in quarrels] between natives and Europeans.'[53] Only those who signed the Treaty acknowledged 'the Queen's sovereignty', Clarke believed, 'and that only in a limited sense'. (Arawa people called it 'that pukapuka [document] which the Ngapuhi signed'.[54]) Most Tangata Whenua allowed *kāwanatanga* to intervene in some cases, but only when Europeans were involved. When Clarke tried to tell Tangata Whenua that they were British, very few agreed.[55] Indeed, not even all colonists agreed. When Willoughby Shortland, temporary governor after Hobson's death, canvassed the Executive in 1842 as to whether the islands of New Zealand were British and whether its indigenous people were all British subjects amenable to British law, the Attorney General, William Swainson, answered no to the first issue and contested the second, arguing that those who had not ceded by signing the Treaty were not British subjects.[56]

These were the problems of juxtaposed and interpenetrating authorities, both of which remained able to assert different, often competing, claims. There was no clear definition or consensus over whose law should apply when, or to whom, and many problems resulted. Fortunately, both parties could see little advantage in direct conflict. Violent incidents (and the Northern War) were unusual. In general, though not always, such conflagrations signalled the failure of authorities to recognize and exercise within tentative, mutually agreed boundaries. There was much negotiation and mediation. One group of *rangatira*, for instance, requested that the government 'provide for us, some friendly adviser, [*sic*] who shall be able to understand both our customs and those of the White People, that he may constantly explain to us . . . the laws of the Queen'.[57] Government deliberately implemented a resident magistrate system which applied law gradually, carefully, locally, with discretion and (hopefully) the support of *rangatira*. Tangata Whenua turned in considerable numbers to these new courts and magistrates to extract debts from Pākehā, though not, as a rule, from each other.[58]

---

[52] Adams, *Fatal Necessity*, pp. 221–2.
[53] CO 211/1, fo. 41: Executive Council minutes, 27 December 1842.
[54] ATL, qMs-0426, Thomas Chapman papers, 2: Journal, 19 January 1852.
[55] CO 211/1, fos. 42–3: Executive Council minutes, 28 December 1842.
[56] CO 211/1, fos. 42–4: Executive Council minutes, 28 December 1842.
[57] CO 209/42, fos. 291–2: Grey to Stanley, 17 February 1846, enclosing Ngatitoa, Ngatiawa, and Ngati Raukawa to Grey (14 signatories).
[58] Ward, *A Show of Justice*, esp. pp. 75–114.

This competition of authorities was obviously significant for all involved. But what is perhaps of most interest to questions of racial amalgamation was the way problems of race and authority were, for colonial government, conflated. The racial taxonomy, the charting of 'native' and 'European' races, was not merely a question of observation, but a way of organizing policy, practices and understandings. Nor was this particular kind of bi-racial taxonomy a foregone conclusion. There was the possibility of classifying 'tribally', of cleaving apart Tangata Whenua into groups distinguishable and amenable to colonial authority, and organizing these into a hierarchy, underwritten by state operations (this was an operation later to be pursued, but within a bi-racial taxonomy). There was also the possibility of a taxonomy of rank, where indigenous leaders would have been separated out, their privileges protected and reified, and allowed to function as a kind of class difference. Both of these possibilities were seriously and explicitly available, and would have recast colonial practices and discourses had they been made operational.

Colonial government policy towards land is perhaps the most striking example of how racial taxonomies shaped practices and discourses. Much like Gladstone's maxim that the government should stand between settler and native, colonial land policy dictated that no land could be sold from indigenous proprietor to settler, except via the government. This stance had been composed for the first governor and was established in the Treaty of Waitangi. As land policy it was both contingent upon, and defining of, racial definitions: Hobson was instructed to make sure that no 'aborigine' could convey or contract land 'to any person of European birth or descent'.[59] Land sales and pre-emption have been much discussed by historians, and this monopoly had important consequences: it allowed government to purchase at low rates and sell at higher ones, and gave it some control over where colonists settled. (Moreover, because Tangata Whenua used land in similar ways, to raise revenue and control settlement, government monopoly and price control impinged on indigenous authority and caused conflict.[60]) But the way that land and 'race' were used to articulate each other was elemental to this policy, and its significance is largely overlooked. In one fell swoop all land had been racialized—it was either native or 'European'—and racial distinctions were made concrete.[61]

[59] CO 209/8, fo. 455: Russell to Hobson (Hobson's 'additional instructions'), 28 January 1841.
[60] Adams, *Fatal Necessity*, pp. 193–206; Hickford, 'Making "Territorial Rights of the Natives"', pp. 104–7.
[61] See especially M.P.K. Sorrenson, 'The Politics of Land', in J.G.A. Pocock, (ed.), *The Maori and New Zealand Politics* (Wellington, 1965), pp. 21–45; 'the government adopted a

As suggested in Chapter 1, 'equality' could, in such a regime, only be nominal. At the same time as colonial law purported to bring all before it equally, a bi-racial colonial regime was enshrined in government. After being admitted, not least by the Treaty, to the full 'rights and privileges of British subjects', 'natives' were still distinguished from what Governor Grey called 'the other classes of Her Majesty's subjects'.[62] Lord John Russell might 'dread any thing which would create a palpable opposition or separation of interest between the White and the Black Colonists', yet there was no question in his mind that the two races were separate and opposite.[63] Grey consistently wrote how he refused to treat 'natives' 'as a distinct race', as if their 'interests and duties were wholly distinct from those of Europeans'; but his administration (as considered below) was characterized by 'special' policies targeting them.[64] There were numerous such professions of 'equality' and incorporation, accompanied by practice in which most colonial laws explicitly or implicitly differentiated the two races.[65] This identification of two races meant different laws and legal disabilities and competencies could be enabled.

These racial distinctions were not by-products of colonial government but virtually prerequisites. They were fundamental and ubiquitous. Racial taxonomies were not only etched on the land but entrenched in related pieces of legislation and policy. Most acts of policy or legislation in this period were predicated on this distinction, even the very idea of 'native policy' or a 'Native Department'. The ordinances issued by the first governors all assumed an 'Aboriginal Native Population' which was recognized and understood, though the limits of the population were (revealingly) never demarcated. Typically, legislation was intended to operate on 'person[s] of aboriginal race' or 'any person of the Native race', but never specified precisely who those people might be.[66] Similarly, the resident magistrate system took the 'native race' as its given field, and the Legislative Council used this same categorization to exclude 'natives', if only for a time, from juries.[67] The categorizations themselves were not necessarily insidious; they could be mobilized 'positively', for example to exempt 'natives' from having

dual policy on land that was to dominate political relations between the races for many years', p. 28.

[62] CO 209/38, fos. 10–11: Grey to Stanley, 21 November 1845.

[63] CO 209/8, fos. 448–9: Russell, minute, 24 December 1840.

[64] CO 209/46, fos. 7–8: Grey to Gladstone, 6 November 1846.

[65] CO 380/122, fo. 88: 'Abstract of General Instructions to Governor Hobson', 24 November 1840.

[66] Native Exemption Ordinance; Ordinance [sale of alcohol], 12 August 1847.

[67] CO 211/1, fo. 347: Legislative Council minutes, 11 January 1844.

to pay dog tax.[68] But as was evident in these ordinances and policies, coming only a few years after the inception of government, racial categories were already indispensable, and not simply a medium, but part of the substance, of colonial government.

Race was a fundamental condition for racial amalgamation. This was obvious in a number of early colonial efforts to institute racial amalgamation. Fitzroy's 1844 Native Trust Ordinance ostensibly aimed at 'assimilating as speedily as possible the habits and usages of the Native to those of the European'.[69] An early attempt at the government of detail, it faced a number of difficulties. Amongst a number of other things the ordinance addressed the predicament of half-caste children, intervening to guarantee the rights of 'half-caste children' to inherit property (land, in effect) from their 'native' mothers (who were not generally married in conformity with colonial law).[70] The ordinance, then, was tasked not with making this transfer occur, for such children were already inheriting land, under the terms of indigenous protocols, kin, and customary law. At stake, then, were not just questions of recognition and succession but the task of converting these indigenous relationships and claims over half-castes into colonial terms. This government preoccupation signalled not only that half-castes were increasingly 'legible', but increasingly important. Moreover, it was explicit recognition that half-castes were people who should not simply, or uniformly, be subjected to the laws that treated natives. The legal contortions undertaken within the ordinance to extend legal benefits to half-castes in spite of a convergence of different racialized laws indicated how serious colonial claims over half-castes were. Finding a path for half-castes between the policy of pre-emption that was aimed at native land and the laws of illegitimacy that addressed Europeans was not easy. But, evidently, it was important enough to be undertaken, even if it was eventually to no avail, as the ordinance was refused at the Colonial Office.[71]

Evidently these racial schemes were not as easily confounded by the complexities and intricacies of New Zealand as might be expected. Certainly colonial government faced seemingly intractable challenges. On

---

[68] CO 211/1, fo. 350: Legislative Council minutes, 11 January 1844; ibid., fo. 356: 23 May 1844.

[69] Native Trustees Ordinance, [29 June 1844].

[70] Such property would be placed in the care of a trust until the children reached maturity.

[71] It was disallowed because of a sectarian reference contravening the Colonial Office's commitment to freedom of religion in New Zealand. PP 1846, xxx (337), p. 85: Stanley to Grey, 13 August 1845; CO 211/1, fos. 372–4, 379–80: Legislative Council minutes, 18 June 1844, 29 June 1844.

the one hand the categories were ambitious, as much prescriptions for government as they were descriptions of whom and what they hoped to govern. On the other hand, they apparently rendered large numbers of people anomalous or troublesome, not least Pākehā living amongst Tangata Whenua, 'natives' who came to town, 'native' wives, their Pākehā husbands, 'Pākehā-Māori' and, perhaps most graphically, 'half-castes'. But these efforts to institute a colonial racial order were not crude, hopeful or intrinsically problematic. These racial categories were constituted and operated in particular ways, ones that were both informed by, and enabled, a strategy of racial amalgamation. To be compatible with racial amalgamation, racial categories necessarily had to be provisional: amalgamationist racial categories had to enact racial difference, but they also needed to provide for individuals, or at least their children, to move from one racial category to another. If it seems odd to cast racial categories as provisional and adjustable, racial amalgamation furnished categories that were, on closer inspection, even more surprising. Far from conceiving of a European racial category that was restricted, exclusive or sacred, in practice the category of 'European' was to prove both expansive and assertively inclusive. (The native category, on the other hand, was to prove far more often the more narrow and exclusive colonial construction.) These provisional and inclusive (in the case of European) qualities, which conformed to the project of amalgamation, charged and empowered government to make bold inclusive claims over multifarious interracial intimacies and crossings.

THE GREAT AMALGAMATOR

More than any other official, Governor Grey (1845–1853) was responsible for enshrining 'racial amalgamation' in New Zealand as a policy and as a policy objective. Grey is worth considering in detail, for he gave 'racial amalgamation' much of its shape, and some of this was to be lasting. Certainly, racial amalgamation contributed to the raising of Grey's stock in the Colonial Office and in Britain itself. He was considered by many, though certainly not by all, to be one of the great British governors of the nineteenth century, an outstanding scholar, collector and correspondent. By historians he has been judged more variously, as an '*Uebermann*', yet also as a 'fake humanitarian' and 'fake explorer'.[72] Regardless, his arrival in

---

[72] James Collier, *Sir George Grey: Governor, High Commissioner, and Premier* (Christchurch, 1909); J.B. Peires, *The Dead Will Arise: Nongqawuse and the Great Xhosa Cattle-Killing movement of 1856–7* (Johannesburg, 1989), p. 51.

New Zealand in late 1845 represented a more active phase of colonial government. He arrived when the Northern War was underway, and there were extensive problems with the New Zealand Company. The post of New Zealand governor was, the Colonial Secretary wrote apologetically, 'a position so full of embarrassment'.[73] But Grey brought military reinforcements, the war was soon to be over and the spectre of the New Zealand Company was about to fade; he also had a lieutenant-governor (Edward John Eyre, known as a humanitarian but later to be notorious after his role in the Morant Bay Rebellion in Jamaica in 1865).[74] It was an opportune time to take the reins. He was advised that if he succeeded in New Zealand the credit would be all his, 'whilst . . . should you unfortunately fail, the blame which can fall on you will be comparatively small'.[75]

Grey had initially made his name through a report on 'civilizing' aborigines which he had submitted to the Colonial Office. He had then become governor of South Australia before his New Zealand appointment. His 1840 report had been greeted with much enthusiasm, and had been included in Hobson's 1840 instructions; it was published in *Parliamentary Papers* and afterward in a number of periodicals in Britain and Australasia.[76] It was widely read and admired: 'Lord John Russell', one newspaper declared, 'saw that [Grey] was a man destined to reclaim an aboriginal race and amalgamate them with civilization'.[77] The report had contained little that was original. Its strength was that it tied together many diverse approaches to which the Colonial Office was already sympathetic, with a few detailed touches that were Grey's own. It particularly emphasized ('British') law as the most effective civilizing influence, a view to which the Colonial Office was very sympathetic. Law facilitated advances in civilization with less chance of regression. Thus, 'British laws' should 'supersede' those of aborigines.[78] Once in New Zealand, Grey announced that his great purpose was 'to give the laws of Great Britain a

[73] CO 380/122, fo. 175: Stanley to Grey, July 1845.
[74] Hall, *Civilizing Subjects*.
[75] APL, Grey Letters (GL), G15(7), Gipps to Grey, 21 December 1845.
[76] One writer read it with 'heartfelt joy'; 'The Aborigines of Australia', *Fisher's Colonial Magazine*, 1, second series, (1843), p. 139; CO 380/122, fo. 74: Russell to Hobson, 9 December 1840; Martin, *New Zealand*, pp. 314–16. Stanley also approved of the suggestions by the Auckland settler William Brown, who wanted the natives to be used for building roads, and to be rewarded for amalgamationist behaviour; PP 1846, xxx (337), p. 85: Stanley to Grey, 28 November 1845.
[77] *New Zealand Journal*, 25 May 1845, p. 172; ibid., 5 February 1842, p. 29. Merivale, *Lectures on Colonization and Colonies*, 2, p. 165.
[78] PP 1841, xvii (311), pp. 43–7: 'Report on the Best Means of Promoting the Civilization of the Aboriginal Inhabitants of Australia', enclosed in Grey to Russell, 4 June 1840.

practical adaptation to the circumstances of the country', to both New Zealand and its 'natives'.[79]

Symbolically, Grey's amalgamation began on the battlefield, when he arrived in the middle of the Northern War. He accompanied the military commander, entering the field with indigenous allies actively in the ranks. *Rangatira* remained in charge of their warriors, and had input into the formulation of battlefield tactics. By such means he hoped that 'the several reverses which have hitherto been experienced may without difficulty be retrieved.'[80] Native troops were to be regularly rationed, and the chiefs treated appropriately. By the time of the key engagement at Ruapekapeka, Grey had a racially amalgamated army. Grey preferred to avoid war (he said), but if it had to be fought (as with the Northern War, he believed), it should be won. He hoped to 'attach' the indigenous population to the European, as he observed, 'an apparent tranquility, based upon anything else than the attachment of the Maori population, must be merely illusory'.[81] Racial amalgamation was to be his way of promoting and regulating such 'attachments'.

Grey quickly made dramatic changes. He was the first governor to begin using the word 'Maori' to describe the category of persons hitherto called 'natives', 'aborigines' or 'New Zealanders'. He abolished the office of Protector of Aborigines and replaced it with the position of Native Secretary. This put paid to the 'Native Exemption Ordinance', which allowed for the arrest and detainment of natives only in severe cases, such as rape and murder. The Colonial Secretary, Lord Stanley, was supportive: he was worried that the 'zeal' for aboriginal welfare 'has rather outrun discretion'.[82] Grey embarked on what appeared to be an ambitious programme of legal and social reform, the kind of 'new institutions' envisioned by his report.[83] He began to use the word 'amalgamation' or the phrase 'racial amalgamation', and it occupied a key position in his descriptions of the 'progress' or 'improvement' of New Zealand aborigines. Grey said he wished to stop treating Māori 'as a distinct race', to hold them rather as fellow subjects with a joint share in the government, which he regarded as working in the interests of both races.[84] But his promising beginnings aside, there was never any sustained attempt by him to allow indigenous political autonomy. As Alan Ward has shown, racial amalgamation under Grey was to be more interventionist, an expansive

---

[79] CO 211/2, fo. 143: Grey's opening address, Legislative Council, 5 October 1846.
[80] CO 209/42, fos. 72–5: Grey to Stanley, 19 January 1846.
[81] CO 209/51, fo. 175: Grey to Earl Grey, 4 February 1847.
[82] PP 1846, xxx (337), p. 85: Stanley to Grey, 13 August 1845.
[83] PP 1841, xvii (311), p. 44: 'Report on the Best Means'.
[84] CO 209/46, fos. 3–9: Grey to Gladstone, 6 November 1846.

kind of *kāwanatanga*, where the transformation of the 'native race' and indigenous polities was more vigorously pursued.[85]

A good idea of what racial amalgamation meant to Grey can be seen in one of his 'classic' statements on racial amalgamation, a dispatch to the Colonial Office in February 1847. Here he first told the Office that he was replacing the 'Protector of Aborigines' with a 'Native Secretary', and that he was beginning the process of disarming the native population. He also announced the opening of savings banks to encourage 'natives' to enter the cash nexus. His major initiative was in the area of justice, where he designed a policy which would 'adapt our laws to the circumstances of this country'. This was the system of 'resident magistrates', licensed officials—a kind of 'legal missionary'—who would go into native communities and attempt, with virtually no coercive power and with some freedom to bend and shape laws, to win 'natives' over to 'the Law'.[86] These were to allow the government greater purchase in regions that were largely beyond their reach, and to remake indigenous societies. Many of these echoed policies directed at the working class in Britain (especially savings banks). This was the political and social amalgamation of the native population.

But Grey also announced policies directed at the 'race' itself, not only as a society and a set of various communities, but as a collection of bodies—a racial 'body'. Notably, there were the four colonial hospitals (at Auckland, Wanganui, Wellington and Taranaki), for both 'Europeans and Natives'. These 'mixed Hospitals', as Grey called them, were calculated 'to gain the regard and esteem of the Natives', to 'produce very beneficial effects on the Native race.'[87] This was a particularly significant example of what was also true of savings banks and resident magistrates, the construction of new kinds of social space in which 'natives' could interact in a controlled yet ordinary way with Europeans. All patients were to share the facilities, and there was to be no racial segregation. In the hospitals—'engines of colonisation' one doctor called them—all would be equal before medicine, at least in principle, just as they were to be before the law.[88] (In actuality

---

[85] Ward, *A Show of Justice*, pp. 125–46.
[86] CO 209/51, fos. 202–8: Grey to Earl Grey, 4 February 1847; cf. ibid., fos. 346–7: Grey to Earl Grey, 29 March 184. The phrase is Belich's: 'The Governors and the Maori'.
[87] CO 209/51, fos. 201–2: Grey to Earl Grey, 4 February 1847; cf. CO 211/1, fo. 357: Legislative Council minutes, 25 May 1844.
[88] DUL, Third Earl Grey Papers, GRE/B86/2/7: J. FitzGerald to Earl Grey, 2 March 1855; also, Damon Salesa, ' "The Power of the Physician": Doctors and the Dying Maori in Early Colonial New Zealand', *Health and History*, 4 (2001), pp. 13–40; Nicholson, 'Medicine and Racial Politics', pp. 66–104.

this was not always quite true, as Europeans with means often preferred local doctors to colonial hospitals.[89])

The singling out of half-castes was, again, perhaps the most striking of the attempts to engage explicitly with questions of race. Grey announced that he was to pursue a course of action which was, in a sense, foreshadowed by the Native Trust Ordinance. He was to regularize and regulate native and European sexual relations. 'I beg further to state', Grey wrote,

> that I have also enacted an Ordinance by which Europeans are prevented from abandoning, in a state of utter destitution and misery, their half-caste children, as they were previously in the habit of doing—A measure which will produce important future benefits to this country.[90]

This was an assertion of government interest and jurisdiction over half-castes. Though by the 1850s there were relatively few half-castes, the shaping of a colonial, racial taxonomy had already made them a consistent and significant concern. The attention which Grey gave the matter was both a part and a proof of this. The question of half-castes lay at an intersection of domestic, economic, sexual and legal concerns, and the Ordinance which Grey described had to address this. Here, in a graphic proof, Grey made it clear that any attempt to police racial boundaries in a colonial New Zealand would necessarily involve disciplining both European and native races, and controlling 'half-castes'.

Grey was preoccupied with half-castes because racial amalgamation had made them disproportionately significant. In the debate over the ordinance to punish those who abandoned their children, Grey declared:

> No greater evil could scarcely be imagined, than a race of half-caste children coming within our circle . . . who, being left without support, would have recourse to every species of impropriety, which would entail the greatest possible evil upon the future circumstances of the country.

Though the language was dramatic, it was addressed to a like-minded audience. No one on the Legislative Council disagreed, and one member, Alfred Domett (a pivotal figure who would later write an epic poem about an interracial love affair), went even further.[91] He suggested that half-castes were too important to be safely entrusted to their native mothers. He argued that half-castes be taken from native mothers and given to the care of 'European women, who would see that they were brought up to

---

[89] See Derek Dow, *Maori Health and Government Policy 1840–1940* (Wellington, 1999), pp. 15–56.
[90] CO 209/51, fo. 208: Grey to Earl Grey, 4 February 1847.
[91] Alfred Domett, *Ranolf and Amohia: a South-Sea Day-Dream* (London, 1872).

our habits and usages.'[92] These were loomings of what were to be many future colonial claims concerning half-castes, and were integral to the larger strategy of racial amalgamation. Within the year Grey had further buttressed colonial claims on mixed families and half-castes through another ordinance that recognized marriages between natives and Europeans (and not, it is worth noting, between natives and natives).[93]

Grey's February 1847 dispatch outlining his plans for racial amalgamation and its progress was received in the Colonial Office as a tour de force. Undersecretary Stephen called it 'very remarkable', noting that it 'w[oul]d seem to demand some laudatory notice'.[94] Parliamentary undersecretary Hawes thought it 'most important & gratifying', deserving of the 'most cordial approbation!'[95] Earl Grey went even further, insisting it be published before Parliament: 'I wish to have a copy of it made for the Queen.'[96] Little wonder that one settler thought 'the Whole of Sir George's administration has been only for Stage effect. Nothing has been done really towards civilizing or amalgamating [the natives].'[97]

Grey's exaggerations emphasized that he was capable of regulating and controlling racial intercourse. In this way he could demonstrate that his legitimate and orderly 'amalgamation' was indeed distinct from irregular and illegitimate 'pandemonium'. This concern with half-castes, even shorn of his self-promotion, was real and persistent. 'And above all', he had told his first Legislative Council, 'I trust that you may be able to devise some means by which you will prevent European fathers from abandoning and leaving in a state of destitution and misery, families of children whom they may have had by native mothers.'[98] The needs of a bi-racial colonial order were conjoined with the interests of the influential missionary organizations, who were both troubled by illicit intercourse and set in favour of orderly, moral and controlled intercourse and intermarriage. Amalgamation could potentially reconcile these concerns. The Colonial Office knew these matters were difficult, common as they were in all the colonies. They were difficult enough even in Britain. Little wonder that Grey's success would have appeared impressive; an 1844 British

---

[92] *New Zealand Spectator*, 13 October 1846: Legislative Council, 13 October 1846.
[93] 'An Ordinance for Regulating Marriages in the Colony of New Zealand', 28 September 1847. The ordinance could be applied to two natives at the governor's discretion.
[94] CO 209/51, fo. 211: Stephen to Hawes, minute, 17 June 1847.
[95] Ibid., fo. 211: Hawes to Grey, minute, 17 June 1847.
[96] Ibid., fo. 211: Earl Grey, minute, 17 June 1847. This was again suggested for one of Grey's later despatches. Ibid., fo. 279: Stephen to Hawes, minute, 28 September 1847.
[97] Henry Sewell, *The Journal of Henry Sewell*, (ed.) W. David McIntyre, 2 vols., (Christchurch, 1980), 1, p. 340: 7 July 1853.
[98] CO 211/2, fo. 143: Grey's opening address, Legislative Council, 5 October 1846.

commission on domestic marriages knew well that one could not legislate against 'mutual attachment'.[99]

The regulation of 'mixed' marriages was significant in a number of ways. It ensured that government would tabulate intermarriages. It placated those interests who saw in unmarried cohabitation a great wrong. But its greatest effects stemmed from aligning these marriages with inequitable colonial gender relations. By entering into a 'legitimate' marriage, a 'native' woman, just like a 'European' one, gave up her property rights to her husband.[100] Marriage inserted 'native' women into a new complex of relations explicitly mediated by the colonial state. Many indigenous women would bring property to a marriage, and an important number would bring a large amount. In practice this property was usually rights to land, and before the later 1860s these rights were mostly held in customary title. But it was not uncommon for the relations of an indigenous woman to attempt to get individualized title for her or her children. Under colonial law, in a way quite foreign to the relations of *hapū*, women gave up these property rights to their husbands. It was a legal domestication, and the nice distinction between a common law and 'legitimate' marriage carried tremendous repercussions.

Highlighting Grey's self-publicity should not paint him as a lone figure. Racial amalgamation was a common concern, structured by colonial categories, and widely endorsed in settler publics, notably by clergy. Two of New Zealand's bishops, Roman Catholic Pompallier and the Anglican Selwyn, are good examples. These two also sought to mediate interracial relations, and these they commonly encountered as they were both great travellers. Pompallier came across different kinds of cohabitation (what he described in one instance as 'a sort of marriage'), and would commonly baptize half-caste children and give 'the nuptial blessing' to interracial couples.[101] But Pompallier was overshadowed by Selwyn, who was something of a southern Prospero, making visitations in his ship, 'regularizing' all the irregular relationships he could, baptizing children and giving them Christian names. Neither gave their sanction freely, but sought to ensure a basic pattern of domestic life and future behaviour. Selwyn, for example, refused to marry those in polygamous relationships

[99] PP 1847–1848, xxvii, p. xii: 'First Report of the Commissioners Appointed to Inquire into the State and Operation of the Law of Marriage'.
[100] Cf. Bettina Bradbury, 'From Civil Death to Separate Property: Changes in the Legal Rights of Married Women in Nineteenth-Century New Zealand', *NZJH*, 29 (1995), pp. 40–66.
[101] Jean Baptiste F. Pompallier, *Early History of the Catholic Church in Oceania*, (trans.) Arthur Herman (Auckland, 1888), pp. 53, 69–70, 77; also, for example, OLC 1/1362: Fr. Jean Petit Baptiste, evidence, [1857?].

or who did not seem settled or committed to each other. In his first journey to the southern parts of New Zealand, where interracial relationships were common, Selwyn was everywhere concerned to marry mixed couples and baptize their 'half-caste' children. At Stewart Island he gathered together all the Pākehā men and their 'native wives':

> Spoke to them in order of the sanctity of marriage and the sin of their mode of life; with reference also to the example upon their children. Most of them had been living many years with the same consort, and apparently were resolved to be faithful to them.[102]

That day Selwyn married twelve couples, and baptized twenty one children. The next day, at a neighbouring island, he married a further four such couples, baptizing eight children. This was a process he repeated; Selwyn was not as fussy as some of his antecedents, and he saw marriage as an essential part of a Christian lifestyle.[103]

The common concern of government and church with half-castes and mixed families is best seen in the development of schools.[104] By 1853 there were disproportionate numbers of 'half-castes' in many of the educational institutions. The school for young women run by Catholic sisters in Wellington, St Joseph's Providence, had many half-castes amongst its pupils as did other schools, such as the institution at Three Kings in Auckland and St Mary's at Freeman's Bay.[105] Much like the colonial hospitals, these schools seemed the epitome of Grey's amalgamation. As a report on the Anglican schools commented, 'A very interesting feature in these Schools is the education of Maori and European children *together.*' The school inspectors came out strongly on the side of 'the system of free association of the children of both races', as a way of overcoming such prejudices in both populations. The reports of the school inspectors were widely published and used to display one of the most obvious 'achievements' of government. In response to strong criticisms about the amount of money being spent on 'native' education, one of New Zealand's main newspapers, *The New Zealander*, reprinted large portions of the reports, thinking they would 'be read with interest by all the friends of Education,

---

[102] Howard, *Rakiura*, pp. 377, 376: Selwyn, journal, 5, 6, 7 February 1844; ATL, MS-Papers-0428–04A, Wohlers, Ruapuke reports, fos. 5–6: December 1844.

[103] Cf. ATL, qMS-1390–1392, John Morgan, Letters and Journals, 1, fo. 262: Morgan, journal, 22 December 1846.

[104] J.M. Barrington and T.H. Beaglehole, 'A Part of Pakeha Society': Europeanising the Maori Child', in J.A. Mangan, (ed.), *Making Imperial Mentalities: Socialisation and British Imperialism*, (Manchester, 1990), pp. 167, 170–1.

[105] OLC 1/41A: Pompallier to Grey and Eyre, 19 March 1853; Sewell, *Journal*, 1, p. 232: 8 April 1853; Buller, *Forty Years in New Zealand*, pp. 311, 294.

especially of the Education of the Native and Half-caste [*sic*] children of New Zealand'.[106]

But one school, more than any other, epitomized both Grey's racial amalgamation and increasing government intervention in the lives of half-castes. This was the Half Caste School at Otawhao in the Waikato. Otawhao was at the junction of two major rivers, at the centre of a region which was consolidating through the 1840s and early 1850s as a heartland of indigenous independence and in which the Kīngitanga would be rooted. It is a sign of how widespread 'race mixing' was that it was at this spot that the CMS missionary John Morgan established the school, and philosophized about the place of half-castes in New Zealand society and its future.[107] Limited in numbers mostly by its capacity, the school opened in late 1849, and by 1850 it had an average roll of around forty students. The rolls increased until disaffection with the government and the Church led towards a falling off of numbers in the mid-1850s. The school was not huge, but nonetheless was at the time one of the largest 'native' schools in New Zealand, and probably the largest boarding institution. Certainly it attracted a lion's share of government funds.

Morgan was the energy and the spark behind the school, using the £40 CMS school allowance to erect a small building which he quickly turned specifically to half-caste purposes. When the CMS ordered that schools were too expensive and had to be stopped, Morgan turned to Bishop Selwyn and Governor Grey for financial aid, and tried to continue his school without cost to the CMS.[108] Morgan thought a mission without a school was like a bird without wings: 'it would fly but it cannot'.[109] Writing to Grey was the critical moment for Morgan. 'His Excellency took a great interest in my proposed Half Caste School', Morgan crowed, and in the following years Grey was to often use his influence and means in support of Morgan and his Half Caste School.[110] Soon enough he had received a special government grant for building extensions, promises of a portion of the annual government grant for education, and a visit from Grey himself. Grey was grateful for Morgan's exertions, and made sure

---

[106] Reprinted in *The New Zealander*, 19 February 1853.

[107] K.R. Howe, 'Missionaries, Maories, and "Civilization" in the Upper-Waikato, 1833–1863', MA thesis, University of Auckland, 1970, esp. pp. 86–104.

[108] Morgan, Letters and Journals, 2, fo. 304: Morgan, Annual Report, 1848; Ibid., 2, fos. 302–3: Morgan to CMS secretaries, 23 December 1847.

[109] Morgan, Letters and Journals, 2, fo. 377: Morgan to CMS secretary, 2 January 1849.

[110] Morgan, Letters and Journals, 2, fo. 368: Morgan, journal, 22 February 1849: ibid., 2, fos. 385–6: Morgan to CMS secretary, 5 July 1849; ibid., 2, fo. 488: Morgan to CMS secretary, 11 November 1850.

they were widely known back in Britain.[111] Morgan, ambitious and
pushy, continued extending his school, adding extra buildings and kitchens,
getting himself into debt, and then looking for help.[112] Fees of £3 were
levied on the students (no small sum, particularly for families with
several children), but the school was often short of funds.[113] By 1852
the school was in debt to the tune of £841, a debt which Grey settled, and
which was more than 10 percent of the government's entire educational
budget.[114]

Morgan was unusual but not unique in his concern for half-castes.
He often discussed their significance with the CMS committee, and
the reasons he used to explain his interest are revealing. 'The Half caste
Children will soon form an important race', Morgan wrote on one occasion, 'and unless watched over may prove very injurious to the colony.'[115]
Quite openly, then, the school was more than simply an educational
institute, somewhere to learn to read and write, and to be Christian; the
school was to 'watch over' half-castes. Though Morgan considered the half-
castes to be dangerous, he had both great hopes and great fears for them.
Morgan believed half-castes 'will no doubt in future years exercise great
influence amongst their respective tribes, either for good or for evil.'[116] The
school was to be 'a blessing to the much neglected Half Caste race'.[117]
They were simply 'too important to be neglected by the [mission] Society.'
They were children of influential people, often the children of daughters
of chiefs. 'If attended to they will form a bond of union between the
Europeans and the Native race, and will be exactly the persons the Society
require to act as Schoolmasters and we may hope that some of them will be
Ministers of the Gospel.'[118]

But the half-castes were not a group immediately apparent in everyday
Waikato life. Whether the children of old Pākehā settlers, or newer ones,
they were ordinarily no different to other children. 'The [half-caste]
children with few exceptions had been brought up in the midst of the

[111] Ibid., 3, fo. 574: Morgan to CMS secretary, 6 January 1853, enclosing Grey to Morgan,
15 November 1852.
[112] Ibid., 3, fos. 558–9: Morgan to Ligar and Sinclair, 20 October 1852.
[113] Ibid., 2, fo. 386: Morgan to CMS secretary, 5 July 1849.
[114] APL, Grey New Zealand Letters (GNZL), M44(18): Morgan to Grey, 27 September
1852; ibid., M44(19): Morgan to Grey, 3 January 1853.
[115] Morgan, Letters and Journals, 2, fos. 302–3: Morgan to CMS secretaries, 23
December 1847.
[116] Morgan, Letters and Journals, 2, fos. 369–70: Morgan, journal, 23 February 1849.
[117] GNZL, M44(17): Morgan to Grey, 1 June 1852.
[118] Ibid., 2, fos. 385–6: Morgan to CMS secretary, 5 July 1849, Morgan papers.
Though some feared education might make them more dangerous; Sewell, *Journal*, 2,
p. 265: 26 August 1856.

maori [*sic*] population', Morgan observed; 'they spoke their language and knew their customs ... their education, religious, moral, and domestic training had in almost every instance been totally neglected, and these Anglo Maori children had descended to the Maori level'.[119] Some were already too old, Morgan thought, to be 'reclaimed'; others, in their early teens, could still potentially be rescued. In a powerful way, if Morgan was not there to constitute the 'Half Caste race' which he saw, they would not have existed to be seen. It was Morgan's 'watching over' the half-castes which constituted them as a group. His words gave them a term to be recognized under; his actions, his school and his 'watching' set them apart.

'The half caste children', Morgan wrote, 'are a fine intelligent and promising race.'[120] By 1853 he was convinced that 'the half caste children [are] so much in advance of the maori's' that it was necessary to keep the two 'races' apart so that appropriate attention could be given to the half-castes.[121] 'It was however evident, for past experience had proved it', Morgan explained, 'that the Anglo Maori children could not occupy a medium state between the Europeans and the Maoris; they must either sink to the Maori level, or rise to that of Europeans.'[122] For Morgan, then, the separation out of half-castes was preliminary to their exclusion from native life, and their inclusion into that of 'Europeans'. If half-castes were figured as a field where colonial government might extend and assert a variety of claims, the kind of institution that epitomized these colonial efforts to claim, remake and realign half-castes was Morgan's school and others like it.

This process was manifest in the education given to half-castes at Otawhao. Unlike the native schools, all the teaching was in English, a language many, perhaps most, knew little of.[123] Morgan 'banished' *te Reo* from his school, and even playground conversation was restricted to English.[124] This made progress often very slow and hard. Morgan was convinced that unless their learning of English was rigorous it would be lost as half-castes were in later life surrounded only by natives.[125] The girls were taught knitting and sewing; 'Shoemaking', he thought, 'would be a good trade for the halfcaste boys.'[126] For the boys it was to be trade and

[119] Ibid., 3, fo. 556: Morgan to Ligar and Sinclair, school inspectors, 20 October 1852.
[120] Ibid.
[121] GNZL, M44(19): Morgan to Grey, 3 January 1853.
[122] Morgan, Letters and Journals, 3, fo. 557: Morgan to Ligar and Sinclair, school inspectors, 20 October 1852.
[123] Ibid., 2, fo. 469: Morgan, Annual Report, 1850.
[124] Ibid., 3, fo. 557: Morgan to Ligar and Sinclair, school inspectors, 20 October 1852.
[125] Ibid., 3, fo. 562.
[126] Ibid., 2, fo. 469: Morgan, Annual Report, 1850; GNZL, M44(8): Morgan to Grey, 6 February 1851.

industry, for the girls domesticity. The savage would, in a single mixed generation, be transformed to wage labourer or homemaker.

Morgan's domestic ideal for his female half-caste students was marriage to a European settler. A small number of girls in the school seemed to find matches which pleased Morgan enough to write about. One married 'the Son of a respectable English farmer' and another 'a steady young man, a squatter'. Morgan was much impressed with the results of their domestic educations (largely overseen by Mrs Morgan), and commented how the former girl kept her house 'neat, clean and comfortable.'[127] The first of the half-caste students that married became Mrs Powdrell, and she was given a piece of land on the Piako river by her *hapū*. Here Morgan used his influence with Grey to get this land confirmed in her ownership while she was in Auckland with 'her Maori relatives'.[128] Grey expedited this process, finding there was no objection to such a confirmation, and within days the land had been accordingly recognized.[129] This speed was remarkable, as the process often took years, and was another example of Grey lending his support to the process of racial amalgamation; and of state and school working cooperatively to this end. In a very real, if targeted, way, government was capable of powerful interventions that could reshape lives and relations.

Another missionary deeply interested in half-castes was J.F.H. Wohlers, a German missionary who moved to the Fouveaux Strait (the deepest south of New Zealand) in 1844.[130] Much like Morgan, Wohlers saw 'half-castes' as a particularly important population, and placed special emphasis on their education and domestic reform. However, unlike Morgan, Wohlers was, in a sense, on the fringes of both colonial and indigenous New Zealand, based in this thinly populated region. Where Morgan was in a heartland of indigenous population, independence and *rangatiratanga*, Wohlers had a scattered maritime population of just over 1,000 (of which over 10 percent were half-caste children).[131] He did not receive the government interest and support of Morgan.

---

[127] Ibid., 3, fo. 563: Morgan to Ligar and Sinclair, 20 October 1852; ibid., 3, fo. 568: Morgan, Annual Report, 1852.

[128] NA, Internal Affairs, (IA) 1 1853/2828: Morgan to Grey, 20 December 1853.

[129] IA 1 1853/2828: Grey to Sinclair, minute, 21 December 1853; ibid., Sinclair to Grey, minute.

[130] ATL, MS-Papers-0428–04C, J.F.H. Wohlers, Ruapuke Reports: 20 July 1849, fo. 13.

[131] Sheila Natusch, *Brother Wohlers: a Biography of J.F.H. Wohlers of Ruapuke* (Christchurch, 1969); J.F.H. Wohlers, *Memories of the Life of J.F.H. Wohlers, Missionary at Ruapuke, New Zealand: an Autobiography*, (trans.) John Houghton, (Dunedin, 1895). MS-Papers-0428–04A, Wohlers, Ruapuke Reports: 31 December 1845, fo. 2.

Wohlers baptized many of the 'native wives' and children of local Pākehā men and remained particularly interested in these children and their education.[132] He was passionate about the need for 'an educational institution for the local halfcaste [sic] children', especially one where they might learn English.[133] Like Morgan, a large part of this education was domestic; after he married, he and his wife often took half-caste girls into their home, in the hope that they might become able wives for Pākehā men.[134] Inside his own house, he and his wife set a domestic example; a half-caste girl who came to live with them became a model of such domestic reform, being well supplied with material for clothes by her father, 'healthy too, and somewhat trained to cleanliness'.[135] This brought considerable comfort to Wohlers, who reflected warmly upon any improvement in the 'morality' or 'cleanliness' of native and half-caste alike. This was a common missionary concern, but typically for Wohlers it was half-caste women who drew most attention, though he also looked to the condition of the native wives of Pākehā (and lamented the drunken state of the Pākehā fathers).[136] Wohlers supported one Pākehā who was trying to prevent his wife from going to the native church service in order to 'civilize' her, endorsed his efforts to make his wife wear 'clothes' and shoes, and compel her to go only to the English service, even though she was lonely around white women. He lamented that 'most of the Europeans who are married to New Zealand women don't lift a finger to civilize their wives.' He saw it as a great mark of progress when local women absorbed these values, and insisted on being 'officially married . . . so that the men cannot leave them again.'[137]

Wohlers saw great potential in half-castes. He thought the children were all 'beautiful to look at', and imagined that 'in ten years time Foveaux Strait will be famous because of its beautiful girls. . . . If these women were to be painted, their portraits could compete well with the pictures of the beauties of Europe.'[138] When this beauty was combined with civilized domesticity, (a then single) Wohlers seemed almost forlorn with longing:

> Mrs Sterling is a half cast, [sic] but she had had the luck to be educated by her father, an Englishman. She is the crown of the women at Foveaux Strait and

[132] Ibid., 7 June 1845, fo. 3, 30 June to 17 July 1846, fo. 16.

[133] Ibid., 31 December 1845, fo. 4, 7 June 1845, fo. 3.

[134] MS-Papers-0428–04C, Wohlers, Ruapuke Reports: January to May 1853, fo. 4, October to December, 1852, fo. 5, July to September, fos. 2–3, 12 January 1852.

[135] Ibid., 31 March 1852, fo. 5.

[136] MS-Papers-0428–04A, Wohlers, Ruapuke Reports: 31 December 1845, fo. 2.

[137] Ibid., [Report of Journey], 9–23 October 1846, fos. 21–3; ibid., 1 May 1845, fo. 16; ibid., Parish register for 1845, marriage register; ibid., 30 June to 17 July 1846, fo. 14.

[138] Ibid., December 1844, fo. 1; ibid., 30 June to 17 July 1846, fo. 16.

one cannot at all notice that she is a half cast. She is so pretty, so friendly, so quick and so clever that one might envy Sterling for her.[139]

The increase of half-castes in the region was especially striking when compared to the depopulation of 'natives'.[140] Wohlers supposed, at least locally, that 'the largest part of the natives will, sad as it is, be mostly recorded in the register of deaths, while the Europeans with their mixed offspring are going to continue the line of the thin population of this region.' From the Europeans 'a new race is emerging which probably will devour and fuse with the remainder of the pure natives.'[141] (This was a point made by other missionaries, such as Walter Lawry.[142]) Over the years Wohlers' original fatalism, which saw this as preordained, gave way to a search for causes. He no longer saw this as 'the decision of God . . . to let the natives die out and create a new race of half-cast[e] children.' Rather, it became an indicator of the superiority of European lifestyle, and the effect that 'civilization' had on improving domestic conditions. For Wohlers this meant that 'if something is to be done . . . it would have to be education of the female sex towards a more civilized way of life.'[143] This conformed with the familiar reasonings of racial amalgamation: the best way to save the pure native race was to marry them off to civilized (white) husbands.

Not all missionaries were of the same mind as Morgan or Wohlers. Morgan's fellow CMS missionary, Richard Taylor, was also given money (£200) by Grey to start a school. He too quickly received 'several applications to admit half casts [*sic*]', but decided that as the building was too small and places were limited, natives would receive priority.[144] In other respects Morgan was also unusual. His CMS superiors and his brethren suspected that Morgan was too concerned with his school and 'civilization' and not enough concerned with the Gospel.[145] Morgan had aided in bringing much of the technology, from seeds, ploughs, horses and carts to mills and millers, to the Waikato. He hoped by these means—'civilization' as he called it—that natives 'might then be led on to form christian

[139] Ibid., [Report of Journey], 9–23 October 1846, fo. 26.
[140] Ibid., 19 February 1846, fo. 15; see also ibid., 26 September 1846, fo. 3.
[141] Ibid., 31 December 1845, fo. 9; ibid., 19 February 1846, fo. 15; ibid., 1 May 1845, fo. 17.
[142] Walter Lawry, *Friendly and Feejee Islands: a Missionary Visit to Various Stations in the South Seas in the Year 1847* (London, 1850), p. 137.
[143] MS-Papers-0428–04A, Wohlers, Ruapuke Reports: 26 September 1846, fo. 3.
[144] GNZL, T5A(2): Richard Taylor to Grey, 25 September 1848.
[145] Morgan, Letters and Journals, 2, fo. 504: Morgan to CMS secretary, 24 March 1851; ibid., 2, fo. 535: Chapman to Morgan, January 1852; ibid., 3, fos. 542–3: Morgan to Chapman, 4 March 1852.

villages, & build neat boarded cottages.'[146] Morgan also actively canvassed support for a resident magistrate, perhaps motivated by the drunkenness new Pākehā settlers were bringing to the prosperous region.[147] Morgan was visibly pro-government. When one local Pākehā said the Waikato had no need for a resident magistrate, and that if they got one they would be known as a '*kainga taurekareka*' (a community of slaves), Morgan responded that a magistrate would be 'a "takawaenga" [mediator] to stand between themselves & the Europeans when disputes arose.'[148] An agent of government and 'civilization', Morgan was appropriately a 'watcher' and 'reclaimer' of half-castes.

Morgan's practices and discourse show how the racial taxonomies were by no means solely the province of colonial government. Moreover, Morgan, Selwyn and Pompallier illustrate the rich ways in which attempts to reshape indigenous and half-caste subjectivities often originated outside colonial government, particularly in the work of the church and missionaries. They facilitated the refinement and implementation of these racial distinctions, however, just as they responded to them. But the efforts of the missions and missionaries were especially important as they addressed racial crossings and intimacies that were consistently beyond the competence or jurisdiction of colonial authority. Mission institutions were, for much of the 1840s and 1850s, the key conduits for colonial engagements with indigenous subjectivities, and one of the few locations where other colonial or even half-caste subjectivities might be nurtured or promoted. Experiences within a half-caste or racially amalgamated school and engagement with other colonial institutions helped realize the very differences a racial taxonomy asserted it was observing. In these contexts half-castes might no longer simply be local children like the others, and this had increasingly meaningful consequences.

Towards the end of his governorship, Grey summed up the progress of racial amalgamation as he saw it. The native population was being brought into the colonial polity, Grey told the Colonial Office (and through them, the British public), 'with a rapidity unexampled in history'. Only a few years 'would suffice for the entire fusion of the two races into one nation'.[149] So successful an impression had Grey conveyed to the Colonial Office (partly through the tactical use of Morgan's school), that he left New Zealand in 1853 to a chorus of praises. Earl Grey, shortly after he

[146] GNZL, M44(8): Morgan to Grey, 6 February 1851.
[147] Morgan, Letters and Journals, 3, fo. 568: Morgan, Annual Report, 1852; GNZL, M44(17): Morgan to Grey, 1 June 1852.
[148] Ibid., M44(16): Morgan to Grey, 14 January 1852.
[149] PP 1852, (1475), p. 21: Grey to Earl Grey, 30 August 1851.

had left office as Colonial Secretary, lamented only that he had not had more Greys to send throughout the Empire. If only Grey had been in charge of 'the Kafirs', wrote the Earl, there would be no 'war of extermination' there, and the Kafirs would be, as he believed the New Zealand natives were, 'becoming useful subjects'.[150] Ironically, Grey was soon at the Cape, and there his policies and his tactical descriptions of them were to meet with less success. There were critics enough in New Zealand, who were alarmed by his 'flashy dispatches', and the few 'real signs of advancement towards the fusion of the two races'.[151]

'ILLICIT INTERCOURSE' AND THE GROUNDING OF RACIAL TAXONOMIES

Education, medical care, and other matters of social policy and law aside, at certain times government had to approach a central question of racial amalgamation, namely intimate and domestic arrangements, more directly. The second governor, Robert Fitzroy, framed the government's approach: he lamented 'the baneful effects of illicit intercourse (so frequently subsisting between the native females and Europeans in or near the principal settlements)'.[152] But if 'illicit intercourse' was to be frowned upon, this was by no means true of 'moral' or 'legitimate' interracial relations. In much the same way as government approached the problems of land purchases and trade relations, it was impolitic and exceedingly difficult to simply wipe the slate clean. 'His Excellency did not come out here to found a colony', one settler advised the governor, 'on the contrary, he found one already formed'.[153] Government's response was circumspect: it aimed to control and regulate, legitimize selectively, to make sexual relations, like relations in trade and land, amenable and compliant to a slowly growing colonial power. Here there was irony: many of the communities which were already 'mixed', the 'New Ground' where Tangata Whenua and Pākehā lived together (mostly under *rangatiratanga*), were to attract criticism and become marginalized under 'racial amalgamation', even as government professed an apparently similar goal. This irony resided in the critical differences between a disciplined and orderly

---

[150] APL, GNZMSS 35(13): Earl Grey to Grey, 28 February 1853.
[151] Sewell, *Journal*, 1, pp. 390, 200: 5 November 1853, 11 March 1853.
[152] PP 1846, xxx (337), p. 11: Fitzroy to Stanley, 24 February 1845.
[153] CO 212/1, fo. 80: Earp in the Government Gazette, 23 March 1842. He is referring to both the informal colonization and the New Zealand Company's efforts.

'racial amalgamation' imagined by government, and the unplanned and unofficial 'pandemonium' that it arrived to find.

It was not just the case that colonialism in New Zealand never sought to *obstruct* interracial sexual relations, as a number of historians have observed. Indeed, government *actively* encouraged and supported interracial marriages, but with the crucial proviso that they were disciplined or 'legal'; that is, subject to colonial surveillance and authority. This aligned with the key difference between pandemonium and racial amalgamation. Hobson's opinion (as phrased by his secretary) was that 'the *legal* intermarriage of Europeans with the Aboriginal Subjects of Her Majesty is highly worthy of every just encouragement'.[154] This was typical of the official attitude. With not only moral and domestic but political and social repercussions, legitimate and disciplined 'amalgamation' was to be supported and facilitated; whereas illegitimate, 'illicit' intercourse was to be criticized and, where possible, either interdicted or reformed.

The racial 'pandemonium' government perceived was, in a primary sense, about intimacy. Carnal and intimate relations between 'Europeans' and 'natives', as in earlier days, continued. Government responded by criticizing native leaders for prostituting their girls to Europeans, and for not conforming to Christian or civilized standards.[155] But these relations were not one-sided, nor very often prostitution: they were, however, deemed by colonial government to be illicit. Settlers were intimately involved with Tangata Whenua, and the soldiers the governors had brought behaved not too differently from soldiers elsewhere. By the mid-1840s the Bay of Islands had seen no significant changes in behaviour; the soldiers picked up where others had left off. An official response ensued:

> Through the influence of Bishop Selwyn orders were decreed, that all military officers must dispense with their young miss's [*sic*] (aborigines, Mauries so-called) young girls from the age of 12 years to 20 years . . . Some with their 6 or 8 wives during their pleasure. . . . The spirit of the just and the honorable [*sic*] sighs in secret over the sordid pollution of so designing a mass of beings. . . . Happy would it be if the Bishops [*sic*] influence would extend throughout the Bay.[156]

The approach was regulatory, seeking to adjust a pre-existent traffic, rather than prohibit: a way of easing a weak government into domestic

---

[154] NA, OLC 1/1362: Willoughby Shortland to Frederick Whittaker, 4 May 1842. Emphasis added.

[155] *Te Karere o Nui Tireni*, 1 May 1843; RHL, Mss. N.Z.r.1, David Burn, Original Letters 1849–1863: Burn to Serle, 24 January 1849.

[156] John Williams, *The New Zealand Journal 1842–1844*, p. 65: journal, 1844.

arrangements. But this regulation attended to class, status and gentility, homing in on government officials, officers and those who claimed gentility in illicit intimate relationships. Amongst common soldiers, natives, and the class of Europeans already living amongst natives, such illicit relations might not be approved of, but they could be expected. Racial amalgamationist policies commonly made such differentiations within the 'European' population, casting certain whites as less moral, civilized and governable than others. (In practice, for instance, many of the whites in racially amalgamated schools were orphans, and many in mixed hospitals were poor.) Moral indignation not only usually stemmed from, but was better directed at, the 'better' classes. As a result there was a huge fuss when a Taranaki magistrate was accused of kidnapping a young indigenous woman.[157] There was also especial vitriol for a government official who worked at the customs office (which was open only from 10 a.m. to 2 p.m.): 'The intervening time is to[o] much taken up with lewd Maurie [sic] women, especially the Sub-Collector J. Guise Mitford, living licentiously with lewd Mauries, and a seducer of innocent young native girls'.[158]

Direct attempts to 'regulate' the races were not often powerful, because colonial government had a loose grasp; such attempts would only be significant in arenas where government had firmer control. The most important area was land. Land was, as argued above, also the starkest and most striking example of the advent of a racial taxonomy. It was a critical issue in the colonization of New Zealand, as a number of historians have shown.[159] As Karl Polanyi observed, the isolating of 'land' into a commodity and forming a market of it was 'perhaps the weirdest of all undertakings of our ancestors'.[160] In Europe this happened intermittently, over the course of centuries; in colonial New Zealand, the brunt of this work was done in about 25 years. The production of a land 'market' imposed a myriad of adjuncts—not least a similar process regarding labour—most of which were complex, and which are in some ways poorly mapped in the historiography (which is particularly driven by historical land claims and grievances).[161] But in New Zealand the land market was constructed in concert with racial classifications, regulated and policed by

---

[157] CO 211/1, fos. 52–7, 65–123: Executive Council, minutes, 25 August 1843.
[158] John Williams, *The New Zealand Journal 1842–1844*, p. 65: journal, 1844.
[159] Adams, *Fatal Necessity*, pp. 175–210; Hickford, 'Making "Territorial Rights of the Natives"'; Sorrenson, 'The Politics of Land'; Sinclair, *The Origins of the Maori Wars*; Ward, *An Unsettled History*.
[160] Polanyi, *The Great Transformation*, p. 178.
[161] See particularly the reports of the Waitangi Tribunal, and I.H. Kawharu, *Maori Land Tenure: Studies of a Changing Institution* (Oxford, 1977).

government monopoly, and positioned half-castes as a field adjacent to European race and colonial rule, and through which the effective jurisdiction of colonial rule might be extended.

Still, it was significant that it remained far easier for half-castes to own land in accordance with indigenous customary law than to have such a property holding recognized by the Crown. Before the Native Land Acts of 1862 and 1865, 'preemption' guaranteed government monopoly on the transfer of indigenous customary title to Crown grant. Private or indigenous attempts to do this were 'declared by law to be absolutely null and void'.[162] This racialized regulation made it more difficult for half-castes (or Tangata Whenua) to access capital or to develop their land, and left tenure vulnerable to both colonial revisions and *hapū* politics. A Crown grant of land had advantages, but most of these stemmed from the advantages it conferred on *kāwanatanga*. This made it possible to gain endorsement from both forms of authority, but ensured that the land was placed under the surveillance and nominal sovereignty of *kāwanatanga*. The impetus behind seeking a Crown grant, though this action had to be supported by the *whānau* (families) of half-castes for it to be successful, often came from their European fathers. They, in particular, were 'anxious to have their [half-caste children's] lands and property given them in right of their mothers, duly registered, and otherwise legally secured to them'.[163]

All the governors seemed to consider the recognition of half-caste titles to land desirable, and made at least occasional efforts to promote this. This was not just their shared patriarchal bent (though this was not unimportant), nor simply the way that it crystallized colonial relationships with, and claims on, mixed families and children. Such half-caste lands typically entered the land market, could be traded and potentially taxed, stabilized within received notions of colonial settlement. By receiving Crown grants half-castes were also marking a relationship with colonial authority that was only available to those who were considered half-castes. Though the import of this may not have been immediately apparent, this was an early benefit selectively extended through racial crossings. However remote the residence of these half-castes, they were now in a relationship with the nascent colonial state that they or their parents had submitted to. This did not mean it was easy, given the starkly racial discriminations in land law, to set aside land for half-castes or mixed race families. Nonetheless, all the early governors made efforts in this direction. Hobson seemed intent on asking the Colonial Secretary to make provision for land grants for 'those

---

[162] CO 211/2, fo. 97: New Munster Executive Council minutes.
[163] PP 1851, xxxv (1420), p. 241: H. Tacy Kemp, 'Statistical Return'.

persons who may have formed connexions of that nature and for their children', but his death prevented this.[164] The government practice that was established in lieu of these formalities was that provided the land had been acquired through a person's 'wife' or her family, was a 'moderate portion' of land and was not actively contested, the holding would be left undisturbed. This was, though it was never framed as such, a tacit recognition of indigenous protocols. Without instruction or sanction from the Colonial Office, over this critical issue of land, Hobson could not go any further.

Colonial rhetoric continued to contrast its vision of orderly racial amalgamation with a supposed disorderly pandemonium over which natives presided. Yet it was apparent that colonial policy was considered by many onlookers as insufficiently articulate or aggressive regarding half-castes, and was effectively surrendering them to natives and native life. A preoccupation with the predicament of half-castes, native wives and, especially, native widows was a feature of colonial publics. One newspaper article captured these sentiments perfectly, fretting over the fate of a recently widowed native woman and her half-caste children (and, of course, their land).

> Have the [half-caste] children of such marriages the rights belonging to the Maories, or those of British subjects; or are they outcasts—without rights of any kind? . . . Is it to be the policy of this Government to encourage lawful marriages, and so promote the amalgamation of the races?—or, . . . Should the Government discourage such alliances . . . and thus aid and promote those irregular, immoral and destructive connexions already so prevalent.[165]

This commentator was sharply proclaiming a need for more decisive and engaged colonial policy regarding half-castes. It was revealing that this was framed in a way that allowed them only to be either 'Maories' or 'British subjects' (though to most officials, natives were British subjects). This call to action was driven by the shared assumption that these intimate unions would occur irrespective of what was done or said. At issue was whether such unions would be a mechanism to promote amalgamation or to surrender to (native) connections which were seen as not just immoral and irregular but actually destructive. The important steps that *kāwanatanga* had already undertaken to compete for, and to try to reposition or realign, half-castes and mixed families appeared not to satisfy this commentator.

There were recurrent efforts to utilize government initiatives in ways that addressed half-castes, which sought better to identify them and either

---

[164] OLC 1/1362: Shortland to Whitaker, 4 May 1842.
[165] *Southern Cross and the New Zealand Guardian*, 15 January 1850.

established or strengthened relations with colonial government. Some initiatives were better fitted for this than others, and one that was unusually relevant was the Old Land Claims Commission. The Commission was set up in 1856 primarily to investigate land purchases before annexation in 1840 and the purchases made during the short periods (in 1844) when Fitzroy had suspended pre-emption. In 1858 the original act was extended, and the commissioner was given new powers, one of which was the ability to grant land title for half-castes without it first having to pass through government ownership.[166] There were over twenty half-caste claims, and nearly fifty 'supplementary' half-caste claims.[167] This resolution was probably due to a board of official experts, convened in 1856, that had been preoccupied with the problem of half-caste lands, and were specifically interested in them as a way for Europeans to 'acquir[e] surplus lands'. But their main statement on half-castes demonstrated just how ubiquitous they thought the influence of land was on colonial life in general and race in particular. Granting colonial legitimacy to half-castes' land holdings, they wrote, was a way of placing

> an increasing and interesting class of individuals in a position of usefulness. The half-caste race, occupying as they do an intermediate station between the European and the native, have neither the advantages of the one nor the other, and whose future destiny may, by proper management, be directed in the well being of the Colony, or by neglect be turned to a contrary course. They are objects of great solicitude to their native relatives, as well as to their European fathers, who desire to secure them sufficient portions of land for their maintenance, and when such is the case there is every reason for the co-operation of the Government.[168]

The committee reiterated earlier government feeling, recommending no distinction be made between those half-castes born in wedlock and those born out of it (this was a point that was not to be resolved until 1860; see Chapter 5). The already familiar colonial theme that half-castes could be a force for either good or ill (which generally conformed with 'native' or 'European') again called for special attention and governmental cooperation. Unsurprisingly, given the textures of colonial and racial discourses, rights to land were to be the principal arena in which these difficulties were both evident and through it was supposed they might be solved.

---

[166] Land Claims Settlement Act, 1856; Land Claims Settlement Extension Act, 1858, section 13.

[167] OLC 1, files 1355–75, 1A-49A.

[168] PP 1860, xlvi (2719), p. 238: C.W. Ligar *et al.*, 'Report of a Board Appointed by His Excellency the Governor to Inquire into and Report upon the State of Native Affairs', 9 July 1856.

Colonial recognition of half-caste land holding was bound up with intimate government interventions in the family, gender and race. This was made plain when George McFarlane sought a Crown grant 'for certain lands given to his half-caste children by the relations of their mother.' McFarlane was told that a grant could be made, but it was conditional on confirmation that 'the natives admit having given this land for the use of the children' and that the land would be surveyed. But most importantly the grant attached explicit conditions regarding to whom, and how, this property would be transferred. Though the land had explicitly been given to the children, the specification was that the land would belong 'to the father for his life, in trust for the children, then to the mother in the same manner, and lastly to the children'.[169] Such conditions seemed matters of course to officials, as they re-enacted legal inequalities and disabilities standard in settler and metropolitan society. But when this intervention was coupled with that of surveying—which opened up indigenous space to the measures and archive of government—the consequences were palpable. Permission had been granted for colonial government to survey the land, but it had gone further and entered intimate domains, inserting itself in relationships *within* the family. This was a clear effort to mobilize colonial hierarchies and relationships in these intimate spaces, and to reconstitute domestic units—even ones (like McFarlane's) that were not recognized, having not been sanctioned by colonial marriage. This was not lost on the people in question. As McFarlane himself stated (and as was often the case) this new regime of ownership went sharply against the wishes of the children's relations to gift the land directly to the children. Such colonial initiatives to transmute relations of *whānau* into those of a patriarchal colonial family were to prove a cutting edge of colonialism.

These were not arcane disembodied concerns, but drew individuals and families into forums and conversations where powerful interests were at work. The Commission daily confronted complex and personal dimensions in such ways. One example was the settler William Anderson, who was much concerned that should he die his wife, Rongi or Rebecca, and his two children would be left destitute. An indigenous relative had given the children 100 acres to provide for the children, and their relatives and father were anxious that this land be confirmed by the government. Anderson petitioned government for recognition, and included the deed.[170] Yet although officials investigated and were quickly aware that Anderson was telling the truth, the troubled nature of land ownership at

---

[169] CO 211/2, fo. 117: New Munster Executive Council minutes, 26 April 1850.
[170] IA 1 1847/1584: William Anderson to Sinclair, enclosing 'The Humble Petition of William Anderson of the Island of Kawau, Miner', 28 August 1847.

the time (mid-1847), then still under review at the Colonial Office, meant that the government had to put the matter aside until further instruction was received.[171]

In another protracted case, the half-caste children of Thomas Maxwell and Ngeungeu sought to gain Crown title to the island of Motutapu, in the Hauraki gulf near Auckland. The sale of the land generated a dispute which took nearly 18 years for government to resolve. The island had apparently been purchased by Maxwell from Ngeungeu's father, Tara, though Maxwell died in 1842 before he had completed full payment for it. The *hapū* concerned, Ngāti Tai, consequently treated much of the land as unalienated, and looked to dispose of it. In 1844 two Pākehā, Williamson and Crummer, asked for government permission to purchase part of the island, which was given. At this point the claims became extremely complex, as within two years title had been given to the Maxwell children: John, James, Robert, George, Patrick and Andrew. (To add even further complications, another settler, Robert Graham, had occupied a part of the land.) This provoked complaints from Williamson and Crummer, which were referred by Grey to the Crown Law Office. After hearing from the Law Office, the Land Claims Commissioner again held up the children's title as valid and prior.[172] Grey decided that year on a compromise, and gave the Pākehā purchasers a grant of as many acres as they had paid pounds.

Successive governors looked kindly upon the plight of the half-caste Maxwell children. Fitzroy was in favour of making some sort of agreement in their favour. Grey, too, felt that government had prejudiced the interests of the children; that the decision to allow Williamson and Crummer to purchase the land in 1844 was 'an act of very great injustice'.[173] Grey wanted the supreme and intestate courts 'to take such steps as might be required to protect the rights of the children.'[174] This claim received an unusual amount of consideration from government, with the governor considering the children's right to title in Executive Council no less than three times. Title had almost been given in 1854, and by the time it finally arrived around 1858, the Maxwell children were adults, spread out around the globe, as well as in the Waikato (where Andrew, or Anaru Makihara, was to become very famous, including as an expert in tattooing), England

[171] IA 1 1847/1584: Sinclair, minute, 3 August 1847; ibid., Symonds, minute, 1 September 1847; ibid., Sinclair, minute, 15 September 1847.
[172] OLC 1/332: [Charles Heaphy or Francis Dillon Bell], 'Motutapu case', c.1858. Also *Daily Southern Cross*, 11 August 1857.
[173] The first purchase was made during the period in which pre-emption had been waived by Fitzroy.
[174] OLC 1/332: [Charles Heaphy or Francis Dillon Bell], 'Motutapu case', c.1858.

and Australia.[175] The commissioner granting the land waived any fees that were due because of 'the peculiar circumstances of the sons of Thomas Maxwell being persons of the half caste race'. Yet this was a double-edged sword, for the grant of land was placed in official custody, not given immediately over to the Maxwells nor to their indigenous kin, presumably due to the same 'peculiar circumstances'.

Colonial strategies of racial amalgamation positioned policies towards land and half-castes as integral to the extension and substantiation of rule. Coupled with increasingly important government institutions of racial amalgamation—other forms of colonial property, civil marriage, courts, schools and hospitals, particularly—the new racialized colonial regime was evermore relevant to Tangata Whenua. Each of these colonial efforts had public, formal, communal components, but in practice it became evident that they were also addressing intimate and quotidian relationships as well. From this early period forward colonial government was, to varying degrees, inaugurating a competition to establish legitimacy and strength of claim not just between *kāwanatanga* and *rangatiratanga*, but between the kinds of intimacies that were manifest in indigenous life and those advanced by colonial practices and models. These approaches to government set forth a strong link between producing colonial subjectivities and ruling colonial subjects. The question of how half-castes would be aligned in this competition, and whether they would be a burden or a boon, was consequently a matter that was not restricted to public policy per se, but inextricably tied up with wider questions concerning subjectivities and intimate relationships. Could half-castes be harnessed to, and advance, the efforts of colonial government, or would they prove complications or even active obstacles?

Evidently, the colonial and the indigenous were not opposite, incompatible polarities, despite the operations and discourses charged with realizing them as such. There remained the kinds of multifarious entanglements between Tangata Whenua and newcomers that made New Zealand profoundly resistant to such easy characterizations. It remained clear, for instance, that indigenous families and leadership sought to consult and accommodate, even include, colonial officials and settlers, and that for the most part there was consensus that differences could be reconciled. Indigenous families were certainly capable of including both half-castes and Pākehā, through the encompassing 'net of relationships' that constituted them. Relatives might walk these 'half-castes' around their lands, showing them the boundaries and telling them of

---

[175] OLC 1/332: Andrew Maxwell, testimony, 20 March 1859. Cf., Maureen and Robert McCollum, 'Rachael Ngeungeu Te Irirangi Zister', *DNZB*.

their 'ownership'.[176] These same relatives then supported these half-castes in their representations to government. Likewise, colonial discourses and agents made it equally clear that there was much about indigenous life that was compatible with, even necessary to, successful colonial rule. Such a concession was central to the colonial recognition given to half-castes' property, which explicitly sanctioned and recognized the relationships between these children and their relatives. Integral to this, of course, was that these relationships might then be regulated and transformed, a sequence that mirrored the colonial approach to land (and much else besides). Indeed, this was to be the central mechanism by which New Zealand was transformed from a disordered 'pandemonium' to the supposed colonization, 'organized and salutary'.

Confronted with supposedly dying or endangered populations of 'aborigines' or 'natives', and with extremes of either segregation or an indiscriminate equality, colonial officials had settled on the 'experiment of amalgamation' as a kind of middle way. This held the promise of both incorporating and marking difference, with the stated aim of erasing it. The colonial strategy regarding 'half-castes' and 'mixed' families understood them as a coalface, a point where colonial efforts to manage racial crossings saw them not as intrinsic dangers but as openings into the most intimate realms of indigenous life, a portal into new opportunities for consolidating colonial rule and advancing racial amalgamation. Half-castes were not simply a symptom of the complicated entanglements existing in New Zealand, but could be used as an engine for disciplining and transforming them. In a sense half-castes and mixed families were a nascent territorial dispute, as colonial government, *kāwanatanga*, sought to claim them away from indigenous kin groups, communities and *rangatiratanga*. The responses were eloquent of what was to come. Racial crossings were not ineffable or ambiguous, not a no man's land, or between the trenches, not between worlds. The people proximate to, or embodying, these racial crossings were usually far from interstitial or marginal, as the efforts of both government and *whānau* showed quite clearly. There were no large numbers of half-castes who were landless, impoverished or alienated from their indigenous kin. Equally, the numerous colonial musings about half-castes, whatever their tone, made sure to mark their urgency and importance, and almost all of these invited or exhorted intervention in the lives of half-castes and mixed families. The varied and important interventions that had already been undertaken by the end of the 1850s were further evidence that these people at racial

---

[176] For example, OLC 1/332: Henry Cook to Dillon Bell, 6 June 1858; OLC 1/1357: Hare Hongi, evidence, 30 March 1858.

crossings were a preoccupation of colonial government, that colonial policy was steeped with these kinds of domestic and intimate inflections, even when grappling with mundane, apparently objective, policy. It was already apparent that half-castes and mixed families were central, though in incommensurate ways, to two different political and communal visions, and their two increasingly competitive forms of authority.

4

Racial Crossing and the Empire:
Scholarship, Science, Politics, and Place

> The question to be decided upon by the jury is this—is it true
> without exception, that any two races of men may produce together
> a mixed race as prolific as those from which it sprang, and equally
> capable of prolonging its existence indefinitely without further
> crossing with either of the parent races?... The question is still *sub
> judice*.
>
> *The Reader*, 1864[1]

Although few in Britain would have questioned the existence of sustainable
mixed races in the 1830s, by the 1860s a journal with a broad readership
could claim it was a matter undecided. In a relatively short period of time
British scholarly, and particularly scientific, circles had apparently transformed their approaches to, and understandings of, human variation.
Similar thoughts could be found in any number of periodicals and were
expounded by a variety of people, in a variety of publics. This striking turn
has been made familiar by recent outpourings in the historiography
of 'race', but the limits of this apparent transformation (and much of this
historiography) have not been sufficiently observed or explored. For
although the question might have been supposed by some to be *sub judice*,
it was only very rarely treated as such in most of Britain's colonies. In the
colonies (and in colonial circles in metropolitan society) proponents of this
view were striking for their scarcity, and were treated as true commodities
amongst adherents of this view, who were themselves not particularly
numerous. Yet this relative scarcity in some places has to be squared with
what seems a disproportionate presence in others, and this can be done by
attending to a fundamental condition of racial discourse (as with other
discourses) that they were specific to place. This was made more dramatic
in the case of empire, as these places could be separated by only an hour or

---

[1] 'Review of Pouchet and Broca', *The Reader*, 4 (1864), p. 476.

by half a year, by a few miles or by 10,000. This chapter argues that reorienting analysis in a way that can attend to the specifics of discursive location and its varying potency is essential to properly engaging the problem of racial crossing, or race more generally. How discourses were embodied and performed—not only in particular texts, but in people, societies, networks of correspondence, and practices—could never be separated from *where* they were embodied and performed. Such an approach does not produce a single coherent narrative of historical development, nor an even terrain through which packaged ideas trickled down or were sent out, but it better accounts for the multiplicity of often conflicting positions, intense debates, and uneven but powerful valence for specific racial projects.

An illustration of these complexities was the work of Paul de Strzlecki, in his popular traveller's account of the Australian colonies. In a widely noticed passage, Strzlecki reported that aboriginal women, once they had borne children to a white father, were no longer able to reproduce with an aboriginal father[2] (an equivalent was commonly believed to occur amongst animals).[3] A surgeon in the Royal Navy, T.R.H. Thomson, was personally moved to investigate these claims in Australia. In a paper he delivered to the Ethnological Society of London, Thomson agreed that many of these women were infertile, but he ascribed this infertility to other causes: concubinage, drinking, tobacco, disease (sexually transmitted and otherwise), and perhaps infanticide. Thomson damned Strzlecki's entire argument, as well as all those who were credulous of it. Throughout the world, he said, 'the traveller will find the half-caste, the mulatto, the creole, too often the brother of the jet black, the brown, the olive, unmixed younger children'.[4] For Thomson it was plain truth, a matter of common sense: he recalled how, when he asked an Australian aboriginal man whether Strzlecki's theory was accurate, the inquiry was treated with disdain. The answer was 'accompanied with remarks in the peculiar jargon used by them in communicating with the white man, neither complimentary to the individual whose name was connected with it, or [sic] my humble self who repeated it.'[5]

These were not simple empirical matters: proximity or experience did not command truth, and could not settle the dispute. Both Strzlecki and

[2] Paul de Strzelecki, *Physical Description of New South Wales and Van Diemen's Land* (London, 1845), pp. 346–7.
[3] Ritvo, *The Platypus and the Mermaid*, pp. 107–18.
[4] T.R.H. Thomson, 'Observations on the Reported Incompetency of the "Gins" or Aboriginal Females of New Holland, to Procreate with a Native Male after having Borne Half-caste Children to a European or White', *JES*, 3 (1854), p. 246.
[5] Ibid., pp. 243–4.

Thomson had been in the field, and both claimed personal experience and observation as authority. Both wrote as modern, even 'scientific' men, free of superstition and privy to the new knowledge of human differences. Not only could substantiated encounters with half-castes not resolve this particular dispute, both of these positions and the arguments they produced would continue well after Thomson and Strzlecki's contributions. Thomson's enthusiastic reception at the Ethnological Society was, in its context, hardly surprising, nor was it surprising that there were many who continued to refer to Strzlecki through the following decades. Evidently, the motility and force of these conceptions stemmed not only from the evidence they gathered nor how they packaged it, but other things.

Discourses about race crossing were mobile, traversing imperial, scientific, scholarly and readerly networks; but their meanings and potency occurred in, and were constrained by, specific environments. Whether it was a London library, a governor's office, the Ethnological Society of London or a colonial missionary school, the actualities of these places shaped and grounded the meanings of these discourses. It was within particular places that imperial networks delivered their cargo of discourse, where traffic in books, conversation and correspondence made purchase on dynamics of power, individual subjects, groups and organizations. Intellectual discursive concerns need to be understood within the locations that invested their meaning, ones sensitive to 'the pragmatics of social space', in James Epstein's felicitous phrase.[6] From the archives in which governmental power and interpretations were consolidated, to parliaments, to gentlemen's societies or the family hearth, meaning was fashioned in place, in encounters with and amongst people and discourse. Whether the writers wrote from, or having been to, the colonies, or whether they remained in Britain, this was equally true. It is useful to understand these developments in racial crossing as, to borrow from D.J. Mulvaney, 'encounters in place'.[7]

With more than 1,400 skulls in his possession, Joseph Barnard Davis seemed to encapsulate the complexity of these discursive encounters. Davis believed it possible to discover all sorts of racial information including, in some cases, the degree and composition of racial hybridity in an individual.[8] If his oeuvre is any indication, his home was an eerie place, and Davis's collecting was compulsive and obsessive. His writings on race and skulls, in

[6] James Epstein, *In Practice: Studies in the Language and Culture of Popular Politics in Modern Britain* (Stanford, 2003), p. 109.
[7] D.J. Mulvaney, *Encounters in Place*; Greg Dening, *Performances*.
[8] Joseph Barnard Davis and John Thurnam, *Crania Brittanica: Delineations and Descriptions of the Skulls of the Aboriginal and Early Inhabitants of the British Islands*, 2 vols., (London, 1865).

impressively illustrated volumes, became touchstones for racial scholars and craniologists. His collection betokened an empire over the globe, but also pointed to an empire over the past. 'Aboriginal' skulls from Britain sat alongside other 'aboriginal' crania, including a dozen skulls of Tasmanians, highly coveted in Europe. Several hundred of his skulls were from the Pacific, and he mobilized his position, connections and wealth to gather more.[9] Davis used Governor Grey as a channel through which to obtain even more indigenous skulls (and skeletons) from New Zealand, adding to the dozens he already possessed.[10] Some of his assets were also invested in the colonies, including a considerable sum in New Zealand. His encounter with New Zealand, even from a distant place, was multi-faceted and complex—not simply that of an intellectual or collector, but as an engaged and entangled investor, patron and correspondent. Through his library, his human remains and his correspondence, the Empire and its colonies weighed heavily on him, and though his encounters were not reciprocal, this was due not to his promixity but to his proclivities.

RACE CROSSING FROM ETHNOLOGY TO DARWIN

From the 1820s into the 1850s James Cowles Prichard was the giant in the study of human variation, 'the father of Ethnographical Science'.[11] He was widely read by learned people in Britain, from scientists like Charles Lyell to historians such as Thomas Arnold. Prichard was a committed monogenist who regarded man as a 'cosmopolite', and although he outlined a definite racial hierarchy (with the European races at the top), for Prichard these were not absolute distinctions.[12] 'All the diversities which exist [among the races of man] are variable, and pass into each other by insensible gradations', he wrote; 'there is . . . scarcely an instance where the actual transition cannot be proved to have taken place.'[13]

For Prichard race crossing was an important topic, and some of his contemporaries thought it the central element of his work.[14] Though

---

[9] Joseph Barnard Davis, *Thesaurus Craniorum: Catalogue of the Skulls of the Various Races of Man, in the Collection of J.B. Davis*, 2 vols., (London, 1867, 1875).

[10] Grey Letters, D11(13): Davis to Grey, 12 December 1867; Ibid., D11(8): Davis to Grey, 5 March 1858; Ibid., D11(10): Davis to Grey, 5 January 1859. Also see J. Barnard Davis, 'Oceanic Races, their Hair etc., and the Value of Skulls in the Classification of Man', *AR*, 8 (1870), pp. 183–96.

[11] G.W. Earl, *The Native Races of the Indian Archipelago: Papuans*, (London, 1853), p. iii.

[12] Prichard, *The Natural History of Man*, p. 3.

[13] Ibid., p. 473.

[14] Smith, *The Natural History of the Human Species*, pp. 113–14.

Prichard's ideas developed, his essential convictions and basic interpretations of race crossing remained largely the same. His most important monograph reflected these changes, as it went through five editions, beginning as a single volume and ending in five. Prichard always insisted that different races could mix, and that different species could not. 'If it be a fact that hybrid races are unprolific', Prichard wrote, 'it follows that mulattoes and other mixed breeds in mankind are not hybrid, and consequently that the parent races are of the same species.'[15] This was the order of the world, and it could not be altered: it was the compelling proof of human unity, one further supported by the similarity of physical characteristics, shared human diseases, and a common moral and intellectual capacity. The mixed race person, healthy and fertile, was proof of original human unity, an exoneration of biblical history.

More than just a biblical proof, Prichard regarded the crossing of races as a potential mechanism for improvement. Typically, he saw racially mixed peoples (or nations), such as the Celt/English people, as improved and superior. More generally, he felt that mixed race offspring, as opposed to the hybrid offspring of different species, 'generally exceed [the parent races] in vigour and in the tendency to multiplication'.[16] If there was any difference in fertility, Prichard thought that it was probable that mixed races were *more* fertile; other advantages might also accrue from their 'double ancestry'.[17]

But Prichard's successors were not as convinced. Robert Latham, his most direct successor, though a monogenist, was far less certain about it (except in a moral or religious sense).[18] Latham agreed that all mixed breeds were fertile and prolific, but believed racial differences were starker and ingrained, and happily read and quoted polygenists. He had a hierarchy of crossings, from 'simple' to 'extreme' intermixture. A mix with an Englishman and an Indian or Arab, who were what Latham called 'intermediate or transitional forms' was a 'simple' intermixture, of the kind to be found in most countries.[19] On the other hand, an intermixture of an Englishman with a negro was an 'extreme' intermixture, because these races belonged to 'two extreme sections of two of the primary divisions'. This extreme intermixture, in a revealing move, Latham called 'hybridism'.

[15] J.C. Prichard, *Researches into the Physical History of Mankind*, 2nd edn., 2 vols., (London, 1826), 1, p. 126. Prichard, *The Natural History of Man*, p. 18.
[16] Prichard, *Researches*, 3rd edn., 1, p. 150.
[17] Prichard, *The Natural History of Man*, pp. 18–26.
[18] Robert Latham, *Man and his Migrations* (London, 1851), pp. 248–9; Robert Latham, *The Natural History of the Varieties of Man* (London, 1850), pp. 564–5.
[19] Latham, *The Natural History of the Varieties of Man*, pp. 555–7.

The arrival of evolution complicated these matters further. In his book, *Origin of Species*, Charles Darwin recognized hybridity as a crucial problem, and tried to reformulate and set new terms of debate. His approach was truly a new one, but failed to strongly inflect that of others, and for decades only a few evolutionists grappled with this concern in the way he had argued they should.[20] In the *Origin*, Darwin had argued that species were not permanent nor absolute; that they were merely 'well-marked varieties', 'artificial combinations made for convenience'.[21] Things were not hard and fast in nature, nor unchanging over time, but constantly varying. All categorical descriptions were inaccurate, Darwin maintained; the only form of 'natural' classification was genealogical.[22] Darwin disagreed that infertility between species was a 'special endowment'. He ascribed this infertility to actual anatomical and physical differences in reproductive organs. Whatever their other differences, if there was sufficient 'systematic affinity' between the two parents, they would reproduce.[23] Darwin disagreed that all varieties could cross, and that all species could not. For him fertility between parents was a fragile and contingent thing; a slight change in the 'conditions of life' could be crucial, fertility was 'incidental on unknown differences, chiefly in their reproductive systems'.[24] Sterility of crosses, be they between supposed species or supposed varieties, was not all or nothing, but graduated, a matter of degree.[25]

To Darwin the distinction between specific and varietal or racial difference was outmoded. But few writers, even among those who supported Darwin, followed the full import of this new view of variation. Even someone like 'Darwin's Bulldog', Thomas Huxley, 'refused to "mix up" evolution with his discrete types, fearing that it would "throw Biology into confusion".'[26] Darwin's friend, J.D. Hooker, and the very successful popularizer G.H. Lewes, were among the few who perceived how Darwin and Wallace had shown that species were indeed 'derivative and mutable',

[20] Charles Darwin, *The Origin of Species by Means of Natural Selection or the Preservation of Favoured Races in the Struggle for Life* (New York, 1979 [1859]), pp. 68, 205–316. See Stepan, *The Idea of Race in Science*, pp. 47–82; Adrian Desmond and James Moore, *Darwin: The Life of a Tormented Evolutionist* (New York, 1991), pp. 467–586.
[21] Darwin, *Origin of Species*, pp. 446, 456. Cf. Charles Darwin, *The Variation of Animals and Plants Under Domestication*, 2 vols., (London, 1868), 2, pp. 100–110.
[22] Darwin, *Origin of Species*, p. 456; George H. Lewes, *Studies in Animal Life* (New York, 1860), p. 125.
[23] Darwin, *Origin of Species*, pp. 273–4.
[24] Ibid., pp. 437, 278; also Darwin, *The Variation of Animals and Plants*, 2, p. 410.
[25] Darwin, *Origin of Species*, p. 288.
[26] Desmond, *Evolution's High Priest*, p. 39; Ibid., pp. 3–100; Adrian Desmond, *Huxley: The Devil's Disciple* (London, 1994), pp. 266–379.

and that therefore the question of species had 'materially changed'.[27]
Lewes told his audience 'that the *thing* Species does not exist: the term
expresses an abstraction, like Virtue, or Whiteness...Nature produces
individuals'.[28] Others understood Darwin fully, though, and simply disagreed. Darwin had predicted that hybridity would be one of the grounds
on which he would meet opposition, and Richard Owen's strong critique
in the *Edinburgh Review* proved him correct.[29]

Perhaps the majority of naturalists in the 1860s continued to see
the questions of hybrids, fertility and the stability of species (or races) in
much the same way as those in the years beforehand. In many respects the
distinctive features of the 1860s were neither particularly Darwinian nor
especially revolutionary.[30] Species were assumed by most scientists to be
stable and rigid. One anthropologist asked: 'What, indeed, would be the
signification of specific differences in nature, and how objectless would
be their permanence; if their obliteration were rendered possible by
continued production of hybrids!'[31]

One of the major monographs devoted to race crossing followed soon
after *Origin of Species*, but might as well have come before. Paul Broca's
1860 work *Recherches sur l'hybridite animale en general et sur l'hybridite
humaine* was translated into English in 1864 as *Hybridity in the Genus
Homo*. Supposedly to reconcile the extremes of debate fostered by monogenists and polygenists, Broca introduced a new terminology that better
described what he saw as a sliding scale of fertility between different
human races.[32] He saw four types of racial crosses: '*agenesic*', which
produced first-generation infertile offspring; '*dysgenesic*' crosses, which
were nearly totally infertile in the first generation, were infertile with
each other and rarely fertile with either of the parent races; '*paragenesic*'
crosses, which were partially fertile in the first generation, had decreasing
fertility through the generations to the point of extinction, and could
breed 'easily' with either parent race and other near, 'allied pure species';
and last, '*eugenesic*' crosses, which were 'entirely fertile' amongst themselves, and could breed, indefinitely, with parent species.

[27] Hooker, *The Botany of the Antarctic Voyage of H.M. Discovery Ships*, III, vol.1,
pp. ii–iii.

[28] Lewes, *Studies in Animal Life*, p. 129; also, p. 151.

[29] [Richard Owen], 'Darwin on the Origin of Species', *ER*, 111 (1860), pp. 487–532.

[30] Peter Bowler, *The non-Darwinian Revolution: Reinterpreting a Historical Myth*
(Baltimore, 1988).

[31] Waitz, *Introduction to Anthropology*, p. 25; also [Henry Holland], 'Life and Organization', *ER*, 109 (1859), p. 249.

[32] Pierre Paul Broca, *Recherches sur l'hybridite animale en general et sur l'hybridite
humaine en particulier* (Paris, 1860); idem, *Hybridity in the Genus Homo*, C. Carter Blake
(trans. and ed.), (London, 1864), pp. 14–15.

Broca's scheme and terminologies were not adopted by many.[33] In France Broca was a major scientific persona, the dominant figure at the Société d'Anthropologie, a stronghold of polygenism.[34] In Britain, though they admired his acumen and his logical and well-informed argument, many British readers remained unconvinced. 'Dr. Broca's treatise is most acceptable', wrote one reviewer, 'although we are by no means satisfied'. Broca's leading supporters were drawn primarily from a group of polygenists, who had not only published him in English, but set up a society to mirror his Parisian one. In other places, such as the *Medical Times*, reviews were circumspect. Their reviewer thought the book 'an able monograph on a highly-interesting and curious subject', but noted his 'strong bias to the polygenist theory' and thought that Broca 'can scarcely be supposed to have satisfied himself—much less to have satisfied his scientific readers— that he has arrived at any certain and well-grounded conclusion'.[35] Five years after Darwin might have radically changed theories of human variation, the arguments about race crossing, even at the cutting edge, were still occurring within the received frameworks of polygenesis and monogenesis, and older ideas of species.

This is not to say that matters were not changing. By the time Darwin published *The Descent of Man* (1871), the scenario was different. That book, J.D. Hooker predicted to the New Zealand governor, George Grey, 'will I expect, turn the scientific & theological worlds upside down'.[36] In some sense it did, but not in the way the *Origin* had. The interval of 12 years had partially inured the reading public to materialism and ape-men: there was, as Moore and Desmond have noted, 'little fire and flair about it'.[37] By the 1860s there was not much that had been left unsaid. Even the word 'hybrid', only recently used to describe people, was becoming common. But still, there was not that much that had been agreed upon. Human variation, race, species, hybridity—all of these remained both intensely political, intricately fractured and dispersed, and interminably debatable. Older conceptions could continue to hold ground, whether biblical literalism or polygenesis, even when assailed by powerful new formations that would later be held to be correct. The multiplication and

---

[33] Other schemes were offered: Cheyne, *Civilized and Uncivilized Races*, p. 28; C.W. Devis, 'Elasticity of Animal Type', *MASL*, 3 (1867–8–9), pp. 81–105.

[34] Elizabeth Williams, 'Anthropological Institutions in Nineteenth-Century France', *Isis*, 76 (1985), pp. 331–48; Michael A. Osborne, *Nature, the Exotic, and the Science of French Colonialism* (Bloomington, 1994), pp. 79–90.

[35] *London Review*, 4 June 1864; *Medical Times*, March 1864; quoted in Vogt, *Lectures on Man*, p. 398.

[36] Grey Letters, H39(7): Hooker to Grey, 31 May 1868.

[37] Moore and Desmond, *Darwin*, p. 579.

complication of scientific discourses was spatialized in fragmentary ways.
The specialized debates of scientists were frequently cordoned off in
particular locales, elite societies and journals, with public interest more
for pyrotechnic than substantial reasons. Yet, as both the monographs of
Darwin and the complicated terminologies of Broca signalled, scientists
were laying claim to a new knowledge of racial crossing, writing about it
and representing it in technical ways that were not easily accessible to the
public, nor easily understood.

THE SPACES OF ETHNOLOGY, THE STUDY OF HUMAN VARIETY AND RACE CROSSING

When the first edition of Prichard's key book came out in 1813, there
were few learned forums where he might specifically have discussed *The
Natural History of Man*. Only 20 years later this was not the case. Key
British institutions such as the (later Royal) Geographical Society (RGS,
founded 1830, Roderick Murchison becomes president 1831), the British
Association for the Advancement of Science (BAAS, first meeting 1831)
and the Geological Society (founded 1807) were founded, and their
concerns explicitly intersected with empire, race and questions of native
peoples.[38] But very quickly the central concerns of these societies gravi-
tated away from those of Prichard and other ethnologists. By 1850 the
historical and racial interests of ethnology were rarely to be found at these
places, under their own banner, except at the British Association, which
was troubled by the controversial and 'non-scientific' demeanour increasingly apparent amongst scholars of race.

In the 1830s and 1840s distinct societies were preoccupied with
ethnological pursuits, and these were very different social spaces: the
Ethnological Society of London (ESL) and the Aborigines Protection
Society (APS). The APS grew out of Buxton's 1837 Aborigine Committee, and the ESL grew out of the APS.[39] Buxton himself was a founding
member of the APS, and Thomas Hodgkin, who was the most influential
of the founding members, gave evidence in front of the committee. The

[38] David N. Livingstone, *The Geographical Tradition: Episodes in the History of a
Contested Enterprise* (Oxford, 1992); Arnold Thackray and Jack Morrell, *Gentlemen of
Science: Early Years of the British Association for the Advancement of Science* (Oxford,
1981); Robert A. Stafford, *Scientist of Empire: Sir Roderick Murchison, Scientific Exploration
and Victorian Imperialism* (Cambridge, 1989).
[39] Stocking, *Victorian Anthropology*, pp. 242–7; George W. Stocking, 'What's in a
name? The Origins of the Royal Anthropological Institute', *Man*, 6 (1971), pp. 369–90;
Sinclair, 'The Aborigines Protection Society and New Zealand'.

APS had numerous 'humanitarian' connections, and these were emphasized by the APS holding its meetings in Exeter Hall, the well-known
home of the missionary societies in London. The APS was foremost a
political lobby group not, in the first instance, an intellectual society. But
it consciously adopted stances on relevant intellectual matters. The APS
resolved in an annual meeting, for example, that aboriginal extinction was
not inevitable but simply a consequence of 'injurious treatment'.[40] It also
reflected on the various differences between races, theorized as to how such
racial differences had arisen, and very often considered the practical and
intellectual problem of how to 'civilize' aborigines, in effect their central
concern.[41]

The same reason the APS is important and interesting—its explicit
political concern with colonies—was one of the chief reasons it was kept
outside a scientific fraternity then trying to fashion itself as disinterested
and dispassionate. The APS formally and vigorously lobbied imperial
and colonial governments, as well as individual officials, in favour of its
own conception of 'racial amalgamation', especially for New Zealand. It
was a marginal organization, with a small membership, that was not a
'popular Society', and which knew its aims did not capture 'the public
mind'.[42] But its lobbying efforts were targeted and persistent: 'There is
not a newly-appointed Governor nor Bishop who is about to take his
departure for a distant Colony, upon whom a Deputation from this
Society does not wait, for the purposes of interesting him in *our views* of
aboriginal government.'[43] It was a 'check Society' or a 'watchman', important not for what it did, but for what it prevented.[44] It was not always
successful, but despite many difficulties proved remarkably resilient, and
convinced of its political and moral necessity. 'If this Society were to go
down', one member asked, 'where was a substitute to be found?'[45]

The APS fashioned their ethnological beliefs into principles and policies. The APS was convinced that 'equal rights' could overcome any racial
differences, because it considered racial differences to be relatively unimportant or changing. The APS advocated the implementation of gradual
steps towards a unified polity, which took no notice of race at all, and
which had one jurisdiction and the same laws for everybody.[46] If colonial

[40] APS, *Annual Report*, 1853, p. 13.
[41] For example, *Colonial Intelligencer*, ix, third series, December 1852, p. 171; Ibid.,
ix–x, new series, January and February 1849, p. 133.
[42] *Colonial Intelligencer*, xvi–xvii, third series, August to December 1853, p. 299.
[43] *Colonial Intelligencer*, xxi, new series, January 1850, p. 323.
[44] *Colonial Intelligencer*, xvi–xvii, third series, August to December 1853, p. 299.
[45] John Burnet, in APS, *Annual Report*, 1856, p. 10.
[46] *The Colonial Intelligencer*, September 1847, p. 165.

government placed 'Natives and Colonists on the same equality of footing', the APS argued, participation in 'like equality' would overcome 'the
differences of race and language.'[47] The APS sponsored practical works
that outlined systems of laws or policies for correct colonial governance,
which were elaborations of this core belief in equality.[48] The link between
'aboriginal' and 'domestic' reform was palpable; and the APS was a
staunch promoter of racial amalgamation. It was never their aim, the
Society made plain, to preserve aborigines 'in the purity of their race'.[49]
If legal equality was the central platform of APS policy, its necessary
concomitant was thus 'racial amalgamation'.

Racial amalgamation, in the eyes of the APS, would obliterate racial
difference. Aborigines, it declared, should 'mingle and intermarry with the
Whites'.[50] Or, as one APS member put it, 'An Englishman claims the right
of amalgamating with anybody he sees ... If England is to occupy strange
and torrid lands, it must be by raising up dark Englishmen, who heaven had
made with the faculties to do it.'[51] The APS advocated racial amalgamation
throughout the 1840s and 1850s, and suggested it as good policy for India,
even going so far as to blame the Indian 'Mutiny' (1857) on the lack of racial
amalgamation.[52] Places where racial amalgamation had apparently pro-
gressed, notably the settlement at Red River in British North America
where the *métis* dominated, were loudly approved of.[53] More than any of
the other 'ethnological' institutions, the APS openly advocated race crossing, and clearly interpreted it within their self-defined brief of 'protection'.

Racial amalgamation was almost an APS crusade in the case of New
Zealand. The APS offered early support for the New Zealand Company,
alienating the mission societies; but these differences were also philosophical, as the missionary preference for a separatism, which kept colonists
and natives apart, was directly counter to APS proposals.[54] The APS was
concerned that if the colonists were kept separate from the aborigines, that
the aborigines would be left unimproved, and thus separation would lead

---

[47] *The Colonial Intelligencer*, September 1847, p. 102; *The Colonial Intelligencer*, March 1847, p. 9.
[48] Standish Motte, *Outline of a System of Legislation* (London, 1840); Saxe Bannister, *Humane Policy; or Justice to the Aborigines of New Settlements* (London, 1830).
[49] Quoted in Stocking, *Victorian Anthropology*, p. 244.
[50] *Colonial Intelligencer*, vii–viii, new series, November and December 1848, p. 102.
[51] Thomas Perronet Thompson, *Audi Alteram Partem, Letters of a Representative to his Constituents*, 2 vols., (London, 1858–1861), 1, p. 30.
[52] APS, *Annual Report*, 1858, p. 6. John Malcolm Ludlow, *British India, its Races, and its History, considered with reference to the mutinies of 1857*, 2 vols., (Cambridge, 1858), 2, p. 261; Ibid., 1, p. 94.
[53] *Colonial Intelligencer*, xii, February 1848, pp. 222–4.
[54] 'Colonisation of New Zealand', *Monthly Chronicle*, August 1839, [reprinted as an APS pamphlet], p. 13.

to conflict and aboriginal extinction.[55] So much were the APS in favour of amalgamation that they even regarded the provision for autonomous native districts in the 1852 New Zealand constitution as a 'very dangerous clause', a clause which others considered an intelligent measure recognizing indigenous independence.[56] The APS did not wish to see *any* racial distinctions it thought unnecessary, certainly not any that were permanent.

The new colony of New Zealand gave the APS hope. 'Surely with such a people you may hope for almost any thing', its journal announced, 'and may look forward to their amalgamating with our own people, instead of decaying and dying off, as all other indigenous races have heretofore done'.[57] New Zealand 'aborigines' treated their women respectably, and their women had property in land; they were thus suitable to marry 'respectable' colonists: 'A legitimate amalgamation of the races will ensue, and peace and prosperity will result.'[58] A problem that the APS recognized was that the alternatives were not simply amalgamation or non-amalgamation, but the possibility of an illegitimate amalgamation, where native women would be treated only as concubines, and then eventually abandoned. Such a situation would generate grave problems, not least what would happen to these children, the fruit of an incomplete amalgamation, one that was sexual and procreative but not social or political. The APS petitioned CMS missionaries to provide for 'the better education and mental culture of New Zealand females.'[59] If these women were correctly cultivated, 'sanctified by grace and adorned by intellectual culture consistent with the sphere in which they should move when taken to be the helpmeets of Europeans the connection would be virtuous and honourable and powerfully conduce [*sic*] to the happiness of the colony'[60] Amalgamation would be completed by the formation of an acceptable domestic unit, within a civilized British polity, where crossing would not be degrading but elevating. But the fears of an illegitimate crossing were to be taken seriously. If not attended to, the children of these crosses 'will be the third element in the future and impending war of races, which must . . . [result if] . . . the British Government . . . discourages a legitimate, honourable amalgamation, and there is no alternative between amalgamation and extermination.[61]

[55] Hodgkin to Hawes, 27 November 1837, in Ibid., p. 42.
[56] *Colonial Intelligencer*, iii–iv, third series, June and July 1852, p. 66.
[57] *Colonial Intelligencer*, v–vi, new series, September and October 1848, p. 86.
[58] *Colonial Intelligencer*, xxiv, new series, April 1850, p. 413.
[59] Hodgkin Papers, WMS/PP/HO/D187: APS to CMS, [1846/1847].
[60] Hodgkin Papers, WMS/PP/HO/D187: APS to CMS, [1846/1847].
[61] *Colonial Intelligencer*, xxiv, new series, April 1850, p. 414.

Such overt involvement with politics and the practices of colonization did not suit everybody. Many APS members were more interested in intellectual, ethnological pursuits, and this less political 'student' party split from the APS and by 1843 had become the Ethnological Society. For the ESL the 'aborigines' were objects of study not protection, even though their sympathies were in precisely this direction. Though there were some tensions between the two societies, many remained members of both. They shared a general tenor, which was unsurprising for it was not a difference of philosophy, but rather of focus, that separated them. The 'first question' with which the ESL was concerned was still the monogenetic unity of mankind.[62]

The APS produced a 'practical' programme of racial amalgamation, while the ESL pursued scholarship that echoed the possibilities and benefits of race crossing. At the ESL it was argued that there was a constant intermixture of races, and that there were no natural barriers to this.[63] Mixed races were 'often superior in physical and psychical qualities to either of the two parent stems', Prichard told the society and most of the ESL luminaries, at least in the 1840s, would have agreed.[64] Thomas Hodgkin (now best known as the discoverer of Hodgkin's disease) was the real force at the ESL, and he was thoroughly convinced that the 'mixed progeny' of amalgamation were critical for a future, improved, colonization.[65]

Both the APS and ESL were marginal to those societies that were coming to define what it was to be 'scientific'. The ethnologists were never fully accepted as scientists by the 'gentlemen of science', the BAAS. Ethnology was enormously popular, yet it was frequently denied its own section at the annual meeting of the BAAS. Many members of the BAAS regarded ethnology as one of 'the unwelcome' or 'fringe sciences', one full of controversy—a distinct liability to men seeking to establish a position of social and intellectual authority.[66] Later, ethnology was forced into the company of zoology and botany in 1843 and 1844, becoming temporarily a subsection only from 1846, a position it then held only intermittently. The lack of patronage and social influence possessed by ethnology compared with other scientific fields was both a cause and a symptom of this.

---

[62] B.C. Brodie, 'Address to the Ethnological Society of London', *Journal of the Ethnological Society*, 4 (1856), p. 99.
[63] Ibid., p. 100.
[64] J.C. Prichard, 'Anniversary Address for 1848', *Journal of the Ethnological Society*, 2 (1850), p. 147.
[65] Hodgkin Papers, WMS/PP/HO/D/D232, Hodgkin, 'On the Progress of Ethnology', fos. 51–2.
[66] Morrell and Thackray, *Gentlemen of Science*, pp. 276, 281; *BAAS Reports*, 1837–47.

This lack of patronage was particularly telling in relations with government. Government officials, including those at the Colonial Office, were willing to patronize and converse with the 'gentlemen of science', like the leaders of the RGS or BAAS. This was not only due to their connections but also their purported disinterest and dispassion, which contrasted with the passion and lobbying of many who had been part of the APS. But scientific disinterest often manifested as racial investigations that were increasingly arcane, specialized and intellectual. These investigations had little apparent applicability to colonial governance. The RGS established its importance for the Empire by circulating maps and geographical discoveries, but it was far less clear what might be done with ethnological researches, even those the RGS published. What use could be made of Prichard's 'On the Ethnography of High Asia', with its turgid study of commonalities between Mongolian, Tungusian, Tartar and Manchurian vocabularies?[67] These were elements of knowledge, to be sure, integral to key discourses, but were not recognized by government officials as instrumental. Unsurprisingly, by the 1850s the Colonial Office was communicating selected materials to the RGS; this was a line it never opened to the APS and ESL.[68]

Most ethnological questions were not legible to colonial officials or governments. For this reason, and due to their lack of a powerful patron who could constitute or operate an influential network (such as Murchison at the RGS), access to government information other than what was in the public domain was consistently denied to ethnological scholars. Such patronage went to other, better positioned and connected, scholars.[69] The ESL's small helpings of official support and information came mostly from Governor Grey. One report he forwarded to the ESL finally prompted them to approach the Colonial Office directly, and this was in 1851, nearly a decade after their establishment. The ESL's letter indicated just how ignorant they were of the reach of the Colonial Office's system, and the extent of its archive. The Society wrote concerning 'the full details of the Ethnology of the British Colonies', asking 'of your Lordship the favor [*sic*] of a copy of any such details as may exist in the archives of the Colonial office.'[70] In just 10 years New Zealand alone had already filled well over 100 folio volumes of as many as 400 leaves each; any amount of these thousands of pages might have been taken to have concerned 'ethnology'. Older colonies, such as New South Wales, the

---

[67] J.C. Prichard, 'On the Ethnography of High Asia', *JRGS*, 9 (1839), pp. 192–215.

[68] CO 209/95, fos. 293, 314–15: Norton Shaw to Hawes, 14 February 1850, Norton Shaw to [Merivale?], 18 November 1851.

[69] CO 209/95, fos. 294, 312: William Hooker to Hawes, 26 March 1851, Francis Hawkins to Hawes, 19 April 1851.

[70] CO 209/95, fo. 313: Richard Cull to Earl Grey, 13 November 1851.

Cape or those in the Caribbean, had archives that were many times larger. Such a request was not only naive, but showed the ESL's social and political disconnect with the Colonial Office. A more effective strategy would have mobilized networks of patronage, and likely would not have led to such a distinctly archived (and easily denied) request.[71]

The Colonial Office was not without sympathy for the scholars of ethnology. Undersecretary Merivale (perhaps showing his own origins as a scholar) thought such societies could be used to communicate colonial information to the public, and that this would be 'very valuable'.[72] His reservations concerned the resources that would be consumed and whether staff could cope; the ESL had done Merivale's argument no favours by being so general, naive and ambitious. But Gairdner was far less sympathetic. He pointed out that it was 'usual to furnish any information which the Office possesses to the Geographical Society, on points connected with Geographical discovery, because it is obviously for the practical benefit of the Colonies as well as of this Country that such knowledge should be diffused'. He was not at all convinced that it was worth forwarding similar information to the ESL, 'a Society of so purely speculative a character', one without the apparent 'practical benefit' of geography.[73] The final word went to Francis Peel, the parliamentary undersecretary for the colonies. He agreed with Gairdner, and instructed that the 'Ethnologicals' request 'need not be taken notice of'.[74] The delineation of social, disciplinary and institutional boundaries—the shaping of particular discursive places—was proving to have some vital purchase on the way these matters were encountered, and how they were to be circulated.

DISPUTING RACIAL CROSSING

The intellectual dispute that dominates the historiography of Victorian racial scholarship was that between polygenesis and monogenesis. This certainly punctuated developments after the 1840s, though only in certain ways. Both monogenism and polygenism were viable propositions given the intellectual context in which they jostled, though only monogenesis remained persistently respectable and orthodox. Both, as Stocking has noted, 'provided alternative answers to the problems of human diversity in the context of Biblical orthodoxy, the Cuverian idea of species, and the

[71] See Laidlaw, *Colonial Connections*.
[72] CO 209/95, fo. 314: Merivale, minute, 15 November 1851.
[73] CO 209/95, fo. 314: George Gairdner, minute, 15 November 1851.
[74] CO 209/95, fo. 314: Francis Peel, minute, 15 November 1851.

data of pre-Darwinian ethnology.'[75] But the pressures were growing on the orthodox, ethnological view of monogenism: the biblical orthodoxy became more questionable; Cuvierian notions of essentially fixed species were increasingly challenged. Scholars investigating these concerns more and more frequently encountered the Empire, the colonies, evidence and texts from beyond, and these frequently highlighted race crossing.

The estrangement between the gentlemanly sciences and ethnology was followed by a fragmentation within this ethnological residue. In 1863 a group broke from the ESL to form the Anthropological Society of London (ASL). Core differences—largely the dispute between monogenism and polygenism—became seemingly irreconcilable, and it was nearly a decade before the two groups eventually reunited, as the (later Royal) Anthropological Institute (1871). The debate was not a detached intellectual contemplation. Polygenesis drew heartfelt fervent reactions: 'this question', one monogenist proclaimed, 'involves the truth or falsity of the Bible, and every interest of Christianity'.[76] Polygenists, wrote another monogenist,

> observe that it cannot be much more criminal to destroy such creatures [i.e. other races] when they annoy us than to extirpate wolves or bears; nor do they strongly reprobate the conduct of some white people in our Australian colony, who are said to have shot occasionally the poor miserable savages of that country as food for their dogs.[77]

Polygenists were sometimes as vigorous in their response, but they were far fewer in numbers, and their reputations were more directly at stake. Polygenesis claimed the sympathies of many scholars, but few public adherents.[78]

In Britain most of the few polygenists that can be found belonged to the ASL. This dearth means that historians who wish to emphasize the importance of polygenesis, such as Robert Young, subsequently lean very heavily on a few mavericks and draw liberally from outside the Empire, particularly from France and the USA.[79] But many nominal

[75] George W. Stocking Jr, 'Review', *Journal of the History of the Behavioural Sciences*, 1 (1965), p. 295.
[76] Smyth, *The Unity of the Human Races*, p. 46.
[77] J.C. Prichard, *The Natural History of Man* (London, 1843), p. 7.
[78] Smyth, *The Unity of the Human Races*, pp. 58–65; see also J.C. Prichard, *Researches into the Physical History of Mankind*, 3rd edn., 5 vols., (London, 1836–1847), 1, pp. vii–viii. See Stocking, *Race, Culture, and Evolution*, pp. 38–41, 44–5; William Stanton, *The Leopard's Spots: Scientific Attitudes toward Race in America, 1815–59* (Chicago, 1960), passim; George L. Mosse, *Toward the Final Solution: a History of European Racism* (London, 1978), pp. 33–4.
[79] The usual suspect is Robert Knox (see below). Also Josiah C. Nott and George R. Gliddon, *Types of Mankind* (London, 1854). See a similar point made by Douglas Lorimer,

monogenists entertained polygenist sympathies. Charles Hamilton Smith, for instance, seemed more convinced by the variety of polygenist evidence than what he felt was monogenist reliance on Buffon and Cuvier's ideas about the sterility of hybrids and the difference of species.[80] Smith was not entirely convinced that mulattoes were perfectly fertile, and argued that mixed races gave way to purer ones, through conquest, absorption or 'decreasing vitality'.[81] Even notorious polygenists, such as Lord Kames, seem in retrospect quite mild.[82]

The remaining 'Ethnologicals' almost universally agreed that all different races could interbreed, while the 'Anthropologicals' denied this or suggested that racial 'hybrids' were unhealthy or lacked fertility. For the first time there was a sustained chorus of polygenist thought in Britain. The Anthropologicals thought race crossing was impossible, unsustainable or degenerative. Unsurprisingly, the Anthropologicals' controversial leader was James Hunt, who was thoroughly convinced that researches into race crossing were critical.[83] Yet the Anthropologicals realized that they were marginal; as one complained, the writers they considered most important, such as Robert Knox and the Americans Nott and Gliddon, were not very often read or heeded.[84] For the Ethnologicals race crossing was important, but largely because the existence and fertility of different races was everywhere to be seen, and was a long-standing historical feature. They pointed to the populations of France and England, 'the most mixed nations of Europe, and the millions of mulattos and Meztizos [sic]'.[85] They saw race mixing in the past, and imagined that it was the way ahead: 'the future human races will be renovated with an infusion of white blood'.[86] Racial crossing was a means of improvement, as one Ethnological argued, '"*half-castes*" very generally combine the best attributes of the two races from whence they originate'.[87] Both communities of knowledge

'Theoretical Racism in Late-Victorian Anthropology, 1870–1900', *Victorian Studies*, 31 (1988), p. 406.

[80] Charles Hamilton Smith, *The Natural History of the Human Species* (Edinburgh, 1848), pp. 113–15.

[81] Ibid., pp. 118–24.

[82] Henry Home, Lord Kames, *Sketches of the History of Man*, 4 vols., enlarged edn., (London, 1779), 1, p. 76.

[83] James Hunt, 'The Presidents Address', *AJ*, 2 (1864), p. xciii.

[84] William Bollaert, 'Observations on the Past and Present Populations of the New World', *MASL*, 1 (1863–4), p. 114.

[85] Crawfurd, 'On the Supposed Infecundity of Hybrids or Crosses', *BAAS Reports*, 1864, p. 142.

[86] A. de Quatrefages, 'The Formation of the Mixed Human Races', *AR*, 7 (1869), p. 39.

[87] Robert Dunn, 'On the Physiological and Psychological Evidence in support of the Unity of the Human Species', *TES*, 1 n.s. (1861), p. 191.

agreed race crossing was enormously significant, but for very different reasons.

The Anthropologicals were deliberately provocative and 'revelled in their repugnance'.[88] In 1860 Britain, the ASL's meetings were one of the few places where it was a slander to call someone an abolitionist; it raised only cheers and not eyebrows to say that taking an African to be a slave in the USA 'is like taking him out of hell and putting him in paradise'.[89] They taunted 'the elder and smaller Society in London'—the Ethnologicals—by claiming (falsely) over 500 fellows.[90] They embarked on an ambitious publishing programme, publishing a *Review*, *Memoirs*, and a *Journal* (as well as for a time a *Popular Magazine*) and translating a number of continental works in a monograph series. But the Society was running at a loss, and it was only a matter of time before the wheels fell off.[91] The Ethnologicals were on the margins of the scientific establishment, but the Anthropologicals were even further on the fringes; symbolically, at the 1869 meeting of the BAAS, they staged an impromptu walkout after not getting a section of their own.[92]

The style of the Anthropologicals reflected their substance. In general they believed that races were fundamentally and historically different, and had a fixity of type and set limits to their abilities. Races were immutable and unequal. Slavery and domestic politics also brought out the contrast between the societies, as did the controversy of Governor Eyre (the Ethnologicals stood against Eyre, while the Anthropologicals supported him vigorously).[93] The Anthropologicals opposed the extension of the franchise to the lower classes: 'if human inequality is a fact of nature', one fellow announced, 'our system of representation should be unequal also'.[94] What amounted to a defence of racial hierarchy was allied with vehement defences of gender hierarchies. The Anthropologicals also opposed political participation for women (a 'hermaphrodite form of government' one labelled it).[95] The Ethnologicals, on the other hand, generally leaned towards political reform, and not only admitted women

[88] Adrian Desmond, *Huxley: The Devil's Disciple* (London, 1994), p. 343.
[89] G. McHenry, *AJ*, 2 (1864), p. xlvi. Winwoode Reade, discussion, ibid., p. xix.
[90] 'Farewell Dinner for Captain Burton', *AR*, 3 (1865), p. 172; C. Carter Blake, in [Anonymous], 'Anthropology at the British Association, A.D. 1864', *AR*, 2 (1864), p. 319.
[91] 'On the Origin of the Anthropological Review', *AR*, 6 (1868), pp. 431–43.
[92] 'Anthropology at the British Association, 1869', *AR*, 7 (1869), p. 428.
[93] James Hunt, 'Presidents Address', *AJ*, 5 (1867), pp. xlviii–xlix; also C.O. Groom Napier, *Anthropological Journal*, 6 (1868), p. lix; 'On the Negro Revolt in Jamaica' and 'The Baptists and the Jamaica Massacre', *PMA*, 1 (1866), pp. 14–20, 20–3.
[94] 'Universal Suffrage', *The Reader*, 7 (1866), p. 5.
[95] Luke Pike, 'On the Claims of Women to Political Power', *AJ*, 7 (1869), pp. xlvii–lxi.

to their meetings but allowed them to become members and give papers (for which the Anthropologicals also mocked them).[96]

The Anthropologicals' belief in natural inequality showed the triangulations between race, class and sex. Both race and class were, in their eyes, policed on the sexual frontier. When one Anthropological confidently announced that 'No white man in America . . . [or] in England, would willingly give his own child in marriage to a Negro', another responded by explaining how this difference related to class:

> We talk of the antipathies of race: you say that a White man will not give his daughter to a Negro; I beg leave to ask whether an English nobleman will offer his daughter to an English peasant. . . . What is that superiority? Is it not parallel to that which constitutes you superior to the peasant who tills your garden?[97]

The answer was in the affirmative. The differences of sex, race and class were not only parallel but were entwined. If inequality was natural, it turned on more than one axis; and crossing, whether of race or class, unsettled them all.

The public dispute between the two societies, a cause célèbre, dramatized the kinds of differences in conceptions of race and race crossing that had been brewing since the early part of the century. Though the two societies had only recently coexisted, after 1863 they conducted themselves so differently that only a handful of people belonged to both societies and attended both meetings, even though they were concerned with the same questions. At the height of the controversy the two societies had trouble even being in the same room. At one meeting of the BAAS, a joint session drew huge crowds (the largest at the meeting) and the room echoed with hissing and booing.[98] These social forms clearly conditioned the discourse that was circulated. The Anthropologicals, in particular, were not averse to mocking and parody, rhetorical forms that jibed poorly with the emergence of scientific protocols for debate. The Ethnologicals, despite their own efforts, had trouble removing themselves from the wider concerns of humanitarians and the position of 'Aborigine's friend'. It is revealing that the two societies often relied on the same sources, the same

---

[96] James Hunt, preface, Carl Vogt, *Lectures on Man: His Place in Creation, and in the History of the Earth*, James Hunt (ed.), (London, 1864), p. viii; Mrs Lynn Linton, 'On the Ethnology of the French Exhibition, as represented by the National Arts', *TES*, 6 (New Series) (1868), pp. 216–26. Not all Ethnologicals were comfortable with this decision; Desmond, *The Devil's Disciple*, p. 343.

[97] C. Carter Blake, discussion, *AJ*, 2 (1864), p. xxviii; Luke Burke, ibid., pp. xliv–xlv.

[98] Roderick Murchison, 'Address', *BAAS Transactions*, 1863, p. 127. 'Anthropology and the British Association', *AR*, 3 (1865), pp. 354–78.

'data', but they encountered and circulated them in profoundly different ways. Vastly different conversations resulted, though ones that seemed to have little impact beyond their own organizations, social and scholarly circles and readerships. One would comb official archives in vain for any corresponding debate over monogenesis or polygenesis, or even the words themselves. Sir Francis Peel of the Colonial Office had dismissed the ESL's concerns as 'speculative' in the 1850s; he would have felt little different in the 1860s, and the great majority of colonial officials, whether in Britain or in the colonies, either thought such questions settled (overwhelmingly in favour of monogenesis) or irrelevant. The abiding questions for them concerned the management or governance of races, questions of policy and law, or the looming extinctions of native populations. This brought to official attention a different set of questions about racial crossing, ones to which no single set or network of scholars appeared to have adequate answers.

PRODUCING COLONIAL KNOWLEDGE ABOUT RACE CROSSING

There were no colonial branches of either the ESL or the ASL or indeed any of the other main London societies. It was expected that papers and people would be returned to London, and that these societies would work as something not unlike 'centres of calculation'.[99] But this model of scholarship was at odds with the way the Empire generally behaved, where colonies were essentially governed locally, mostly through authority delegated to autocratic Crown representatives or colonial parliaments, with only oversight and general guidance from London, and where the traffic between colonies resembled an intricate web more than the spokes on a wheel. It would be surprising if colonial governments surrendered their capacity to gather and construct knowledge to distant, scholarly, often private, realms. And they did not.

In New Zealand, as elsewhere, colonial government had set about constructing an archive to enable rule, as we have seen, an archive that sought to fashion a particular racial, colonial, taxonomy. A great deal of effort was directed at making the land and its peoples legible and governable, and colonial agents and employees gathered writings and knowledge omnivorously, from historical manuscripts to protocols and

---

[99] Bruno Latour, *Science in Action: How to Follow Scientists and Engineers Through Society* (Cambridge, MA, 1987), pp. 215–57.

oral traditions. The documenting and classification of natives and native land and resources was undertaken enthusiastically, and with considerable resources, but remained partial and flawed. For instance in New Zealand it was not until 1871 that a complete national census of the New Zealand population was taken. Before then, only 'Europeans' were counted not 'natives'—and even then, as for many decades afterward, the native figures were unreliable and inaccurate.[100] The practical operation of colonial government enabled and created colonial knowledge, often with indigenous consent, but not infrequently through the use of coercion.

Signal among these myriad official efforts was a panel of native 'experts' convened by Thomas Gore Browne, the New Zealand governor who arrived in 1855. These expert opinions were bolstered by solicited contributions from resident magistrates and missionaries, and compiled by Francis Fenton (resident magistrate in the Waikato) as the volume *Observations on the State of the Aboriginal Inhabitants of New Zealand.* This volume was essentially a search for the causes of 'aboriginal' population decline, and it produced standard answers for the time, such as war, infanticide, alcohol, poor hygiene and general social conditions. (Prostitution was suspected to be a cause, but the number of half-caste children made it apparent that this was not sufficient.[101]) Importantly, the work compiled tribe by tribe population statistics, and though these were often only estimates, they produced a taxonomy of 'tribes' that was to prove of lasting influence, shaping the thoughts of people from judges to historians. These native population figures included half-castes, and the apparent increase in half-caste numbers that they tabulated provided food for thought. In several places they seemed to be the only portion of the indigenous population still increasing. Fenton suspected that the native race might have 'run out', that 'an infusion of fresh blood' might be necessary in order to once again make them profligate.[102]

The colonial government was proud of this document, and disseminated it widely throughout the Empire, as well as to both the WMS and CMS, the Statistical Society, the Society of Arts, Manufacturers and Commerce, and the British Museum. The APS pronounced it 'the most important document of [its] kind we have yet seen.'[103] It sparked debate domestically and overseas. An Anglican bishop was moved to write his own report, agreeing that dress and food were part of the problem, but

---

[100] *Results of a Census of New Zealand, taken for the night of the 27th February 1871* (Wellington, 1872), p. v.
[101] Francis D. Fenton, *Observations on the State of the Aboriginal Inhabitants of New Zealand* (Auckland, 1859), pp. 30–1.
[102] Ibid., p. 31.
[103] *Colonial Intelligencer*, January to June 1859, pp. 80–81.

arguing that the main cause was 'Scrofulous affections'. He also observed that the children of white fathers seemed to be more robust and numerous. This view was already shaping to be, as it was in the report, increasingly important.[104] Half-castes, who were commonly under scrutiny, were being generally depicted as healthy and increasing. In some ways this was accurate; the mixed population (as it was seen at the time) was burgeoning, the native population was reducing. Yet it is clear that a cornerstone of government policy of racial amalgamation was the belief that half-castes would be an improvement, a view that found increasing support owing to various encounters in the colony.

Still, it is easy to overstate the potency or coherency of colonial discourses and spaces. Though the colonies were places of encounter, in New Zealand at least, it proved difficult to create spaces to share and process encounters with 'natives'. Newspapers, the major form of publication in New Zealand's early decades, had little concern in such things. Although there were several scholarly societies formed in New Zealand (one was even formed on one of the first ships out), there was no real scientific or 'ethnological' society until 1871, and then only with government intervention. Prior to this the leading light was perhaps the 'New Zealand Society', and this was dim light indeed. But there was a rich collection of settlers, a high proportion of whom were from the middle and upper classes. They fared unevenly, as is apparent with William Swainson, a New Zealand Company colonist who was one of the best-known popular naturalists in Britain. Ensconced on one of the Company's most suspect purchases in the Hutt Valley, Swainson and his family had struggled to even keep their land; Swainson, possibly the colony's sole FRS (Fellow of the Royal Society), was almost forced to labour on the roads— and his predicament was symbolic of the vicissitudes of metropolitan scholarship in the colonies.[105]

The missionaries had been the first and most prolific correspondents on matters of natural history, but by the 1840s and 1850s these networks were more varied. Such a network of correspondence and patronage could be potentially huge. Governor Grey was the best example, and he wrote on scientific and ethnological matters to an enormous variety of naturalists and ethnologists, from Richard Owen to Charles Darwin.[106] A regular

[104] IA 1/1860/1223: Tancred, minute, 26 April 1860.

[105] Ibid., 2: William Gisborne to Sinclair, 10 December 1855. Sinclair chanced upon a former gardener from Kew, who was working in New Zealand; ATL, Ms-Papers-1947, Andrew Sinclair, Letters and Journals 1844–1856, 2: diary, 17 March 1860.

[106] Grey Letters, O10(3): Owen to Grey, 7 November 1845; Ibid., D8(1): Darwin to Grey, 10 November 1846; Ibid., D8(2): Darwin to Grey, 13 November 1847. Stocking uses Grey as an example; Stocking, *Victorian Anthropology*, pp. 81–7.

donator to the British Museum, Grey managed to maintain active membership of the ESL while governor in New Zealand and Cape Colony.[107] Grey used his official position to patronize a number of ethnological works, and plugged into the patronage networks of scientific London; Murchison, for example, used Grey to find work for a nephew of his.[108] Grey also corresponded with missionary scholars like William Ellis, a fellow member of the ESL.[109] Grey's widely read and admired publications about New Zealand and Australian aborigines, and his relations with notables (such as Latham and Frederick Max Müller), was proof that distance and delay were no intrinsic barrier to participating in London and British intellectual life by means of letters, friendships and thoughtfully used patronage.[110]

The multi-faceted operations of these networks—of sociability, publishing, patronage and scholarship—shaped which texts came to be viewed as authoritative. First amongst these was the work by Ernst Dieffenbach, the 'scientific man' on the New Zealand Company's first expedition, the fruit of two years' research in New Zealand. Dieffenbach wrote in a way amenable to a scholarly and scientific audience; his book could not be mistaken for a simple traveller's account. Dieffenbach had solid societal and scholarly connections: he made a relatively high-profile return to Britain, where he was praised at the BAAS, published by the RGS, and was the first invited speaker at the ESL (where he mused on the links between imperialism and scholarship, and the significance of race crossing).[111] His position of authority was typified by both Prichard and Darwin's adoption of him as the authority on New Zealand.[112]

Dieffenbach was uniformly positive about race crossing in New Zealand and the half-castes he encountered there. From him the mixed race families, 'the inhabitants of the beach', healthy looking half-castes and

[107] Ibid., C59(1), C59 (2): John Crawford to Grey, 16 July 1854, 28 June 1856. Ibid., E13(2), E13(3), E13(4), E13(5), E13(7), E13(14): Henry Ellis to Grey, 4 May 1849, 8 November 1849, 20 February 1850, 19 July 1851, 24 February 1851, 16 October 1852.

[108] *Correspondence of Charles Darwin*, 2, pp. 359, 371: Darwin to Gideon Mantell, 21 [April 1843]; Darwin to Gideon Mantell, 13 May [1843]. Grey helped look after Roderick Murchison's nephew, who Murchison feared would be 'an idler'; Grey Letters, M54(2): Murchison to Grey, 2 August 1853.

[109] Grey Letters, E14(1), E14(2): Ellis to Grey, 7 September 1857, 5 April 1859.

[110] Ibid., L7: Latham to Grey, 4 August 1854; Ibid., M51: Müller to Grey, 6 January 1850; George Grey, *Ko Nga Mahi a Nga Tupuna Maori, ha Mea Kohikohi Mai* (London, 1854); George Grey, *Polynesian Mythology, and Ancient Traditional History of the New Zealand Race as Furnished by their Priests and Chiefs* (London, 1855).

[111] Ernst Dieffenbach, *On the Study of Ethnology* (London, [1843]).

[112] Prichard, *Researches*, 3rd edn., 5, pp. 129–33. *Correspondence of Charles Darwin*, 2, pp. 391, 423: Darwin to Dieffenbach, 2 October 1843, Darwin to Dieffenbach, 16 December 1843.

hardworking native mothers, drew only approving comments.[113] He felt race crossing was well underway; in parts of New Zealand 'intermixture . . . between Europeans and natives is complete.' The half-caste children were healthy and well behaved, often were as light as European peasants, were bilingual and all were 'uncommonly well formed'.[114] Dieffenbach counted at least several hundred such children in New Zealand, and he thought they were 'one of the finest half-castes that exists'.[115]

To Dieffenbach this was more than a biological accident, but had enormous social consequences. Like the Company, Dieffenbach thought mixed marriages should be encouraged (he was critical of the missionaries whom he felt regarded these connections with contempt). He thought these crossings were 'very good marriages', and that they took advantage of a greater number of women in the native population. It promoted what he thought 'very desirable—an ultimate blending of the races.'[116] Such a stance was enabled by his assessment that New Zealand natives were 'a people decidedly in a nearer relation to us, than any other; they are endowed with uncommonly good intellectual faculties . . . They mix easily with Europeans, which has been effected to such a degree, that by future immigrations an entire mixture must be foreseen.'[117] Dieffenbach's account, which was critical of the implementation (if not the principles) of colonization and racial amalgamation, was the most influential of early New Zealand texts.

The other main work to be held in a similarly authorative light before 1860 was Arthur Saunders Thomson's *The Story of New Zealand*. Thomson, too, had a scientific background, and had spent 11 years as an army surgeon in New Zealand. He was a well-connected imperial soldier, and came to New Zealand after a posting in India, which shaped his interest in 'climate' and race.[118] He had a wide-ranging interest in the colony and its native peoples, and was also drawn particularly to racial amalgamation. He soon noted that British soldiers died and were hospitalized in fewer numbers in New Zealand than in Britain, and he argued that New Zealand was an unusually healthy place for the British.[119]

[113] Dieffenbach, *Travels in New Zealand*, 1, pp. 38, 40.

[114] *New Zealand Journal*, 7 August 1841, pp. 202–3; Ibid., 18 September 1841, p. 239.

[115] Dieffenbach, *Travels in New Zealand*, 2, p. 41.

[116] Ibid., 2, pp. 41–2.

[117] Dieffenbach, *New Zealand and its Native Population*, pp. 27–8.

[118] Arthur S. Thomson, *Prize Thesis: Observations on the Influence of Climate on the Health and Mortality of the Inhabitants of the Different Regions of the Globe* (Edinburgh, 1837).

[119] qMS-1809-1812, Sinclair Papers, 2: Thomson to Sinclair, 15 November 1859, [Thomson] to Sinclair, 9 January 1860.

Like Dieffenbach, Thomson was convinced that racial amalgamation represented the best and brightest hope for the future. His assessment of indigenous people was positive, but not as full. Then again, in the 15 years or so between Dieffenbach and Thomson's books, times had much changed. Dieffenbach estimated the native population at over 100,000, Thomson at just over 56,000.[120] By 1860 settlers were more strident, and *hapū* more careful of their independence: there was clearly trouble brewing. Thomson might have been forgiven had he thought the policy of racial amalgamation to be failing.

But Thomson could give more specific and precise reasons for pursuing racial amalgamation than most of his predecessors. He counted six causes for the decrease in native population, each of which, especially consanguinity or 'inbreeding', he argued could be ameliorated or reversed by racial amalgamation. Māori (he used the word) were too 'closely intermingled', and consequently scrofulous intermarriage was both more likely and more dangerous. Animal breeding, argued Thomson, had shown that after several generations of close breeding, crossing with a new breed was necessary. 'The same result has been observed in man, when families have confined their alliances within limited circles', he argued, 'Look at the royal and noble houses in Europe.' Few such families had survived to the present day, because inbreeding produced scrofula and sterility, and aggravated other diseases. He claimed that one in three Māori couples were similarly sterile, and their children were 'sickly and scrofulous'; in comparison, only one in five couples of 'native women and European men' were infertile, and their half-caste offspring were 'numerous, singularly healthy, and seldom scrofulous.'[121] The best solution, Thomson submitted, was racial amalgamation, and he found it 'satisfactory to find that Caucasian blood already flows in the veins of two thousand of the native population.' By the third generation, Thomson argued, the dark features bequeathed by Māori blood were all but invisible. Effectively the 'law of amalgamation' meant that Māori blood would be lost in a sea of Caucasian blood, and 'the features of the Maori race will disappear from among the half-castes'.[122] As in other official and scholarly incarnations, racial amalgamation had become a process and policy of erasure and invisibility, not unlike the 'euthanasia of savage races' that Merivale had earlier imagined.

---

[120] Thomson, *The Story of New Zealand*, 2, p. 336.
[121] Ibid., 2, pp. 285, 290.
[122] Ibid., 2, pp. 305–6. Thomson called all ensuing generations of racially mixed people 'half-castes', and not just the first: this had become customary in the colony.

RACIAL CROSSING AS HISTORY, IMPROVEMENT
AND REFORM

The interests of the ASL, the ESL and the BAAS were generally unrecognizable in those of colonial authorities and colonial government. But such elite intellectual scholarly circles were hardly the sole discursive spaces where racial crossings were considered a compelling interest. By the 1830s British radical scientific and medical circles had been attracted to these concerns, and these were not the 'philosophic radicals' of the New Zealand Company, who argued from the safety of their studies that the system could be used to alter itself, but the common variety to be found on the streets and in Chartist movements.[123] Theirs were 'democratic' sciences, as Roger Cooter has called them, often evolutionist and materialist, invested with a different politics to the kind of science being consolidated by the BAAS.[124] These radical investigations consistently saw crossing as a means of reform or improvement, and this was an assessment that was shared in other places as well, particularly by those concerned with the racial past, from novelists to historians.

Alexander Walker was a leading radical physician who wrote the fullest radical account of race crossing, *Intermarriage*. This focused on the intermarriage of individuals from different backgrounds in class and race, and with different but compatible faculties. This was an extremely popular concern, from those dismissed as 'lowlife in the medical schools' to the home-grown phrenologists, practitioners of the nineteenth century's 'most popular and most popularized "science"'.[125] Walker's approach to intermarriage was that it was a practical 'reforming science' aimed at educating children, maximizing individual ability and preventing disease.[126] Strongly influenced by phrenology, Walker's ideas were materialist and focused on heredity; yet along with most phrenologists he argued that these matters were not solely determined by heredity, and that 'the means of improvement are in the power of every family'.[127] Walker roundly abused the aristocracy as the most terrible of in-and-in breeders; he compared

---

[123] See Thomas, *The Philosophic Radicals*.
[124] Adrian Desmond, *The Politics of Evolution: Morphology, Medicine, and Reform in Radical London* (London, 1989); Stepan, *The Idea of Race in Science*; Roger Cooter, *The Cultural Meaning of Popular Science: Phrenology and the Organization of Consent in Nineteenth-Century Britain* (Cambridge, 1984).
[125] Desmond, *The Politics of Evolution*, p. 21. Roger Cooter, *Phrenology and the Organization of Consent*, p. 2.
[126] Walker, *Intermarriage*, p. 185.   [127] Ibid., p. 284.

kings who had 'intellectual faculties so low, as always to border on fatuity' with the manly and intellectual figure of the well-bred but not inbred Napoleon.[128] Walker advised his readers that by careful selection of marriage partners it was possible to correct any deficiencies in the offspring (he believed he understood the details of human heredity).[129] Walker did not advocate indiscriminate intermarriages but rather 'judicious crossing' that resulted in easy and stable improvement.[130]

In short, Walker considered that selective intermarriage or race crossing was an improvement over inbreeding and relentless purity. To endorse such a belief he could call on more 'respectable' scientists such as Prichard, and others who saw 'a divine command that near relations should not intermarry' as this would 'prevent diseases'.[131] Walker also perceived a natural principle among people that he called the 'love of difference'.

> This beneficial tendency of this love of difference...leads to those slight crosses in intermarriage between persons of different organization, which are as essential to the improvement of the races of men as we have found them to be in animals.[132]

Walker could consequently discuss crosses between the European and an 'African negro' and between the African negro and the native American with some approval, describing the ways in which the different elements in their parentage had combined. Walker's conclusion was that although knowledge was not perfect, it was obvious that the advantages of crossing were 'generally observed and acknowledged'.[133] The boundaries which some ascribed to God or to Nature, and which conservative scientists felt underpinned the very nature of society, the radical reformer felt could be crossed, or at least negotiated, by the enlightened plebeian.

Walker's view was probably the majority view amongst phrenologists and radical scientists—favouring crossings, but not indiscriminately. As another medic put it, 'Nature wishes marriages between different families and nations, because these intermarriages, or crossings of the races are the true means of improving and invigorating the species.'[134] Phrenology and radical science were never simply about explanation or observation, but also a programme of self-help reform: this might include careful

---

[128] Ibid., pp. 188–90; Michael Ryan, *The Philosophy of Marriage, in its Social, Moral, and Physical Relations* (London, 1837), p. 192.

[129] Walker, *Intermarriage*, pp. xxviii–xxix, 198–9, 201–26, 357–60.

[130] Ibid., pp. 282–8.

[131] Steinau, *Essay on Hereditary Diseases*, p. 2; Walker, for instance, quotes Prichard: *Intermarriage*, p. 203.

[132] Ibid., p. 125.

[133] Ibid., pp. 203–5, 365.

[134] Ryan, *The Philosophy of Marriage*, p. 94; also Walker, *Intermarriage*, p. 125.

intermarriages of people with different but compatible capacities.[135] Their objective was not purity, but neither was it continual and random crossings, which could lead to racial instability.[136] Crossings were to be chosen thoughtfully, and the last word came from Nature itself, which set natural boundaries; most followed Virey (after Galen) to argue that the woman had to enjoy sex to conceive, and if there was a natural repugnance this could not take place.[137] The working class bastard could reassure himself that 'illicit love' could breed genius; and love itself—well, *amor omnibus idem—omnia vincit amor*, love conquered all.[138] In this science there were few barriers, and those of race were attacked alongside those of class.

The radicals did, on occasion, turn such thought specifically to the colonies. 'The health of the colonies', the radical medical journal *The Lancet* wrote, 'can never be a matter of indifference to the mother country.'[139] Race was already established in physiological courses and treatises, where race crossing was often seen as beneficial. This was itself a reason for colonization which, wrote one physiologist, was a 'commingling and interaction of different races and communities...whether by positive admixture of blood, or by the reflected influence of language, thought, and ideas'.[140] The phrenologists, too, showed a concern in racial amalgamation. One popular phrenological journal, for example, examined the plans for racial amalgamation in New Zealand. Managing to gain access to some 'native' skulls they anticipated danger from a race with such clearly visible 'animal instincts' and over-developed 'organs of Destructiveness'. 'The mixed race between an English felon and a ferocious savage not destitute of intelligence, will be formidable neighbours' it warned. They might be advocates of intermarriage generally, but these intermarriages they were loathe to condone.

> It may seem a cold and mercenary calculation; but we must say, that instead of attempting an amalgamation of the two races—Europeans and [New] Zealanders—as is recommended by some persons, the wiser course would be, to let the native race gradually retire before the settlers, and ultimately become extinct.[141]

---

[135] Ibid., pp. 149, 198, 357–60, 418; Ryan, *The Philosophy of Marriage*, pp. 163–75.
[136] Steinau, *Essay on Hereditary Diseases*, pp. 37–40; Walker, *Intermarriage*, pp. 200–1.
[137] Ibid., p. xxvii; Ryan, *The Philosophy of Marriage*, p. 141.
[138] Ibid., p. 183.
[139] 'Editorial', *The Lancet*, 1841–2, ii, p. 762.
[140] Robert Verity, *Changes Produced in the Nervous System by Civilization Considered According to the Evidence of Physiology and the Philosophy of History* (London, 1837), p. 35.
[141] 'The New System of Colonisation—South Australia and New Zealand', *The Phrenological Journal and Magazine of Moral Science*, n.s. 1 (1838), pp. 256–8.

These were serious matters, not least because the readership of phreno-logical literature was partly drawn from the 'uneasy classes', from whence came many New Zealand colonists. Clearly, the phrenologists had no intrinsically humane disposition towards aborigines. Indeed, one of the most famous radicals was repeatedly outspoken on the preordained extinction of aboriginal races.[142]

Robert Knox, the most prominent British polygenist, is best situated in this context of radicalism and popular science. Having been cut adrift from Edinburgh after purchasing corpses from the murderers Burke and Hare in 1827 and 1828, Knox was forced (from about 1842) to make a living as a touring lecturer.[143] On the intellectual foundations of Geoffrey St Hilaire's 'transcendental anatomy', Knox built a unique complex of scientific and political ideas, which Evelleen Richards describes as a 'moral anatomy'.[144] Knox became increasingly disillusioned, impoverished, angry and radical—in idiosyncratic ways.[145] He was one of the few who openly denied that the different races could mix:

> Nature produces no mules: no hybrids, neither in man nor animals. When they accidentally appear they soon cease to be, for they are either non-productive, or one or the other of the pure breeds speedily predominates, and the weaker disappears.[146]

Yet, on the other hand, his belief that races were fixed to their native climate led him to be profoundly anti-imperialist. It was no use seizing New Zealand, he cautioned, as 'no Saxon race can ever hold a colony long.'[147] His morality and sensibilities differed from the majority of polygenists, not least due to his unusual and profound secular pessimism. He deplored the excesses of colonialism and the destruction of the 'coloured' races, and was sure that the European races would be pushed out of the colonies eventually. Knox argued that all races were already 'perfect' in a sense, and none was intrinsically any better than any other. Moreover his commitment to 'transcendental anatomy', which saw in all creatures a 'unity of plan' and through which Knox felt all aspects of nature could be comprehended, meant that he believed that underlying

[142] John Arthur Roebuck, *Life and Letters of John Arthur Roebuck, with Chapters of Autobiography*, (ed.) Robert Leader, (London, 1897), pp. 156, 248, 300–01.
[143] Ruth Richardson, *Death, Dissection and the Destitute* (London, 1988), pp. 131–41; Evelleen Richards, 'The "Moral Anatomy" of Robert Knox: the Interplay between Biological and Social Thought in Victorian Scientific Naturalism', *Journal of the History of Biology*, 22 (1989), pp. 378–9.
[144] Knox, *Races of Man*, p. 429.
[145] Richards, 'The "Moral Anatomy" of Robert Knox', p. 390.
[146] Knox, *Races of Man*, 1850, pp. 65–6; also, ibid., pp. 48–9, 89, 148–9, 260–4, 346.
[147] Ibid., p. 222, also pp. 309, 471n.5.

nature there was an essential unity. But his was a 'doctrine of despair': 'Man's gift is to destroy', he wrote, 'not to create'.[148] He was convinced that a global war of races had already begun, and would continue so long as races existed.[149] So marginal and complex was Knox that he struggled even to gain membership of the ESL, who initially blackballed his application.[150]

The extreme ideas of Knox were also difficult to reconcile with widespread and popular notions that both Britain and England were themselves racially crossed. These were long-standing and common beliefs. Folklorist and antiquarian interest had ensured they remained popular, as is well seen in Walter Scott's *Ivanhoe*. This finishes with the marriage of Wilfred and Rowena, 'a pledge of the future peace and harmony betwixt two races [Norman and Saxon], which, since that period, have been so completely mingled that the distinction has become wholly invisible.'[151] For Scott, and most others, race crossing appeared to be simple fact. The Englishman was a breed 'more or less hybrid'.[152] For Scott this mixture was a good thing, a progress, where a 'hostile distinction' was erased and both sides benefitted: the Saxons lost their 'scorn', the Normans 'their rusticity', and the 'mixed language' that is English was born, a fruit of intermarriage.[153] Indeed, it was a commonplace to explain the superiority of the English as due to their racially crossed history, or to observe a 'struggle, silent and ceaseless', 'betwixt the genuine descendants of the ancient Celt—the Welsh, the Irish, and the Highlanders, of pure blood— and the more intelligent mixed races of England and Scotland.'[154] Previously popular views of English purity had, by the nineteenth century, become concentrated in certain circles, where there was a 'zeal for Anglo-Saxonism', particularly after mid-century.[155]

It was more difficult to dispute the racial crossings that had constituted the British: 'the mixture already taken place still goes on . . . the blood [is]

---

[148] I Richards, 'The "Moral Anatomy" of Robert Knox', p. 388; Knox, *Races of Man*, pp. 27–8; Knox, *Races of Man*, p. 464.

[149] Ibid., p. 348.

[150] James Hunt, 'On the Origin of the Anthropological Review', *Anthropological Review*, 6 (1868), p. 432; Richards, 'The "Moral Anatomy" of Robert Knox', pp. 409–11.

[151] Walter Scott, *Ivanhoe* (London, [1819] 1994), p. 515.

[152] Latham, *The Ethnology of the British Islands*, p. 260.

[153] Scott, *Ivanhoe*, p. 515; Asa Briggs, *Saxons, Normans and Victorians* (Hastings, 1966), p. 10.

[154] 'Destiny of the British Race', *The Phrenological Journal and Magazine of Moral Science*, n.s. 1 (1838), p. 376.

[155] Thompson, *Audi Alteram Partem*, 3, p. 121. Hugh A. MacDougall, *Racial Myth in English History: Trojans, Teutons, and Anglo-Saxons* (Hanover, New England, 1982), p. 3; cf. pp. 31–50; Curtis, *Anglo-Saxons and Celts*, p. 31.

in full flow'.[156] By and large this was simply a given. 'Romans first, then the Anglo-Saxons, Danes, Scandanavians, and the Normans, have min- gled their blood, habits and manners, and civilization, with those of the population which was aboriginal to Britain', noted one scholar. 'We are indeed a compound community.'[157] The basic narrative was outlined in the 1842 edition of *Encyclopaedia Brittanica*. This detailed how the Romans (in small numbers) came and drove the Celts 'into the interior and more inaccessible parts of the island', and this 'aboriginal population' was thus removed from the southern coasts making way for the later Teutonic or Gothic settlers. This later Saxon invasion, which aspired to political supremacy, did not have to deal with such a radical difference in 'physical conformation, habits, and customs'. The Saxons accordingly 'forebore from exterminating or utterly expelling the natives; a gradual amal- gamation took place'.[158]

In the majority of contemporary narratives about British and English pasts, writers identified racial 'intermarriage', 'mixtures' or 'amalgamation' that echoed those in certain colonies. The two cases were often differ- entiated, and the races involved in Britain were often declared to be similar or already related. Both the Celts and the Teutons, one writer declared, were 'Caucasians' (and the Caucasians 'were everywhere gaining the ascendancy, and slowly but surely renovating the population of the world').[159] Other factors, such as the British climate, were sometimes thrown in. It was instructive to compare North America with Britain. In Britain climate and the correct type and extent of mixture had combined to produce 'the finest known type of man'; yet too much mixture in North America, and a very different climate, meant that the American future was uncertain.[160]

The surface similarities between British and colonial race crossing ran deeper. As in New Zealand, in nineteenth-century Britain a political amalgamation was underway, drawing new elements into a central polity.[161] These surface similarities were mobilized in more profound ways, and the British historical experience was directly employed to

---

[156] Latham, *The Ethnology of the British Islands*, p. 259.
[157] Williams, *Distribution of the English Race of Men* (Swansea, 1859), pp. 4–5.
[158] [James Brown], 'Britain', *Encyclopaedia Brittanica*, 5, p. 295.
[159] 'New Zealand and its Recent Progress under Governor Grey', *Fraser's Magazine*, xxxix (1848), p. 89.
[160] Williams, *Distribution of the English Race of Men*, pp. 8–9, 64; also Latham, *The Ethnology of the British Islands*, p. 142.
[161] Keith Robbins, *Nineteenth-Century Britain: England, Scotland, and Wales; the Making of a Nation* (Oxford, 1988); Michael Hechter, *Internal Colonialism: The Celtic Fringe in British National Development 1536–1966* (London, 1975); Linda Colley, *Britons: Forging the Nation 1707–1837* (New Haven, 1992).

explain New Zealand. In Britain had not the ancient Britons been raised from barbarity by Roman colonization and race crossing? Even the vocabulary was revealing: the Victorians called the ancient Britons 'autochthones', 'indigenes' or 'aborigines'.[162] Writers told of how the Romans had rescued 'our aboriginal ['British'] fathers... from native barbarism'.[163] The Roman/British and British/Māori parallel was already well established by the 1840s.[164] Indeed, at times Roman and British imperialism were seen as so much a part of each other that they were confused. One writer tried to explain the New Zealand predicament through a story taken from Livy about 'Carthaginian colonists and the Numidian aborigines'. He unblushingly referred to the directions the Carthaginian colonists received from 'the colonial office in Rome'.[165] This was not just what Raymond Betts has called 'a heuristic reinforcement, a magnificent historical reference in a historically-conscious age'.[166] By analogy writers might find not only a common sense of development, but actual understanding: steeped in the ancients as many writers were, most knew more of ancient Rome than modern New Zealand. The racially mixed past was no less an obsession for many ancient historians than it was for their contemporary scholars of empire.[167]

The deep parallels between representations of the British and English racial pasts and that of New Zealand's were obvious. In particular, it became widely understood that New Zealand natives were themselves *already* a mixed race. This drew upon the common observation that there was, or had been, more than one race in New Zealand prior to European arrival. The earliest European voyagers suggested the idea of multiple 'native' races in New Zealand long prior to any European arrivals.[168] Most often this was interpreted as the two races authorities

---

[162] James Brown, 'Celtae', in Napier, (ed.), *Encyclopaedia Brittanica*, 6, p. 274; Piggott, *Celts, Saxons, and the Early Antiquaries*, pp. 15–16.
[163] Jameson, *New Zealand*, p. 266.
[164] Thompson, *Audi Alteram Partem*, 1, p. 29; Chamerovzow, *The New Zealand Question*, p. 15; Thomas Cholmondeley, *Ultima Thule; or, Thoughts Suggested by a Residence in New Zealand* (London, 1854); Charles Hursthouse, *New Zealand, or Zealandia, The Britain of the South* (London, 1857), 1, p. 155.
[165] 'New Zealand Colonization', *Christian Observer*, February 1838, p. 133.
[166] Raymond F. Betts, 'The Allusion to Rome in British Imperialist Thought of the Late Nineteenth Century and Early Twentieth Centuries', *Victorian Studies*, 15 (1971), p. 158.
[167] See, for instance, Ronald Hingley, *Roman Officers and English Gentlemen: the Imperial Origins of Roman Archaeology* (London, 2000), pp. 86–95.
[168] Julien Crozet, *Crozet's Voyage to Tasmania, New Zealand, the Ladrone Islands and the Philippines in 1771–1772*, (trans.) Henry Roth, (London, 1891), pp. 28–9. See especially J.M. Booth, 'A History of New Zealand Anthropology During the Nineteenth Century', MA thesis, University of New Zealand, 1949, pp. 17, 68–80; also M.P.K. Sorrenson, *Maori Origins and Migrations: the Genesis of some Pakeha Myths and Legends* (Auckland, 1979), p. 13.

were convinced could be found throughout the Pacific, one black and one brown.[169] John Lubbock, Thomas Huxley, Darwin, the Australian James Bonwick, the Frenchman Quatrefages and the American Charles Brace, amongst many, all thought there were two races in New Zealand. But there were very different explanations as to the history of these coexistent races. Robert Brown gave one rendition:

> The black division has frizzly hair, and appears to have been first . . . and the brown, or higher race, seems to have come afterwards, as conquerors: for, wherever we find the black and brown races of Oceanica together, we are sure to find the former occupying the interior, where they seem to have been driven by the more warlike brown people.[170]

This was strikingly parallel to most accounts of Britain's history, where the invading Romans were supposed to have pushed the primitive Celts into the fastnesses of Scotland and Wales. Indeed, often the 'brown' race of New Zealand was talked of as almost white, to some was even a 'master race'.[171] In other versions the two races actually lived together, and the brown race had become the chiefs and rulers, while the black race were the ruled.[172] In these instances, race *was* class. But a third kind of explanation, and by far the most common, was that the two races had mixed. This was, for instance, Charles Darwin's interpretation—that the Polynesians were a 'heterogeneous people . . . formed by the crossing of two distinct races, with few or no pure members left'.[173] Each of these types of narrative was homologous to narratives recounted about Britain, and the homology provided the ground for a complex traffic through which British and New Zealand histories could elucidate each other.

The idea of the already mixed New Zealand native was broadly convincing. Even detractors had to acknowledge that there were 'good grounds of conjecture', 'that the present inhabitants of New Zealand have sprung from two distinct races . . . a darker and inferior variety . . . and a later race, superior in intelligence and physical character, who . . . amalgamated

---

[169] See Nicholas Thomas, 'Melanesians and Polynesians: Ethnic Typifications Inside and Outside Anthropology', in his *In Oceania*, pp. 133–55; Nicholas Thomas, *Out of Time: History and Evolution in Anthropological Discourse* (Cambridge, 1989), pp. 29–32. The 'hard'/'soft' distinction is Smith's, *European Vision in the South Pacific*.

[170] Robert Brown, *The Races of Mankind*, 4 vols., (London, 1873–6), 2, pp. 14–15; cf. ibid., 2, p. 112.

[171] Smith, *The Human Species*, p. 231.

[172] Charles Loring Brace, *The Races of the Old World* (London, 1863), p. 161; John Lubbock, *Pre-historic Times* (London, 1865), pp. 355–65; Quatrefages, *The Human Species*, pp. 197–8; Wood, *The Natural History of Man*, 2, pp. 107, 110.

[173] Darwin, *Descent of Man*, 1, p. 241.

with the aborigines.'[174] The racial narrative was made hierarchical, and was also frequently construed in terms of conquest.[175] Joel Polack, an early trader in New Zealand, described at length how the 'dark brown... well formed... muscular' race had overwhelmed a 'second and inferior race' that was woolly haired and 'brown-black' Polack even called the modern aborigine a 'mulatto race', on account not only of their skin colour but of their mixed or amalgamated origins.[176] Many others described the situation in the same or similar way.

This interpretation gained a new potency when it was correlated with the moa, an extinct giant bird (perhaps over 12 feet high) whose remains were found in New Zealand. The first discoveries were in the 1830s, and Richard Owen famously deduced the size and nature of the moa (or *Dinornis*) from a small fragment of bone brought from New Zealand in 1840 (though only after a surgeon connected with the New Zealand Company had forcefully insisted to him that the bone was from a bird). The reconstructed moa became emblematic of New Zealand, which became the land of the moa and the 'Māori', two exotic and strange beings. When it became apparent, from the late 1840s, that people had hunted some species of moa to extinction, it became an easy interpretive step to associate those who had killed moa with this first primitive race.[177] 'I shall call the race which was contemporary with the Dinornis', the prominent New Zealand-based geologist Julius von Haast announced, 'Moa-hunters.'[178] Haast was confident in 'the fact that the Maories are a mixed race, in which Malayan, Papuan, and (in a minor degree) Mongolian blood are apparently blended', and that a later group of arrivals had overtaken and amalgamated with the Moa-hunters.'[179] News of Haast's Moa-hunters travelled quickly, and found considerable support.[180]

A narrative familiar to both settlers and those in Britain was mobilized to account for New Zealand, and was quickly current in places as far removed from the academy as *The Times*. The new racial narrative disturbed not only

[174] Angas, *Savage Life and Scenes*, 1, p. 305.
[175] Power, *Sketches in New Zealand*, p. 143.
[176] J.S. Polack, *Manners and Customs of the New Zealanders; with Notes Corroborative of Their Habits, Usages, etc.*, 2 vols., (London, 1840), 1, pp. 6, 9.
[177] Walter Mantell discovered the cooked moa bones in 1847. Gideon Mantell, 'Notice of the Remains of the Dinornis and Other Birds', *The Quarterly Journal of the Geological Society of London*, August 1850, p. 339.
[178] Julius Haast, 'On certain Prehistoric Remains discovered in New Zealand, and on the Nature of the Deposits in which they occurred', *Journal of the Ethnological Society* (*JES*), 2 (New Series) (1869–70), p. 391. *Nature*, 27 January 1870, p. 391.
[179] Haast, 'Prehistoric Remains discovered in New Zealand', p. 110.
[180] 'Miscellaneous', *NHR*, n.s. 5 (1865), p. 282. *Correspondence of Charles Darwin*, x, p. 592: Haast to Darwin, 9 December 1862; Ibid., xi, p. 208: Darwin to Lyell, 6 March 1863.

other scholarly accounts, but more popular ones. It was also deployed with a specific gravity, as it was used to undermine Tangata Whenua claims to indigenousness and even to property. A *Times* editorial read:

> The title of the New Zealanders to their land is simply that of any savage to the soil on which he happens to be found. In the case of the Maoris, we happen to know that they came within the last hundred years to the spot where we now find them, and there, after killing and eating the former proprietors, established themselves by forcible possession. . . . English lords who did in past times what the Maoris habitually do now, were pretty sure to lose both their estates and their lives altogether.[181]

Politically charged, the prehistoric New Zealander could be mobilized to influence public opinion and to justify policy (in this case, the confiscation of several million acres of land from Waikato *hapū* after the Waikato War).[182] What cause for complaint was there if the natives had themselves dispossessed a different race, 'an inferior people, whom they hunted down like wild beasts'?[183]

Such interpretative manoeuvres, Ranginui Walker has argued, were colonial ideological responses which endured as an 'endorsement of colonisation and Pakeha dominance'.[184] Certainly they were that, but they were not only, nor even primarily, that. For one thing they hinged on a British domestic racial past that had not yet naturalized *English* dominance: the discovery of homologies or parallel situations, whether overseas or in the past, actually aided the domestic racial project. For another, these narratives of the prehistoric New Zealanders or Moa-hunters were not universally accepted. As Atholl Anderson and John Andrews have shown, Haast's 'Moa-hunters' were rebutted by James Hector, the most senior government geologist, and a man well connected in Britain.[185] Hector argued that Haast had misinterpreted key evidence, and this conflict initiated an intense controversy, one in which the Royal Society eventually intervened. The result was important, as Haast was chastened, and retreated from his position on the Moa-hunters.[186] The idea has had little 'scientific' or scholarly credibility since, and had been openly and quickly contradicted by the most senior official colonial expert. Yet it is telling that the idea remained current amongst laypersons (even to this day, in some quarters), and was to be reinvigorated around the turn of

---

[181] *The Times*, 23 September 1865. [182] See next chapter.
[183] Frederic W. Farrar, 'Aptitudes of Races', *TES*, 5 (New Series) (1867), p. 117.
[184] Walker, *Ka Whawhai Tonu Matou*, p. 42.
[185] Anderson, *Prodigious Birds*; John Andrews, *The Southern Ark: Zoological Discovery in New Zealand, 1769–1900* (London, 1987).
[186] Jacob Gruber, 'The Moa and the Professionalising of New Zealand Science', *Turnbull Library Record*, 20 (1987), pp. 61–100.

the century, transformed into the persistent illusion of the prehistoric
'Moriori'—a new iteration of a race prior to 'Māori'—despite never again
being integral to official or scientific calculations.[187]

*****

Perhaps the most striking thing that a study of racial crossing reveals about
these myriad discussions is the absence of indigenous or other colonized
actors. This was entirely consistent with the texture of scholarly and
scientific debate, which was understood to be, and constructed as, a
topography of internal conversations. It is doubtful there would have
been indigenous agency or voice even had 'natives' turned up to meetings
and spoken or voted. When the runaway US slave and noted orator William
Craft spoke at the Anthropological Society, his poignant and powerful
oration was followed by a discussion where he was analysed as if he
were an exhibit, and his intellectual and personal faculties dissected as if
he were mute or absent.[188] There is no reason to think that 'aborigines'
would have fared any differently; as far as Society members were concerned,
the role of Craft, as with that of 'natives', was to be put into discourse, not to
create or shape it. An encounter with living people of other races paralleled
encounters in textual forms—as occasions needing translation or transcrip-
tion or analysis: conversion into what was legible and recognizable.

    To try to resurrect indigenous agency from the writings and discourses
of these societies is misleading. The discursive silence reflects an absence
in place and power. There were no indigenous voices present in these
places, and what visibility or legibility there was came only after they were
subjected to editing, editorializing and translation—after they had been
converted, for instance, from Tangata Whenua to 'aborigines'. These
societies profoundly excluded indigenous people from both their physical
and subjective spaces; the few 'Others' that entered, such as Craft, were
subject to the most rigorous and searching regulation, recontextualization
and representation. It is necessary to comprehend the profundity of the
'pragmatics of social space' in this instance, for the exclusion of indigenous
participation in meetings, correspondence and other readerly and writerly
networks was definitive. Without question 'natives' could speak, but
they would not be speaking at the BAAS or the RGS, and even if they
had, they would not have been heard.

---

[187] It was reinvigorated primarily by the scholars associated with S. Percy Smith. See
Ranginui Walker, *Ka Whawhai Tonu Matou: Struggle Without End* (Auckland, 1990),
pp. 39–42.
[188] 'We can find nothing in Mr Craft's paper on "Dahomey" which is worth
printing.... Mr Craft has a certain amount of African blood in his veins, and this must
influence his innate ideas.' *AR*, 1 (1863), p. 462.

These scholarly societies and conversations were not realms in which indigenous people frequently desired to take action; indeed, they were all but unknown to most. Nor, this chapter has argued, were they places that were very often tactically or strategically important for colonialism—it was hardly a faulty analysis of colonialism to ignore them. These scholarly and scientific social spaces were exclusive, and excluded the majority of voices, not just indigenous ones. The growth of radical science and scholarship was one response to this, and in many respects, perhaps even with regard to race crossing, this radical domain was more significant than its mainstream counterparts. But the societies and discourses shared some common features: they congregated certain kinds of people, concentrated their ideas, disciplined their thought and writing, and regulated their language and forms of discourse; they organized the circulation of discourse; and they cordoned off certain locations from others.

These distinctions made visible the substantial divide between the significantly closed circles of colonial governance and the public and private circuits of science and scholarship. The traffic between the two kinds of space was regulated and disciplined not by scientists and scholars but by officials, as was only too apparent in the Colonial Office's choice to maintain a link to the RGS, for instance, and share nothing with the ESL. These processes were governed by the rules, proprieties and sensibilities of office: the discursive centrality of law and policy, and practicalities such as expense and distance. Other connections were still possible by navigating private, personal relationships, subject to the mores of individuals and the colonial service. The other, critical but intangible, overlap was in the shaping of the subjectivities of colonial officials, particularly their religious, historical, reformist, legal sensibilities.

The terrain over which discourses about racial crossing circulated was a myriad of fragmented and uneven fields. Discourses were grounded in complicated but specific ways, and no single coherent approach to the problem of race crossing could emerge. Between scholarly societies, not least the ASL and ESL, but also within them, there was a great deal of variation. Critical texts, or developments, not least the publication of *Origin of Species* or the collapse of radicalism after 1848, were consequently of limited impact beyond certain spaces, and their meaning differed from place to place. After Prichard, no single text, nor any single person or society, could claim authority over multiple audiences and societies. The increasingly technical complexity of scientific writing about race might have helped moderate the controversy that had previously accompanied their topics, making them seem less emotive and more exacting. This symbolized new boundaries in knowledge, and signified communities of knowledge—smaller and more specialized. But it also ensured that other audiences, not least the Colonial Office and various nineteenth-century publics, came to consider little of what these communities knew to be of 'practical' use. In such instances the social geography of empire and the 'pragmatics of social space' were regularly vital.

The discourses of racial crossing that bore the most resemblance to official discourses were to be found broadly in shared discourses about history and race. Because these discourses bridged different constituencies and societies, they were able to concatenate different places into discursive spaces in ways that eluded the more specialized and active communities, such as the scholarly societies. These larger constituencies agreed that racial crossing did not result in infertility and was not intrinsically degenerative. They posited crossing as a means of improvement or reform, a means consonant with the preoccupations of colonial and imperial politics, and compatible with contemporary empire, and undergirded by (as well as undergirding) the domestic racial project of amalgamating Britain. This is not to say that colonial rule and discourse was somehow softer or more humane just because the more virulent rhetoric of racism was concentrated in a few, visible but distinct, locations. Just as the most stark and violent forms of race might make their proponents anti-imperialists (such as Robert Knox), more gradated, nuanced and mobile approaches to race, which emphasized the improving potential of racial crossing, could be (and were) taken as invitations to colonize, and to colonize aggressively. The apparently humane position with regard to race crossing that prevailed in key places in the Empire was proof of this: acknowledgement of the viability and desirability of racial amalgamation (or even crossing more generally) was commonly accompanied by a commitment to expansive and intensive colonization. Such 'liberal' views on race, then, were integral parts of Liberal views of empire. As was apparent in the discourse and governance of New Zealand, racial crossing (and in particular, racial amalgamation) could easily be separated from the mutuality that characterized some of the radical thought about crossing. The amalgamated community of the colonial future would encompass natives or aboriginals, but would not be constituted by them in any substantial way. Rather, crossing could become a method of erasure, extinction by quieter racial mechanisms, naturalized in historical, scholarly and scientific ways.

5

A Tender Way in Race War

'It is time', declared *The Times* of London in 1863, 'to consider whether the English or the Maories are to be masters of New Zealand.' By then the wars in New Zealand were over two years old, their scale was becoming apparent, and the costs to Britain were becoming public. At least 700,000 imperial pounds, and perhaps as much as 1.5 million, had already been spent, and there was no end in sight to the fighting (which, as it turned out, continued into 1872). These years were tough enough for the imperial treasury, still dealing with the Indian Mutiny and about to contend with a coterie of other imperial troubles from Jamaica to Canada. Now war in New Zealand was being ramped up to an unprecedented scale. War was proving intensive and expensive, and it seemed the policies and precepts that had characterized racial amalgamation had been abandoned. This was 'the first great conflict of the races', cautioned *The Times*, likely 'also to be the final struggle between them.'[1]

But race war in New Zealand did not end colonial and imperial aspirations for racial amalgamation.[2] Rather than simply receding from war and its multiple setbacks and difficulties, the project of racial amalgamation evolved. War disrupted many aspects of colonial government, and in the short term sharply hampered some dimensions of racial amalgamation.[3] But more broadly, and over the longer term, the wars had an opposite effect. Racial amalgamation transformed: a decade of war provided the settings through which racial amalgamation was reconfigured and revivified, expanded and intensified. War extended the provinces of colonial government, claiming new jurisdictions and territories, and leaving its mark in new places. Whatever else the wars undoubtedly were, they were also wars *of* racial amalgamation.

---

[1] *The Times*, 23 October 1863, 19 November 1863, 15 March 1862.
[2] Dalton, *War and Politics in New Zealand*, p. 179.
[3] Sorrenson, 'Maori and Pakeha', p. 157.

During the war years there was a pronounced change in colonial conceptions of racial amalgamation. The perceived failures of two decades of colonial government were not as often laid on the policy of racial amalgamation per se, but rather on the failings of either officials or natives, or both. Racial amalgamation, settlers consistently argued, would only work if officials got out of the way and natives behaved as they were supposed to. Most settlers, though far from all, continued to attend the broad church of racial amalgamation, and most alternatives were not held to be moral or proper, although they might be expedient. Indeed, settlers castigated natives for not recognizing colonial beneficence, for not conforming to colonial logics. Officials were castigated for not 'amalgamating' when they might have, particularly for standing between the proper intercourse of natives and settlers. As a result a fundamental reconfiguring of the timing and forms of racial amalgamation was widely apparent. In these new settler iterations racial amalgamation appeared more like the 'admission' of natives to a reified colonial society, and native incorporation into the colonial polity was increasingly moved into the future (often the distant future). The war made explicit what had often been implicit: native *admission* became conditional on native *submission*, and as a result racial war could become integral, not antithetical, to this end. The waging of war could assuage both critics and proponents of racial amalgamation.

Proponents of colonialism in New Zealand had claimed it was to be 'reformed', even gentle, not least due to its strategy of racial amalgamation. In this racially amalgamating, reformed colonization, it was widely understood that the British Empire had dealt (as *The Times* put it) 'much more tenderly with the New Zealand natives than the first American colonists ever did with the redskins'. Yet, it was ominously lamented, 'we have nursed them into dangerous enemies in much less time.'[4] The imagery was revealing: a feminized colonialism, tender and nursing, with relationships of intimacy and kinship, had both failed and been betrayed. These analyses and moments seemed to invite a re-visioning of racial amalgamation, one that recalibrated its processes, if not its ends and central assumptions. Racial amalgamation might still be operable, but required new masculine and muscular trajectories, less inclined to spoil the child. These new views could integrate violence with the aspects of 'tender' colonialism: there could be a tender way in wars of race.

Colonial understandings of race war, like those of race, were expansive, and encompassed the intimate and domestic, not merely the political or military. The conduct of race war could include natural, political and

---

[4] *The Times*, 19 November 1863.

cultural acts, projects on small and massive scale, material developments as well as those aimed at sentiments. As a result colonial war-making was kaleidoscopic, operating in different but interconnecting modalities and domains. Political language might oscillate between larger strategies of policy and the most intimate details of colonial and native life. One loud critic of the governor, for instance, railed that he had wasted 'every chance of a mixture of the races'. Had Sir George Grey worked to 'save' natives? 'Did he sanction the amalgamation of the races?' In this critic's eyes the signal proof of Grey's failure was not some large-scale anti-amalgamation policy, not the war violence nor the ensuing land confiscations, but the case of 'Widow Meurant'. Grey had failed to secure land title for Eliza Meurant (Kenehuru) and her half-caste children, lands given by their *whānau*.[5] These were expansive understandings of colonial conflicts, where the quotidian was inseparable from the official or the gubernatorial. Such conditions require a measuring of the ways in which colonial warfare, as race war, was not just political and military, but a conjuncture of the political, economic, social, cultural and domestic.

Throughout the Empire a variety of local wars were understood as 'wars of race', and this frame of 'racial war' served as a way of organizing and integrating diverse imperial conflicts. 'As I write', lamented one English commentator in 1866, 'English soldiers are in the field in four distinct wars of race in as many great divisions of the globe.'[6] Crucially, these 'wars of race' were also understood in terms at once expansive and intimate: never entirely, or even centrally, about military campaigns and actual fighting. Race shaped not just how these wars were depicted and understood, but how they were fought. Supposedly 'natural' or innate differences, racial sentiments, climate, social forms and economy were all actors in race war, which in many instances encompassed the oft-predicted 'extinction' of certain races.[7] The discourses of 'race war' shaped local understandings and practices. Racial amalgamation remained a powerful alternative to ceaseless race war, yet one that likewise promised an end to race war, through the erasure of a race. Merivale's tender 'euthanasia of savage communities' encapsulated this vision, but racial amalgamation was still subject to rigorous critique. One radical MP dismissed it as a 'transcendental scheme', that was weak, ineffective and belabouring the necessary: 'the sooner the Maori is destroyed', he blasted in the imperial

---

[5] *Daily Southern Cross*, 14 December 1867.
[6] Frederic Harrison, 'England and France', in *International Policy: Essays on the Foreign Relations of England*, (London, 1866), p. 104; also, for example, Parris to Rolleston, 7 February 1866, in Ward, *A Show of Justice*, p. 194.
[7] Brantlinger, Patrick, 'Victorians and Africans: the Genealogy of the Myth of the Dark Continent', *Critical Inquiry*, 12 (1985), pp. 166–203.

parliament, 'the better.'[8] As race war became increasingly understood to be the reality in New Zealand, contention turned to the meaning of this violence: would it be directed towards annihilating the race or could it facilitate 'tender' colonialism, as envisaged in racial amalgamation. The questions were not just about political or military strategy, but the direction and future of colonialism. As one colonial agent wrote, the New Zealand situation had 'forced the Government into a war of extermination and the natives into a desperate struggle for existence.'[9] The discourses of race war made colonial war appear to be existential.

War, and the project of colonizing New Zealand and its 'natives', seemed all encompassing, consuming much of the energy and resources of officials and settlers. As one settler bemoaned, 'even the expense and manner of paving the footpaths of Auckland, like every other sublunary question affecting this wonderful colony, merges into the "native question".'[10] Colonialism spanned the lives not just of natives but of settlers, and settler footpaths really were entangled with colonial battlefields and indigenous homes. Earlier attempts to discipline and shape indigenous groups, subjectivities and polities had seen limited results. The renewal of war went forward with the renewal of these ambitions, now augmented by both new techniques and capacity for governance and violence. Only a few years earlier there were many dimensions of indigenous life that were left undisturbed by colonial rule, but during and immediately after the wars this began, mostly, to rapidly change. Many lands, populations, practices, property and subjectivities which colonial government had previously either been unable or unwilling to engage commonly became targets for official and private wartime operations. Interventions into the quotidian, domestic and intimate dimensions of indigenous societies were no longer fleeting or occasional, but systematized, if far from universal or effective.

Colonial officials and settlers already regarded violence as a routine dimension of colonialism. This was in keeping with Britain itself where, as historians have observed, violence was accepted as a legitimate political technique, and the 'worshipping of force' was commonplace.[11] Recognizing these imperial actualities reminds us that the wars in New Zealand should not be reckoned as failures in the policy of racial amalgamation or even in native policy more generally. The New Zealand Wars did not tragically end a prior period of peace or coexistence between colonialism

---

[8] J.A. Roebuck, in *The Times*, 15 March 1862.
[9] J.E. Gorst to *The Times*, 17 December 1863: reprinted in *Nelson Examiner*, 5 March 1864.
[10] *Daily Southern Cross*, 5 November 1862.
[11] Walter E. Houghton, *The Victorian Frame of Mind, 1830–1870* (New Haven, 1985), pp. 196–217.

and indigenous groups, nor close a window on a 'better' colonialism. Agents of the British Empire had practised violence for a variety of symbolic and instrumental reasons—to demonstrate, communicate, discipline, coerce and interact—since first encountering the islands' peoples. Military and paramilitary colonial violence was not constant or inevitable, but it was ordinary. The central debate that has occupied historians regarding the New Zealand Wars—whether they were wars of sovereignty, 'New Zealand Wars', or wars to acquire resources, 'Land Wars'—struggles to take this into account.[12] These conversations delimit 'war' as a subject that excludes the ongoing practices of colonial and imperial violence that were integral to colonialism. Violence was only a policy of 'last resort' in the discourses of colonizers who could conveniently define where the 'last resort' began. The 'origins' of the New Zealand Wars lie as much in ordinary practices of colonialism as in specific political aims or policies.

Operationally the Wars can be divided into an overlapping sequence of five or six major wars or campaigns. Chronologically the first was the Taranaki War, which lasted from March 1860 to March 1861. The immediate cause of war was the purchase of a piece of land by the Crown, which Wiremu Kīngi Te Rangitāke (William King) had opposed. Kingi began with not more than 300 warriors, and his Te Āti Awa people were later joined by Taranaki and Ngāti Ruanui, adding another 400 or 500. This compared with the initial 800 that the British had, which by June 1860 was nearly 2,000 and by the end of the war was perhaps 3,500.[13] This conflict was not the quick, obvious victory which had been desired, and its indecisiveness was at least partly responsible for Governor Gore Browne being replaced by Sir George Grey, who became (for the second time) governor of New Zealand. It was Grey who engineered the invasion of the Waikato, which began what was to be the largest and most important of the wars, generally known as the Waikato War (July 1863 to April 1864), where the colonial enemy was the largest of all pan-tribal indigenous polities, the King Movement or Kīngitanga. The invasion of the Waikato, which pitted the British Queen against the Maori King, was interpolated with other smaller conflicts, most importantly a war on the east coast near Tauranga.

Three more protracted wars followed, which are often named for the respective leaders of colonial opposition: Te Ua Haumene (1864–1868),

[12] The key texts are Keith Sinclair, *Origins of the Maori Wars* (Wellington, 1957); Alan Ward, 'The Origins of the Anglo-Maori Wars: A Reconsideration', *New Zealand Journal of History*, 1 (1967), pp. 148–70; Belich, *The New Zealand Wars*. Belich has also attracted some strong, but unsophisticated, criticism, e.g. Matthew Wright, *Two Peoples, One Land: the New Zealand Wars* (Auckland, 2006).
[13] Belich, *New Zealand Wars*, p. 82.

Riwha Titokowaru (June 1868 to February 1869) and Te Kooti (June 1868 to *circa* May 1872). These were different in kind from earlier engagements. Particularly against Te Kooti, fighting was often less dependent on major earthworks and military setpieces. Titokowaru, argues James Belich, was the most successful of all indigenous military leaders, and he (to a limited extent), Te Kooti and Te Ua were religious leaders as well. By the time of these later wars the bulk of imperial troops had gone. Gone, too, was the indigenous unity that had been palpable during the Waikato War, and again substantial contingents of Tangata Whenua fought against those opposing the Crown. Te Ua was not actively involved in the fighting, although the new religion he fostered, Pai Mārire, inspired followers on both the east and west coast of the North Island, which the government answered militarily. Te Kooti founded his own religion, Ringatū, and Titokowaru's leadership was also spiritual.[14] Te Kooti and Titokowaru had much smaller armies, no more than a few hundred for Titokowaru, and smaller still in the case of Te Kooti. But the opposing forces too were smaller, sometimes a little over 1,000, and by then, after the departure of the imperial troops, dependent on colonial militia and other *hapū* to make up their numbers. Neither Te Kooti nor Titokowaru was captured during the course of the wars, and in late 1868, having to fight two wars at once, colonial New Zealand was stretched to breaking point.

The Wars occasioned a fundamental shift from imperial to colonial (and 'self') government. Before and during the Wars, governors, settlers and colonial officials regularly butted against the limits of their rule, not just at the boundaries with natives, but with each other. The Wars began under the aegis of colonial governors, but ended in a politically remade, largely self-governing, colony. The changes in the understanding of, and plans for, racial amalgamation were packaged with these many changes. When Thomas Gore Browne arrived to be governor in 1855, a central charge of his was the implementation of the 1852 Constitution Act, one that empowered settler government but which also gestured towards formalizing native self-government. Browne quickly realized that racial amalgamation was not going as Grey's progress reports had suggested, and that the prospects for closely governing natives seemed poor.[15] Government, he complained, did not so much rule indigenous people and

[14] On *Ringatu*, see Judith Binney, *Redemption Songs: a Life of Te Kooti Arikirangi Te Turuki* (Auckland, 1995); William Greenwood, 'The Upraised Hand', *JPS*, 51 (1942), pp. 1–81; Bronwyn Elsmore, *Mana from Heaven: a Century of Maori Prophets in New Zealand* (Tauranga, 1989).
[15] PP 1860, xxxviii (2719), p. 194: Gore Browne to Labouchere, 15 April 1856.

communities but 'conducts its relations with the Native Tribes by occasional *negociation* [*sic*]'.[16] Native self-government did not need to be created, as implied in the 1852 Constitution Act: it was still the case, de facto. The problem for Gore Browne, then, was less the creation or regulation of native self-government, but the reduction of indigenous independence into forms and subjects that were within the ambit of colonial government.

On many occasions the Colonial Office had found New Zealand's settlers as unruly and intractable as its 'natives'. But unlike 'natives', settlers had leverage in the imperial parliament, a voice in the metropolitan press, and a broadly recognized claim on colonial rule. It was becoming clear that imperial compromises with settler demands had proven both ineffective and enormously expensive, and the transfer of further political powers to settlers, especially control of 'native affairs', was initiated. This had strong metropolitan criticisms, uniting church and Colonial Office elements, who knew that it would 'appear to the Natives that the Queen is delivering them over to the rule of the "Pakeha".'[17]

The 'rule of the "Pakeha"' concretized the political exclusions and inclusions that defined racial amalgamation's enduring local forms. It concentrated colonial rule in the franchise of propertied white male colonists, but did not restrict it to them. Critically, 'native' men were enfranchised in limited and limiting ways through the 1867 Maori Representation Act. The limits were clear in the allotment of four parliamentary seats, which if they had been assigned in accordance to proportion of population would have been around fourteen to sixteen. Many in Parliament also expressed their preference that Maori would elect 'European' members to represent them, a development largely avoided because of fears about what *kind* of Europeans might then come to Parliament. The measure itself was intended to be temporary, and its purpose was largely for Parliament to work on native communities rather than the new MPs to be effective in Parliament.[18] In Parliament the small native delegation could be at once quarantined and encircled. Enfranchisement, meanwhile, claimed indigenous political leaders and ambitions as subjects of colonial authority, and appropriated them to new colonial systems of credentialling and conducting native politics. This was both a model for, and centerpiece of, racial amalgamation: a strategy of incorporation organized through racial difference, a provisional political means of erasing 'the native'. These

[16] CO 209/156, fo. 168: Fortescue, memo, 12 March 1861.
[17] CO 209/156, fo. 131: Chichester Fortescue, 21 February 1861.
[18] For the most recent treatment, see Neill Atkinson, *Adventures in Democracy: a History of the Vote in New Zealand* (Dunedin, 2003), pp. 47–51.

political means conjoined violent and institutional ones, and the settler men who had been at once both colonizers and (in some ways) colonized, decolonized themselves by claiming and intensifying their colonization of 'natives'.

When Grey returned as governor in 1861, he consolidated dual campaigns: one prepared for a massive military campaign, while the other was a programme of 'new institutions'.[19] These were not contradictory efforts, but harmonized both violent and 'tender' colonial strategies. For instance, at the same time as roads were constructed to enable the invasion of indigenous territory, Grey promised to empower *runanga* (councils) and put under them the control of roads, medical care and schools.[20] The tender and violent modalities of racial war both worked on targets consistent with the larger project of racial amalgamation. For two decades the colonial norm had generally been that natives would voluntarily amalgamate themselves on largely colonial terms, but by the 1860s the voluntarism of racial amalgamation was increasingly dispensable. Grey told a meeting of northern *rangatira* that he proposed to establish law and order throughout the country, and 'to put the country into such a condition that it may be possible for Europeans and Maories [*sic*] to mix with one another and mutually benefit each other.'[21] Such 'mutual' benefits, as before, were not mutually decided upon, but were familiar encodings of racial amalgamation.

Racial amalgamation had not previously been so closely and openly connected to colonial violence. This invited new and acute problems, particularly when colonial efforts, which appeared to depend on willing sentiments amongst 'natives', were so clearly articulated with instruments of force and violence. Violence might disaffect those whom it was directed at and transform those who practised it. A central fear, voiced time and again in official circles, in both London and the colony, was that unless settlers adopted the proper approach the war would descend into a 'war of extermination'. 'The colonist', cautioned the *Pall Mall Gazette*, 'takes possession of a land, hitherto occupied by another race, and his first anxiety is to sweep that race off the face of the earth.'[22] Only cool and good government could temper such hotness, and few officials anticipated such qualities would characterize the 'rule of the "Pakeha"'.

[19] Lachy Paterson, *Colonial Discourses: Niupepa Maori, 1855–1863* (Dunedin, 2006), pp. 178–83; Ward, *A Show of Justice*.
[20] MA 1 1861/150: [Drafted by Gorst], memo, 6 November 1861.
[21] Ibid., Memo, 7 November 1861.
[22] *Daily Southern Cross*, 16 November 1868.

Tensions between officials and settlers were long-standing, but the war drew attention to the struggles not only with indigenous polities and subjectivities, but the politics and subjectivities of settlers. 'Natives' were by no means always the most difficult people, and there was often a stark contrast between imperial and colonial officials, who were often sympathetic to 'natives', and the public sentiments of settlers. Settlers had often advocated the intensifying of colonial violence, and it was easy to discern among them a visceral hostility towards natives, whom they frequently called 'niggers' or 'bloody Maories'. 'This epithet [nigger]', mourned one critical voice, 'is freely applied to the natives of New Zealand by colonists, and even by the officers of our regiments.'[23] In these developments the racial organization of colonialism could ally with ordinary racial affect amongst settlers. Moreover, by the 1860s there were many colonial publics where such language and sentiments could be freely expressed and shared. Settlers could happily use the word 'nigger' at public meetings, and papers could defend the use of the word by doubting if more than twenty natives 'would know what "nigger" meant'.[24] These sentiments infused the practices of colonial life and neither began nor ended on the battle-field. In one dramatic instance, a group of indigenous prisoners of war was so severely harassed by settlers that the Bishop of New Zealand had to physically defend them. This did not stop the crowd, and 'so enraged were the people that they would have done [Bishop Selwyn] some bodily harm had not some of the more respectable people come to his assistance.'[25] Racial abuse, taunting and other forms of personal harassment and intimidation were common experiences of Tangata Whenua who ventured into colonial towns.[26] In Auckland Tangata Whenua (including those allied with the Queen) were so indiscriminately abused during the Waikato War, and the lead-up to it, that notices were hung instructing settlers to treat them with civility.[27] By 1864 the killing of wounded Tangata Whenua was widespread and widely known about, yet any public discussions of it centred on settler justifications or denials, or extravagant counter depictions of native savagery.[28]

---

[23] J.E. Gorst, letter to *The Times*, 17 December 1863 and widely reprinted in the colonial press.

[24] Mr Upjohn, in *Taranaki Herald*, 19 July 1862; ibid., 5 March 1864.

[25] Mandeno, 'Journal', p. 31: 4 August 1863.

[26] Grey Letters, N1(5): Newcastle to Grey, 26 May 1862; Ward, 'The Origins of the Anglo-Maori Wars', pp. 160, 163–4; Sinclair, *Origin of the Maori Wars*, passim; J.E. Alexander, in APS, *Annual Report*, 1871, p. 11.

[27] Alexander, *Incidents of the Maori War*, p. 126.

[28] John Bilcliffe, *'Well Done the 68th': the Story of a Regiment* (Chippenham, 1995), p. 175: Grace, diary, 13 March 1865; Scholefield (ed.), *Richmond-Atkinson Papers*, 2, p. 125: A.S. Atkinson, journal, 8 October 1864. See the controversy around the letter by

Settlers were routinely inflammatory, comparing natives with former slaves in Jamaica and finding them wanting, or pushing for soldiers, armaments and war. The first basis of peace, the settler Charles Southwell opined, should be Wiremu Kingi's head.[29] One official confessed he was too ashamed to take indigenous leaders with him to Auckland because of how they would be treated, and when Wiremu Tāmihana went to Auckland in an attempt to avert the Waikato War, he was treated appallingly.[30] As one settler remembered:

> The Pakeha travelled through Maori country enjoying the most distinguished hospitality; the Maori who stayed in a Pakeha township had to pay for his entertainment at a public-house. The great chiefs commanded in their settlements the respect due to sovereignty and blue blood; in the Pakeha streets they were niggers.[31]

These settler sentiments were obvious to many Tangata Whenua. As Governor Browne observed, indigenous leaders 'see that if amalgamated with the English they must take their place only among the lower ranks, and they observe that a chief, however great his rank may be among themselves, is made of no account when he visits the English towns.'[32] A key challenge remained for colonial government: how could they make war and keep racial amalgamation. The Wars presented a critical conjuncture for colonialism in New Zealand, and the practices of the British Empire more generally. Could a violent, aggressive colonial war advance a wider colonial project that had cast itself as reformed, even gentle? Could war be a humane 'euthanasia of savage communities' and not a savage butchery?

As the centre of gravity in New Zealand's colonialism passed from imperial officials to settlers, the future of racial amalgamation was negotiable. Many Tangata Whenua had already noticed the important differences between 'New' and 'Old Pākehā', and this move was substantiated with the constitution of the 'rule of the Pākehā'. That this crystallized new developments amongst Tangata Whenua was not accidental. Indigenous people and groups had been very far from standing still, and now, in moments of crisis, activated new networks of indigenous politics and publics. In unprecedented ways indigenous relations were remaking communities, polities, *hapū* and other kin relations to form new alignments. But colonialism was proving innovative and ambitious also. The Wars

'Exterminate' suggesting such an incident: 27 November to 3 December 1868, *Daily Southern Cross*.

[29] *Auckland Examiner*, 21 April 1860.
[30] Gorst, *The Maori King*, pp. 50–51.
[31] R.A. Loughnan, *New Zealand at Home* (London, 1908), p. 195.
[32] CO 209/145, fo. 131: Gore Browne to Labouchere, 18 February 1858.

demonstrated the breadth of its ambitions for governing indigenous people and groups. The Wars were not simply assaults on the boundaries or edges of indigenous societies, nor even just their lands or territories: a new horizon of targets opened up, as war advanced colonial claims on indigenous hearths and homesteads. These new horizons converged, disproportionately, on racial crossings.

'DANGEROUS PROXIMITY'

The Wars were a workshop for many of the larger and sustained projects of racial amalgamation. The decade of war forged the new self-governing colonial polity, critically shaped settler subjectivities and institutions, all while violently engaging indigenous communities and economies, in many cases expropriating their territory and property. Half-castes and racially mixed families were not the only targets of these discursive, military and governmental operations, but they were concentrated fields of such activity, and the racialized modalities of colonialism and war produced them not only as targets but as subjects. The wartime operations of colonial warfare and politics literally reclaimed many of these half-castes and mixed families and rendered them safe as a strategy of colonialism— reinvigorating racial amalgamation and defusing the prospects of curtailed colonial rule and integration of settlers into indigenous communities (derided earlier as 'pandemonium'). This necessarily coincided with assaults on indigenous independence. The Wars critically advanced the colonial racial order, clarifying colonial categories and substantially inscribing them in the actualities of colonial life. Invasive colonial prac- tices were pushed into the realm of the hearth, and colonial institutes and practices began to contest not only indigenous politics but one of their key animating forces—*whanaungatanga* (family relationships, kinship, sense of family connection and responsibility).

At the start of the 1860s many of colonialism's categories in New Zealand were more prescriptive than descriptive. People, land, property and discourse did not fall so easily into the kind of legible, monochrome categories that were pivotal in governmental discourse. Individuals and groups of people were not generally ordered in ways that were demon- strably or unequivocally 'racial'. The crucibles of settler colonialism, the 'six colonies of New Zealand', provided a few places where race seemed to be relatively straightforward, but on the margins of those towns (and sometimes at their centres), as well as in the majority of locations beyond, things were far less certain. Time and again all kinds of people would lament, as one colonel did, that settlers and native tribes were 'mixed up in dangerous proximity'. 'I should have preferred', this officer went on to say, 'to have seen the settlers and Maories entirely apart, with well defined limits.' This colonel, and many others, worried that it would be impossible for a British soldier to discern a 'friendly' native from an enemy.[33] The fighting men would have agreed, and from 1861 there were requests for special uniforms so that soldiers could tell their (native) friends from the enemies—it was already costing soldiers their lives. Other attempts were frequently made to mark friendly from unfriendly natives (one general reportedly cursed, 'Damn the friendly native.')[34]

Colonial war multiplied these 'dangerous proximities', and these proximities were understood in opposing but related ways. On the one hand, the mobilization of settlers and their substantial engagement with native allies and indigenous communities presented new opportunities to be seized, new grounds for colonial rule and order. On the other hand, these promixities could truly be dangerous, threatening the stability and success of colonial rule, undermining colonial authority, making visible its limits, or cohering in forms it could not govern or claim. Correspondingly, the very practices of war, where these dangers were most evident, also provided key opportunities. 'We confess', editorialized one commentator,

> that we should prefer to see the volunteers of the Maori and Pakeha races amalgamate and stand shoulder to shoulder, and the whole able-bodied men of the country turn out irrespective of any clannish feeling, to withstand any acts of aggression; and we are convinced that the desirable union of the two races would be much facilitated by free union and mutual co-operation in a force like that of a volunteer rifle corps.[35]

There remained a pivotal and ongoing tension between desires for regulated and disciplined intimacy and comity with natives on the one hand, and dreams of 'well-defined limits' and fears of proximity on the other.

'Half-castes' and racially mixed families appeared to embody 'dangerous proximities' because of their place in colonial understandings and practices. This situation was not 'natural', nor simply because these people did not easily conform to colonial categories or jurisdictions—this was also true of many people in a complicated and messy world, be they quarrelsome settlers, idiosyncratic chiefs, single settler women or white critics of

---

[33] Alexander, *Incidents of the Maori War*, pp. 56, 223–4; GNZ MSS 246: Fulloon to Native secretary, 24 October 1863.
[34] Scholefield, (ed.), *Richmond-Atkinson Papers*, 1, pp. 515–16: J.C. Richmond to C.W. Richmond, 9 February 1860; ibid., 1, p. 653: H.A. Atkinson to A.S. Atkinson, 11 November 1860.
[35] *Daily Southern Cross*, 24 March 1869.

empire. Rather, the strategies of racial amalgamation and colonialism produced conjunctures where half-castes and mixed families were configured as an important colonial coalface—a project considered critical to larger successes of colonial policy. The horizons of colonial authority were significantly expanded during the Wars, and these expanded horizons consistently brought half-castes and racially mixed families into the very centre of colonial views.

For important reasons, colonial government did not have reliable figures on the number of half-castes nor the number of marriages between settlers and Tangata Whenua. There was not, until the end of the Wars, a broadly observed official statistical category of 'half-caste', nor were there very reliable colonial censuses of the 'native population'. In addition, most 'interracial' marriages were 'common law' marriages, or were contracted according to indigenous protocols. Nonetheless, the large number of these families that can be identified suggest very clearly that their number, particularly as a proportion of the largely stagnant indigenous population, was increasing. Many of these intermarriages were durable, a characteristic less widely observed of their precedents in the 1830s and 1840s. Moreover, particularly in Murihiku (the Deep South) and in some parts of Muriwhenua (the Far North), intermarriages, or marriages amongst those with Pākehā ancestry, were not only common but perhaps even in some places normative, at least for Tangata Whenua. Angela Wanhalla has documented these complexities in and around Taieri in the south, Judith Binney has observed some similarities on the east coast, and there are many other locations, such as Hokianga, where local developments had similar dimensions.[36]

Mixed families and half-castes during the Wars were a characteristically complex and diverse population. As a population that was discursively constituted—having no necessary ties of relationship, community or locality—this was perhaps unsurprising. These differences marked the partiality of colonial efforts to organize both half-caste, and 'native', subject positions, and their limitations in ordering or inflecting the majority of these peoples' subjectivities. However, it was increasingly obvious that these categories and labels were no longer irrelevant to indigenous people, communities and discourses. Earlier chapters have shown that there were long-standing and concerted efforts to wrest half-castes and native wives from their families and make them institutional subjects, and these often had powerful effects. By the 1860s a significant

[36] Wanhalla, 'Transgressing Boundaries', idem, '"One white man I like very much": Intermarriage and the Cultural Encounter in Southern New Zealand, 1829–1850', *Journal of Women's History*, 20 (2008), pp. 34–56; Binney, '"In-Between Lives"'.

minority of half-castes had spent time with, or even within, these institutions, although usually in sporadic or limited ways. These institutions,
most significantly schools, churches and individually waged occupations,
were often weak or unreliable. But when synergized with other 'engines' of
racial amalgamation—from hospitals, shifts into the colonizing spaces of
colonial towns and, not least, marriages (particularly of young women)—
the texture of changes amongst these people can be appreciated.[37] The
Wars represented both the maturation of an early generation of people
who had engaged these colonial institutions, chiming with an increase in
the ability and reach of the colonial state, which was now able to archive
and organize far more effectively. Critically, colonial government could
increasingly offer benefits to subjects, even 'natives', and not only seek
to expropriate indigenous possessions. The state could distribute its goods
and benefits unequally, and thus substantiate its own taxonomies of
difference.

In New Zealand (as in many British colonies of settlement) a critical
mark of colonizing institutions was producing an ability to speak English.
This was the colonial tongue, and admitted persons to routine social and
economic opportunities, providing new chances to access and experience
colonial institutions and practices. These opportunities, in turn, fashioned
new relationships and engagements, and colonial institutional connections
and experiences were often durable producers of subjectivity and further
opportunities. Perhaps the most critical engagements, though, came
through the legal, social and cultural paternity of settler fathers and
husbands. The fundamentally gendered nature of colonial law regulated
access to property and courts, and altered one's relationship with the state
and its institutions. When one unscrupulous official accused a half-caste
woman married to a European of constituting a wartime threat, her
husband, Edward Hill, defended her, and his, 'good behaviour'. He had
ensured his wife had led a European lifestyle. 'I must add that my wife has
resided all her life amongst Europeans, and that I have systematically
prohibited the visits of any Natives to my house for the last five years.'
Hill was affronted and demanded that either 'all Halfcastes of whatsoever
class or position should be subject to this supervision' or he would hand in
his gun and quit the militia.[38] All in the Colonial Secretary's department
agreed that this official had overstepped his mark, and whatever his
instructions were, such an 'intrusive "surveillance" over the half-caste
wife of a gentleman and [government] officer' was completely unjusti-

---

[37] Damon Salesa, 'The Power of the Physician": Doctors and the Dying Maori in Early
Colonial New Zealand', *Health and History*, 3 (2002), pp. 13–40.
[38] IA 1 1863/2140: Edward Hill to the colonial secretary, 29 July 1863.

fied.[39] 'An Englishman's wife is an Englishwoman and not subject to any "loi des suspects", or domiciliary visits.'[40] In this case, both the patriarchal energies of a husband, with his systematic prohibitions, and of the colonial state, which made an Englishman's wife English, worked to realign a subject, and potentially to remake her subjectivity.

Increasingly important were colonial regimes of licit conjugality and domesticity. These assigned value, and rewarded and enabled marriage according to colonial norms, with its proper gender roles, rules of property and propriety, and colonial subjecthood. An indicator of this was one persistent feature, that formal 'mixed' marriages were overwhelmingly between European men and non-European women. This echoed the assumptions of racial amalgamation from even before 1840, but was now integral to the real inequalities in colonial marriage, with its resolute attachment to patriarchy with cultural and legal disabilities for women. There were only ever a few marriages that did not conform to this type, and the kinds of treatment they received in settler publics was revealing. Kamariera Wharepapa returned from England with an English bride, Elizabeth Ann Reid, who was six or seven months pregnant.[41] She chose to live with Wharepapa in his *kainga*, and was almost completely forgotten by colonial government and the settler publics. On the other hand, the most prominent of these marriages was that of Hirini (Sydney) Taiwhanga to a white woman in around 1874 or 1875. Taiwhanga was a good speaker of English, a trained carpenter and surveyor later prominent for leading an indigenous delegation to England.[42] Coverage of the Taiwhanga nuptials extended as far as Australia, and there was 'much surprise' at this 'instance of miscegenation'.[43] Taiwhanga and his wife became favoured targets: she was described by one official as 'an Irishwoman of not too excellent a character' (in a familiar turn that mobilized a different vocabulary of race and class distinction), and there was widespread coverage of her arrest for smashing windows, one of them under the sarcastic title 'A Nice Couple'.[44] There were also indications that some half-caste women, particularly those who were educated and of status, might also be

---

[39] IA 1 1863/2140: Gisborne, minute, 29 July 1863, Dillon Bell, minute, 30 July 1863, Domett, 2 August 1863.

[40] Ibid., Gisborne, minute, 29 July 1863.

[41] Brian Mackrell, *Hariru Wikitoria! An Illustrated History of the Maori Tour of England, 1863* (Auckland, 1985), pp. 85–92.

[42] MA 23/1: Clendon to undersecretary for native affairs, 27 September 1882.

[43] *Evening Post*, 14 June 1877.

[44] MA 23/1: Resident Magistrate, Russell, to undersecretary for native affairs, 27 September 1882; *Hawera & Normanby Star*, 30 August 1883. Also Clementine Fraser, '"Incorrigible Rogues" and Other Female Felons: Women and Crime in Auckland 1870–1885', MA thesis, University of Auckland, 1998, passim.

operationally in this category of settler or 'European' woman.[45] At any rate, the hostility directed at Mr and Mrs Taiwhanga was rarely, indeed almost never, evident in any similarly public accounts of marriages between settler men and indigenous women.

Settler perceptions of how other putative norms of colonial marriage might be breached or violated through certain kinds of racial crossing were revealing. In one case, H.B. Brown was hauled before a colonial court. 'The offence he. . . committed [was] that of running away with somebody else's [a settler's] wife—a young half-caste woman'. This act was not, in itself, a criminal offence. Instead Brown was 'charged by the husband with stealing his wife's clothes', the only legal option available to him.[46] Here a husband used the gendered legal disabilities and inequalities to discipline a domestic relationship, and assert a variety of ownership over his wife— through her clothes. In another instance, a similar but potentially more dangerous violation was held up in the settler public: fears of an inversion of proper gendered and racial roles within a marriage. Fears that a native or half-caste wife might usurp or exploit a vulnerable settler man were occasional, but persistent, and again illustrative of the presumed make-up of a proper colonial marriage and intermarriage. One newspaper article, for instance, made a fuss over 'May to December' marriages that were suspected of being exploitative, arguing that such alliances were designed by half-caste or native women and their families to secure settler property and privilege.[47] This indexed the way in which marriage, with specific gendered and racial parameters, was a central institution for colonial strategies.

Relationships with other colonial and allied institutions were to prove especially important for many half-castes and mixed families during the wars. The half-caste Benjamin McKay, for instance, was at a school at Te Kohanga attended mostly by half-castes that closed with the outbreak of the Waikato War in 1863. He stayed on and acted as a 'runner' for the British.[48] He was just one of many such half-castes who were in demand as interpreters and guides. Many of these individuals, though by no means all, had been repositioned; they were bilingual and often bi-cultural, but were not solely or primarily shaped by the sentiments of *aroha*, *whanaungatanga* and propriety that marked indigenous subjectivities. It was rumoured that one of the major fortifications in the Waikato War, the

---

[45] Barry Mason and John Hitchen, *One Hundred and Fifty Years of the Mason Family in New Zealand, 1837–1987*, 2nd edn., (Christchurch, 1988), p. 45.
[46] DSC 31 July 1868.
[47] *Evening Post*, 14 June 1877.
[48] Rex and Adriene Evans, comp., *The Whanau of Irihapeti Te Paea (Hahau)*, 2, p. 543.

Paterangi line, had been neutralized by just such half-caste guides. One narrative talked explicitly of such people as 'traitors'. 'A half-caste, for a few shillings, betrayed us, and offered to show the general a way around our pas'.[49] James Edwards (also known as Himi Manuao) and John Gage were half-castes who had grown up in the Waikato and worked for the invading army as interpreters and guides.[50] At Te Awamutu some local women gave voice to their disgust with one of these men. ' "You dog", said the women, "you slave; you led the pakeha [sic] to kill your mother, your sister, and", holding up a pretty little girl, "your cousin, too. Stand off! Stand away!" '[51] During the Waikato War, which through the means of the King consolidated indigenous sentiments and polities in unprecedented ways, there was very little access to local and indigenous knowledge. General Cameron found 'that venal agents and half-caste interpreters were his only sources of information'.[52]

Eloquent of these new kinds of subjectivity was James Te Mautaranui Fulloon, a young but well-known and widely respected surveyor, translator, advisor and government agent.[53] Fulloon had been Donald McLean's secretary, was consequently present at important land purchases, and was well known to officials as an accomplished orator and translator.[54] Fulloon's *whakapapa* was also distinguished, and he descended from an important leader of Tūhoe and Ngāti Awa. On the one hand Fulloon had a long history of working for, and with, colonial government, advancing colonial policy, particularly in the form of land sales. Yet, on the other, Fulloon worked hard to conciliate with and protect a variety of indigenous interests, including those to whom he was not related. This complexity was manifest intimately, as he had a common law marriage and son with Teni Rangihapainga, but with whom he did not keep house, reputedly because his own sister objected to such a relationship with a native. This complicated subjectivity was to lead him to his fate: he used both his official connections and his relationships with Ngāti Awa to gain a commission. He proposed a mission to raise a troop of half-castes and natives, chiefly amongst Ngāti Awa, to fight against the adherents of the

---

[49] Thomas McDonnell [and Kowhai Ngutu Kaka], 'Maori History: Being a Native Account of the Pakeha-Maori Wars in New Zealand', in Thomas Gudgeon, *The Defenders of New Zealand* (Auckland, 1887), p. 518.

[50] Cowan, *The New Zealand Wars*, 1, p. 51.

[51] Thomas McDonnell, 'Incidents of the War: Tales of Maori Character and Customs', in Gudgeon, *The Defenders of New Zealand*, p. 571.

[52] Lomax, *The Late New Zealand War*, p. 25.

[53] See W.T. Parham, *James Fulloon: A Man of Two Cultures* (Whakatane, 1985).

[54] ATL, Micro-MS0535-094, Donald McLean Papers: Thomson to McLean, [undated]; MA 1 1861/18, J. Fulloon, 'Notes of native speeches at the Bay of Islands', 12 February 1861; GNZL, B31: Brown to Grey, 29 April 1862.

new religion, Pai Mārire, on the east coast.[55] As he was on his way to pursue this mission, on 22 July 1865, he was killed. Though Fulloon's was not the only death in the incident, his was the most widely reported and lamented; he was not merely a half-caste, but well known to many settlers as a gentleman.[56] Despite Fulloon's richly textured life and complicated subjectivity, his death largely reduced it to a much simpler and clearer narrative about supposed native fanaticism and savagery. Other contemporaries, with a more nuanced sense of Fulloon's multiple entanglements, hoped his death would generate new support amongst his mother's family against the adherents of Pai Mārire.[57]

Lucy Lord, who was also known as Lucy Grey and Takiora Dalton, is equally instructive.[58] During the war against Titokowaru she supplied information to colonial officials and soldiers. Though she did so secretly, many were suspicious, and even years after the fighting had ended, many of her relatives would not shake hands or greet her. She initially survived because Titokowaru had protected her despite what Titokowaru called her 'evil-doing'. She wrote of these tense relations to a senior government official:

> Titokowaru talked to me; he taught me that that was enough of my talk to the Government. His word is that he had heard at Whanganui I was the worker of the Pakehas, that is of the Government side. . . . His word was that I should be taken to Waitara in case I stayed here and talked of their words and thoughts to the Government. 'Because you were born from my sister you have been allowed to live like this. [He said.] You would have been killed by now if I were a different man.' He didn't look at me, but the point of his gun will look at me.[59]

These strong ties of kinship were critical, and they demonstrated how complicated and encompassing indigenous kinship might be. Lord's mother was Kotiro Hinerangi and her father was William Lord, and her

[55] GNZ MSS 246: Fulloon to 'military secretary', Queen's redoubt, Pokeno, 22 October 1863. Fox, *The War in New Zealand*, p. 226; cf. Thomas Gudgeon, *Reminiscences of the War in New Zealand* (London, 1879), p. 47–8.

[56] Bilcliffe, 'Well Done the 68th', p. 165: Shuttleworth, diary, 31 July 1865; Donald Stafford, *Te Arawa: A History of the Arawa People* (Wellington, 1967), pp. 394, 400–11.

[57] Binney, *Redemption Songs*, p. 338; Scholefield, (ed.), *Richmond-Atkinson Papers*, 2, p. 176: J.C. Richmond to Maria Richmond, 18 August 1865; ibid., 2, p. 175: J.C. Richmond to Gore Browne, 14 August 1865; ibid., 2, p. 178: A.S. Atkinson, journal, 29 May 1863.

[58] See, in particular, Tui MacDonald, 'Takiora, Lucy Lord', in Macdonald *et al.*, (eds.), *The Book of New Zealand Women/Ko Kui Ma te Kaupapa*, pp. 650–2; Keith Sinclair, *Kinds of Peace*, pp. 24; James Belich, *I Shall Not Die: New Zealand, 1868–9* (Wellington, 1989), passim.

[59] ATL, MS-Papers-0032-0694D-12, Donald McLean Papers: Grey to Maclean, 26 September 1870, (trans. Curnow).

half sister was later to become famous as the guide Sophia, or Te Paea.[60] Though a 'half-caste', Lord had deep and broad kin connections in the area through Hinerangi, and was also rooted in the community through her adopted parents (*matua tiaki*), Tito Te Auataua and Te Ngohi.[61] Her adopted parents had proven critical in protecting her in the wake of her actions, as had her husband Te Mahuki. For her information she was paid up to £10 per month, and McLean gave her two blocks of confiscated land (which at one point she was evicted from).[62] Though she had complicated sentiments regarding kinship, her relatives supplied her with the knowledge she trafficked in, and which later kept her alive. But these ties were, in important ways, reciprocal. Subsequent to her marriage to Te Mahuki, after the Wars, Lord had been received back by many of her relatives, and appeared ready to enter arranged marriages—particular to Pākehā men, several of whom showed a strong interest in her—in order to cement relationships and advantages for her people.[63]

But it was not only in interstitial capacities that the racially mixed participated. Significant numbers were effectively regularized as 'settlers'—incarnating one model of amalgamation—entering units or operating in capacities that were not positioned as 'native'. Thomas Bartlett, a son of Takotohiwi and William Bartlett, was a private in the 3rd Waikato regiment, with whom he was involved in the pursuit of Kereopa, and for which he received the New Zealand medal.[64] Others were attracted to the centres of the wartime economic boom. Marianne McKay, daughter of Irihapeti Hahau and John Horton McKay, married the Scotsman Robert Oliphant Stewart who became resident magistrate at Whaingaroa (Raglan). Around the time of the Waikato War they moved to the mouth of the Waikato river; Stewart became interpreter and magistrate, and both were public figures in the burgeoning small town that channelled supplies up the river to the battlegrounds.[65] (Marianne later became a licensed interpreter of the Native Land Court.) One of the key officers of the Arawa in the war against Titokowaru was Captain William Gundry, a man of Arawa descent but who was often styled as a 'European officer'. One of the units was known simply as 'Gundry's

[60] Her mother Kotiro was reputed to have been the one who compared Hone Heke to the head of a dead hog, precipitating an inter-*hapū* war: Cowan, *The New Zealand Wars*, 1, pp. 16–17.

[61] ATL, MS-Papers-0032-0694D-12, Donald McLean Papers: Grey to Maclean, 26 September 1870, (trans. Curnow).

[62] ATL, MS-Papers-0032-0695A-08, Lucy Grey to Maclean, 12 January 1871.

[63] ATL, MS-Papers-0032-0178: Charles Brown to Maclean, 21 June 1876.

[64] Mere Whaanga-Schollum, *Bartlett: Mahia to Tawatapu* (Mahia, 1990), p. 17.

[65] F.J.W. Gascoyne, *Soldiering in New Zealand* (London, 1916), p. 89; Harrop, *England and the Maori Wars*, p. 344.

Arawas'.[66] These positions modelled, to a greater or lesser degree, reconfigured colonial subjectivities, ones difficult to reconcile with indigenous counterparts.

Indigenous subjectivities were themselves very far from straightforward during the Wars. Particularly after the Waikato War, numbers of 'native' troops entered the (usually paid) service of the Queen. Despite this apparent alliance, these troops did so mostly in *hapū* or *whānau* groupings, under *hapū* or *whānau* leadership, with only the looser guidance of European officers. The British troops who fought alongside them, as one of the militia officers observed, acted as a contingent to indigenous forces, not the other way around.[67] These people were known as *kūpapa*, a word which in modern times has come to mean 'traitor' but which in the nineteenth century connoted both allied and neutral.[68] *Kūpapa* leaders often gained the rank of officers, and the most prominent, Rāpata Wahawaha and Mete Kīngi, were famous. Though *kūpapa* had the greatest impact against Te Kooti and Titokowaru, even during the Taranaki War some were quick to recognize the opportunities these colonial wars presented as a means of gaining satisfaction for older concerns. For example, the Taranaki leader Ihaia was only too ready to lend his expertise to the British. He gave lengthy instructions in a letter to imperial troops on how to invade Wiremu Kīngi's *pā*, an old enemy of his.[69] (This meant, as one indigenous commentator opined, that the governor was attaching himself 'as a tail' to Ihaia, in his dispute with Kīngi.[70]) 'Natives' entered the war as allies of the Queen and fought other groups of Tangata Whenua for reasons that were fundamentally indigenous—because of, not in spite of, indigenous subjectivities.

Distinctions in half-caste subjectivity were important to, and targeted by, colonial government. During the Wars official practices and policies increasingly addressed these subjectivities, and in the Wars' aftermaths efforts to identify and tabulate them were consolidated. The most striking instance was in the inscription of a statistical dyad inscribed in each colonial census from 1874 until 1921. Here colonial government crafted two categories of half-castes: 'half-castes living as natives', who were often, after enumeration, generally treated as an addendum to the 'native'

---

[66] Belich, *I Shall Not Die*, p. 233.
[67] McDonnell, 'Incidents of the War: Tales of Maori Character and Customs', Gudgeon, *The Defenders of New Zealand*, p. 580.
[68] For example, 'a kupapa is one who is sitting still, taking no part with either side'; Robert Burrows, *Extracts from a Diary Kept by the Rev. R. Burrows During Heke's War in the North in 1845* (Auckland, 1886), p. 24: 1 May 1845.
[69] Alexander, *Incidents of the Maori War*, pp. 168–9.
[70] *Te Hokioi*, 26 April 1863.

category; and 'half-castes living as Europeans', who were enumerated separately from either Europeans or natives. This second category formalized the racial amalgamation project of reclaiming or appropriating half-castes, levering half-castes away from Tangata Whenua. Most half-castes were in the first category, aligned through these indigenous subjectivities and their intimate and kinship ties to *whānau*, a category that was contrasted pejoratively with those 'half-castes living as Europeans'. Even those half-castes who had spent time in the colonial schools, workplaces, churches and towns continued very firmly to 'live as natives'. This was despite the often heavy-handed ways in which the goods of colonialism, its unequally distributed benefits, might hinge on precisely the indexing or performance of certain subjectivities. The status of 'European' was explicitly figured as property, a 'high estate' from which one had to 'descend' to be amongst 'the Maoris', and a proper colonial subjectivity defined ones access to certain benefits and rights.[71] These developments were commonplace, but one of the most public of these was the effort to provide a pension for the native wife and half-caste children of Edward Broughton, who had died while a colonial official. A petition to this end made it as far as the floor of Parliament, and made colonial subjectivity a precondition of such an award. The petition specified that his surviving family would only receive it 'provided that the children be educated as European children to the satisfaction of trustees to be appointed by the Government'.[72] It was more than symbolic that in lieu of a settler father, the state and settler community could act over half-castes in his stead, enacting a certain licit form of legal and social paternity.

Colonial rhetoric paralleled these distinctions, ushering in a new rhetorical figure: half-castes whose colonial subjectivity was only partial or superficial. This was strongly gendered. These 'partially' amalgamated half-caste men or boys were typically sullen, difficult and untrustworthy, 'educated half-caste youths' who could be blamed for everything from explaining the intricacies of colonial and imperial government to founding 'perverted' native cults.[73] Meanwhile their female counterparts were typically coquettish, improper and knowing, diverting both native and settler male attentions and money in frivolous ways—'crinolines for the half-caste ladies'—or sitting ostentatiously outside the Native Land Court—'half-caste girls discussing the fashions'.[74] In both cases these half-castes

[71] *Daily Southern Cross*, 15 August 1867.
[72] *Otago Witness*, 1 September 1866.
[73] *Daily Southern Cross*, 29 June 1860: Sydney *Empire* correspondent; ibid., 26 April 1865.
[74] *Nelson Examiner*, 15 Sept 1864; *Daily Southern Cross*, 9 January 1865.

usually spoke English, but were not clearly aligned with the colonial government and settler culture, and often attracted criticism:

> We have among us some half-castes, chiefly girls, who speak English pretty well. A few of them were educated in Auckland, but prove the old saw of 'what's bred in the bone'. They are as much Maori as the oldest *waihine* [*sic*] in the place, the only advantage they derive from their education being the doubtful one of being able to translate for ignorant visitors the very questionable conversations and songs going on.[75]

This rhetoric, and the tabulation of two essential kinds of half-castes, crystallized a new dimension to the colonial treatment of half-castes. By so clearly asserting that appearances could be superficial or deceptive there was a specification that outward appearances were insufficient grounds for assessment. What was required was the adjudication of proper colonial subjectivities by colonial agents.

Time and again colonial officials and settlers declaimed various incantations about the spectre of half-castes. In its most common form these comments supposed that if half-castes were not claimed by settlers and the colonial state, not only might they be lost to native families and communities, they might prove a 'curse' to colonial plans.[76] The Wars seemed to offer plenty of examples to those with enough patience to register them. Every campaign generated a number of half-castes, typically male, who were a routine feature of the 'native' landscape during the Wars. There was the 'venerable half-caste chief Pou-patate Huihi, of Te Kopua', as Cowan remembered him, who had his jaw shot off in the Taranaki campaign, but who lived long afterwards.[77] Or Henry Phillips, a Waikato half-caste, who came across a party of 'rebels' in Taranaki on their way to kill Pākehā, and ended up as their interpreter, leaving the only surviving account of their action.[78] Perhaps the most famous of all was Heni Pore (Jane Foley). Pore's experiences are so complicated and contradictory, however, they make it clear that any simple formulations of half-caste lives—some of which have been uncritically accepted by some historians—are wrongheaded.

Pore was the daughter of an Arawa woman, Maraea, who had been taken north in a raid by Hongi Hika, and William Thomas Kelly.[79] Pore

---

[75] St John, *Pakeha Rambles Through Maori Lands*, pp. 170. This is St John's version of a trader's narrative.

[76] Morgan, Letters and Journals, 2, fos. 476–7: John Morgan to Sec. Venn, 3 July 1850.

[77] Cowan, *The New Zealand Wars*, 1, p. 193; also Scholefield, (ed.), *Richmond-Atkinson Papers*, 2, p. 47: A.S. Atkinson, journal, 29 May 1863.

[78] Belich, *I Shall Not Die*, p. 223.

[79] She was also known as Heni Te Kirikaramu, adds Stafford; *Te Arawa*, p. 406. Her second husband was a Pakeha, Dennis Foley (or Pore, in *te Reo*).

had been present at the start of the war in the north when Kororareka had been 'sacked' (1845), and had been educated at several institutions, working for a time at Three Kings College in Auckland, where many half-castes were schooled. She married an Arawa man, Te Kirikaramu, and bore five children. After the breakout of war in 1863, she went with her children, mother and sister to fight for the King. She was an active warrior, and is reported to have fought in the Waikato War while carrying her baby in a blanket on her back. It seems that she had a rifle (when others generally had muskets and shotguns) and was a crack shot.[80] She was also a talented embroiderer and made one of the most famous of New Zealand flags, later captured by colonial troops. She was immortalized for her role in the disastrous British action at Gate Pa. There, after the British had suffered heavy casualties and been repulsed from the *pā*, many British wounded were left in no man's land, close enough to their comrades for their sobbing and cries for help to be heard, but where they could do nothing. Pore took water out to the dying, and comforted them.[81] This unique moment was made symbolic of the war and, as Belich points out, was enshrined in a historiography that privileged a few moments of chivalry over commonplace brutality.[82] Pore was later a well-known hotelier at Maketu, gained her licence as an interpreter, and was known as an expert on matters of Maori land.[83] The siding of Pore with kin despite her long engagement with colonial institutions is instructive in the partiality and particularity of these institutions and the limits of colonial government and discourse. Producing colonial subjectivities was not as straightforward as claiming new colonial subjects.

Few campaigns illustrate how these complexities intertwined messily than the war against Te Kooti. New indigenous and colonial subjectivities were criss-crossed with established colonial and indigenous subjectivities. These were sites of decisive differences that colonial practice and discourse struggled to refine and tabulate, and that encumbered colonial attempts to make them clear and stable. For the most part, as Judith Binney has shown, 'race' offered no particular insight into the experience or practice of living and violence during these times. For instance, Paku Paraone, son of William Brown and Hine Whati-o-Rangi served as the local militia commander's dispatch messenger while his sister, Mere Kīngi Paraone,

---

[80] Ibid., p. 406.

[81] She 'had borne a rather conspicuous part in the war. . . she was in the Gate Pa. . . when she had humanely administered water to the wounded.' St John, *Pakeha Rambles Through Maori Lands*, pp. 129–30.

[82] Belich, *The New Zealand Wars*, pp.

[83] Tui Macdonald, 'Heni Pore', in Macdonald, (ed.), *Book of New Zealand Women*, pp. 531–3.

married Komene, Te Kooti's brother.[84] (Mere Kingi went on to have three marriages, and apparently later forsook the Ringatū religion founded by Te Kooti to become a strict Anglican.[85]) One of Te Kooti's leading generals was Eru Peka Te Makarini (Edward Baker McLean). He was understood to be, and likely was, the son of the Native minister Donald McLean, but his father had little to do with his upbringing and he had been imprisoned on the Chatham Islands with Te Kooti. Consequently he was one of the *whakarau*, the original prisoners who had escaped from the Chatham Islands with Te Kooti (he was also reputedly married to Te Kooti's sister).[86] Peka Te Makarini died in 1870, killed by colonial militia while carrying one of the most famous of Te Kooti's flags.[87] Te Makarini did not, as one historian has claimed, appear 'to lend confirmation to a British belief that half-castes inherited the worst qualities of both races... A belief that appeared to be given sanction by the new scientific reasoning of Charles Darwin'.[88] This did not happen because in colonial eyes there were many, many more prominent half-castes fighting as, or allied to, settlers. The most prominent of these, the Tapsell brothers, were prototypical examples of gentlemanly half-caste subjectivities: unlike more powerful indigenous leaders working with colonial militias, they were feted by settler society. Race was not straightforward, but mediated in elaborate ways by settler discourses of subjectivity, class, gender and politics.

The intricate ways in which such encounters might both complicate and iterate the 'racial' were woven in the most infamous of incidents during the war against Te Kooti: the raid he led upon the small settlement of Matawhero. Variously called a 'reprisal', a 'massacre' and an 'incident', in a one night raid over fifty people were killed by Te Kooti's followers. As Binney has emphasized, the action was both alarmingly violent and carefully planned. (Binney counts twenty nine Pākehā and half-caste victims, as well as twenty two Tangata Whenua).[89] The fate of the half-caste Goldsmith siblings is one illustration.[90] Sixteen-year-old Maria Goldsmith was shot and bayonetted, possibly because her father (a Pākehā store owner) had been responsible for an early arrest of Te Kooti, or

[84] Binney, *Redemption Songs*, p. 96.
[85] Heni Sunderland and Cushla Parekowhai, 'Mere Kingi Paraone', in Macdonald, (ed.), *Book of New Zealand Women*, pp. 493–6.
[86] Binney, *Redemption Songs*, pp. 86, 96, 132.
[87] Gascoyne, *Soldiering in New Zealand*, p. 103.
[88] Butterworth, *Maori/Pakeha Intermarriage*, p. 5.
[89] Binney, *Redemption Songs*, p. 121.
[90] Kararaina married Charles George Goldsmith, but he also had children with her sister, Makere.

perhaps because he owned some contested local land, and had become increasingly supportive of the colonial government.[91] Four-year-old Albert Edward, who was with Maria, was also killed. Rapata (Robert) Goldsmith had already skirmished with Te Kooti and been injured, and was convalescing when his siblings were killed, and soon after he rejoined the militia in their pursuit of Te Kooti; he was present at some of the most notorious reprisals against Te Kooti, and later made a successful half-caste land claim.[92] (In the same raid, the half-caste woman Heni Kumukumu, in danger of attack herself, took Maria Goldsmith's horse and rode off. Instead of riding, as others were, into the bush and away from Te Kooti and his people, she rode up to him, becoming his favourite wife.[93]) Another family of a Pākehā, the Frenchman Jean Guérin, also suffered in the raid. Guérin and his child were killed by Te Kooti, and his half-caste wife was taken.[94] The sins of the father were visited upon their sons and daughters, and their partners. No wonder that an indigenous veteran of the campaign reflected upon Matawhero: '*He nui nga tangata i mate i a Te Kooti ki reira, Maori, pakeha, hawhekaihe* [sic]' (many persons were killed there by Te Kooti, Maori, Pākehā, half-caste.)[95]

Half-castes and mixed families were a central and recurrent concern, but not an isolated one. The shoring up of colonial government, and colonial uneasiness with various domestic, racial and gender arrangements, was by no means restricted to 'the native question'. The War gave sharp rise to these concerns amongst settlers, most critically with respect to young or single settler men widely understood to be troublesome. Ruling elites, both in the metropole and the colonies, regularly entertained concerns about colonial societies dominated by such undomesticated white men. This had itself been a critical impulse in early ideas of reform, and not only colonial reform. Racial amalgamation drew very strongly upon these concerns, which could interpret intermarriage as both domesticating men and colonizing women, families and property, through unified 'natural' processes. One of systematic colonization's many failures was to not produce the new, more gender-balanced colonialism it had aspired to, meaning by the late 1850s—even before the massive influx of

[91] Binney, *Redemption Songs*, pp. 23–4, 122.
[92] 'Life seemed of very little consequence', Goldsmith reminisced, 'and we thought little more of shooting down a Hauhau than a farmer does now of killing a fat sheep to supply his household.' Rapata Goldsmith, in Mihi Keita Ngata and Katerina Te Reikoko Mataira, *Taura Tangata: Te Whakapapa o Nga Kiore o Ohinewaiapu* (Raglan, 1988), p. 33; also ibid., pp. 8–11; OLC 1/1371: Curnin, note, 22 July 1869.
[93] Binney, *Redemption Songs*, pp. 122–5.
[94] St John, *Pakeha Rambles Through Maori Lands*, pp. 154–5.
[95] Nihoniho, *Narrative of the Fighting*, p. 12, 39. (A slightly modified translation.)

gold miners and soldiers in the 1860s—there were fears about the well-being of New Zealand's settler societies. It was widely understood that wartime threats, as one colonial official outlined, lay not only on the frontiers.

> We have not only Maories to fear in case of a rupture but also loafers & vagabonds, black sheep of all sorts with white skins who [would] seek to suck advantage out of our confusion. I am going to get a muster roll of the rogues and vagabonds that as far as possible they may be kept under surveillance & at innocent amusements as militiamen.[96]

War might have located most of its violence in specific militarized theatres, but there were widespread fears that this might not always be the case. Colonial commanders understood that successful colonialism required watchfulness both within and without.

Desertion demonstrated the pivotal ways in which colonial subjects were not intrinsically or naturally aligned within the developing colonial order. Colonial government had to persistently police large populations of subjects, and this was heightened at the moments it was attempting to amalgamate natives. Deserters presented a number of challenges for the colony, especially when the majority of deserters left their regiments for the booming towns, where the settlers welcomed them. This was compounded by the persistent colonial difficulty in raising and training settlers to fight in the Wars. In 1867 colonial militias were no longer the 'innocent amusements' of 1860, as the withdrawal of imperial troops had already begun. The want of volunteers, and their lack of commitment, was serious and persistent. One settler lamented the small and fickle militia: 'if they could only get 50 who would honestly stick to it'.[97] These later campaigns were particularly rife with desertion, notably the war against Titokowaru, where men not only left in great numbers but were also discharged in large numbers as unsuitable.[98] Yet the deserters who left the colonial and imperial forces to live amongst Tangata Whenua, and even fight for them, compounded these problems.

The number of colonial soldiers who changed sides was not large, but was disproportionately significant. It could also be put alongside large indigenous groups whose allegiance to colonial forces also shifted during the course of the Wars. At any rate, despite their relative scarcity, accounts

---

[96] Scholefield (ed.), *Richmond Atkinson Papers*, 1, p. 516: J.C. Richmond to C.W. Richmond, 9 February 1860.
[97] *Otago Witness*, 15 February 1862.
[98] As was mutiny: Gorton disbanded a unit with 42 mutineers. Edward Gorton, *Some Home Truths Re the Maori War 1863 to 1869 on the West Coast of New Zealand* (London, Greening and Co, 1901), p. 65.

of these rogue 'Europeans in the bush with the rebels' were common-place.[99] Kimble Bent left the fullest account of such a desertion, which took him from the 57th Regiment of the British Army into the forces of Titokowaru, where he was active in the field.[100] But Bent was by no means unique, and there were as many as four other 'white' deserters who at one time fought or lived with Titokowaru or his allies: Humphrey Murphy, Charles Kane (or King), William Moffat and John Hennessy.[101] By and large those deserters who fought against colonial forces are archived only because they were apprehended or killed, their deviance profound and disturbing to settlers and soldiers alike. Such deserters were likely to be subject to far harsher treatment than those deserters appre-hended in Auckland. In Auckland even deserters who resisted arrest violently and who escaped multiple times were placed in shackles and taken to the police court. Deserters who came quietly in from the 'rebels' were routinely brutalized. Peter Grant, who was captured while fighting for Pai Mārire forces in early 1867, was given fifty lashes 'and was branded with a cross on his hip.'[102] (The cross seems to have been a deliberate statement about the heathen nature of Grant's adopted community; most deserters were branded with a 'D'.) Public disgust for these kinds of deserters meant that no censorship was needed. When a deserter from the 65th and 12th Regiments was found dead amongst the indigenous defenders of Rangiriri, his death was commemorated as 'the fate he so richly deserved'. At least one other deserter had been amongst the defen-ders of Rangiriri but escaped: 'it is to be hoped that vengeance may yet overtake him.'[103]

Indigenous communities incorporated these deserting individuals and produced powerful ties of sentiment. On the occasions that these men were captured, they often claimed abduction and imprisonment, but few could make versions of such a history compelling. The reasons were at times obvious. Thomas Purdan had been living at Mokau for over 8 years and working as a sawyer when he was captured in 1864. John Brown was caught at Poverty Bay, having deserted hundreds of miles away, on the other side of North Island, from the 57th at Taranaki. These were subject positions enabled and anchored by intimate and enduring relationships

[99] For example *Daily Southern Cross*, 6 August 1866.
[100] James Cowan, *The Adventures of Kimble Bent: A Story of Wild Life in the New Zealand Bush* (London, 1911); W.H. Oliver, 'Kimble Bent', *DNZB*, 1.
[101] Gudgeon, *Reminiscences of the War in New Zealand*, pp. 189–90; Cowan, *The Adventures of Kimble Bent*, pp. 75–6; James Bodell, *A Soldier's View of Empire: the Reminiscences of James Bodell 1831–92*, (ed.) Keith Sinclair, (London, 1982), p. 166.
[102] *Nelson Examiner*, 4 April 1867.
[103] *Daily Southern Cross*, reprinted in *Taranaki Herald*, 5 December 1863.

with indigenous people and communities. 'Fox', a suspected deserter from the 65th, was found living on the fringes of Pai Mārire forces. Entrusted with a letter to Pai Mārire from colonial forces, he made clear his preference for the former over the latter: he 'forgot to return'.[104] The power of these relationships was demonstrated in the reciprocal willingness to fight and die. Just as the British deserters fought at Rangiriri for the Maori King, when Peter Grant was captured his Pai Mārire associates attempted to rescue him, sending word 'that if he were not brought back in five hours, they would come down and fight.' The engineer of his capture, Hans Tapsell (a 'half-caste' and Te Arawa), knowing the seriousness of this declaration, quickly left to return to the nearest colonial stronghold.[105]

The differences between the racial order envisaged in official discourses and governance, and more complicated and kaleidoscopic actualities, were apparent in various kinds of racial crossings, from desertion to intermarriage to half-castes. If the immediate problem the Wars presented for colonialism seemed to be independent or 'rebel' natives, racially crossed families and people were no less a warfront. The attention they attracted revealed that colonial goals were not just political subjection, but social transformation and the assertion of new kinds of subjectivity. Clearly these developments showed that the Wars did not simply bring into collision an already aligned set of populations and polities, but were critical in their actual formation.

'GROWING INTO THE SOVEREIGNTY OF NEW ZEALAND'

Few things better illustrate the entangled races, discourses and practices during the war than an incident with George Gage (known in *te Reo* as both Te Kehi and Hori Keeti). In April 1862 Gage, a 'half-caste', appeared before John Gorst then the resident magistrate in the Upper Waikato. Gorst had been completely without influence, living essentially in a foreign land, in what he described as 'a condition of perfect harmlessness'. The only complaints he fielded were almost always of Europeans amongst themselves.[106] For almost the entire time he was magistrate, before he was

---

[104] *Taranaki Herald*, 10 March 1866; *Daily Southern Cross*, 28 February 1866.
[105] *Daily Southern Cross*, 28 February 1867; *Otago Witness*, 16 March 1867; *Nelson Examiner*, 4 April 1867.
[106] John Gorst, *The Maori King*, pp. 163, 189; Gorst, *New Zealand and Recollections of it*; also, *Te Pihoihoi*, 9 March 1863.

finally expelled by the Kīngitanga, it seems only one 'native' ever brought a case to Gorst—against George Gage. Gage responded to Gorst's court summons, but arrived at the court accompanied by two Kīngitanga men. Initially these two men seemed to prevent Gage from answering Gorst's questions. Finally they left Gage alone, but only briefly; upon Gage's return to court, these two Kīngitanga men, this time joined by others, 'took away the defendant without leave or license.'[107] Gage was no longer a subject of the Queen, it was made clear, but under the *mana* of the King.[108] As was being made clear, Gage's removal from Gorst was not simply an individual matter, a question limited to Gage's own subject-hood or belonging, but a question of both sovereignty and *mana*, a staking of the limits of competing claims to rule.

In court Gorst had asked Gage 'whether he did not consider himself a European?' Gage had initially answered yes, though this was not the first time a magistrate had put this question to him. Prior to appearing before Gorst, Gage had navigated the Kīngitanga's legal system. He had been taken in front of the Kīngitanga's Wahanui Huatare, where he had claimed exemption from the jurisdiction of the King.[109] For this reason, in an uncomfortable air of military escalation, the plaintiff (a Kīngitanga himself) had been allowed to take his case against Gage to the colonial magistrate. Gage's subsequent removal from Gorst's jurisdiction was not a local or particular intervention, then, but another moment in a tangled series of encounters. Nor was it a simple reaction: as early as November 1859 the King's *runanga* had issued an edict that none of its people would be placed in a government gaol, and in Gage's case there appears also to have been a specific order from the *runanga* at Kihikihi to reclaim Gage for the King.[110] 'We cannot allow [Gorst] to interfere with those who join our king.'[111]

The case of Gage was not unique. Time and again, especially in 1861 and 1862, a variety of individuals and families raised questions over the extent and legitimacy of different authorities. Most 'Europeans' would not allow themselves to be brought before the King's magistrates, and the King's people were forbidden from going in front of a colonial magistrate. This was the case, for instance, in a long-standing dispute over Robert

---

107 *Daily Southern Cross*, 9 May 1862.
108 Ibid., 3, fos. 726–7: Morgan to CMS secretaries, 1 July 1862.
109 *AJHR*, 1862, E-9, III, p. 8. This names Waharoa (Reihana), but almost certainly means Wahanui Huatare, also known as Reihana Te Huatare, Te Reihana Whakahoehoe and Te Wahanui.
110 *Daily Southern Cross*, 26 July 1862: J.E. Gorst, 'General Report', June 1862.
111 Morgan, Letters and Journals, 3, fo. 727: Morgan to CMS secretaries, 1 July 1862.

Ormsby's horses, and the non-payment of rent by Louis Hetet.[112] But there were ways that these difficulties could be negotiated. In one case, for instance, a Pākehā man was unable to have his case heard by the 'King Magistrate' and was actually cautioned by them for trying. He had lost sheep to local dogs, and was seeking redress. However, when his wife, a 'half-caste', took the case forward, it was adjudicated in her favour.[113] To those colonials inclined to see it, on the other side of the Kīngitanga border or *aukati* was not a vacuum of law and order, but an intensifying centre of a different law and order, with its own printed gazettes, magistrates, councils, led by men of great *mana*, such as Hapemana and Wahanui.[114]

The limits of two species of rule, and the contest between colonial sovereignty and the *mana* of indigenous leaders and their communities, were neither uniform nor universal, but tussled in specific locations. Previously, it had often been the case that sovereignty and *mana* could coexist, even cooperate. *Mana* was broader even than sovereignty, and many dimensions and aspects of *mana* lay beyond the ambitions of colonial government. But war showed dramatically that in certain ways colonial sovereignty and *mana* could not coexist as it had in years before. Both were to claim jurisdiction over, and through, people and their bodies, as Gage showed clearly. However, these competing jurisdictions were perhaps most clearly signalled by the expanding territorial dimensions of colonialism—over indigenous lands and resources. Just as significantly, though less obviously, colonial sovereignty began incursions into the government of the hearths, families and relationships of its 'native' subjects. Colonial sovereignty sought to rule these people and communities—as subjects and bodies—as well as their lands and property. The debacle over Gage, and his position within these contesting regimes, demonstrated how specific local problems of race or practice were keyed to strategic or larger ones.

As the case of Gage suggested, during the Wars half-castes and mixed families could be a key, highly competitive, theatre. This was less apparent in the colonial towns and settlements, and was most marked in the centres of indigenous resistance, especially the Waikato, a crucible of resistance to colonial rule. In the Waikato half-castes were to prove an important and enduring problem in the 1860s. Colonial authorities expended great energy in the Waikato not just to claim and demonstrate interest in half-castes, but to regulate and produce particular kinds of half-caste

[112] *Daily Southern Cross*, 13 May 1862. Hetet's name is given as 'Lewis Hettit'.
[113] *Taranaki Herald*, 5 October 1861.
[114] *Daily Southern Cross*, 26 July 1862: J.E. Gorst, 'General Report', June 1862.

subjectivity. By the middle of the 1850s the Half-Caste School at Otawhao in the Waikato was by far the largest of its kind in the colony. It had a roll of nearly 100 students, even though it was charging parents two to three pounds per student. Though some tried to insinuate that half-castes ran wild 'like dogs or pigs', and were a sign of 'the wrong and dishonour done them by the white man', these were clearly not disposable or uncared for half-castes.[115] Rather, as the expenditure of all involved showed, the colonial government and the mission, as well as the families of the children, valued them highly. But the values were different. The schoolmaster plainly stated his, and the state's, interests:

> If attended to [half-castes] will form a bond of union between the Europeans and the Native race... We may reasonably expect that these children will under proper training and Gods [sic] blessing form a superior race, but if left and neglected in their education, they will often prove a curse to those whom they ought to be a blessing.[116]

By managing the subjectivity of half-castes, aligning them with settlers, producing them as 'a bond of union', the limits of colonialism could be both extended and stabilized.

These intimate developments correlated with more strategic efforts to consolidate and stabilize political boundaries. The Kīngitanga had already established a boundary line, the *aukati*. Governor Grey went further, and on 9 July 1863 ordered that all natives living between Auckland and the Waikato should be expelled unless they took an oath of allegiance to the Queen. Within days General Cameron began the invasion of the Waikato, crossing the *aukati* from the north. Many 'natives' were sufficiently scared to relocate south. The King responded to the Queen, issuing an equivalent order that Pākehā were to leave the King's country, an Act that had been previously comtemplated.[117] But this shoring up of jurisdictions and boundaries had as much impact on the edges of these territories as on the domestic and intimate arrangements of certain people and families. The families and people that crossed race, not those near the borderlands, were those most explicitly targeted. Wives parted with husbands, communities with 'their Pākehā', parents with their children. Political and strategic boundaries fingered the domestic lives of people, and matters of sentiment and affect.

There are scores of accounts of the deep disruptions these political developments had on domestic lives of families and persons who crossed

---

[115] Gorst, *The Maori King*, p. 51.
[116] Morgan, Letters and Journals, 2, fos. 476–7: John Morgan to Sec. Venn, 3 July 1850.
[117] *Nelson Examiner*, 18 June 1862.

races. These disruptions began with the targeting of Pākehā and indigenous men now potentially out of place.[118] But the issue was negotiable. In colonial domains Tangata Whenua could take the oath of allegiance to Victoria. Inside the *aukati* the Kīngitanga would permit Pākehā men to stay, but they 'were required pay £1 as a poll tax for this year, to acknowledge the authority (mana) of the Maori King, and to disclaim the authority of the Queen, or leave his Majesty's dominions'.[119] This was not indiscriminate: Louis Hetet, married to a local woman Paeata Mihinoa, was a Frenchman not allowed to leave but instead sent to Otorohanga for the War's duration.[120] Other Pākehā men did comply, though most did not, often demonstrably refusing one part or other. Reverend Reid refused completely, for example, while Robert Ormsby paid the tax but refused 'to curse the Queen'.[121] Imperial troops began patrolling their territories and the Kīngitanga began to consolidate theirs, and regulate their borders. The colonial mail was stopped and taxed, and a gate erected at Te Ika Roa a Maui, which listed tariffs, was quickly notorious in the colonial press.[122] Pākehā men who would not commit to the Kīngitanga began to be called 'broken bottles'.[123]

The domestic situations of these Pākehā men showed how colonial control was as much a matter of hearth as frontier. The colonial press was fascinated with these developments, documenting in detail the predicaments of the racially mixed families of the Waikato, mirroring and intensifying the earlier interest in the Half-Caste School. In case after case Pākehā fathers tried to take their wives and families with them out of the Waikato into colonial territory, and were prevented. It was confirmation of how colonial audiences considered racial amalgamation legitimate. Native or half-caste wives and children enmeshed in 'proper' domestic relationships with European men could be considered settler entities threatened by natives, native society and culture. Again, the social paternity and patriarchy of settler husbands was critical: they were, as one commentator put it, 'the natural guardians of Maori women and half-caste children', and without them their families would 'be exposed to the lawless violence of the native race.'[124] Occasional dramatic 'rescues'—successful

---

[118] See also Riddell, 'A "Marriage" of the Races?', pp. 77–85.
[119] *Nelson Examiner*, 12 May 1863.
[120] C.W. Vennell and Alan Taylor, 'Louis Hetet: Government Agent in the King Country', *Historical Journal Auckland-Waikato*, 30 (1977), pp. 12–16; Te Muri Turner, *Hetet Reunion* (Te Kuiti, 1995), pp. 3–5, 19.
[121] *Nelson Examiner*, 12 May 1863; *Daily Southern Cross*, 12 December 1867.
[122] *Taranaki Herald*, 7 June 1862; *Nelson Examiner*, 4 July 1863.
[123] *Daily Southern Cross*, 6 May 1863, 19 May 1863; *Taranaki Herald*, 9 May 1863. This appears to come from warnings that they should leave, 'Lest they cut their feet on broken bottles.' *Taranaki Herald*, 25 April 1863.
[124] *Daily Southern Cross*, 16 May 1863. Cf. *Nelson Examiner*, 20 September 1862.

extractions of entire families by their fathers—were well publicized.[125]
John Allen, for instance, had sought to leave Rangiaowhia and been
allowed to take his cattle, but not his family. He covertly returned to
find his family distributed around the community, and after a great deal of
effort secreted them away (often with the aid or tacit consent of their
indigenous relatives).[126] But in the majority of cases, especially after late
1862, Pākehā fathers left without wives and children. Many seemed to
think this was a temporary arrangement; others were unable to convince
wives or children to join them. Most had little choice. Nathaniel Barrett,
for instance, made it part way with his sons before his wife's relatives
intercepted him, and simply took his sons away.[127]

The situation of these half-caste and native wives and children was
uniformly depicted in colonial publics as one of forced captivity, savagery
and danger. For many colonists this was akin to an invasion of the most
sacred intimate colonial realms, and was inflamed by calls for war. 'I look
upon this', wrote one newspaper commentator,

> as a more daring act by the Waikatos than the murder of the soldiers by the
> Southern savages. They violated every tie of friendship and blood, and it is
> well known that they turn the unhappy half-caste females to the vilest of
> purposes which their brutal lusts and savage habits suggest. If this great crime
> goes unpunished, the sooner the settlers take the law into their own hands
> the better.[128]

In the colonial newspapers were to be found lists of such incidents,
and inflammatory accounts of these 'outrages' by observers and even
officials.[129] These accounts were never contextualized in ways that
acknowledged indigenous ties to family—which were dismissed as mere
'pretence'—but instead used the language of captivity and imprisonment,
and some even suggested white women and children might be next.[130]
Much was made of a young European boy living at Mahoetahi amongst
'natives'. Wihona Te One had refused to give him up 'when demanded',
though the boy had been abandoned by his settler parents and had been
starving and uncared for prior to Wihona's care of him. The boy was
apparently happy, and even the *Nelson Examiner* acknowledged that 'they

[125] *Daily Southern Cross*, 5 May 1863.
[126] *Nelson Examiner*, 13 May 1863.
[127] Pani Aranui and Henry Barrett, in Te Rongotoa Barrett, *Ngati Te Maawe: the Barretts of Waiharakeke Kawhia, New Zealand* (Wellington, 1986), p. 10.
[128] *Nelson Examiner*, 30 May 1863.
[129] *Taranaki Herald*, 9 May 1863, 13 June 1863; *Daily Southern Cross*, 16 May 1863.
[130] *Taranaki Herald*, 14 May 1864; *Nelson Examiner*, 30 May 1863; *Daily Southern Cross*, 23 May 1865.

treat him kindly, at least according to Maori ideas'.[131] But the boy was now being claimed as a colonial subject, and attempts to lever him into colonial jurisdictions and domestic life were being made.

Amongst Tangata Whenua, these detentions or reclamations of kin by family and community were not new. Nor were they limited to the Waikato, although these ones, in particular, attracted a good deal of settler interest. Beyond the *aukati*, in other indigenous domains, these reclamations were also common, and had been occurring since long before the New Zealand Wars. They were a common *hapū* response to conflict, both between and within families. In the far north and outside Wellington, for instance, a number of these incidents occurred, even though these communities were not ostensibly at war.[132] A number of indigenous parties showed themselves perfectly willing to travel to distant colonial townships and settlements to try to reclaim half-caste *whanaunga* for their relatives. The family of Whatahoro Jury (later an outstanding scholar) went as far as Wellington to get him back after his Pākehā father had sent him there.[133] The indigenous relatives of the prominent Jenkins sisters also sought the return of their relatives, though from their Pākehā father's custody, most ardently after he had remarried a Pākehā woman.[134]

Equally, the attempts by white fathers and colonial and missionary institutions to lay claim to half-caste children had begun before 1840. Half-caste children were put in schools, sent away or even overseas, removed into the colonial towns, and certain relations with natives (especially marriage) prohibited. Half-caste and native wives had often worked as domestics in missionary and settler households, gone to these schools, and were regularly supposed to be subject to close husbandly monitoring of their behaviour and family connections. Colonial critics of indigenous living often focused on the supposed limitless 'province of [native] government; their regulations extend to the minutest details of private life... [and] the runanga is a grievous tyranny'.[135] This view was shaped by a belief in the domestic remedies of settler patriarchy: 'A man who hopes to educate his half-caste children with any idea of respect for their intellectual welfare or moral training, must either doom his wife to perpetual banish-

---

[131] *Nelson Examiner*, 20 September 1862.

[132] *Daily Southern Cross*, 28 June 1860; *Nelson Examiner*, 21 September 1861; HBWeekly Times, 5 October 1868; OW 3 October 1868. West Coast Times, 21 May 1866; ANZ LE/1/32/1861/248, 'Correpondence relating to the taking away of a half-caste child from Oruru by a chief from Kikihi'.

[133] J.M. Jury, manuscript, in D.R. Simmons, *Great New Zealand Myth: A Study of the Discovery and Origin Traditions of the Maori* (Wellington, 1976), appendices A and C (transl.), pp. 335–7, 351–3.

[134] *Otago Witness*, 3 October 1868; *Hawkes Bay Weekly Times*, 5 October 1868.

[135] *Daily Southern Cross*, 26 July 1862: Gorst, 'General Report', June 1862.

ment from her own people, or separate the mother.'[136] Domestic disputes were entangled with far broader political, cultural and social contestations.

In these ways the Wars broadened and intensified the colonial government's engagement with indigenous lands and property. Government renewed and extended its strategies to make land and property legible, but this legibility was cast in relatively stark terms: 'native' or 'European'. These classifications were never innocent, and it was clear that one integral part of this process was that more and more would be transferred from the former classification ('native') to the latter ('European'). Indeed, there was almost no capacity to do otherwise. Neither during nor after the Wars were there 'half-caste lands' as such (except in the case of some important reserves resulting from some large sales in South Island).[137] The parallels between the claiming of land and of people and their purported transfer were deeply significant. It was not just land that was being transferred from the 'native' to the 'European' categories, but people too.

During the Wars the mechanisms through which land was surveilled, sorted and otherwise processed by colonial government and its agencies were varied and numerous. The Treaty of Waitangi had established 'pre-emption'—Crown monopoly on the alienation of 'native' land—in 1840, but this approach was radically altered during the period of the Wars. In 1862 the Native Land Act shifted the government's role from being initial proprietor to being adjudicator and guarantor—deciding and issuing title—a move that symbolized a change in sovereignty, and sovereign ambition, as well as speeding up the transfer of land to settlers.[138] This had uneven and differentiated effects on many communities, combined as they were with other contexts, from war, economic stress, large increases in settler numbers to confiscation.

Prior to the Wars there had been few formal processes specifically treating the lands and property of half-castes and racially mixed families. Previous governors (particularly Governor Grey) mostly used their own discretion, occasionally choosing cases or moments to personally intercede.[139] The Wars expanded both the jurisdiction and ambition of colonial government, and these instances became more numerous and more complex. To get a measure of the extent and the ramifications of these developments it is necessary to take in more than any single venue or

---

[136] *Taranaki Herald*, 10 January 1863.

[137] See, especially, Angela Wanhalla, 'Women "Living Across the Line": Intermarriage on the Canadian Praires and in Southern New Zealand', *Ethnohistory* 55 (2008), pp. 29–49.

[138] David Williams, '*Te Kooti Tango Whenua' : The Native Land Court 1864–1909* (Wellington, 1999).

[139] For example ANZ, AAAC 706/123b/53, Sinclair to Superintendent, 8 November 1854; ditto, 18 March 1856.

development, but to triangulate the Native Land Court with the Compensation Court (which adjudicated the losses of 'innocent' parties due to the War), and revisit the Old Land Claims Commission, as well as to consider some other policy and bureaucratic developments.

These institutions were independent but connected. Of them, only the Old Land Claims Commission was specifically charged to investigate land claims 'arising from the setting apart of land for the maintenance of half-caste children', which was but one of its duties.[140] (A few other institutions also specifically concerned themselves with half-caste claims.[141]) Half-caste claims could be settled by the Old Land Claims Commissioner, but it was generally easier, faster and cheaper for those involved to have the matter settled in the Native Land Court.[142] The Native Land Court was tasked with converting complex clusters of often overlapping use rights into durable colonial land titles.[143] Its many other requisite practices—lands had to be surveyed (and surveyors paid), large parts of *hapū* had to reside in the (often distant and expensive) townships for prolonged periods of time to attend the court, and subjection to colonial authority—ensured it was one of the most insidious acts of colonial government. It was commonly called 'the land taking court' (*te Kooti tango whenua*). But compared with the Old Land Claims Commission, where the commissioner's decisions often took years and the claimants were left in what one half-caste called 'disagreeable suspense', the Native Land Court was often preferable.[144]

Half-castes were consequently appearing in the Native Land Court from its inception. The Acts which established the Native Land Court stipulated that the Court was to look at *native* lands, although in keeping with much government legislation it did not clearly define who was and was not a 'native'. Yet the half-castes who appeared often did so not surreptitiously or in camouflage as natives but, conscious and assertive of the difference, as half-castes. For instance, Annabella Webster's claim, which was settled in her favour by Judge F.E. Maning, resulted in a certificate specifying she was 'Annabella Webster a half Caste'. This was literally against the form of the court; on the certificate was printed

---

[140] CO 209/153, fos. 132–4: Dillon Bell, memo, 21 February 1860, enclosed in Gore Browne to Newcastle, 22 February 1860.

[141] Notably the Poverty Bay Commission, though it had not been specifically empowered; OLC 2/7, facing fo. 88: Curnin's register, notes; also CO 209/153, fos. 132–4: Dillon Bell, memo, 21 February 1860, enclosed in Gore Browne to Newcastle, 22 February 1860.

[142] OLC 1/1356, 1/1356A: O'Rorke to Munro, 18 April 1874; OLC 1/1366: Curnin, note, undated; OLC 1/1370, Curnin, memo, 24 January 1872; s.83 of the 1865 Native Land Act.

[143] Ballara, *Iwi*, p. 195.

[144] OLC 1/1362: James Berghan to minister of native affairs, 6 October 1863.

'Aboriginal Native', which in her case had been crossed out.[145] There were other reasons for half-caste cases going to the Native Land Court and not the Commission, not least because potential claimants found it easier to contest the case in the Native Land Court.[146] The Commission did not always pay very much attention to the kinds of objections considered by the Native Land Court.[147] Native Land Court judges were more experienced in dealing with the intricacies of local custom, *whakapapa*, and customary law. As one of the clerks for the Commission observed: 'All these Kororareka Claims have become so confused and entangled, that it is impossible to settle them anywhere except upon the spot. I would recommend, therefore, that all of these claims, such as are half caste [*sic*] claims be remitted to the Native Lands Court for adjudication by Judge Manning [*sic*]'.[148] This was by no means always a point against half-caste claimants.

Court hearings were specifically tasked with interrogating relations within and amongst kin as a part of the process of granting Crown titles. The efforts of *whānau* were critical to ensure that half-castes had their land claims endorsed.[149] Other times divisions amongst locals were revealing, as when Hare Hongi supported the award of a land title to the half-caste children of Henry Snowden, and Wi Hongi Te Ripi later opposed.[150] Such disputes were an indication that half-castes and their families were within the ordinary dimensions of *hapū* and community life. But there were inequalities and unevenness in these places too. Many half-castes appearing in these colonial venues seem to have been unusually well connected, and these colonial forums were ways in which this status within indigenous communities could be confirmed and their property acknowledged—a means by which indigenous legitimacy could be, almost literally, capitalized. One of the most famous indigenous leaders, Tamati Waka Nene, did this by gifting a piece of land to his half-caste grandchild, as did Paora Patete Ururoa when he wrote to Grey to tell him that his half-caste relations had their piece of land conveyed to them *tika* (correctly).[151]

[145] OLC 1/1368: Maning to Land Claims Commissioner, 6 May 1874. Other examples: Ngaki-a-Totara: Murray Parsons, *John and Te Aitu Jury: The Jurys of the Wairarapa* (Christchurch, 1986), p. 30; Waiomu: *Daily Southern Cross*, 5 July 1865.

[146] OLC 1/26A: Te Whiwhi Hopohia to Domett, 20 May 1871, Te Whiwhi to Domett, 21 May 1871. Te Whiwhi was the son of George Cook, a half-caste.

[147] OLC 1/44A: Maihi Te Uaua to Fenton, 19 April 1869.

[148] OLC 2/7, facing fo. 91: Curnin, comments.

[149] OLC 1/1367: John White, memo, 12 November 1860, W.J. Woodhouse, report, 28 May 1872.

[150] OLC 1/1357: Hare Hongi, evidence, 30 March 1858; Wi Hongi Te Ripi to Gore Browne, 7 July 1868.

[151] OLC 1/1360: Waka Nene to Gore Browne, 21 January 1862: 'ki te whenua o aku mokopuna nau i tuku atu ki a ratou ma ake tonu atu'; OLC 1/1362: Paora Patete Ururoa to

Many other cases were of similar kinds, where parents or kin, or the half-castes themselves, sought to ensure and protect their advantage. This population of half-castes were hardly marginal creatures, but people confident of their place and connections, and with a great deal to lose. One Pākehā father of a large half-caste family was adamant about his wife's land: 'The natives there cannot dispute her title—because my children's relatives would maintain it if any of them did.'[152]

If ever there was a reminder of how the colonial archive was not simply *of*, but *for*, colonial rule (as Nicholas Dirks observed), it was in land titles.[153] These certificates spun out of an intensive process where not just land, but people, communities and relationships had been surveilled with the explicit purpose of archiving them. Few colonial texts were ever to approach the power and apparent finality of a land title. These were claims over both the past and the future, and which structured the present. But what has not been emphasized sufficiently in the large historiography about colonial land tenure is how this visibility extended not just into the past—indigenous history and *whakapapa*—but into the domestic lives of families and individuals. Court decisions not only rearranged lives on the macro level, dispossessing and forcing people to move, making decisions *between* families; they rearranged relationships *within* families, rewarding certain kinds of kinship and refusing others. This was most evident in the gendered archiving of land title. Though the right of women to hold land was recognized, grants consistently favoured men. So it was when judge Francis Fenton objected to one woman's request to have her name added, in addition to that of her sons (and also the half-caste Andrew Maxwell). Fenton remarked 'that he wished to discourage those Maori notions as much as possible'. There was no need for 'two names representing one interest', Fenton continued; and, in conformation with colonial practice, the single named interest was not her but her son.[154] In these ways, and many others, the certification of indigenous property became another means of reforming indigenous domestic life and subjectivities.

The Old Land Claims Commission and the Native Land Court embody two different tactics within larger strategies of grappling with half-castes and 'mixed' families. The Native Land Court simply treated half-castes and mixed cases, in the first instance, as natives. In such a

Grey, 15 July 1863 ['Harae' sic]; 'ua ma tou [sic] ana tamariki ua to ma tou [sic] tuahine ini te whenua he mea tuku tiki ki aua tamariki.'

[152] OLC 1/21A: Faulkner, evidence, 12 January 1865.
[153] Dirks, *Castes of Mind*, p. 107.
[154] *Daily Southern Cross*, 14 March 1866. The land was Mataitai 'No.1', at Wairoa, about 10,000 acres. Also *Daily Southern Cross*, 2, 4 October 1867.

manner they could bring their claims in front of the courts. Thereupon the discretion of the judge and the 'native assessors' operated to ensure that the law was applied in an appropriate way, without having to acknowledge its anomalous characteristics. The Old Land Claims Commission, on the other hand, enabled 'half-castes' as a special case, a marked population, which, within strict limits in terms of time and jurisdiction, could be ruled on according to different protocols. Through both of these tactics, the complex and fraught problem of land was rearranged into categories subject, and responsive, to colonial rule. Both sets of tactics were consistent with, and advanced, the wider project of racial amalgamation.

A third critical institution was the Compensation Court, established in 1863 by the same Act that began the confiscation of indigenous lands from those 'engaged in rebellion'.[155] Its relationship with half-castes and mixed families is instructive. Though not frequently the explicit targets of expropriation, many mixed and half-caste individuals lost property and wealth during the War and as a result of it. Half-castes regularly, and it seems disproportionately, appeared in the Compensation Court. This was sometimes a function of their ability to navigate colonial institutions, and sometimes because they were better able to establish a sense of property legible to the court, property convertible into compensation. But perhaps a chief reason was that it seemed to be easier for half-castes and mixed families to assert their innocence: that they were not 'engaged in rebellion', but innocent, righteous, victims. Mrs Turner, widow, 'mother of a large and respectable family of half-caste grown-up children', testified to her suffering from 'treatment said to be received from some soldiers, who... took her prisoner and burnt all the crops collected in front of her house, while she was alone in the house at the time.'[156] Many other cases seemed to have similar characteristics, particularly when European husbands had parted from their wives. This was clear in the case of Robert Ormsby, who lived in the Waikato. 'The rebels put it to me whether I would be a Kingite or leave; I preferred to leave.' He offered as evidence of his and his family's loyalty that his son had joined the militia—at the time he had been aged only 10.[157]

It was evident after the War that not all half-castes or mixed families could extract themselves from the categories targeted by colonial authorities. Making this situation more difficult was that a few did, and did so publicly and very successfully—in some cases not just protecting their

---

[155] New Zealand Settlements Act, 1863 (amended and continued 1865, 1866).
[156] *Daily Southern Cross*, 30 July 1864.
[157] *Daily Southern Cross*, 12 December 1867.

holdings, but extending them. These instances were a small minority, but were often mobilized or understood to represent the majority. This widespread belief moved one half-caste to protest how those cases were exceptional, and that after the War the majority of the large half-caste population in the Waikato was suffering:

> I am a half-caste; my wife is a half-caste. The land awarded to me would not be a mote in the eye of a miromiro [a small bird]. You said that half-castes got a great number of acres… there were many half-castes at Ngaruawahia, but I did not see one of them who received land amounting to a thousand acres. Our claim upon the land of our mothers was great… there are many persons annoyed about their lands, which were taken as payment of the sin of the people.[158]

This individual again asserted the correctness and fairness of their land-holding, arguing legitimate claims to property through their mothers. After the Waikato War, however, these were not the measures by which colonial authorities made their assessments. Lands were to be confiscated, as one act notoriously declared, from natives 'in rebellion against Her Majesty's authority'. Exemptions were not for those who had legitimate claims, but for those who were 'well-disposed'.[159] This required a different species of evidence, put in colonial framings of proper colonial, half-caste, subjectivity, and whether claimants had set themselves sufficiently apart from native communities and practices and aligned themselves with colonial power and institutions. Yet in many cases, even conformation to these criteria was not always sufficient. Half-castes had to have been strongly and demonstratively aligned with colonial authority. By making oneself a governable colonial subject one supposedly could avail oneself of the colonial governments legitimating and protective capacities. These capacities remained partial and discretionary, and were only occasionally as powerful as they claimed: but the Compensation Court and Native Land Court demonstrated how real, and broad, these effects could be.

The unfinished colonial undertaking to claim half-castes and native wives meant many were of uncertain status when the frame of reference was 'natives in rebellion'. The ravages of war, and then the massive confiscations afterward, gravely affected tens of thousands of people. The claims of the Power (or Paoa) family illustrate this only too well. Thomas Power, an Englishman who was originally a miller, had lived in the King Country since at least 1850. He was married to Tehauata Rahapa, and together they had five children, owned a store, and farmed a variety of horses, chickens, cattle and

---

[158] *Daily Southern Cross*, 9 September 1867.
[159] New Zealand Settlements Act, 1863.

pigs.[160] After the expulsion of Pākehā and with little choice but to leave, Power left for Auckland with three of their children, leaving two with Tehauata. Power did not return until May 1864. In the meantime soldiers had arrived at their home in late February 1864. Tehauata had heard them coming and had put a white flag on the roof; regardless, she stated, when the soldiers arrived they started killing the fowls and pigs, kicked in the store and looted. By her account they even took the account books and deeds to land. 'I was so frightened, almost fainting', wrote Tehauata, 'my children crying and I not knowing what would happen to us, the soldiers cursing at me and my children and threatening that if I complained against them to the Officers they, the soldiers, would come at night and kill us.' The soldiers looted much of their property and tried to force her out of their home (later colonial accounts asserted she had been 'protected' by the soldiers). Soon after the soldiers had left, the Bishop of New Zealand arrived; he advised her not to leave, and carved messages in English (which she did not understand) to the soldiers on all the doors of the house. After the war the Power's troubles only multiplied, and they brought multiple cases before the Compensation Court. Some of them were evidently inflated, and an initial award of £365 was followed by a claim of £1,973, a truly enormous sum. This was dismissed as 'monstrous', and another claim, when reinvestigated, was declared 'altogether dishonest'.[161] The family situation appeared dire, and Thomas Power begged the governor, '[I] ha[ve] been thrown upon the world without a home for [my]self and family'.[162]

The 1860 Half-caste Disability Removal Act was an explicit example of how this concern with proper half-caste subjectivity was important and could be institutionalized.[163] This Act legitimized all 'the issue of mixed blood' whose parents were then unmarried but had subsequently married, so long as these parents were of the 'European and Maori race respectively'. This recognized the maturation of a generation of half-castes raised under nominal colonial rule, marking them as subjects of special interest to be levered into proper subject positions. These half-castes were aligned with colonial practices but unable to access key benefits, particularly succession to property. This relatively small population was virtually an ideal category for racial amalgamation, one incrementally being cleaved

---

[160] IA 1 1865/3021: Power to Grey, 25 October 1865, Paoa to Grey, 20 April 1865 (trans. by Vinoy, no original).
[161] *Daily Southern Cross*, 18 October 1866, 20 October 1866, 19 July 1869.
[162] IA 1 1865/3021: Power to Grey, 25 October 1865, Paoa to Grey, 20 April 1865 (trans. by Vinoy, no original).
[163] 'An Act to Legitimatize [sic] in certain cases the Issue of Mixed Blood born before Marriage of Parents of the European and Maori Race respectively subsequently Married.' [3rd November, 1860].

from indigenous communities, families and contexts, whether through schools, relocation orders, paternal direction or legal acts. The Act even left open a twelve-month window for parents to get married and thus legitimize their children. This was an unusual tinkering with the laws of legitimacy and succession, laws usually subject to an iron discipline, and created an opportunity denied to the children of settlers. Critically, the Act specified its racial categories in a way that broadened race beyond simple questions of descent. 'Maori', for instance, was held to include half-castes and all mixed people 'unless there be something in the context repugnant to such construction', presumably if they lived as 'Europeans'. Coming as it did just prior to the Wars, this was a clear proclamation of colonial intentions regarding half-castes aligned with settlers and colonial government. They would be recognized by the state, and key privileges and abilities would be extended to them.

Amongst the governing class the Half-caste Act was not controversial. Most of the debate in Parliament was over details: should the Act expire at some point, or should it only apply to marriages between 'full Maoris' and Europeans, to ensure that there was not confusion in later generations?[164] Other politicians worried that gendered inequalities in colonial law were acting as a disincentive for native or half-caste women to marry settler men. One member observed:

> As matters now stood a Maori woman possessing any property in land retained those rights so long as she remained only the mistress of a European, but the moment she married she forfeited those rights, because our laws did not recognize the tenure by which her property was held. Thus, in fact, a premium existed in favour of concubineage.[165]

Frederick Weld agreed that this was 'manifestly unjust', but knew that it was a function of a multiplicity of gendered inequalities, in both English and colonial law. Legitimate marriage conferred upon indigenous women the loss of property rights that settler or English women experienced when they married (which remained in New Zealand until the Married Women's Property Act in 1884). The inequality was, in itself, less important to legislators than its deterrent effect. The recurrent themes of licit and illicit intimate relations, and the work of marriage as a kind of engine of transformation, not just for racial amalgamation but the legal domestication of natives (especially native women), was here openly hitched to the harnessing of property.

---

[164] NZPD, 1860, p. 641: Henry Sewell and C.W. Richmond.
[165] NZPD, 1860, p. 640: Forsaith.

In was indicative of the broader strategies of colonial officials and settlers that there was a disproportionate redirecting of activity to those populations seen to lie at racial crossings. These moves were neither mistaken nor idiosyncratic, but rather owed to the increasingly important linkages between racial crossings, the texture of territorial expansion of colonial sovereignty, and the ambitions of colonial sovereignty in new cultural and social realms, especially indigenous intimate spaces and domains. In other words, the disproportionate colonial investments in racial crossings both heightened and reflected their disproportionate significance. Settlers and officials knew well their own rationales for the significance of half-castes, friendly natives and native wives—or deserters and other 'black sheep... with white skins' for that matter. The investment was not just because these populations might be 'dangerous', but because their proximities presented new possibilities, occasions or locations where colonialism might progress. When settler newspapers vigorously condemned natives who refused to let their mixed relatives be taken away by their settler fathers, they understood the stakes. This was not simply about individuals, wives or children, but progress and sovereignty—and was thus condemned, being of 'as black a hue as even the murders at Taranaki.'[166] At racial crossings the future, and political utility, of key colonial strategies was at stake. The fate of half-castes and mixed families could not be separated from racial amalgamation and colonization. As one newspaper put it, 'It is a very grievious [*sic*] matter that so many half-caste children, who have been brought up and educated carefully, should be kept prisoners by the Maoris to grow up savages, whilst we are "growing into the sovereignty of New Zealand".'[167]

HE TAUĀ PEPA/A PAPER WAR

Indigenous understandings of purportedly 'mixed' *whānau*, their children, and the ways of governing or ordering them neither simply opposed nor corresponded with colonial and settler formulations. The problem of race crossing during the Wars makes clear that 'family' and *whānau* were not equivalents, and that conflicts in these intimate domains were not simply about the right to govern or rule them, but how they were constituted and understood. In the 1860s the category of 'half-caste' became increasingly important in governmental and settler circles, and a critical means by which the capacity and reach of colonial sovereignty could be extended.

---

[166] *Daily Southern Cross*, 16 May 1863.
[167] *Nelson Examiner*, 12 May 1863.

These settler, missionary and official efforts to distinguish and address these 'half-castes' and 'intermarriages' broadened the problem of racial crossings beyond conversations with and amongst Pākehā, and precipitated sustained engagements within indigenous practices and understandings. As colonial discourse and institutions directly mobilized to reclaim half-castes, for an increasing number of Tangata Whenua 'half-caste' was no longer an esoteric term or a distant figure of imperial imagining, but visceral embodiments of colonial developments that could not be ignored. Settler and colonial formations of race had to be engaged and could no longer be simply excluded or quarantined by Tangata Whenua. Just as vitally, Tangata Whenua understandings of *hāwhe kāehe*—or others recognized by settlers as lying at racial crossings—could prove critical not just for indigenous but colonial activity.

Indigenous discourses did not make the fetish of race crossing that colonial discourses did. The people that settlers and officials addressed as half-castes were only occasionally addressed by their own kin and communities as *hāwhe kāehe*. Indigenous relationships with 'half-castes' were generally ordinary, everyday relationships of kinship, politics and sociability. These relationships were subject to the same configurations that ordered the lives of their indigenous parents and cousins; half-castes and mixed families were not, by and large, the subjects of exceptional institutions, practices, customs or laws. In the small but important ways that this was beginning to change by the 1860s, it was clear that the impetus for change did not originate inside indigenous communities and kin groups, but stemmed from engagements with colonial agents and discourses. By this time most indigenous communities had decades of experience in negotiating the quirks and vagaries of having Pākehā men amongst them; colonial claims and assertions about these men were commonplace, and many indigenous strategies—both concessions and assertions—had evolved to deal with them. But the constitution of 'half-caste' as an operational colonial category, and the targeting of mixed families, had made clear the expanded horizons of colonial rule. In many corners this had led to an urgent and necessary revisiting of indigenous strategies regarding these people and realms. It was already clear that these indigenous intimate domains were ones that would be staunchly protected: the sheltering of families, the claiming and reclamation of half-castes, and the full-throated assertion of these people's indigenous kinship and belonging were all matters of record. But indigenous strategies were both more nuanced and complex, not merely a conservative reaction to colonial interloping, but creative, innovative and nimble. New, and newly empowered, colonial claims were engaging indigenous arrangements both traditional and innovative; in no place was this complicated mix as evident as in relevant indigenous discourses.

Already changes in the contours of colonialism had contributed to reshaping the spaces of indigenous discourses. The settler towns, and their many offshoots, had produced large-scale spaces that had both appropriated indigenous property and alienated 'natives'. Important, large and durable settler institutions and publics were characterized by the practical exclusion of 'natives' and their singular conduct in English. Still, the spaces of effective colonial and settler jurisdictions remained importantly limited in large parts of indigenous domains. New 'colonial' forms had tended not simply to replace indigenous public and community spaces, practices and places of discourse, but to be appropriated into, or as supplemental to, them. Because the independence of *hapū* was still commonplace, Christian and colonial practices had been appropriated by Tangata Whenua as much as they had 'colonized' them. The central public space for Tangata Whenua and *hapū* remained the *marae* but it was now articulated with much that was distant or new, for instance new trade networks and means of transportation as well as the church, stores, mills and other new places of work.[168] These articulations might be initiated and regulated by Tangata Whenua, but they could not always so easily control them. Perhaps the most powerful indicator of these new articulations was the inauguration of new indigenous communities, religions or polities such as the Kīngitanga, Pai Mārire or Ringatū.

New polities and new religions remade the dimensions of indigenous life, and ushered in expanded realms of indigenous discourse. Though most developments originated within particular *hapū* relations, these new 'pan-tribal' groups began to accumulate adherents from beyond and were enabled by new discourses broadly shared by Tangata Whenua, not least Christianity and commerce. These new groupings became stunningly successful in allying different, even in some cases warring, *hapū*. The Kīngitanga was the largest and most striking of these, but throughout the later 1850s they were evident through much of New Zealand. These themselves began to produce what we might call new 'publics', which both drew upon and transcended the specificities of individual locations, or local places of discourse such as *marae*. Tony Ballantyne and Lachy Paterson have both shown how literacy and print were mobilized by Tangata Whenua in ways that were complicated and often conflicted, but which were responsive to their own purposes: as Ballantyne puts it, 'to disembody Pakeha knowledge and to fashion new powerful religious

---

[168] Hazel Petrie, *Chiefs of Industry: Maori Tribal Enterprise in Early Colonial New Zealand* (Auckland, 2006).

identities and political idioms that challenged Pakeha claims to hegemony.'[169] Central to this was different ways of texting *te Reo*: not just the advent of extraordinarily widespread literacy, the translation of the Bible and numerous newspapers and periodicals, but the rise of both political, kin and social letter writing, written forms of sermons, instruction, *waiata* (songs) and even what seem to be innovative forms of commentary and creative narratives.[170] The early domination of these realms was by the missionary churches, and this gave way quickly to official publications that drew upon this body of discourses and attempted to turn it to more specific colonial ends. Yet, by the 1850s, despite the monopoly of colonial and religious bodies over printing presses and even the post, writing circulated in indigenous channels and publics beyond missionary and official control. Leaders and kin were commonly writing letters to each other, records of business and *whānau* were being kept, letters to the editor frequently contested official views, and many indigenous networks were trafficking paper and discourse. By the time the Kīngitanga consolidated, beginning in 1858, there were overlapping multiple and distinct domains of discourse that were not just spatial, practical and oral, but written.

Te Hokioi e Rere Atu Na (The Hokioi [a mythical bird] Flying Towards You) was indicative of this new development. It was published by the Kīngitanga irregularly for two years when resources allowed, until the War finally forced its abandonment in late 1863. It was printed on a press given to two Waikato men who had travelled to Austria with an Austrian exploring expedition, and was edited by Patara Te Tuhi. *Te Hokioi* was a publication that was not only completely independent of colonial government, but was actively in opposition to it. This was a publication that marked the developing coherence of a new indigenous public. It was unsurprising, then, that within months of the first appearance of *Te Hokioi*, the government had given the local resident magistrate, Gorst, enough resources to start his own newspaper. His production was *Te Pihoihoi Mokemoke i Runga i te Tuanui* (The Pihoihoi [groundlark] that Sits Alone on the Roof). This newspaper was much more in keeping with Pākehā convention, though it was also responsive to the format of *Te Hokioi*, though longer and more frequent. The first edition, though edited by Gorst, was written almost entirely by the New Zealand Governor, Sir George Grey. The two birds of the Waikato conducted an unusual press war, and *Te Pihoihoi* openly promoted *te taha Pākehā*, the Pākehā

---

[169] Ballantyne, *Orientalism and Race*, p. 168. Paterson, *Colonial Discourses*, pp. 37–48.
[170] Bradford Haami, *Putea Whakairo: Maori and the Written Word* (Wellington, 2004); Paterson, *Colonial Discourses*, passim.

side or viewpoint, in distinction to *Te Hokioi*, which gave *te taha Māori*, the Maori side or viewpoint.[171] Before the military invasion of the Waikato, the two newspapers were at each other's throats in what *Te Hokioi* described as *he tauā pepa*, a paper war.[172]

This 'paper war' was in effect a discursive confrontation, and one front was the problem of the half-castes, whose bodies were themselves literally being fought over. Half-castes were, as has been seen, an urgent conjuncture of Kīngitanga practice and discourse, and *Te Hokioi*'s treatment of them makes this clear. In the issue dated 24 March 1863, *Te Hokioi* began what was intended as the first in a series of articles on the *tikanga*, or customs, of other lands. The first of these was entitled 'Korero o Haiti', a discussion of Haiti. The article gave a brief history of the island, from its discovery by the Spanish through to its French takeover. It began with an account of how the Spanish had slaughtered the original inhabitants in order to take their treasures, and because of the colour of their skin. It went on to describe how the French had then defeated the Spanish, and had taken from their homes '*nga mangumangu o Awherika*' (blacks of Africa) or '*te iwi kirimangu*' (the people with black skins) and had enslaved them. 'Those people, the French', *Te Hokioi* said, 'slept with their female slaves and the result was the half-castes.'[173]

Te Hokioi told a history of Haiti that hung on the slave rebellion and which played up both its parallels with New Zealand and the crucial role of 'half-castes'. In the war against the French, over 70,000 French had been killed or expelled from the island, *Te Hokioi* contended. And although the French had looked after their half-caste children, and had sent them to Europe to be educated, *Te Hokioi* emphasized that the half-castes had fought alongside the people with dark skins: during the struggle half-castes had killed their fathers. This was symbolic, powerfully so, when the Waikato had hundreds of half-castes in their midst. In other important ways besides these, similarities between Haiti and New Zealand were drawn out, but the overarching theme of the article was that the dark people of Haiti had overturned a European power, and that they now had their own country.[174]

By the account in *Te Hokioi* Haiti was a rich country and the people were happy. The issue following the original article on Haiti reiterated that

---

[171] *Te Pihoihoi Mokemoke i Runga i te Tuanui*, 4, 9 March 1863. Essential reading regarding this is Lachy Paterson's *Colonial Discourses*, particularly pp. 183–96.
[172] *Te Hokioi e Rere Atu Na*, 26 April 1863.
[173] 'No, ko taua iwi ko te wiwi, ka moe ki o ratou wahine taurekareka, puta ana he Hawhe kaihe.' [sic]
[174] Laurent Dubois, *Avengers of the New World: the Story of the Haitian Revolution* (Cambridge, MA, 2004).

the *rangatira* or chiefs were content, and the *runanga* or councils were working for the good of the country. Law was established, and they were making a great revenue from their many wharves.[175] However, Gorst, Grey and *Te Pihoihoi* never got to contest *Te Hokioi*'s version of Haiti's past as within weeks of that issue's publication, the government press had been confiscated and Gorst had been expelled from the Waikato.[176] This was another reminder of the physical, spatial dimensions of discourse. Gorst was then taunted by *Te Hokioi*, which now apparently had the last word, rejoining that if the Kīngitanga's system of government was let alone, it would be effective, and one day New Zealand would be prosperous like Haiti.[177] As *Te Hokioi* reminded its readers, formulating a system of law and order was not the work of a few years. Pākehā had been working at theirs for hundreds of years, and were still going.

The seriousness with which colonial government engaged in this *tauā pepa* was consistent with long-standing efforts by officials, missionaries and settlers to contest both the limits of these developing indigenous spaces and the discourses they circulated. Colonial government and established churches already dominated publications in *te Reo*, and edited and produced these texts in ways amenable to their aims. But a near monopoly on print did not grant privileged access to indigenous publics. This was because indigenous literacy, by itself, was not autonomous of communities and so did not constitute a single public: colonial publications were in many ways interlopers or adjuncts in a complex of indigenous discursive spaces. Tangata Whenua used newspapers in a variety of ways. They used them as venues for their own pronouncements and conversations, for instance, and as a way of learning more about Pākehā, their activities and their ways.[178] Tangata Whenua were aware of the regulation practised by these official organs, as were colonial officials and settlers. Violations of these colonial norms were taken very seriously. One European, Charles Davis, occasionally published independent newspapers in *te Reo* and was widely derided for his independence. A settler and colonial official complained in the strongest possible fashion that Davis's coverage of the Indian 'Mutiny' was an incitement for natives to take up arms. Davis had described the Mutiny as a war between India and England, and said that 50,000 Indians had killed all the wives and children of Pākehā there. This, the settler continued, was 'Not a good move—no comment, not a

[175] *Te Hokioi*, 26 April 1863.
[176] The fifth and last issue of *Te Pihoihoi* had been the day before the article on Haiti, 23 March 1863.
[177] 'E hoa, e kae ana pea ae mo tau mana kua taka nei'; (Friend, perhaps you are jealous because your influence has fallen).
[178] CO 209/153, fos. 409–10: Gore Browne to Newcastle, 25 April 1860.

word of our victories—of the hanging and blowing from guns.' It would inspire 'contempt' for the British, and depicted Europeans as 'little sheep just at the option of the Natives of India'. Though this critic thought that this might be accurate, 'the mere truth is not to be told at all times, or to all persons'; you simply could not tell them 'without comment that we are butchered here and massacred there as if we were sheep or hares.' 'Blowing from guns is rather in fashion now, and I think it would be a good thing to blow Mr Charles Oliver Davis from a field piece as quick as possible.'[179]

These contests over discourse and discursive spaces were integral to the extent and nature of the Wars. The Kīngitanga was able, briefly, to disrupt specific colonial publications, through its control of people, material and space. But over the longer term this capacity proved limited, uneven and unsustainable. By the 1870s not only the greater part of indigenous territory, but many indigenous public spaces, had come under recurring and sustained attacks. The King himself had shifted into exile, and other places of resistance had been reshaped into insurgencies. The autonomy that had previously characterized indigenous discourse in many of these places could no longer be so easily assumed. There was no simple relationship between the storming of indigenous territory (or the appropriation of indigenous bodies) and colonial invasions of indigenous discourse: the Wars did not end indigenous autonomy, nor fully establish colonial sovereignty nor erode *mana* or *rangatiratanga*. But the violent dimensions of war critically transformed the material conditions of the majority of indigenous communities and discourses.

Indigenous politics had not been unified by the advent of this overlapping array of emerging publics. But the forging of these new publics made it possible to navigate indigenous relationships differently, and contributed to the consolidation and extension of pan-tribal groupings. The differences between indigenous leaders were apparent, for instance, at a large 1860 meeting about the Kīngitanga's involvement in the Taranaki War. There, some leaders said they were embracing the Queen, others suggested 'let us build a house for three' (Māori, Pākehā, God). Some argued for a separation of peoples ('Let not the Pakeha cross to us... Let not the Maori cross to the Pakeha'), and some warned of the rapacity of Pākehā ('Do not permit the Pakeha to trample us under his feet... Let him take his mana back to England).[180] Colonial observers doubted that the different leaders could agree on anything, and many mistakenly suggested that the Kīngitanga would fall apart if left alone. To be sure, at no point

---

[179] CO 209/145, fos. 143–5: Maning letter, undated, enclosed in Gore Browne to Labouchere, 18 February 1858.
[180] Buddle, *The Maori King Movement*, pp. 46–54.

were all Tangata Whenua united in either leadership or purpose. But neither did a lack of uniformity constitute a lack of unity, and the Kīngitanga stood, powerfully, as did many pan-tribal forms—all pointing to the integrative power of these publics, despite important differences, when they were conditioned by shared indigenous sentiments, politics and practices.

A concern for half-castes was one of many that was shared in these indigenous discourses. At the great conference at Kohimarama, organized by the colonial government in 1860, Te Makarini Te Uhiniko put forward his own solution to the plight of half-castes, one consonant with both earlier and subsequent indigenous formulations. He was adamant that half-castes were *takawaenga*, mediators, between Maori and Pākehā. But he was particularly concerned about the fragile position they occupied, which he likened to birds on a sandbank: soon enough such birds were forced by the tide to take flight. Te Makarini was insistent that the conference attend to half-castes, that Maori manifest *aroha* (compassion, love) for them, and give them a share of the land of their maternal ancestors. He was particularly concerned that others might take the lands of half-castes and their children and leave them landless.[181] The significantly different freight of Te Makarini's words, as compared to the colonial translation offered alongside it, marked the fundamentally different cultures and discourses. The colonial translation was free, inserting a passage that 'they are neither Pakeha nor Maori', and making the word 'regard' hold the place of the far more powerful '*aroha*'. The translation also converted some idiomatic phrases into ones recognizably racial, using the term 'half-Maories', for instance, a sense not communicated in the original. The difference was more than one of transparency of meaning, but pointed to deep, apparently irreconcilable, differences.

There is little evidence that Tangata Whenua felt other than that *hāwhe kāehe* were *whanaunga* and needed to be recognized as such. As Tomika Te Mutu put it, 'This is my word about the half-castes. I think that when the father and the mother die, and the children survive, the children should occupy the land which belonged to the mother.'[182] Examples of

---

[181] 'Ko te taha ki nga hawhe-kaihe, ta te mea be takawaenga ia no nga Maori no nga Pakeha. E penei ana ratou me te manu e tau ana ki te tahuna, ka pa-ria e te tai ka rere noa. Kia whakatikaia tenei e to tatou runanga, no te mea he taha ia no tatou no nga Maori; me aroha ano tatou ki te taha ki a tatou. Me whakaatu he pihi, i te whenua o ona tupuna o tona matua wahine; kei riro te whenua i te tangata ke, ka waiho tona uri kia rere noa ana.' *The Maori Messenger*, 1 September 1860.
[182] 'Tenei ano toku kupu mo nga hawhekaihe, ki toku whakaaro ka male te matua tane me te matua wahine, ka ora ko nga tamariki, e mea ana ahau, me noho ano i te whenua o te whaea.' *The Maori Messenger*, 3 August 1860.

people acting to try to apportion land or include half-castes in property are so common as not to be noteworthy. Oftentimes, of course, unless one knows the details of individuals' fathers, they are not marked within indigenous discourses as half-castes. *Hāwhe kāehe* were generally treated as part of *hapū* by other *hapū* who opposed them, whether the contexts were indigenous or colonial. Tangata Whenua sought to include *hāwhe kāehe* within indigenous regimes and understandings of kinship and intimacy, even as they recognized the need to make these practices legible to Pākehā and, particularly, to the emerging forms of colonial government.

Because Tangata Whenua understood their world as largely proper and ordered—even as they commonly admired much about Pākehā—they were willing to contest Pākehā discourses on the few occasions they were allowed entry to Pākehā discursive arenas. A dramatic example was in England, in 1863, where a group of *rangātira* were touring. While they were there, one of their number, Horomona Te Atua, offered, in a speech he gave, his thoughts on the subject of intermarriage and the failures of colonial government:

He had not seen that laws had had the effect of making the English and Maori nations one nation. In his opinion, the best plan to unite them would be that the two races should marry together (laughter and applause). They might laugh at the suggestion, but those were his thoughts. That would be the best way to make them keep the laws. It would greatly improve them in every respect (laughter and hear, hear). Some of the New Zealand women had married English settlers, but the British ladies had not married with the Maories (laughter). They were taught in the Word of God that they should do unto each other as they would be done by and that they should love one another, and they could not do this in a better manner than by doing as he had recommended (laughter and cheers). They must not blame him for what he had said, for he was sure that his countrywomen, had they been present that evening, would have approved of his observations. New Zealanders were anxious to give their females to Europeans, but their example had not been followed by the English (cheers and laughter).[183]

Though the amusement Te Atua gave the English crowd marked the work of race in popular discourses, there was much more that was striking. For one there was the inability of indigenous interventions in metropolitan spaces to find discursive purchase, a point consistent with the reception William Craft had received at the ESL (Chapter 4). For another, there was the concordance between Te Atua's comments and early formulations of

[183] *Australian & New Zealand Gazette*, 3 October 1863; cf. Mackrell, *Hariru Wikitoria!*, p. 72.

'racial amalgamation'. Neither the premise nor the actualities Te Atua described were laughable: racial crossings had long been at the centre of British colonialism in New Zealand and, as if to prove this, by the time Te Atua's party departed England one of his kin had married an English-woman, who would return to New Zealand and live with his people. But the spaces of discursive encounter conditioned and disciplined Te Atua's attempt to engage, and his experience was common. On the few occasions when Tangata Whenua entered colonial spaces to engage they were reduced to being 'natives'. These colonial spaces customarily exoticized and infantilized their presence: literally, in this case, 'possessing the other with a laugh'.[184]

Within indigenous discourses the half-caste was also emerging as a rhetorical or symbolic figure. As Lachy Paterson has shown, indigenous discourses about differences between groups of people were multiple and shifting, and did not operate through a single architecture for describing cultural and social variety.[185] But across many of these discourses the trope of the half-caste became commonly used. Castings of the half-caste as *takawaenga*, a go-between or mediator, were particularly common (as with Te Makarini). The half-caste *takawaenga* was unlike the half-caste at the centre of colonial or racial discourses. The *takawaenga* or go-between was, critically, mobile, mediating and moving between, whereas the 'half-caste' that inhabited colonial discourses was intentionally the opposite, singular and static, and increasingly assignable to one or other category. The inclusive, genealogical, impulses recognized as central in *te Reo* were foreign to the typological, bureaucratic, ones that predominated in colonialism. This feature of indigenous discourses was evident in how the vocabulary of difference between *whānau*, *hapū* and *iwi* was commonly used to describe differences between settlers and Tangata Whenua.[186] The common elements in these concepts were of descent, relationship and connectedness, less of visible features (such as eye or hair colour, or noses) or taxonomies and typologies. In indigenous speeches and texts it was appropriate that even differences between Pākehā and Maori (a word that was commonly in use by the 1860s) might be presented as malleable, changeable or ironic. Sometimes Tangata Whenua referred to themselves as Pākehā, or called the Pākehā their fathers. The Maori King himself, Pōtatau, called upon these matters in rich, ironic, ways: 'I am black', he once mused, 'but though the skin is black outside, the inside of my heart is

[184] cf. Dening, *Mr Bligh's Bad Language*, pp. 262ff.
[185] Paterson, 'Kiri Ma, Kiri Mangu', pp. 78–97.
[186] See also [Anonymous], 'A Maori Comment on Race Relations Since the Treaty', (trans.) L.F. Head, *Te Karanga*, 5 (1989), pp. 20–22.

white'.[187] This was an inclusive language of difference that many colonial agents inhabited when talking *te Reo*, but was rarely visible in English other than in translation. This was not, however, the only sense entertained amongst Tangata Whenua for they were not blind to the complexities concerning half-caste. Many Tangata Whenua had observed that government efforts specifically targeted those they labelled half-castes. It was clear that *hāwhe kāehe* were not only mediators but the subjects of competing claims and potentially subject to competing loyalties. Tamati Ngapora understood that this was evident to Pākehā too, and used it to frame his explanation of why a part of the Kīngitanga had gone to fight in the Taranaki War. 'They are halfcastes', he asserted, 'they came from Taranaki [as well as Ngāti Maniapoto, of Waikato] and have gone to see their friends.' In addition to naming a cohering new feature in indigenous life, the term *hāwhe kāehe* also indexed new engagements and entanglements between colonialism and indigenous discourses.

Although by the 1860s half-castes and mixed families were frequently visible within indigenous families and communities, this visibility was not connected to exceptional political and cultural activities. Amongst *hapū* there was no real counterpart to half-caste schools, differentiated laws or other institutions. Although in some circumstances *hāwhe kāehe* presented difficulties to indigenous leaders and kin, they did not radically disrupt *whanaungatanga* and other indigenous sociabilities. Particular half-castes who had been engaged with or immersed in colonial institutions were often individually distinctive, particularly those whose subjectivity was, in some sense, 'colonial'. These half-castes were more likely to be able to speak English, often fluently.[188] These people, and their families, were also more likely to identify themselves—in public and in the colonial archive—as half-castes.[189] This was a way to signify a different relationship to the colonial state, as well as to differentiate them from those who surrounded them, their land and property. Increasingly this differentiation, in terms legible to colonial agents, was a step in making political, legal and cultural claims. More and more of these claims were land claims, the kind of claim most carefully documented by the colonial state. At the same time, these claims fundamentally rested on relationships within or amongst *whānau* that were recognized by government. The indigenous relatives of the Bennett family, for instance, signed a deed for Pokuru, a

[187] Buddle, *The Maori King Movement*, pp. 48, 59. Different *hapū* who were closely intermarried might be referred to as 'mixed' or 'half-caste'; Ballara, *Iwi*, pp. 156–7, 193.
[188] For example, OLC 1/1362: James Berghan to minister of native affairs, 6 October 1863.
[189] Ibid., James and Joseph Berghan to the minister of native affairs, 22 July 1864.

piece of land specifying it was '*ma nga tamariki hawhe kahi* [*sic*] *o Hare Peneti*' (for the half-caste children of Harry Bennett).[190] It was also indicative of an increasing awareness of the power of colonial discourses, particularly legal ones, that news of a piece of legislation that had been passed concerning half-castes quickly spread, and generated a significant number of enquiries to officials.[191] Pākehā fathers, too, were careful to specify that their children were 'Half Caste children'.[192] *Hāwhe kāehe* was clearly one of a number of technical colonial terms that entered ordinary indigenous use (another interesting one was 'Crown Grant' or '*Karauna Karati*'). But the official uses of *hāwhe kāehe*, as we have seen, were only ever one species of a variety of indigenous usage.[193] As much as 'half-caste' was often a point of intersection between indigenous and colonial discourses, it was proof that neither of these discourses or discursive communities could straightforwardly define the other. The differences and incommensurabilities remained, even as they were increasingly entangled. A sharp reminder of this point came in many texts that were in both *te Reo* and English, where half-caste was in the English text, but *hāwhe kāehe* was omitted in *te Reo*.[194]

The complex assemblage of subjectivities and subject positions at these racial crossings was always present but, as developments in the Waikato showed, often became acute in a time of war. This was not only true of *colonial* warfare, but could be seen in conflicts between indigenous parties in the context of colonialism 'growing into sovereignty'. Perhaps the most interesting of these moments came in the far north. There, though far from the formal prosecution of colonial war, the writ of colonial rule was still distinctly limited, and colonial government was—as in the King Country and on the east coast—often hesitant to exercise a fragile power.[195] Even faced with a series of local wars between different *hapū*, government proved reluctant, and probably unable, to intervene. In 1867 and 1868, elements of Ngāti Kurī and Te Rarawa came into conflict at Whirinaki, in southern Hokianga. This boiled over into a number of armed engagements, resulting in multiple deaths. The central conflict arose between rival claimants to a piece of land: Nuku of Ngāti Kurī and John Hardiman of Te Rarawa. Each was strongly supported by their

---

[190]   OLC 1/1373: Tomika Te Mutu *et al.*, deed, 4 December 1860.
[191]   OLC 1/1359: Cook to Dillon Bell, 3 May 1858.
[192]   OLC 1/1375: John Smith to Dillon Bell, 8 January 1863; OLC 1/42A: Wybrow to Pearson, 27 March 1871.
[193]   OLC 1/1360: Waka Nene to Gore Browne, 21 January 1862.
[194]   For example, [G.S. Cooper], *Journey to Taranaki/Haerenga ki Taranaki* (Auckland, 1851), pp. 57–60.
[195]   James Belich, 'The Governors and the Maori', pp. 75–6.

people, and armed fortifications were constructed proximate to the disputed land. The conduct of the war followed shared protocols very different from those of colonial war. Visiting between enemies was common, fighting was reserved for pre-announced days, and on all but those days the immediate vicinity was safe and peaceful. John Hardiman, as suggested by his name, was a half-caste, but forcefully asserted both his descent from the Te Rarawa ancestor and his belonging with them: 'I reside at Hokianga and am a Rarawa', he declared before the Supreme Court. Hardiman's claim was over land his mother had herself cultivated, and in this he was strongly supported by his people, in customary ways, not least the scores of armed kin that accompanied him.[196]

The space in which this war occurred, and which it was partly about, was at once thoroughly indigenous and filled with half-castes. A large number of Pākehā men had settled in the district, and all had married either native or half-caste women. As one observer pointed out, 'their sons are [now] grown up men, about fifty in number, many of whom are the acknowledged chiefs of their respective sections'.[197] These people were descended from both Tangata Whenua and Pākehā, and apparently understood themselves to be half-castes, but not only half-castes. Especially prominent were Hardiman's chief offsider, his 'half-caste friend', Tawake, and a Ngapuhi half-caste mediator, Hori Rewhi. The conflict had been immediately precipitated by a case appearing before the Native Land Court, but the dispute was long-standing. Nonetheless, indigenous orders of politics, practice and discourse prevailed. By these lights the war was understood to be proper, and conducted properly, and had even seemed to come to an appropriately negotiated settlement. Then Tawake violated these shared norms, shooting and killing Nuku in an act understood as improper (*kohuru*). Because of this recognition, through the careful work of indigenous actors on all sides and entrepreneurial colonial officials, fully-fledged hostilities did not break out, and Tawake was placed under the jurisdiction of colonial government.[198] The significance of this for colonial government was immense, and not lost on the colonial press, where it was proclaimed as 'a triumph incalculably more brilliant than has ever been achieved by gallant British generals and their armies, aided by saps, Armstrong guns, large commissariats, bloodshed, and all the thou-

---

[196] *Daily Southern Cross*, 10 September 1868; also see *Te Rarawa: Historical Overview Report*, vol. 1, pp. 97–9; Evelyn Stokes, 'The Muriwhenua Land Claims Post 1865, Wai 45 and Others', pp.

[197] Maning to the editor, *New Zealander*, August 1864, in Jack Lee, *Hokianga* (Auckland, 1987), p. 181.

[198] These developments were closely followed in press and official reports, e.g. *Nelson Examiner*, 15 September 1868, *Daily Southern Cross*, 15 August 1868, 8 September 1868.

sand and one concomitants of a New Zealand campaign.'[199] Indigenous protocols that unequivocally integrated 'half-castes' into indigenous life nonetheless produced a conjuncture that enabled a small but pivotal assertion of colonial governance.

Half-castes, both as subjects to be governed and as subjects of discourse, illustrated how indigenous discourses were also 'encounters in place'. These two dimensions were inseparable, of course, and *hāwhe kāehe* drew together both the bodies that were claimed and the spaces and discourses in which those claims were articulated. This at a time when indigenous spaces and discourses were under stresses that were unimaginable in the scientific and scholarly publics and societies in domestic Britain. In Britain the pressures of new ideas, women, or groups and classes to enter spaces of privileged discourse, from Parliament to the BAAS, were strong and had great effect; but in New Zealand colonial efforts marshalled armies, tenurial revolutions, dispossessions and institutions on a societal scale, all tasked to control indigenous bodies, resources and not least discursive places, aiming to usurp or erase the efficacy of indigenous discourses. The extent and intensity of colonial warfare and government had rapid and substantial effect on indigenous lives and discourses: the invasion of the Waikato, for instance, forced the Maori King to relocate his capital, with its *marae*— embodying a key Kīngitanga public—out of his lands and into those of his ally. The invasion also enabled the colonial seizure of his printing press, and the reopening, to a significant degree, of the lands and people to the colonial mail, missionaries and government discourses of law, land tenure and governance. As indigenous communities and spaces became subject to multifarious, often violent, incursions from soldiers, officials, settlers and other indigenous groups, the kinds of careful regulation and deliberate appropriation that characterized earlier indigenous approaches to encounter were less sustainable. Colonial interventions had often been chronic, but the War made them acute.

The leveraging of half-castes by colonialism made some indigenous response necessary, but the complexity and vigor of these responses was striking. Tangata Whenua did not simply appropriate 'half-caste' into a new tongue and new discourses, but integrated competing notions of 'hāwhe kāehe' into indigenous discourses, and contested colonial configurations with indigenous ones, marked by kinship, belonging, and *aroha*. The key contexts for this were the cohering of indigenous publics that retained much of their autonomy, even under tremendous, often unprecedented, pressures. The competition to claim and rule half-caste bodies and mixed families that

---

[199] *Otago Witness*, 18 July 1868.

so diverted the colonial press was an outgrowth of this preceding discursive struggle over the substance and meaning of *hāwhe kāehe* and half-caste: extensions of the 'taua pepa' or paper war. In this *taua* colonial conceptions of half-castes—that they would be realigned with settler society and brought under the purview of colonialism—were only partially successful. The capacity of indigenous life and discourse to produce subjectivities amongst *hāwhe kāehe* that resisted this, and that led to most people being strongly aligned with their *whānau*, their *mātua wahine* or maternal ancestors, was remarkable. In the face of strategic and military losses, population reduction, resource alienation and new colonial institutions this capacity was critical for the sustainability of *hapū* and *whānau*. Despite the unenviable and precipitous positions in which many Tangata Whenua found themselves after the War, a capacious remodelled terrain of indigenous discourses remained. This ability to be indigenous in new ways, in new places, amongst multiple communities and generations, survived the battlefields because it was sustained around the hearth, and in indigenous discourses that militias, armies and indigenous allies did not defeat. Though some half-castes had proven to be important points through which colonial access and challenges were advanced, the efficacy and power of indigenous discourses and the political, kin and social relationships they embodied had substantially challenged and circumscribed this colonial strategy.

*****

The Wars were neither an easy nor a complete success for colonial or imperial rule. On the one hand, effective government was largely relocated to settlers, a shift some imperial officials felt keenly. On the other hand, colonial sovereignty was still significantly truncated, and indigenous *mana* and autonomy were evident through much of the colony. Whole regions of the North Island were still, in practice, held to be independent and ruled by 'natives'. Even after the Wars officials openly acknowledged these restrictions: one official dismissed a settler's claim to a piece of land in the East Cape by explaining that it 'Might as well be within the walls of the holy city of Mecca'.[200] Grey's successor as governor, George Bowen, still thought not only that the split between natives and Europeans was complete and irrevocable, but that natives were destined to become a separate nation under their own sovereignty. He even proposed British sovereignty formally retreat and extend a 'modified recognition, within certain districts, and to an extent not inconsistent with the Suzerainté of the Queen—of the so-called "Maori King".'[201] Even the thought of this

---

[200] OLC 4/20: Curnin, memo, 27 February 1872.
[201] ATL, Ms-0253, Bowen to Lord Lyttleton, confidential report, draft, 4 August 1869.

chilled Bowen, who considered the King an 'insolent barbarian'; 'but as he was not conquered by Generals Chute & Cameron with 10,000 regular troops, it is absurd to suppose that he can be conquered by the raw and scanty Colonial levies alone.'[202] Bowen's point of view is understandable, but his conflation of the parameters of colonial rule with military success meant he did not appreciate the ground colonial sovereignty had made through other, tender, yet no less intrusive, colonial manoeuvres.

In this sense, and in other kindred ones, the Wars were a workshop for colonial activities and projects, especially for 'race-making'. The work of transforming race largely from prescribed categories of government into operational categories integral to ordinary colonial discourse and practice was greatly advanced by war. As proved to be the case with other imperial and colonial wars, the 1860s New Zealand Wars presented unprecedented opportunities for altering the dimensions of colonialism, with the massive movement of people, the appropriation or destruction of resources, and the political opportunities that warfare occasioned. The intense jostling described in this chapter, whether over marriage, jurisdiction, discourse, subjecthood, rights, loyalty or the ambit of the state, were peculiarly (but not uniquely) manifest in the half-castes and mixed families. The racial crossings at which these people were thought to be found remained highly contestable intersections, and colonial perceptions of danger that often accompanied these proximities illustrated this. As the colonial state was indeed 'growing into sovereignty', the difficulties and unevenness apparent at racial crossings marked both growing pains and stunted growth, but the capacity and reach of colonial sovereignty and the state nonetheless dramatically increased.

A keystone of the continued integrity of indigenous communities, kinship, subjectivities and polities was the sustained efficacy of *whānau*. This was despite the broad opportunities the War provided for government to intrude and intervene in these crucibles of indigenous life. By targeting material dimensions of indigenous life colonial government could clearly alter the circumstances of *whānau*: land, resources, location, and opportunities for peace. But the most invasive colonial tactic in this realm proved to be none of these so much as the Native Land Court, and this was not due directly to its purpose of assigning title to land, but owed to the processes and modes it adopted: the breaking up of alliances and communal groupings, the fostering or reawakening of rivalries, the recognition or valuing of only certain relationships, and other processes intended to reorder indigenous resources and lives. But even in the face

---

[202] ATL , Ms-0253, Bowen to Lord Lyttleton, confidential report, draft, 4 August 1869.

of all this, not only did the independence of some indigenous polities persist, the *whānau* and *whanaungatanga* that both undergirded and exceeded indigenous politics retained their integrity. The disposition of half-castes remained a good measure of this. Guides, informants, soldiers, troublemakers and double operatives who worked chiefly for colonial government were amongst the most celebrated half-castes, but there is no question that they were in the minority. That the greater number of *hāwhe kāehe* aligned themselves with their mother's family, with indigenous discourses and practices, and with their maternal ancestors, was a key aspect of the continued communal vitality and integrity that survived the multiple traumas of the Wars. For most this was directly forged in the *whānau*, where they might be nursed in *whanaungatanga*, indigenous community and politics at a remove from colonial discourses, institutions and practices. But even when this education was faced with direct colonial or religious competition, it remained consistently powerful and successful. The majority of *hāwhe kāehe*, when presented with choices, made ones that engaged them with indigenous orbits, rather than aligned them substantially with colonial spaces, discourses or institutions.[203] Hori, a half-caste captured in the Wars and put on trial for murder, illustrated this power perfectly. Though from the north, he had decided to join the Taranaki people in their war against the colonial forces. He was not even amongst his relatives, and originally he had wanted to go home, but he eventually made up his mind, as he put it, 'to be a Maori with the Maoris'.[204]

Settlers and officials had known since before they left Britain that the management of people through race, gender and sexuality was fundamental for successful colonialism. Racial amalgamation had institutionalized particular kinds of approaches to these problems as policy, and the Wars bore out their continued significance. These strategies ensured that racial crossings mattered for colonialism. On the one hand this was clear as the settlers were 'growing into the sovereignty of New Zealand', and native policy touched every element of colonial life, not only governing the grand strategic questions of the day. On the other hand, the management of these concerns also shaped the intimate dimensions of settler life, and colonial ambitions. Racial crossings entangled and concentrated these activities. In both of these two seemingly very different scales, racial

---

[203] One can see a colonial recognition of this in the Qualification of Electors Act, 1879. Not only did it count most half-castes as Maori, but it also hinged on the mother: 'An aboriginal inhabitant of New Zealand and includes any half-caste living as a member of a native tribe according to their customs and usages and any descendants of such a half caste by a Maori woman.'
[204] *Daily Southern Cross*, 5 June 1863.

crossings seemed to be integral to the processes of colonizing, both in the largest of racial and policy terms, and in these very intense and intimate moments of war—the dangerous proximities. As one commentator mused, 'nothing will save the Maori race but amalgamation or incorporation with our own', regardless of whether these marriages remained 'a matter of taste, or want of taste'. 'Let the two races be interwoven', it was declared.[205] Racial crossings were a distinct and intense point of application for colonialism.

One story that was both keenly watched and gently mocked can serve as a parable of the broader problem of race crossing during the Wars. This was the powerfully professed love of an imperial soldier for a young woman. This was not of course unusual, though the circumstances were. The soldier had met the young woman while out in the field, and she was not a settler woman but a half-caste. Complicating matters further was that the woman in question had sided with anti-colonial forces, and was likely active on the battlefield. This young half-caste woman had been shot and wounded and, if this were not enough, the soldier who subsequently became her suitor had fired this shot. In a rush of tenderness afterwards, the soldier had taken her wounded from the field of battle, and nursed her back to health. He then made plain his desire to marry her. This promised to be a fable of the War, a colonial romance of racial amalgamation where conflict (with some injury but no lasting damage) was set aside for love and a mixed family, under the rule of a patriarch and colonial sovereignty. What could have been more fitting or more tender? One of the newspaper headlines declared it 'Chivalry in War'.[206] But evidently such chivalry, such tenderness in the contexts of violence and colonialism—and the charms of the soldier himself—could not draw such an attachment. The half-caste woman refused both the proposal and the attention.

---

[205] *Daily Southern Cross*, 5 November 1862.
[206] 'Chivalry in War': *Daily Southern Cross*, 29 July 1864; fuller account, *Evening Post*, 22 February 1865.

Conclusion: Dwelling in Unity

Behold, how good and pleasant it is
For brethren to dwell together in unity!
It is like the precious oil upon the head,
Running down on the beard,
The beard of Aaron,
Running down on the edge of his garments.

In October 1862, in the uneasy quiet between the Taranaki and Waikato Wars, indigenous groups from throughout the North Island gathered at Peria, in the Waikato. Peria was a new kind of indigenous space, a Christian community founded by Wiremu Tamihana Tarapipipi and named for the Biblical town of Beria (Acts 17: 10). Peria was 'a land of abundance' before the War, with all the trappings of a prosperous and modern community including a post office, school house and flour mill.[1] Tamihana was a devout Christian and pacificist and had sought to avert war, even visiting the governor in Auckland, only to be disrespectfully neglected: 'We are treated like dogs', Tamihana had remarked of that visit, 'I will not go again.'[2] By 1862 Tamihana had largely abandoned hopes of reasonable negotiation, but not his faith. At the Peria meeting Tamihana's most important speech took the form of a sermon on Psalm 133: 'Behold, how good and pleasant it is for brethren to dwell together in unity.'[3] The sermon was widely admired, and Tamihana's call for unity had, according to one colonial observer, 'great effect' in 'relating the benefits produced by

---

[1] Cowan, *The New Zealand Wars*, 1, p. 455.
[2] B.Y. Ashwell to C.M.S., 1 May 1861: tss, AIM. John White, *The Ancient History of the Maori*, XI, p. 233.
[3] Henry William Tucker, *Memoir of the Life and Episcopate of George Augustus Selwyn, D.D.*, London, 1879, vol. 2, pp. 181–2. In the Bible in *te Reo*, Psalm 133 has a different quality to it. Rather than the gendered 'brethren' for instance, which has no specific equivalent, it uses the words for older and younger siblings, and pivots on the verb *whakaaro*, namely 'Na, ano te pai, ano te ahuareka o te nohoanga o nga teina, o nga tuakana I runga it te whakaaro kotahi!'

the union of Maori tribes'.[4] The audience was a large and important group of indigenous leaders and representatives, and many had come great distances. This unity of brethren was already much realized in the Kīngitanga, but was both far from complete and under tremendous pressure from settlers and colonial government. Tamihana called for others to join.

Tamihana had opposed inviting the governor, as some of his allies had suggested, but in his audience was George Selwyn, Bishop of New Zealand. Struck by the artfulness and power of Tamihana's speech, and knowing firsthand his *mana*, Selwyn reacted strongly to this sermon and asked to deliver his own in the afternoon. Rather than put forward another text, or move to another theme, Selwyn's sermon returned to Psalm 133. Its purpose was not to oppose unity, nor argue for fracture, but to contest the vision of unity that Tamihana had put forward. Selwyn's sermon was a sermon, in effect, on racial amalgamation, and the chosen figure, embodying that vision of unity, was the half-caste. 'Here am I, a mediator [*Takawaenga*] for New Zealand', Selwyn preached, in *te Reo*.

> This is my work, mediation, I am not a Pakeha, neither am I a Maori; I am a half-caste. I have eaten your food, and I have slept in your houses: we have eaten together, talked together, travelled together, prayed together, and partaken of the Lord's Supper together; and therefore I tell you that I am a half-caste. My being a half-caste cannot be altered (or uprooted). It is in my body, in my flesh, in my sinews, in my bones, and in my marrow. We are all half-castes; your clothes . . . Your strength . . . Your soldiers are half-caste . . . Your 'mana' (power or authority) is half-caste; the 'mana' is Maori 'mana', but the name [King] is Pakeha. Your religion is half-caste . . . Hence, I say to you, we are all half-castes; therefore let us live together in one religion, one love, and one law.[5]

Selwyn sought to specifically answer Tamihana's powerful rhetoric. Rather than concede Tamihana's vision of unity amongst 'brethren', Selwyn had used the figure and position of the half-caste and recast both himself and his audience as embodiments of a new kind of unity. Selwyn had contested the limits of Tamihana's vision of unity with the language and undergirding rationales of racial amalgamation. He had not only challenged Tamihana's use of the Bible, but had appropriated a common Kīngitanga expression—one faith, one love and one law—and not as a Kīngitanga aphorism, but as a tenet of racial amalgamation. It was evident Selwyn imagined that this 'one law', as well as one love and faith, would be governed by colonial churches, laws and institutions. More than this, with

[4] Gorst, *The Maori King*, pp. 318–19.
[5] Bishop Selwyn, speech, Peria, 27 October 1862, AJHR, E-12, 1863, pp. 4–6. The speech was widely reprinted in the colonial press.

the same rhetorical moves he simultaneously reaffirmed colonialism and difference, even as he expressed solidarity.

Selwyn's self-fashioning as a half-caste was particularly striking, because he was a consummate Victorian. A stellar graduate of Eton and Cambridge (and for whom Selwyn College, Cambridge was later named), a friend of Gladstone, one of the original 'muscular Christians', and one of the most celebrated churchmen of his age, Selwyn was about as English, and as Victorian, as they came. But these dimensions and connections were hardly relevant to the discourses that prevailed in Peria. Using the most intimate and affective language available to him, Selwyn was trying for something radical and far-reaching, through access to an arena of discourse that was mostly closed to Pākehā. The point was not that Selwyn was being disingenuous when he declared himself a half-caste. His identification with Tangata Whenua was genuine, and amongst many the affection was mutual. Nor was Selwyn's claim that the 'one faith' belonged to all contradicted by his riding, only a few months later, in the train of the colonial and imperial forces as they went to battle. In making his case for a different conception of unity, one that was relevant and recognizable to Tangata Whenua and in indigenous discourses, Selwyn was doing so through a different conception of the half-caste, and a different evaluation of the meaning of racial crossings. Half-castes, for Selwyn, as for many other settlers and officials, may have been go-betweens, but only in ways consistent with racial amalgamation. Their work of mediation was legitimate only if aligned with, and framed by, colonialism, and half-castes were destined to be claimed by the church and the state, and racially amalgamated.

Selwyn's declaration that he was a half-caste seems to have been thoughtfully received at Peria; it had a very different impact in colonial circles. In settler publics Selwyn had many critics: they had long dismissed him as unduly sympathetic to natives, and disdained him as the 'Maori Bishop'.[6] For them, his claim to being a half-caste was given a wildly different construction. Selwyn-the-half-caste was openly mocked.[7] Already seen by most settlers as overly gentle, weak and wrongheaded, Selwyn's new turn as a half-caste confirmed to many that he was 'scrupulous to folly', and that the 'natives' were 'Bishop Selwyn's pets'.[8] Selwyn was even blamed for the war, supposedly because he had 'indulged ['natives'] beyond any example in the history of colonisation'. Selwyn, his critics urged, had failed to understand that 'these are questions which

---

[6] *Taranaki Herald*, 13 June 1863.
[7] *Nelson Examiner*, 7 January 1863.
[8] *Taranaki Herald*, 13 June 1863.

will have to be decided by war and its inevitable attendants and consequences.' Only the most thoughtful of colonial responses were more
careful and willing to entertain the situation in which it was given, and
the import of his sermon:

> We are not all aware how far Bishop Selwyn may be excused in speaking in
> language which seemed to strip him of something of his national character,
> and in adopting a tone not very creditable to British civilisation. What can the
> Bishop mean when he speaks of himself as a 'half-caste'. If he be so, then in
> what relation does he stand to his own countrymen? We are aware that a
> meaning may be imposed upon these words which it may not be improper to
> tolerate, though there is but small dignity in such condecension [*sic*]; but . . .
> they were as little creditable to his judgment as to his taste.[9]

The dangerous line Selwyn was held to be crossing was being carefully
staked. He was risking his 'national character' and potentially discrediting
the project of British civilization. Where would he then stand with 'his own
countrymen'—settlers and Britons? How could such speech be dignified,
or befit a Bishop? Even though this writer could imagine the usefulness of
the rhetoric, the figure of the half-caste was held to be sufficiently marginal
and questionable, with a status that was at least potentially improper, that
merely placing oneself in such a rhetorical position was an impugnable
offence. Yet such strong language had to be reconciled with durable
notions—in the very same newspapers, no less—that invested half-castes
and mixed marriages with an abiding and urgent legitimacy.

In his own experience, then, Selwyn was discovering it was easier to be a
half-caste amongst Tangata Whenua than amongst settlers. The same
position he had claimed—as half-caste—and which he argued put him
in a position of mediation, had in the eyes of many settlers made him
marginal and suspect. Settlers themselves considered half-castes to be of
peculiar importance to both settler patriarchs and colonial government,
and actively pursued both individual half-castes and half-caste policy. Yet
these inclusive claims over half-castes were thoroughly provisional, and
allocated half-castes to visible positions where they could easily (and
ordinarily) be made marginal. Selwyn's experiences, and his self-fashioning
as a half-caste, were indicative of the perils of acting as *takawaenga* even
when one was not a 'real' half-caste.

While trying to navigate post-war Taranaki, Selwyn was so unpopular
with settlers that he was openly booed, or 'hooted', by a settler mob.
Selwyn answered the mob that it was 'more English-like to look me in the
face and tell me your grievances'. A lively debate then ensued. Leaving the

---

[9] *Taranaki Herald*, 7 February 1863.

township and its 'hoots' Selwyn then went about the country of the Ngāti Ruanui, one of the principal anti-colonial combatants of the Taranaki War. One Ngāti Ruanui man confronted Selwyn and told him he must leave, that he should not travel in their lands, and that he would be seen as a spy. Selwyn's reply carried, no doubt, great feeling: 'I am like wheat. The Pakeha at Taranaki were the upper-stone grinding me there, and now you grind me here.'[10] This would have been a classic rendition of being caught in the proverbial middle, except that after this discussion Selwyn was invited to continue, and was left unmolested by Tangata Whenua to investigate the War and its aftermath. Again, the position of mediator seemed to be easier amongst the People of the Land, even lands torn by war.

But the question was not just whether half-castes would be *takawaenga* or whether they would be ground 'like wheat'. Colonial practices recognized them conditionally, in both ways, and others besides. Rather than turning on an announced exclusivity, it worked substantially through an inclusivity, though one that was always provisional. Half-castes would be included, under the right circumstances, and would be allowed access to certain colonial privileges and protections. But this was conditional on their removal from native categories and particular 'native' situations and allegiances, and was subject to their alignment with colonial institutions, sovereignty and strategies of rule. Such unity was not intended to, and evidently did not, make half-castes invisible: the 'racial' did not end with 'amalgamation', but the processes and instruments of amalgamation worked to make race identifiable and enduring. Nor did racial amalgamation produce the equality that purported to inhere in the project, its policies and laws. Selwyn's fashioning of himself as a half-caste and the predictable settler responses made this clear. In such a provisional manner half-castes and mixed families could be incorporated, levered out of indigenous communities and the native categories, yet would remain discernible from settlers or colonists, and susceptible to interventions on this basis. Inclusivity was conjoined with powerful and abiding racial differentiations. Half-castes might be mediators, *takawaenga*, provided they were aligned with colonialism; otherwise they were often prone to inhabit the predicament Selwyn mourned, and be ground 'like wheat', just as if they were 'natives'.

Half-castes and mixed families were indeed important to many different parties in New Zealand, but these interests were not equivalent. Rewi Maniapoto and Sir George Grey, for instance, contested over half-castes,

[10] G.W. Rusden, *The History of New Zealand* (Melbourne, 1883), vol. 2, p. 103, n. 1.

but would not have agreed on why they were important, nor how, where or with whom they should live their lives. The conflict was not that competing claims, interests and understandings were identical, similar or equivalent, but that they could no longer be made to coexist. This was made dramatic as this conflict came to centre, intensely, on particular individuals and bodies and their kin. This was a conflict distinguishable from, but entangled with, that between colonial sovereignty and *mana*; it was evident in Selwyn and Tamihana's sermons, and in myriad other places, in increasingly intense ways. It is also evident that these different understandings of racial crossings were not *inevitable* sources of conflict: 'half-castes' had emerged in the fray of encounters between indigenous and settler or colonial encounters, and the great majority of these were peaceful. The particularities of settlement, indigenous living, and political and cultural strategies—and much else—had shaped what these racial crossings could mean, and set their stakes. For colonial and imperial government racial crossings had been shaped and loaded as fields where power and rule might be applied or transferred; indigenous polities and families regarded these same people and groups as integral to their own domains. Neither set of interests could afford to give way, yet neither had it entirely their own way.

Racial crossing was not only a ground for discursive contests, but an illustration of the unevenness and particularity of how discourses circulated and were distributed. This was true even within the relatively constrained boundaries of the New Zealand colony, and characterized the fractured and particular terrains that these discourses traversed across the Empire (and between empires). On the one hand, even the words of articulate, powerful, public imperial men such as Selwyn and Grey in New Zealand or Wakefield and Stephen in London were profoundly conditioned by their particular locations. The varied understandings of Selwyn's speech at Peria serve as a powerful example of how 'the production of meaning [was] never independent of the pragmatics of social space.'[11] On the other hand, though, the powerful conditions of locality were neither total nor fatally restrictive: discourses relevant to the problem of racial crossing were also remarkably, though never uniformly, mobile and durable. Local particulars were defining, but not singularly so; these localities were unevenly and intermittently drawn into empire's connections and disconnects. The problem of racial crossing, broadly construed, continued to have an integrative capacity, cohering different discourses into conversation, as well as opening up to new fields and relations of

---

[11] James Epstein, *In Practice*, p. 109.

power. The chief agents in this were diverse groups and political parties: missionary societies, businesses, patrons, private and scientific societies. In the New Zealand case, the first consolidated approach to the problem of racial crossing had been by the joint stock New Zealand Company, working with the patronage of key Colonial Reformers, and the backing of key societies and officials. However, by the mid-1840s it had become clear that official and institutional practice were to be the most salient.

These official concentrations of discourse were epitomized, in both their qualities and their limitations, by colonial archives. Though colonial archives were hidden, sprawling and immense, they were not boundless accumulations of knowledge, but specific discursive formations occupying actual places (that a fire at one time destroyed a significant portion of New Zealand's colonial archive illustrates this). The archive responded very closely to colonial rules and protocols, and its 'encounters in place' could be mediated by colonial government and organized accordingly. This was in line with the work of archives, which was not just to document colonial rule but to enable and organize it. Official sanctions were deliberately given to certain texts and genres of texts, and official eminence lent to certain discourses. From the inception of colonial rule in New Zealand race had been enshrined—in ways that were considered mere matters of course—as an archival principle, one significantly drawn from other colonial experiences, discourses and archives. As a result race profoundly conditioned the New Zealand colonial archive: everything from the colonial land regime to the purchasing of liquor and the taxing of dogs. This had the abiding effect, too, of naturalizing race, and substantiating many of the claims previously embodied in the archive. Race was an *archival principle*, and it was a matter of course that it guided the increasing capacity of government to rule, and made these distinctions and differences self-evident and natural. Within this archive, racial amalgamation was a continuing preoccupation: not always starkly evident, but retaining an expansive and lasting influence. Racial amalgamation spanned a variety of archival divisions, and was fundamental to a variety of policies, but also educated the archive, which was attentive and thickened accordingly at relevant moments. But the markedly limited effective jurisdictions that were evident to colonial rule—most powerfully the continued independence of Tangata Whenua—were embodied within the archives, whose limits echoed those constraining government.

The colonial archives made the dispute between Tangata Whenua and 'Europeans' seem vividly political, but underlying cultural and epistemological differences were at least as important. A focus on racial crossings brings this firmly into view, as explicitly political developments make sense only when put alongside distinctive cultural formations and intellectual projects. Moreover, when different concepts or understandings came into competition or conflict, it was clear that they were not resolved by power of argument, but in more prosaic or material ways or, often, did not necessarily need to be resolved at all. More often relations of power and material dimensions, rather than the content or persuasiveness of argument—between Tangata Whenua and Europeans as much as between the Ethnological Society and the Anthropologicals—were decisive or critical. There were few better illustrations than the response to Charles Darwin's call for a return, in effect, to 'natural history'—that all classifications needed to be genealogical. In the wake of *Origin of Species* the main streams of public colonial and imperial discourse went in very different directions, reifying and freezing typologies in humans and nature. These typologies had much in common with statistics and bureaucracy, but were fundamentally contrary to Darwin's evolution. What makes this ironic was that in New Zealand, where the decades after 1859 were supercharged with producing colonial categories of rule that were racial, typological and monochrome, indigenous understandings of difference were much more compatible with those advanced by Darwin. Indigenous discourses, as has been seen, were primarily historical, genealogical and sought to describe relationships rather than place individuals in classificatory schemes of type. Darwin followed a similar path when he sought to organize groups by 'community of descent', and argued for a system that was, in his own words, 'genealogical'.[12] The apparent harmony between these new Darwinist views and indigenous ones was an important illustration that it was the operations of power that were decisive, rather than the acuity of ideas or their ability to account for the 'realities' of the world.

As a problem racial crossing continued to maintain the capacity to focus and concentrate different kinds of attention, to preoccupy texts and practice, and to integrate otherwise separate or even disparate discourses. The lack of a single unanimous or hegemonic position with respect to racial crossing contributed to, rather than undermined, this durability. Equivocating over whether half-castes would be an influence for 'good or evil', for instance, focused discursive and governmental attention, and shaped the distribution of resources and relationships of power. Irrespective of which answer you felt was correct, the common result was a focusing of attention: half-castes needed to be (as one missionary had put it) 'watched over'.[13] The problem of racial crossing continued to make the differences between races, mixed families, half-castes and other mixed

---

[12] Darwin, *Origin of Species*, pp. 420, 455.
[13] Morgan, Letters and Journals, 2, fos. 302–3: Morgan to CMS secretaries, 23 December 1847.

people, visible, legible and relevant—to government, scholarship, law, history and much more. The problem itself, while setting the parameters of the intersection, did not however make any particular response necessary. The problem provided the grounds to accommodate vigorous and opposing views, and could refine, focus and support purportedly incompatible positions, not least segregation, amalgamation and racial extinction. The problem of race crossing marked the field, charged it with significance, but left pivotal questions open, while in the process foreclosing the possibility of others. It was this organizing power that meant race could at once be unified and conflicted, diverse and dispersed—pregnant, and in certain ways, impregnable.

Consistent with this understanding of the problem of racial crossing is the striking prominence of racial amalgamation, which might otherwise seem counter-intuitive in the face of the so-called 'hardening' of race in the 1860s. The seismic events that serve as waymarks in this—the Morant Bay Rebellion, the Indian 'Mutiny' and the New Zealand Wars— unquestionably reshaped the topography of racial discourses and the publics and spaces that produced and trafficked them. As before, racial amalgamation was clearly not the only approach tailored to the problem of racial crossing, yet as before it was entrenched in crucial fields of empire. Treating racial amalgamation as whimsy or a mere cover for colonial brutality explains neither its particulars nor its success in the face of a number of other possibilities, many of which were attached to powerful publics and political communities (not least in the case of the 'Jamaica Controversy' in Britain following the Morant Bay 'Rebellion'). Racial amalgamation's proponents drew from varied constituencies of settlers, officials, missionaries and scholars, who advanced racial amalgamation in serious and determined ways. These proponents crafted a racial amalgamation that was compatible with a range of projects and rhetoric: from reform, humanitarianism and Christianity to specific forms of colonialism such as land tenure and free labour, or sovereignty and the law. As a result, racial amalgamationists cannot be easily typed by political allegiance, religion, occupation, class or (so far as can be discerned) gender. Even New Zealand settlers, so long held as bogies by the Colonial Office, were themselves by and large racial amalgamationists. Racial amalgamation was a critical strategic convergence, and this can be seen if consideration is given to its entanglements with liberalism. This was an important conjuncture, given the origins of some of the leaders of racial amalgamation: Colonial Reformers, Liberal Anglicans and Liberals more generally. Like racial amalgamation, liberalism was gradual and progressive, and assumed what Uday Mehta has called the 'provisionality' of other races. Both called for the privileged classes and the better races 'to complete that which was incomplete, static, backward, or otherwise regnant, and to guide it to a higher plateau of stability, freedom, and purposefulness—to hitch it to a more meaningful teleology': progress.[14]

John Stuart Mill's 1865 *Considerations on Representative Government* captures the sustained and vigorous relevance of racial amalgamation, decades after its early iterations in the 1830s. In this key work Mill argued for the desirability of representative government, but considered that there were certain situations where it was 'inapplicable'. Representative government was only for those 'of [Britain's] own blood and language', people 'ripe' to receive it. For other races, notably those in India, such days were 'still at a great distance'. Mill fundamentally assumed racial difference and inequality, but coupled this with a strong advocacy for the necessity and desirability of racial amalgamation. Mill argued that there was great advantage in different populations crossing: that 'when it was originally an inferior and more backward portion of the human race, the absorption is greatly to its advantage.' Offering a scattering of examples of various inferior races (Basques, Welsh, Breton, Highlanders) lifted to British or French nationality, Mill continued to argue the desirability of crossing, and called upon the familiar analogue of animals. 'The united people, like a crossed breed of animals . . . inherits the special aptitudes and excellences of all its progenitors, protected by the admixture from being exaggerated into the neighbouring vices.'[15] Mill was hardly an advocate of revolutionary racial equality and made it clear that 'representative government' by a small portion of population over a majority was entirely proper, if that minority were 'markedly superior' because of 'difference of race, [or] more civilized origin'. As Mill himself put it, 'the first lesson of civilization [is] that of obedience.'[16] As a result Mill's arguments not only accorded with prevalent Liberal arguments and projects, but were compatible with those of many of his most vehement opponents. (Neither were Mill's greatest disputes, not least over Jamaica, always about what they seemed to be.[17]) Such arguments were instructive, not only in the way colonial practices and discourses were fashioned and consumed, but in partially accounting for the continued valence of racial amalgamation.

Resonances between British metropolitan reforms and colonial racial amalgamations were sharply evident in 1867. That year both New Zealand and metropolitan Britain extended their electoral franchise: in Britain,

---

[14] Uday Mehta, *Liberalism and Empire: a Study in Nineteenth Century Liberal Thought* (Chicago, 1999), p. 191.
[15] John Stuart Mill, *Considerations on Representative Government* (London, 1861), pp. 131, 122.
[16] Mill, *Representative Government*, pp. 33, 30.
[17] Hall, *White, Male and Middle-Class*, pp. 255–94.

through the second Reform Act, and in New Zealand via the Maori Representation Act. In Britain reform was a way, as with its 1832 predecessor, of relieving political pressure, appropriating political energy and reconstituting the polity in limited and controlled ways.[18] In New Zealand, reform addressed the racial definition of the franchise. The opening of parliament to 'Maori' (the Act, importantly, used the word, though it was still common amongst settlers to use 'native') was designed to incorporate 'native' leadership while both limiting and controlling it, and to subject natives to a variety of colonial institutions and surveillance. Discriminatory inclusivity remained a defining strategy: Māori representation reinscribed and reified, rather than erased, racial difference on the floor of Parliament. This controlled opening to 'natives' also marked the real security that New Zealand settlers and officials now felt. Nonetheless, given the circumstances elsewhere in the Empire and world, and with the majority of adult men without the franchise in Britain (and many 'European' men still without the vote in New Zealand), colonial and metropolitan observers alike could remark that this development appeared unusually progressive—a 'happy augury' of New Zealand's 'future harmony'.[19]

Racial amalgamation did not hinge on exceptional developments—such as a uniquely humane and beneficent cast amongst the settlers of New Zealand—nor did it stem from a proven track record. Racial amalgamation remained a widely shared strategy despite multiple high-profile failures: the New Zealand Company, Durham's mission to the Canadas, the Cape Colony's abortive attempts to racially amalgamate, and the most turbulent wars New Zealand had seen. A little evidence literally went a long way, and small marks of success in New Zealand had been trumpeted elsewhere as proof of racial amalgamation progressing 'with a rapidity unexampled in history'.[20] Racial amalgamation could consequently be appropriated as successful regardless of its actual record, and made available and transferable. Grey, as has been shown, was quickly dispatched to the Cape Colony to amalgamate populations there, and the Colonial Office wished only that it had more Greys to send. Policies and individual papers were held up as models, and supporters of racial amalgamation from Charles Buller to Bishop Selwyn acted as consultants, critics or even oracles. Helping to make racial amalgamation transferable, and give it further valence in the discourses of empire, was a cohering of New

[18] Catherine Hall, 'The Nation Within and Without', in Hall *et al.*, *Defining the Victorian Nation*, pp. 179–233.
[19] *New Zealand Parliamentary Debates* (1867), 1, p. 465: Donald McLean.
[20] GBPP 1852, (1475), p. 21: Grey to Earl Grey, 30 August 1851.

Zealand's reputation. New Zealand was *the* example of reformed and tender British colonization, and was explicitly governed in accord with racial amalgamation. Such a reputation not only exceeded its actual record but, as Chapter 1 showed, it preceded it. Yet all this further provided for the circulation of racial amalgamation as a tender, model, form of British colonialism, a claim not simply due to its local practices in New Zealand, but enabled and shaped by its relationship with a number of effective discourses.

By the 1870s, racial amalgamation was broadly, though not universally, persuasive in colonial and imperial circles. Central to these understandings of racial amalgamation was a broadly conceived intermarriage or fusion of races under a unified domain of sovereignty, government and law. What made racial amalgamation even more distinctive, however, was that it was not just any kind of crossing. Racial amalgamation was not just any combination. A proper amalgamation did not combine two races into a 'new' race that was substantially mixed or intermediate; rather the process of amalgamation projected, very baldly, the *disappearing* of one race into another. This was what Merivale had imagined as early as 1841, and had called 'the only possible Euthanasia of savage communities'.[21] Yet, although the other race would then no longer exist *as a race*, race itself would still pertain, still visible in individuals. An entire race might disappear, but racial markings lingered, enabling at the same time both the continued sorting by race and its disavowal. A complete racial amalgamation would make 'native' polities, families, legal structures and communities disappear, leaving only remnants or relics. Racial amalgamation was an *inclusion* through which the other race would be consumed or absorbed, ceasing to exist yet still visibly and practically different. The inclusion was unequal, and its processes and mechanisms fashioned and enabled continuing inequities. It was precisely this professed inclusivity and intimacy that were critical to the self-understandings of racial amalgamation's protagonists and promoters, who understood it to be humane, benevolent, Christian and generous. Would they not be man and brother-in-law?

Racial amalgamation, then, was not just a grandiose ascription given to a set of loosely combined policies, but a coherent and identifiable strategy. It was more than just a policy platform, but presented readings of law, history, nature, races and theology, readings that diverse and competing people and groups found compelling. It was, as a result, well fitted to address the complicated and distributed problem of racial crossing. This

---

[21] Merivale, *Lectures on Colonization and Colonies*, 2, pp. 180–1.

was helped by the comparative temper pervasive amongst proponents of racial amalgamation, who were attuned not just to different spaces and races but different times. Promoters of racial amalgamation repeatedly cited races that had been successfully amalgamated, such as those in Britain or in the ancient world; they ordinarily pointed pejoratively to places in North or South America, or even sometimes to Australia, Africa or India, to make their negative contrasts explicit. The distinctiveness of racial amalgamation as strategy stemmed not only from its internal characteristics, but also from such contrasts with both past examples and its chief competitors: those who augured (or, less often, advocated) racial extinction, and those who set forth agendas of enduring racial separation, segregation or exceptionalism (often, but not always, married to readings of innate interracial hostility or permanent difference). Read against these alternatives, the tenderness and appeal, as well as the malleability, of racial amalgamation is apparent. Racial amalgamation could be naturalized, it could engender colonial expansion (of a purportedly inclusive variety), inspire active and intensive government, disappear entire races and cultures and yet remain apparently compatible with claims of liberty and Christian morality.

The strategic qualities of racial amalgamation addressed not only different policies, even different colonies, but had intergenerational dimensions. Even comparatively early articulations of racial amalgamation were cast in *generational* terms. Fifty years or longer is a duration not normally relevant to policy-making, yet it was commonly a setting, or reference, in racial amalgamationist discourse. This would be best read as grandiosity—as indeed it often also was—were it not for the demonstrable record, especially in New Zealand but also elsewhere, that it *was* a strategy sustained across generations of government. The durability of racial amalgamation, during some of the Victorian empire's most tumultuous and challenging events, foreshadowed what was to prove a formidable persistence. Such a sustained relevance was enabled by an equal durability for key dimensions of racial discourse, and particularly the broader problem of racial crossing, one whose genealogy was to continue to be significant deep into the twentieth century. These problems and discourses each retained their distributed and connected qualities. The enduring relevance and power of racial amalgamation can be seen in its continuing centrality in New Zealand.

Racial amalgamation proved central to the abiding settler belief that the native race in New Zealand would soon no longer exist—one that was to prove powerful well into the twentieth century. In retrospect it was reasonable to imagine that the censuses of the early twentieth century would have ended these arguments, as they showed clear increases in the tabulated population of 'Māori' (by then a term ordinarily used in both indigenous and official circles). But racial amalgamation conditioned the way this disappearance was apprehended and understood. The disappearance of Māori was not to be the kind of extinction seen elsewhere, but one specified in the discourses of racial amalgamation: intermarriage and inclusion would slowly but surely erase racial difference, and natives would be absorbed by the white race. An increasing 'Māori population' could be reconciled, or even demonstrate, the teleology of disappearance. As a result, in the face of increasing native numbers, European New Zealanders (and even some Tangata Whenua as well) could exercise themselves in mourning for the passing of Māori. Folklorists, artists, collectors and local historians began archiving and documenting the last of the pure-blooded, old-time, or 'real Māoris' (as they were called) in order to, as one leading practitioner put it, do 'justice to the brave race whom we have supplanted.'[22] Monuments were erected. Even the most distinctive voice in these discussions, that of Te Rangihiroa Peter Buck (himself mixed), embraced these views. In 1921, in a soon-to-be-famous lecture, Te Rangihiroa indisputably showed that the Māori population was increasing and youthful. Then he turned this analysis into yet another proof of this familiar narrative, asserting that this increase of population was disproportionately of mixed race, with perhaps as many as 50% of Māori already not 'full-blooded'. This 'miscegenation' (a word that had not previously been widely used in New Zealand), with its cultural and physical dimensions, was 'the stepping-stone to the evolution of a future type of New-Zealander in which we hope the best features of the Maori race will be perpetuated for ever.'[23] His lecture was titled 'The Passing of the Maori' and his argument was that Māori *would* pass away as a race, but that the means of passing was miscegenation. In Buck's, and scores of other kindred accounts, the disappearance of Māori was not only compatible with the purported tenderness of New Zealand race relations, but the result of it.

Racial amalgamation had a heavy investment in the study of Māori racial origins, an investment already apparent in arguments that New Zealand natives were themselves racially mixed. As settlement intensified, and new colonial spaces of discourse were inaugurated, this led to a remarkable outpouring of scholarship, chiefly by settler and imperial

---

[22] James Cowan, 'Maori Place Names', *New Zealand Illustrated Magazine*, 1 June 1900; Chris Hilliard, 'James Cowan and the Frontiers of New Zealand History', *NZJH*, 32 (1997), pp. 219–33.
[23] Te Rangi Hiroa (P.H. Buck), 'The Passing of the Maori', *TPNZI* 55 (1924), pp. 362–75.

scholars, on the 'whence of the Maori'.[24] These were almost always highly compatible with racial amalgamation, and could be powerful reiterations or revivifications of racial amalgamationist discourse. A striking example was the scholarly project to substantiate Aryan origins for New Zealand Māori. This 'discovery' of ancient Indian origins—the 'Aryan Maori' as Edward Tregear put it—was only one of many colonial scholarly efforts that were entangled with racial amalgamation.[25] This enterprise (which was not entirely well received) was yet again a sign of how even apparently idiosyncratic developments were articulated in both imperial and global networks, as Tony Ballantyne's study of Aryanism has revealed.[26] The valence of an Aryan Māori was, of course, also local; Aryan Māori were uniquely positioned and amenable to be amalgamated with settlers. Such findings were no mere coincidence, and the Aryan Māori was no exception. Not just reconciling or legitimating, but naturalizing, racial amalgamation was integral to the work of New Zealand scholars. If Te Rangihiroa's assessment that one could witness 'the passing of the Maori' seemed a little premature, already it had been cast as history. Such developments had begun before 1860, and became cliché in the twentieth century, where national histories often ruminated on this theme. As one important history argued, to a greater or lesser degree Māori would be absorbed in 'the dominant white race', leaving 'a people rich in the stories and traditions of both races, looking back with equal pride to the Maori explorers and navigators and the great leaders of the British people.'[27]

These recapitulations of racial amalgamation again charged the racially mixed as a special population for colonial discourses and government. This was not because half-castes actually lay 'between two worlds', for the territory and spaces of New Zealand were never, and never became, monochrome and bipolar. Rather, these articulations of 'half-castes' were part of the discursive project of racial amalgamation: erasing or disappearing the 'native' or Māori race while preserving racial difference. The stakes, then, remained formidable. But this was a multi-faceted project: in the twentieth century as much as in the nineteenth century it required not only discursive, but other concurrent developments. With respect to half-castes, perhaps the chief set of tasks was levering those identified as half-castes away from alignments with Tangata Whenua and their communities towards colonial subjectivities and institutions. In many respects,

[24] A brief history can be found in K.R. Howe, *The Quest for Origins: Who First Discovered and Settled the Pacific Islands* (Auckland, 2003).
[25] Edward Tregear, *The Aryan Maori* (Wellington, 1885).
[26] Ballantyne, *Orientalism and Race.*
[27] J.B. Condliffe and W.T. Airey, *Short History of New Zealand*, 6th edn revised and expanded: Auckland, Whitcome and Tombs, 1938, p. 2.

and in ways that addressed individuals, this had some significant success. But despite repeated and ongoing claims to the contrary, it was substantially unsuccessful. Despite a great number of tabulated Māori being classified as not 'full-blooded', the majority were unequivocal as to with whom and where they belonged, and how they saw themselves: they were Māori. This was a development that was considered by non-Māori to be remarkable, and was to prove fascinating to scholars, who wondered why, if given access not just to the colonial polity but the white race, literally thousands of people apparently refused, and not just day after day but (by the 1930s and 1940s) generation after generation.

Such developments were inseparable from larger indigenous efforts to sustain, forge and assert distinctive kinds of indigenous unity, symbolized by, but not limited to, the tenor of Tamihana's efforts and increasingly known as *kotahitanga*.[28] It was not the case that this was a natural or simple state of affairs; nor did it reflect some innate biological preference. Rather, it rested on the continual production of indigenous subjectivities, as well as sustained affinities amongst Tangata Whenua for each other, and commitments to a set of shared political, cultural and social values and practices. In the nineteenth century colonial government had also, as has been shown, consistently designated half-castes as a point of entry into indigenous polities, cultures and families. But for a majority of *hapū*—as had happened in the struggle of the Kīngitanga with colonial government for their half-castes—half-castes were equally a field of reassertion and maintenance of independent indigenous domains. By the 1860s colonial government had intensified its attempts to remake indigenous domestic and intimate relations, but indigenous relationships with half-castes and mixed families consistently proved resistant to these colonial activities. As has been argued, of all the conflicts that indigenous polities and communities were to be engaged in, this intimate domestic contest was paramount: and this assessment holds in the decades that follow. The practice and vitality of relationships and discourses that were housed and fostered within *whānau*, particularly in distinctive forms that expressed, maintained and developed indigenous subjectivities, were durable and capacious. Indigenous families and groups were under no illusions that their indispensable resource was people: many knew this more sharply than most, for much else that they had once possessed was already expropriated. *Whānau* could not, and did not, simply give up their *whanaunga*.

These indigenous practices and understandings were not irreconcilable with understandings half-castes came to have of themselves, that distin-

[28] Lindsay Cox, *Kotahitanga: The Search for Māori Political Unity* (Auckland, 1993).

guished themselves as half-castes. Te Rangihiroa proclaimed, as we have seen, that mixed race people were the 'future type' of New Zealander. Harry Dansey agreed, regarding half-castes 'truer New Zealanders than those of full blood of either of the other races', and consequently tasking them as 'pro-consuls extraordinary' (amongst whom he counted himself).[29] The idea of the exceptionality or futurity of half-castes could be, and was, accommodated amongst Tangata Whenua, even as it was appropriated in racial amalgamationist narratives as signalling that one was *not* 'fully' native. But the experiences of half-castes who engaged with settler society and discourses were perforated with moments or signs that showed the indelibility of their own racial markings. Bishop Selwyn had learnt it was easier to 'be' a half-caste amongst Tangata Whenua than settlers, and many subsequent half-castes were to find likewise. This predicament was noticed by a number of observers, including a young Janet Frame growing up in the 1920s and 1930s, and who remembered learning that half-castes were supposed to be subjects of a certain kind of shame, to be 'spoken of as unclean' and also somehow lacking or incomplete—such a person was 'only a half-caste'.[30] Such actualities could not be concealed from the colonized, and placed even more of a premium on the indigenous sociabilities, values and practices to which half-castes retained a full claim.

The complexities of history subsequent to the 1870s make it clear one should not idealize or overstate the continuity or power of *whānau* or other indigenous sociabilities. In the decades after 1900 *whānau* were disproportionately impoverished, comparatively much poorer than they had been before the 1860s wars, and drastically poorer than the average settler domestic unit. The assault continued, through means sometimes brazen and imposing, other times more tender. Though some *hapū* remained integral and powerful presences, the colonial assault on indigenous politics was broadly evident. Colonial government, now with active and often vigorous indigenous participation, had a real presence in most indigenous lives, from 'Native Schools' to land development schemes, from the police force to the Māori battalion. Yet, irrespective of these chronic and acute pressures, the *whānau* remained—in abiding and new forms alike, in 'traditional' settings, and in cities. Moreover, 'half-castes' and other 'mixed' families remained integral to *whānau*. It is indicative that in the twentieth century the figure more often depicted in indigenous writing as troublesome, dangerous or misguided was not the mixed race person, but the 'brown Pakeha' (as Dansey called them)—people who had

---

[29] Introduction, and Harry Dansey, 'Of Two Races', *Te Ao Hou*, 28 September 1959, pp. 6–9.

[30] Janet Frame, *To the Is-land* (New York, 1982), pp. 96, 198.

a *whakapapa* but were more comfortable in Pākehā than indigenous settings, those who occupied 'Pākehā' subjectivities, or did not claim their share in indigenous relationships, responsibilities and values. There were relatively few efforts amongst indigenous groups to expel or purge or to police boundaries (with some notable exceptions around tribal or urban developments). There was no sustained politics of purity, but rather for the most part an abiding politics of inclusion, in keeping with genealogies of indigenous practices evident in the nineteenth century. One marker of this was the relative scarcity of the term *hāwhe kāehe* in twentieth-century publications published in *te Reo*. This indexed the rise of English as a communal language for Tangata Whenua but, more importantly, showed that by this time Pākehā ancestors were commonplace and unexceptional possessions for Tangata Whenua.[31]

The centrality of the *whānau* instructs not only in the fundamental role of gender in conditioning both colonial and indigenous societies and the ways they interacted, but in how the problem of racial crossing was understood and approached. The gendered regime of colonial activity had, as has been shown, delivered single settler men and not single settler women to be the chief participants in racial intermarriage. This had both enabled and limited racial amalgamation. It had also enabled a patriarchal mode of social, legal and political participation to be extended interracially. The gendered inequalities within colonial marriage were used to service racial difference and inequality, and to aid in the inclusion and disappearance of natives within the strategy of racial amalgamation. But this strategy butted against the gendering within the settler family, which largely apportioned the labour of child-rearing to mothers. In a 'mixed' family, where the mother was typically Tangata Whenua, indigenous practices could be central in a purportedly 'settler' family. In the face of this, patriarchal control required shoring up, to assume or discipline gendered labour within settler families, or to attempt to restructure indigenous practices more broadly. There certainly were examples of these paternal interventions: relocation or divorce were not uncommon, other kinds of reductions in a wife or child's *whānau* ties, forbidding *te Reo*, banning of certain practices. Though it is not easy to judge with complete authority, the evidence suggests these instances were very unusual, even exceptional. Particularly if the mixed family was itself living within indigenous spaces or communities, proximate to or constituted as *whānau* (and this was common, as we have seen, for land was commonly provided), the children seem to have usually been educated into what are

---

[31] Indeed, Pākehā ancestors could themselves be understood as *tīpuna/tupuna*, ancestors, or even founding ancestors for *whānau*: cf. Ballara, *Iwi*.

best understood as indigenous subjectivities. At any rate, it is evident that the durability of *whānau* drew substantially on the work of indigenous (including those considered by some to be 'half-caste') women, as well as the private, domestic work of indigenous men. The public political leadership of indigenous politics was to prove disproportionately male, from the nineteenth century until the 1970s, but these public political dimensions were often those most directly targeted by colonialism. Interventions into indigenous domestic life, despite their increasing intensity and power, were to meet with limited, partial kinds of efficacy. The energy of these realms, *whānau*, came disproportionately from indigenous women, and many of the most successful and durable indigenous political activities were based or drew upon precisely these gendered, *whānau* formations.[32] That this work was not always visible, or legible, to government and its archives—or subsequently to historians—is instructive. These limits stem not just from the shortcomings of historians, but from precisely the same qualities that allowed women and indigenous sociabilities at the time to evade or powerfully resist colonial rule and its archives.[33]

Crucially, racial amalgamation not only mobilized intellectual and political resources to the problem of racial crossing, it oriented colonialism towards the intimate dimensions of indigenous and settler lives. As productive and energetic as racial amalgamation proved, it was also critical in framing colonial interest not only in the 'subjecthood' of 'natives', but in their *subjective* transformation. This altered the nature of colonial rule as well as occasioning new ways of contesting or evading it. There are few better illustrations of this than the life of Maria Aminta Maning. Maning (1842–1892) was a half-caste strongly disciplined into a colonial subjectivity, in her case largely because her mother, Te Hikutu Moengaroa, had died when she was young. Many fathers in this situation left their children to be raised by their *whānau*, but Maria's father, the prominent settler (and self-proclaimed Pākehā-Māori) Frederick Maning, tried to sever these *whānau* ties and sent her to be raised by her paternal grandparents in Tasmania. She grew up away from any 'dangerous proximities' in a life of some colonial privilege, as a young colonial woman, with a proper colonial education and with little contact with her *whānau*, even her siblings. Not until she was 23 did she return to New Zealand and again

---

[32] For just one example, see Anna Rogers, Miria Simpson and Mira Szaszy, *Early Stories from the Maori Women's Welfare League/Te Tīmatanga Tātau Tātau: Te Rōpū Wāhine Māori Toko i te Ora* (Wellington, 1993).

[33] Cf. Binney, *Nga Morehu*, and my commentary on her work in this respect: Salesa, 'Korero', *NZJH*, 38 (2004), esp. pp. 286–7.

meet her maternal family, by then strangers to her. Her expectation was that she would also be a stranger to them: she did not know her mother's language, and she assumed her relatives did not know her. But matters proved different. Her first encounter with some of her *whanaunga* was one that Maria considered profound, and it proved transformational. Her careful lifelong colonial upbringing, with its French lessons and domestic finishing, was complicated in just a day. 'I was greeted by my Mother's name & had her dying *Waiata* sung to me', she wrote. 'I was welcomed as befitted *her* & I became mixed in my mind'.[34] Maning would later develop facility in *te Reo* Māori, and even composed *waiata* herself.[35]

No doubt Maria's experiences were unusual— certainly her circumstances and upbringing were—but by this time there was much about her life that resonated with others. Maria's life cast light on much of what both attracted and cautioned colonials about racial crossings. On the one hand, the way in which Maria was configured as part of a racial crossing had made her susceptible to her father's control as well as colonial rule, institutions and sensibilities: it had led to her move to Tasmania, and a certain kind of life. Yet by the same lights these racial crossings could be threatening: despite attempts to mitigate and regulate them, Maria's encounters with her *whānau* troubled, contradicted or opposed the efforts of her father and her settler family, as well as the larger purposes of colonial government. But as Maria moved from one colonial location to another, it harkened to the ways in which racial and colonial discourses were themselves mobile and circulating, conditioning and framing how many understood her (including, perhaps unusually in the case of Maria, how she understood herself). Yet for all the visible and measurable power of race, empire and colonialism, these moments in Maria's life showed how they did not encompass men and women like her. Colonial advantages in material, political and cultural resources were critical, but were not always decisive. It was not so simple to educate, control and claim Maria. Even the most careful regimes of colonial order and control, of settler domesticity and education, could not govern her fully. In the cadence and rhythm of a song, and in *aroha*, Maria could become, almost instantly, 'mixed in mind'.

[34] Hocken Library, Dunedin: MISC MS 0082: Maria Amina Maning, Papers and Reflections on Maori Life: 'A Maori Mother'. See also John Nicholson, *White Chief* (Auckland, 2006), passim.
[35] APL, Special Collections, NZMS 393, Maria Amina Maning, 'He Tangi mo Hauraki i Mate ki Waikare/Lament for Hauraki Who Fell at Waikare'.

Bibliography

PRIMARY SOURCES

Unpublished

Alexander Turnbull Library, Wellington, New Zealand (ATL)
J.W. Barnicoat, journal 1841–1844; qMS-0139
George Bowen, confidential report; MS-0253
Robert Fitzroy, papers; qMS-0795
Octavius Hadfield, letters; qMS-0895
James Heberley, 'Reminiscences'; qMS-0942
Henry Hill, papers; MS-Papers-0004
'The Story of Whaler Jenkins and Wharemauku'; qMS-1900
Donald McLean, papers; Micro-MS-0535-094
R.D.D. McLean, papers; MS-Papers-0032-0930
John Morgan, letters and journals; qMS-1390-1392
New Zealand Government, Department of Internal Affairs, Centennial Publications
    Branch, Historical Atlas Material, 1938–1952; MS-Papers-230, folder 9
Florence Nightingale, letter; MS-Papers-2280
Searancke collection; MS-Papers-0879
Edward Shortland, report on a visit to the South Island; qMS-1801
Andrew Sinclair, letters and journals, MS-1947
Andrew Sinclair, papers; qMS-1809-1812
James Heaton von Sturmer, papers; MS-78-024
Hori Kerei Taiaroa, 'Family Tree and Notes on Robinson and Brown Families';
    ref-77-124
Tapsell papers, 'Events in the Life of Phillip Tapsell'; qMS-1980
Toms family Bible; MS-2151
Charles Williams, 'The Whangamumu Whaling Family'; MS-Papers-2122
Johann Friedrich Heinrich Wohlers, papers; MS-Papers-0428-03 through 05C

Auckland Institute and Museum (AIM)
James Fulloon, papers and letters
Colin Henderson, papers on the Fulloon family
Alexander Macdonald, 'Reminiscences 1840–ca.1910'
Rangi Mawhete, papers
Miscellaneous clippings; MS 98/101

Auckland Public Library (APL)
James Fulloon, correspondence
Sir George Grey Letters
Sir George Grey New Zealand Letters (GNZL)
Richard Taylor papers

Arthur Thomson, 'Questions Relative to the System of Generation Among the Natives of New Zealand'

British Library, London (BL)
William Gladstone, papers; vols. ccxiv, cclxxviii
Richard Owen, papers
Robert Peel, papers; vols. cccxciv, ccccxxi
'Sketches of Scenery, Portraits of Natives'; Add.Ms.19,954
Edward Gibbon Wakefield, letters; BL 35,261

Durham University Library (DUL)
Henry George Grey, third Earl Grey, papers

National Archive of New Zealand, Wellington (NA)
(Selected files)
Governor's Office (G)
Internal Affairs (IA)
Old Land Claims Commission (OLC)
Maori Affairs (MA)
New Zealand Company papers (NZC)
Sir Thomas Gore Browne papers. (These are missing, presumed stolen; the detailed handlist is all that remains.)

Public Record Office (PRO)
Colonial Office 167, vol. 143
Colonial Office 208, vols. 30–35, 180–193, 295, 301
Colonial Office 209, selective consultation, vols. 1–180
Colonial Office 211, vols. 1–5
Colonial Office 212, vols. 1–34
Colonial Office 323, vol. 1512/2
Colonial Office 325, vol. 47
Colonial Office 380, vol. 122
Colonial Office 847, vol. 1/5
Colonial Office 854, vols. 1–8

Rhodes House Library (RHL)
Anti-Slavery Society Papers (ASS), C122/13, C122/5, C122/11
David Burn, original letters, 1849–1863
Thomas Fowell Buxton Papers, vols. 14, 15
John Newland, diary 1841–1873 (tss)

Wellcome Institute Library, London (WIL)
Hodgkin Family Papers, WMS/PP/HO

Published

Official publications
Appendices to the Journals of the House of Representatives (*AJHR*) (1854–1872)
Great Britain, *Parliamentary Debates* (selected consultation)

Great Britain, *Parliamentary Papers* (PP) (1836–1870)
New Zealand, *Parliamentary Debates* (*NZPD*) (selected consultation, 1854–1870)
Historical Records of Australia (Sydney, 1914–)
Historical Records of New Zealand (*HRNZ*), (ed.) Robert McNab, 2 vols.,
    (Wellington, 1908)
Historical Records of Victoria, (Melbourne, 1981–)
Results of a Census of New Zealand (1871–)

Periodicals consulted
(With dates consulted; where dates not given, selected consultation)
Annals of Natural History, 1840
Anthropologia, 1873–1875
Anthropological Journal (*AJ*), 1863–1870
Anthropological Review (*AR*), 1863–1870
Auckland Examiner, 1860
Australian and New Zealand Gazette
BAAS Reports (and *Transactions*), 1831–1870
Chambers's Edinburgh Journal
Christian Observer, 1838–1840
Church Mission Society, *Proceedings*, 1818–1841
Church Mission Society, *Reports*, 1816–1842
Daily Southern Cross
Dublin Review, 1840, 1845
Edinburgh Review (*ER*), 1840–1870
The Ethnological Journal: A Magazine of Ethnography, 1848, 1854
*The European Review; or Mind and it Productions, in Britain, France, Italy,
    Germany &c.*, 1824–1826
The Evening Post (Wellington, New Zealand)
Fisher's Colonial Magazine (*The Colonial Magazine and Commericial Maritime
    Journal*), 1840–1845
Fraser's Magazine, 1848
Hawera and Normanby Star
Te Hokioi e Rere Atu Na, 1862–1863
Journal of the Ethnological Society (*JES*), 1847–1870
Journal of the Royal Geographical Society (*JRGS*), 1840–1870
The Lancet
Memoirs Read Before the Anthropological Society of London (*MASL*), 1865–1869
Natural History Review: A Quarterly Journal (*NHR*), 1854–1865
Nature, 1869–1870
Nelson Examiner
New Monthly Magazine and Humorist, 1848
New Zealand Journal, 1840–1849
Otago Witness
The Phrenological Journal and Magazine of Moral Science, 1838–1848
The Phrenological Journal and Miscellany, 1825–1840

Te Pihoihoi Mokemoke i Runga i te Tuanui, 1863
Proceedings of the Zoological Society of London
The Quarterly Journal of the Geological Society of London, 1850
The Reader, 1863–1866
Southern Crosxs and the New Zealand Guardian
Taranaki Herald
Transactions of the Ethnological Society (TES), 1863–1869
Transactions of the New Zealand Institute
Te Karere Maori/The Maori Messenger
Te Karere o Nui Tireni

Books and pamphlets

[Aborigines Protection Society], *Colonisation of New Zealand*, [originally from *Morning Chronicle* (August 1839)].

Aborigines Protection Society, *Annual Reports* (1839–1875).

——, *Report of the Parliamentary Select Committee, on Aboriginal Tribes, (British Settlements); Reprinted with Comments* (London, 1837).

——, *The New ZealandGovernment and the Maori War of* 1863–64 (London, 1864).

A Corrected Report of the Debate in the House of Commons, 17th, 18th and 19th June, on the State of New Zealand and the Case of the New Zealand Company (London, 1845).

Adderley, Charles, *Some Reflections on the Speech of the Rt. Hon. Lord John Russell* (London, 1850).

——, *Review of 'The Colonial Policy of Lord J. Russell's Administration,' by Earl Grey, 1853; and of Subsequent Colonial History*, 2 vols., (London, 1869).

Alexander, James, *Incidents of the Maori War, New Zealand in 1860–1861* (London, 1863).

Alison, William, *Outlines of Physiology and Pathology; with a Supplement to the Physiology, Embracing an Account of the Most Recent Additions to that Science* (Edinburgh, 1836).

Algar, Frederic, *A Handbook to Auckland (New Zealand)* (London, 1867).

Angas, George French, *The New Zealanders Illustrated* (London, 1846).

——, *Savage Life and Scenes in Australia and New Zealand*, 2 vols., (London, 1847).

[Anonymous], *Suggestions on the Ancient Britons* (London, 1852).

——, *The Case of New Zealand* (London, 1865).

——, 'A Maori Comment on Race Relations Since the Treaty', (trans.) L.F. Head, *Te Karanga*, 5 (1989), pp. 20–22.

Anson, F.A., (ed.), *The Piraki Log (E Pirangi Ahau Koe) or Diary of Captain Hempleman* (London, 1910).

Arnold, Thomas, *The Effects of Distant Colonization on the Parent State; a Prize Essay Recited in the Theatre at Oxford, June 7, 1815* (Oxford, 1815).

——, *An Inaugural Lecture on the Study of Modern History* (Oxford, 1841).

——, *History of Rome*, 3 vols., (London, 1838–1843).

———, *The Miscellaneous Works of Thomas Arnold, DD.*, (ed.) A.P. Stanley, (London, 1845).

[Ashwell, B.Y.], *Recollections of a Waikato Missionary* (Auckland, 1878).

Ball, Robert, (ed.), *A Manual of Scientific Inquiry; Prepared for Use in Her Majesty's Navy, and Travellers in General*, 5th edn., (London, 1886).

Bannister, Saxe, *Humane Policy; or, Justice to the Aborigines of New Settlements* (London, 1830).

[Barlow, John], *The Connection Between Physiology and Intellectual Philosophy* (London, 1846).

———, *British Colonization and Coloured Tribes* (London, 1838).

Beard, L.E., *Our Colonies and Foreign Possessions; including their Physical Features* (London, 1872).

Beddoe, John, *The Races of Britain: A Contribution to the Anthropology of Western Europe* (Bristol, 1885).

Beecham, John, *Colonization: Being Remarks on Colonization in General, with an Examination of the Proposals of the Association Which has been Formed for Colonizing New Zealand*, 4th edn., (London, 1838).

Blackie, W.G., (ed.), *The Imperial Gazetteer; a General Dictionary of Geography, Physical, Political, Statistical and Descriptive* (Glasgow, 1855).

Blair, William, *Anthropology: or, The Natural History of Man* (London, 1803).

Blumenbach, Johann, *The Anthropological Treatises of Johann Blumenbach*, (trans.) Thomas Bendyshe, (London, 1865).

Bodell, James, *A Soldier's View of Empire: the Reminiscences of James Bodell 1831–92*, (ed.) Keith Sinclair, (London, 1982).

Bonwick, James, *Geography of Australia and New Zealand*, 3rd edn., (Melbourne, 1855).

Boultbee, John, *Journal of a Rambler: the Journal of John Boultbee*, (ed.) June Starke, (Auckland, 1986).

Bourne, H.R. Fox, *The Aborigines Protection Society: Chapters in its History* (London, 1899).

Brace, Charles Loring, *The Races of the Old World: a Manual of Ethnology* (London, 1863).

Brande, W.T., *A Dictionary of Science, Literature, & Art* (London, 1842).

Bray, Charles, *The Science of Man: A Bird's-Eye View of the Wide and Fertile Field of Anthropology* (London, 1868).

———, *A Manual of Anthropology, or Science of Man, Based on Modern Research* (London, 1871).

Broca, Pierre Paul, *Recherches sur l'hybridite animale en general et sur l'hybridite humaine en particulier considerees dans leurs rapports avec la question de la pluralite des especes humaines* (Paris, 1860).

———, *On the Phenomena of Hybridity in the Genus Homo*, trans. C. Carter Blake (London, 1864).

Brown, Robert, *The Races of Mankind: Being a Popular Description of the Characteristics, Manners and Customs of the Principal Varieties of the Human Families*, 4 vols., (London, 1873–1876).

Brown, William, *New Zealand and its Aborigines* (London, 1845).

Buckle, Henry Thomas, *History of Civilization in England*, 2 vols., (London, 1857, 1861).

Buddle, Thomas, *The Maori King Movement in New Zealand, with a Full Report of the Native Meetings Held at Waikato, April and May 1860* (Auckland, 1860).

Buffon, George Louis de Clerc, Comte de, *Barr's Buffon: Buffon's Natural History, Containing a Theory of the Earth, a General History of Man, of the Brute Creation, and of Vegetables, Minerals, &c.*, (ed.) James Smith Barr, 10 vols., (London, 1810).

Buller, Charles, *Responsible Government for Colonies* (London, 1840).

——, *Systematic Colonization* (London, 1843).

Buller, James, *Forty Years in New Zealand* (London, 1878).

[Burford, Robert], *Description of a View of the Bay of Islands, New Zealand* (London, 1838).

Burns, Barnet, *A New Zealand Chief* ([London?], 1835).

Burrows, Robert, *Extracts from a Diary Kept by the Rev. R. Burrows During Heke's War in the North in 1845* (Auckland, 1886).

Burton, Richard, *Wanderings in West Africa, from Liverpool to Fernando Po* (London, 1863).

Butler, John, *Earliest New Zealand: the Journals and Correspondence of the Rev. John Butler*, (ed.) R.J. Barton, (Masterton, 1927).

Butler, Samuel, *A First Year in Canterbury Settlement* (London, 1863).

——, *The Family Letters of Samuel Butler 1841–1886*, Arnold Silver (ed.), (London, 1962).

Byrne, J.C., *Twelve Years' Wanderings in the British Colonies from 1835 to 1847*, (London, 1848).

Campbell, John Logan, *Poenamo: Sketches of the Early Days of New Zealand* (London, 1881).

Campbell, Pamela, *Martin Tobin: a Novel*, 3 vols., (London, 1864).

[Carleton, Hugh], *A Page From the History of New Zealand* (Auckland, 1854).

[Chambers, Robert], *Vestiges of the Natural History of Creation* (London, 1844).

Chamerovzow, Louis, *The New Zealand Question and the Rights of Aborigines* (London, 1848).

Cheyne, Thomas Kelly, *The Relations between Civilized and Uncivilized Races, a Prize Essay* (Oxford, 1864).

Cholmondeley, Thomas, *Ultima Thule; or, Thoughts Suggested by a Residence in New Zealand* (London, 1854).

Chouvert, J.A.M., *A Marist Missionary in New Zealand, 1843–1846*, (ed.) Jinty Rorke, (trans.) Patrick Barry, (Whakatane, 1985).

Clarke, George, *Notes on Early Life in New Zealand* (Hobart, 1903).

Coates, Dandeson, *Notes for the Information of those Members of the Deputation to Lord Glenelg, Respecting the New Zealand Association* (London, 1837).

——, *The Present State of the New Zealand Question Considered in a Letter to J.P. Plumtree* (London, 1838).

——, *The New Zealanders and Their Lands: The Report of the Select Committee of the House of Commons on New Zealand, Considered in a Letter to Lord Stanley* (London, 1844).

Cockburn, Alex, *Nationality: or, The Law Relating to Subjects and Aliens, Considered with a View to Future Legislation* (London, 1869).

Coke, Charles, *Census of the British Empire: Compiled from Official Returns from 1861*, 2 vols., (London, 1863–1864).

Colenso, William, *The Authentic and Genuine History of the Signing of the Treaty of Waitangi* (Wellington, 1890).

Combe, George, *The Constitution of Man Considered in Relation to External Objects* (Edinburgh, 1828).

[Cooper, G.S.], *Journey to Taranaki/Haerenga ki Taranaki* (Auckland, 1851).

[Craik, George], *The New Zealanders: The Library of Entertaining Knowledge* (London, 1830).

Crawfurd, John, *The Plurality of the Races of Man: A Discourse Delivered by John Crawfurd* (London, 1867).

[Croly, D.G. and Wakeman, G.], *Miscegenation: the Theory of the Blending of the Races Applied to the American White Man and Negro* (London, 1864).

Crozet, Julien, *Crozet's Voyage to Tasmania, New Zealand, the Ladrone Islands and the Philippines in 1771–1772*, (trans.) Henry Roth, (London, 1891).

Cruise, Richard A., *Journal of a Ten Months' Residence in New Zealand* (London, 1823).

Darwin, Charles, *The Origin of Species by Means of Natural Selection or the Preservation of Favoured Races in the Struggle for Life* (New York, 1979 [1859]).

——, *The Variation of Animals and Plants Under Domestication*, 2 vols., (London, 1868).

——, *Descent of Man, and Selection in Relation to Sex*, 2 vols., (London, 1871).

——, *The Correspondence of Charles Darwin*, (eds.) Frederick Burkhardt and Sydney Smith, (Cambridge, 1985–).

Davis, C.O., (ed.), *Maori Mementoes* (Auckland, 1855).

Davis, Joseph Barnard, *Thesaurus Craniorum: Catalogue of the Skulls of the Various Races of Man, in the Collection of J.B. Davis*, 2 vols., (London, 1867, 1875).

——, *On the osteology and peculiarities of the Tasmanians, a race of man recently become extinct* (Haarlem, 1874).

——, and John Thurnam, *Crania Brittanica: Delineations and Descriptions of the Skulls of the Aboriginal and Early Inhabitants of the British Islands*, 2 vols., (London, 1865).

Dieffenbach, Ernest, *New Zealand and its Native Population* (London, 1841).

——, *On the Study of Ethnology* (London, [1843]).

——, *Travels in New Zealand; with Contributions to the Geography, Geology, Botany, and Natural History of that Colony*, 2 vols., (London, 1843).

Dilke, Charles, *Greater Britain: A Record of Travel in English Speaking Countries during 1866 and 1867*, 2 vols., (London, 1868).

Dillon, Constantine, *The Dillon Letters: the Letters of the Hon. Constantine Dillon, 1842–1853*, (ed.) C.A. Sharp, (Wellington, 1954).

Dillon, Peter, *Narrative and Successful Result of a Voyage in the South Seas, Performed by Order of the Government of British India, to Ascertain the Actual Fate of La Perouse's Expedition*, 2 vols., (London, 1829).

———, 'Extract of a Letter from the Chevalier Dillon, to an influential character here, on the advantages to be derived from the establishment of well-conducted Commercial settlements in New Zealand', 1 May 1832, London, tss in RHL.

Domett, Alfred, *Ranolf and Amohia: A South-Sea Day-Dream* (London, 1872).

———, *The Diary of Alfred Domett 1872–1885*, (ed.) E.A. Horsman, (London, 1953).

Durham, Lady, [Louisa Elizabeth Grey], *Letters and Diaries of Lady Durham*, (ed.) Patricia Godsell.

Durham, Lord, [John George Lambton], *The Life and Letters of the First Earl of Durham 1792–1840*, (ed.) Stuart J. Reid, 2 vols., (London, 1906).

———, *Lord Durham's Report on the Affairs of British North America*, (ed.) C.P. Lucas, 3 vols., (Oxford, 1912).

D'Urville, Dumont, *New Zealand 1826–1827*, (trans.) Olive Wright, (Wellington, 1950).

———, *The New Zealanders: A Story of Austral Lands*, (trans.) Carol Legge, (Wellington, 1992).

Earl, G.W., *The Native Races of the Indian Archipelago: Papuans* (London, 1853).

Earle, Augustus, *A Narrative of a Nine Month's Residence in New Zealand in 1827* (London, 1832).

Egerton, Hugh Edward, (ed.), *Selected Speeches of Sir William Molesworth, on Questions Relating to Colonial Policy* (London, 1903).

Elder, John Rawson, (ed.), *Marsden's Lieutenants* (Dunedin, 1934).

Ellis, George, *Irish Ethnology; Socially and Politically Considered; Embracing a General Outline of the Celtic and Saxon Races* (Dublin, 1852).

Fenton, Francis D., *Observations on the State of the Aboriginal Inhabitants of New Zealand* (Auckland, 1859).

Finch, John, *The Natural Boundaries of Empires; and a New View of Colonization* (London, 1844).

Fitton, Edward, *New Zealand: Its Present Condition, Prospects and Resources* (London, 1856).

Fitzroy, Robert, *A Narrative of the Voyage of the H.M.S. Beagle*, (ed.) David Stanbury, (London, 1977).

Fox, William, *The Six Colonies of New Zealand* (London, 1851).

———, *The War in New Zealand* (London, 1866).

Forster, John Reinhold, *Observations Made During a Voyage Round the World*, (eds.) Nicholas Thomas *et al.*, (Honolulu, 1996).

Galton, Francis, *Hereditary Genius: An Inquiry into its Laws and Consequences* (London, 1869).

Gascoyne, Frederick *Soldiering in New Zealand, Being Reminiscences of a Veteran* (London, 1916).

Gibbon, Edward, *The Decline and Fall of the Roman Empire*, (ed.) J.B. Bury, 5 vols., (London, 1901).

Gobineau, Arthur, *The Moral and Intellectual Diversity of Races, with Particular Reference to their Respective Influence in the Civil and Political History of Mankind*, (trans.) Henry Hotz, (Philadelphia, 1856).

Gorst, John, *The Maori King, or, The Story of Our Quarrel with the Natives of New Zealand* (London, 1864).

——, *New Zealand Revisited* (London, 1908).

Gorton, Edward, *Some Home Truths Re the Maori War 1863 to 1869 on the West Coast of New Zealand* (London, Greening and Co, 1901).

Grace, Thomas, *A Pioneer Missionary Among the Maoris 1850–1879, Being Letters and Journals of Thomas Samuel Grace*, (eds.) S.J. Brittan *et al.*, (Palmerston North, 1928).

Grey, Earl, [Henry George Grey], *The Colonial Policy of Lord John Russell's Administration*, 2 vols., (London, 1853).

Grey, George, *Ko Nga Mahi a Nga Tupuna Maori, ha Mea Kohikohi Mai* (London, 1854).

——, *Polynesian Mythology, and Ancient Traditional History of the New Zealand Race as Furnished by their Priests and Chiefs* (London, 1855).

Gudgeon, Thomas, *Reminiscences of the War in New Zealand* (London, 1879).

——, *The Defenders of New Zealand* (Auckland, 1887).

[Haliburton, T.C.], *A Reply to the Report of the Earl of Durham* (London, 1839).

Harvey, Alexander, *On a Remarkable Effect of Cross-Breeding* (Edinburgh, 1851).

——, *Man's Place and Bread Unique in Nature and His Pedigree Human Not Simian* (Edinburgh, 1865).

Hawtrey, Montague, *An Earnest Address to New Zealand Colonists, with Reference to their Intercourse with the Native Inhabitants* (London, 1840).

——, *Justice to New Zealand, Honour to England* (London, 1861).

Heale, Theophilius, *New Zealand and the New Zealand Company: Being a Consideration of How Far Their Interests are Similar* (London, 1842).

Heaphy, Charles, *Narrative of a Residence in Various Parts of New Zealand* (London, 1842).

Herschel, J.W., (ed.), *A Manual of scientific enquiry, prepared for the use of Her Majesty's Navy and adapted for Travellers* (London, 1849).

Hinds, Samuel, *The Latest Official Documents Relating to New Zealand; With Introductory Observations* (London, 1838).

Hochstetter, Ferdinand von, *New Zealand: Its Physical Geography, Geology and Natural History* (Stuttgart, 1867).

Home, Henry, Lord Kames, *Sketches of the History of Man*, 4 vols., enlarged edn., (London, 1779).

Hooker, J.D., *Handbook of New Zealand Flora* (London, 1864).

——, *The Botany of the Antarctic Voyage of H.M. Discovery Ships* Erebus and Terror *in the Years 1839–1843*, 6 vols., (London, 1844–1860).

Hotz, Henry, *Analytical Introduction to Count Gobineau's Moral and Intellectual Diversity of Races* (Mobile, 1855).

Howitt, William, *Colonization and Christianity: A Popular History of the Treatment of the Natives by the Europeans in all Their Colonies* (London, 1838).

Hunt, James, *On the Negro's Place in Nature* (London, 1863).

Hursthouse, Charles, *New Zealand: The Emigration Field of 1851, An Account of New Plymouth; or Guide to the Garden of New Zealand*, 3rd edn., (Aberdeen, 1851).

——, *New Zealand, or Zealandia, The Britain of the South*, 2 vols., (London, 1857).

Huxley, Thomas, *Evidence as to Man's Place in Nature* (London, 1863).

Jameson, R.G., *New Zealand, South Australia and New South Wales* (London, 1842).

Johnes, Arthur, *Legislation Applied to Infant Colonies, A Letter Addressed to the Commissioners of the Association for the British Colonization of New Zealand* (London, 1838).

——, *Philological Proofs of the Original Unity and Recent Origin of the Human Race* (London, 1843).

Kendall, Thomas, *Grammar and Vocabulary of the Language of New Zealand* (London, 1820).

Kennedy, John, *The Natural History of Man; or, Popular Chapters on Ethnography*, 2 vols., (London, 1851).

Kerry-Nicholls, J.H. *The King Country; or, Explorations in New Zealand* (London, 1884).

Kingsley, Charles, *The Water-Babies: A Fairy-Tale for a Land Baby* (London, 1863).

——, *The Roman and the Teuton: A Series of Lectures Delivered Before the University of Cambridge* (London, 1864).

Knox, Robert, *The Races of Men: A Fragment* (London, 1850).

——, *The Races of Men: a Philosophical Inquiry into the Influence of Race over the Destinies of Nations*, 2nd edn., (London, 1862).

Lang, John Dunmore, *New Zealand in 1839: or Four Letters to the Right Honourable Earl Durham* (London, 1839).

Latham, Robert Gordon, *The Natural History of the Varieties of Man* (London, 1850).

——, *Man and His Migrations* (London, 1851).

——, *The Ethnology of the British Colonies and Dependencies* (London, 1851).

——, *The Ethnology of Europe* (London, 1852).

——, *The Ethnology of the British Islands* (London, 1852).

——, *The Natural History Department of the Crystal Palace Described: 'Ethnology'* (London, 1854).

——, *Descriptive Ethnology*, 2 vols., (London, 1859).

——, *The Nationalities of Europe*, 2 vols., (London, 1863).

Lawrence, Sir William, *Lectures on physiology, zoology and the natural history of man* (London, 1819).

Lawry, Walter, *Friendly and Feejee Islands: a Missionary Visit to Various Stations in the South Seas in the Year 1847* (London, 1850).

Leslie, J.F., *The Early Races of Scotland and Their Monuments*, 2 vols., (Edinburgh, 1866).

Lewes, George H., *Studies in Animal Life* (New York, 1860).

Lewis, George Cornewall, *An Essay on the Government of Dependencies* (Oxford, [1841] 1891).

Leys, Thomson, (ed.), *Early History of New Zealand* (Auckland, 1890).

Livingstone, David and Charles, *Narrative of an Expedition to the Zambesi and its Tributaries* (London, 1865).

Lomax, Hugo, *The Late New Zealand War, or, Facts Revealed and Slanders Refuted* (London, 1866).

Long, Edward, *The History of Jamaica*, 3 vols., (London, 1774).

Long, George, (ed.), *Penny Cyclopaedia*, 30 vols., (London, 1833–1858).

Lonsdale, Henry, *A Sketch of the Life and Writing of Robert Knox* (London, 1870).

Loughnan, R.A., *New Zealand at Home* (London, 1908).

Lubbock, John, *Pre-historic Times, as Illustrated by Ancient Remains, and the Manners and Customs of Modern Savages* (London, 1865).

——, *The Origin of Civilisation and the Primitive Condition of Man*, (ed.) Peter Riviere, (Chicago, 1978 [1870]).

Ludlow, John Malcolm, *British India, its Races, and its History, considered with reference to the mutinies of 1857*, 2 vols., (Cambridge, 1858).

Lyell, Charles, *Elements of Geology* (London, 1838).

——, *Principles of Geology: or, the Modern Changes of the Earth and its Inhabitants, Considered as Illustrative of Geology*, 3 vols., 6th edn., (London, 1840).

——, *Travels in North America; with Geological Observations on the United States, Canada and Nova Scotia*, 2 vols., (London, 1845).

——, *The Geological Evidences of the Antiquity of Man* (London, 1863).

Lyson, Samuel, *Our British Ancestors: Who and What Were They? An Inquiry* (Oxford, 1865).

Mackay, James, *Our Dealings with Maori Lands; or, Comments on European Dealings for the Purchase and Lease of Native Lands, and the Legislation Thereon* (Auckland, 1887).

Malthus, Thomas, *An Essay on the Principle of Population, as it affects the Future Improvement of Society* (London, 1798).

——, *An Essay on the Principle of Population; or, a View of its Past and Present Effects on Human Happiness*, 2nd edn., (London, 1826).

Mandeno, J.H., 'Journal, 1860–1863', *Journal of Te Awamutu Historical Society*, 9 (1974), pp. 22–33.

Mangles, Ross, *How to Colonize: The Interest of the Country, and the Duty of the Government* (London, 1842).

Markham, Edward, *New Zealand or Recollections of It*, (ed.) E.H. McCormick, (Wellington, 1963).

Marsden, Samuel, *The Letters and Journals of Samuel Marsden 1765–1838*, (ed.) John Rawson Elder, (Dunedin, 1932).

Marshall, William Barrett, *A Personal Narrative of Two Visits to New Zealand, in His Majesty's Ship Alligator, A.D. 1834* (London, 1836).

Martin, Robert Montgomery, *The British Colonies; Their History, Extent, Condition and Resources*, 12 vols., (London, 1850).

Martin, S.M.D., *New Zealand in 1842; or The Effects of a Bad Government on a Good Country In a Letter to the Right Hon. Lord Stanley* (Auckland, 1842).

——, *New Zealand; in a Series of Letters* (London, 1845).

Martin, William, *The Taranaki Question*, 2nd edn., (London, 1861).

Mathew, Felton, (ed.) James Rutherford, *The Founding of New Zealand: the Journals of Felton Mathew* (Dunedin, 1940).

Matthew, Patrick, *On Naval Timber and Aboriculture: with Critical Notes on Authors who have Recently Treated the Subject of Planting* (Edinburgh, 1831).

——, *Emigration Fields: North America, the Cape, Australia, and New Zealand; Describing these Countries, and Giving a Comparative View of the Advantages they Present to British Settlers* (Edinburgh, 1839).

[Matthew, Patrick], *Prospectus of the Scots New Zealand Land Company* (Edinburgh, 1839).

Maynard, Felix, *The Whalers*, (ed.) Alexander Dumas, (trans.) F.W. Reed, (London, 1937).

McKillop, H.F., *Reminiscences of Twelve Months' Service in New Zealand* (London, 1849).

McLennan, John, *Primitive Marriage: an Inquiry into the Origin of the Form of Capture in Marriage Ceremonies* (Edinburgh, 1865).

Melville, Henry, *The Present State of Australia, Including New South Wales, Western Australia, South Australia, Victoria and New Zealand* (London, 1851).

Melville, Herman, *Moby Dick* (London, 1900).

Merivale, Herman, *Introduction to a Course of Lectures on Colonization and Colonies* (London, 1839).

——, *Lectures on Colonization and Colonies Delivered Before the University of Oxford in 1839, 1840, and 1841*, 2 vols., (London, 1841–1842).

Mill, John Stuart, *Dissertations and Discussions, Political, Philosophical, and Historical, reprinted chiefly from the Edinburgh and Westminster Reviews* (4 vols, London, 1859–1875).

——, *Considerations on Representative Government* (London, 1861).

Miller, Hugh, *First Impressions of England and its People* (London, 1848).

Mills, Arthur, *Colonial Policy in New Zealand: Speeches* (London, 1864).

Morrell, Benjamin, *A Narrative of Four Voyages* (New York, 1832).

Morton, Samuel, *Crania Americana; or, a Comparative View of the Skulls of Various Aboriginal Nations of North and South America* (Philadelphia, 1839).

Motte, Standish, *Outline of a System of Legislation* (London, 1840).

Napier, Charles O.G., *Miscellanea Anthropologica, or Illustrations of Races* (London, 1867).

Napier, Macvey, (ed.), *Encyclopædia Brittanica*, 7th edn., 21 vols., (Edinburgh, 1842).

New Zealand Company, *Reports* (1840–1849).

Ngata, Apirana, (ed.), *Nga Moteatea He Maramara Rere No Nga Waka Maha*, 3 vols., (Wellington, 1972–1974).

Nicholas, John Liddiard, *Narrative of a Voyage to New Zealand: Performed in the Years 1814 and 1815, in Company with the Rev. Samuel Marsden*, 2 vols., (London, 1817).

Nicholas, Thomas, *The Pedigree of the English People: An Argument, Historical and Scientific, on English Ethnology, Showing the Progress of Race-Amalgamation in Britain From the Earliest Times; With Especial Reference to the Incorporation of the Celtic Aborigines*, 2nd edn., (London, 1868).

Nihoniho, Tuta, *Narrative of the Fighting on the East Coast 1865–1871* (Wellington, 1913).

Nordau, Max, *Degeneration* (London, 1895).

Nott, Josiah C., *Two Lectures on the Natural History of the Caucasian and Negro Races* (Mobile, 1844).

——, and George R. Gliddon, *Types of mankind: Or, Ethnological Researches, based upon the Ancient Monuments, Paintings, Sculptures, and Crania of Races* (London, 1854).

Oliver, Richard Aldworth, *A Series of Lithographic Drawings From Sketches in New Zealand* (London, 1853).

Petre, Henry William, *An Account of the Settlements of the New Zealand Company*, 3rd edn., (London, 1841).

Pickering, Charles, *The races of man and their geographical distribution* (London, 1851).

Pike, Luke Owen, *The English and Their Origin: A Prologue to Authentic English History* (London, 1866).

Pim, Bedford, *The Negro and Jamaica* (London, 1866).

Polack, Joel, *Manners and Customs of the New Zealanders; with Notes Corroborative of Their Habits, Usages, etc.*, 2 vols., (London, 1840).

Pompallier, Jean Baptiste F., *Early History of the Catholic Church in Oceania*, (trans.) Arthur Herman (Auckland, 1888).

Porter, Frances, (ed.), *The Turanga Journals 1840–1850: Letters and Journals of William Williams and Jane Williams Missionaries to Poverty Bay* (Wellington, 1974).

Pouchet, Georges, *The Plurality of the Human Race*, (trans.) Hugh J.C. Beaven, (London, 1864).

Power, W. Tyrone, *Sketches in New Zealand, with Pen and Pencil* (London, 1849).

[Pratt, W.T.], *Colonial Experiences; or, Incidents and Reminiscences of Thirty-Four Years in New Zealand* (London, 1877).

Prichard, James Cowles, *Researches into the Physical History of Mankind* (London, 1813).

——, *Researches into the Physical History of Mankind*, 2nd edn., 2 vols., (London, 1826).

——, *Researches into the Physical History of Mankind*, 3rd edn., 5 vols., (London, 1836–1847).

——, *Researches into the Physical History of Mankind*, 4th edn., vol. 1, (London, 1841).

——, *The Natural History of Man* (London, 1843).

Prichard, James Cowles, *The Natural History of Man*, 2nd edn., (London, 1845).

——, *On the Relations of Ethnology to the Other Branches of Knowledge*, (Edinburgh, 1847).

[James Cowles Prichard et al.], *Queries Respecting the Human Race, to be Addressed to Travellers and Others* (London, 1841).

Quatrefages de Brèau, Jean Lois Armand de, *The Human Species* (London, 1879).

Rainy, William, The Censor Censured: or, the Calumnies of Captain Burton on the Africans of Sierre Leone Refuted (London, 1865).

Ray, John, *The Wisdom of God Manifested in the Works of the Creation* (London, 1691).

Rhodes, W.B., *The Whaling Journal of Captain W.B. Rhodes: Barque* Australian *of Sydney 1836–1838* (Christchurch, 1954).

Ritter, Carl, *The Colonization of New Zealand* (London, 1842).

Robarts, Edward, *The Marquesan Journal of Edward Robarts 1797–1824*, (ed.) Greg Dening, (Canberra, 1974).

Roebuck, John Arthur, *Life and Letters of John Arthur Roebuck, with Chapters of Autobiography*, (ed.) Robert Leader, (London, 1897).

Ross, Alexander, *The Red River Settlement: its Rise, Progress, and Present State* (London, 1856).

Rusden, G.W., *History of New Zealand*, 3 vols., (London, 1883).

Russell, A., *A Tour Through the Australian Colonies in 1839* (Glasgow, 1840).

Ryan, Michael, *The Philosophy of Marriage, in its Social, Moral, and Physical Relations* (London, 1837).

Savage, John, *Some Account of New Zealand* (London, 1807).

Scholefield, Guy, (ed.), *The Richmond-Atkinson Papers*, 2 vols., (Wellington, 1960).

Scott, Theodore, *Description of South Australia; With Sketches of New South Wales, Port Lincoln, Port Philip, and New Zealand* (Glasgow, 1839).

Scott, Walter, *Ivanhoe* (London, [1819] 1994).

Sewell, Henry, *The Journal of Henry Sewell*, (ed.) W. David McIntyre, 2 vols., (Christchurch, 1980).

Sewell, William, *The Ordeal of Free Labor in the British West Indies* (NewYork, 1861).

Sinnett, Mrs Percy, *Hunters and Fishers: or, Sketches of Primitive Races in the Lands Beyond the Sea* (London, 1846).

Smith, Charles Hamilton, *The Natural History of the Human Species, its Typical Forms, Primaeval Distribution, Filiations, and Migrations* (Edinburgh, 1848).

Smith, Samuel Stanhope, *An Essay on the Causes of the Variety of Complexion and Figure in the Human Species* (Edinburght, 1788).

Smyth, Thomas, *The Unity of the Human Races Proved to be the Doctrine of Scripture, Reason, and Science: with a Review of the Present Position and Theory of Professor Agassiz* (Edinburgh, 1851).

Snow, W. Parker, *British Columbia, Emigration, and Our Colonies, Considered Practically, Socially, and Politically* (London, 1858).

Spencer, Herbert, *The Principles of Biology*, 2 vols., (1864, 1867).

———, *Descriptive sociology; Or, groups of sociological facts, classified and arranged* (London, 1873–1881).

———, *Descriptive sociology: Lowest races, Negrito races, and Malayo-Polynesian races* (London, 1874).

Steinau, Julius Henry, *A Pathological and Philosophical Essay on Hereditary Diseases with an Appendix on Intermarriage* (London, 1843).

Stephen, Caroline Emelia, *The Right Honourable Sir James Stephen: Letters with Biographical Notes* (Gloucester, 1909).

Stephen, James, *Addresses of Sir James Stephen on the British Colonies and Colonization* (Liverpool, 1858).

St John, J.H.H., *Pakeha Rambles Through Maori Lands* (Wellington, 1873).

Strachan, Alexander, *Remarkable Incidents in the Life of the Rev. Samuel Leigh* (London, 1853).

Strzelecki, Paul, *Physical Description of the New South Wales and Van Diemen's Land* (London, 1845).

Swainson, William, *New Zealand: The Substance of Lectures on the Colonization of New Zealand*.

Taylor, Henry, *Autobiography of Henry Taylor*, 2 vols., (London, 1874).

Taylor, Richard, *Te Ika a Maui; or, New Zealand and its Inhabitants*, 2nd edn., (London, 1870).

Tikao, Teone Taare, *Tikao Talks: Treasures from the Ancient World of the Maori*, (ed.) J. Herries Beattie, new edn., (Auckland, 1990).

Thompson, Thomas Perronet, *Audi Alteram Partem, Letters of a Representative to his Constituents*, 2 vols., (London, 1858–1861).

Thomson, Allen, *Syllabus of Lectures on Physiology* (Edinburgh, 1835).

Thomson, Arthur S., *Prize Thesis: Observations on the Influence of Climate on the Health and Mortality of the Inhabitants of the Different Regions of the Globe* (Edinburgh, 1837).

———, *The Story of New Zealand: Past and Present – Savage and Civilized*, 2 vols., (London, 1859).

Topinard, Paul, *Anthropology* (London, 1876).

Tregear, Edward, *The Aryan Maori* (Wellington, 1885).

Turner, J.G., *The Pioneer Missionary: Life of the Rev. Nathaniel Turner* (London, 1872).

Turton, H., (ed.), *An Epitome of Official Documents Relative to Native Affairs and Land Purchases in the North Island of New Zealand* (Wellington, 1883).

Tylor, E.B., *Researches into the early history of mankind and the development of civilization* (London, 1870).

———, *Anthropology: An introduction to the study of man and civilization* (London, 1881).

———, 'Notice on the Asian relations of Polynesian culture', *Journal of the Anthropological Institute*, 11 (1881), 401–4.

Verity, Robert, *Changes Produced in the Nervous System by Civilization Considered According to the Evidence of Physiology and the Philosophy of History* (London, 1837).

[Victoria Institute], 'Prospectus of an Institution for the Maintenance and Education of Children, the Offspring of English Fathers by New-Zealand Mothers', broadsheet, printed at Paihia, 29 July 1839, ATL.

Vogt, Carl, *Lectures on Man: His Place in Creation, and in the History of the Earth*, (ed.) James Hunt, (London, 1864).

Wade, William, *A Journey in the Northern Island of New Zealand* (Hobart, 1842).

Waitz, Theodor, *Introduction to Anthropology*, (trans.) J. Frederick Collingwood, (London, 1863).

Wake, C.S., *Chapters on Man, with the Outlines of a Science of Comparative Psychology* (London, 1868).

Wakefield, Edward Gibbon, *The New British Province of South Australia; or a description of the Country with an Account of the Principles, Objects, Plan and Prospects of the Colony* (London, 1834).

———, *Mr. Dandeson Coates and the New Zealand Association; in a Letter to Lord Glenelg* (London, 1837).

———, *Popular Politics*, (London, 1837).

———, 'A View of Sir Charles Metcalfe's Government of Canada, by a Member of the Provincial Parliament' [1844], in (ed.) M.F. Lloyd Prichard, *The Collected Works of Edward Gibbon Wakefield* (Glasgow, 1968), pp. 721–52.

———, *The Southern Colonies; their Municipal Annexation, or their National Independence* ([?], 1849).

———, *A View of the Art of Colonization: with Present Reference to the British Empire* (London, 1849).

[Wakefield, Edward Gibbon], *A Statement of the Objects of the New Zealand Association, With Some Particulars Concerning the Position, Extent, Soil and Climate, Natural Productions, and Natives of New Zealand* (London, 1837).

Wakefield, Edward Jerningham, *Adventure in New Zealand, from 1839 to 1844 : with some Account of the Beginning of the British Colonization of the Islands*, (ed.) Robert Stout, (Christchurch, 1908 [1845]).

Walker, Alexander, *Intermarriage; or the Mode in which, and the Causes why, Beauty, Health and Intellect Result from Certain Unions, and Deformity, Disease and Insanity, from Others*, 2nd edn., (London, 1841).

Wallace, Alfred, *Australasia* (London, 1879).

Walton, John, *Twelve Months' Residence in New Zealand* (Glasgow, 1839).

[Ward, John, and Edward Gibbon Wakefield], *The British Colonization of New Zealand* (London, 1837).

Ward, John, *Information Relative to New Zealand, Compiled for the Use of Colonists* (London, 1840).

Ward, Stephen, *The Natural History of Mankind* (London, 1849).

Whately, Richard, *Thoughts on Secondary Punishments in a Letter to Earl Grey* (London, 1832).

———, *On the Origin of Civilisation* ([Dublin?], 1854).

———, *Miscellaneous Lectures and Reviews* (London, 1861).

Whewell, William, *History of the Inductive Sciences, from the Earliest to the Present Times*, 3 vols., (London, 1837).

Wilberforce, William, *An Appeal to the Religion, Justice, and Humanity of the Inhabitants of the British Empire, in Behalf of the Negro Slaves of the West Indies*, new edn., (London, 1823).

Wilkes, Charles, *Narrative of the United States Exploring Expedition, During the Years 1838, 1839, 1840, 1841, 1842*, 5 vols., (New York, 1856).

Williams, Henry, *The Early Journals of Henry Williams: Senior Missionary in New Zealand of the Church Missionary Society 1826–1840*, (ed.) Lawrence Rogers, (Christchurch, 1961).

Williams, John, *The New Zealand Journal 1842–1844 of John B. Williams of Salem, Massachusetts* (Salem, 1956).

Williams, Thomas, *The Present Geographical Movement and Future Geographical Distribution of the English Race of Men* (Swansea, 1859).

Wohlers, J.F.H., *Memories of the Life of J.F.H. Wohlers: Missionary at Ruapuke, New Zealand: An Autobiography* (Dunedin, 1895).

Wood, John, *Twelve Months in Wellington, Port Nicholson* (London, 1843).

Wood, J.G., *The Natural History of Man, Being an Account of the Manners and Customs of the Uncivilized Races of Men*, 2 vols., (London, 1868).

SECONDARY SOURCES

Articles and books

Adams, Peter, *Fatal Necessity: British Intervention in New Zealand, 1830–1847* (Auckland, 1977).

Anderson, Atholl, *Prodigious Birds: Moas and Moa-Hunting in Pre-Historic New Zealand* (Cambridge, 1989).

——, *Race Against Time: the Early Maori-Pakeha Families and the Development of the Mixed-Race Population in Southern New Zealand* (Dunedin, 1991).

——, *The Welcome of Strangers: An Ethnohistory of Southern Maori A.D. 1650–1850* (Dunedin, 1998).

Anthony, Frank, *Britain's Betrayal in India: The Story of the Anglo-Indian Community* (Bombay, 1969).

Appel, Toby, *The Cuvier-Geoffrey Debate: French Biology in the Decades Before Darwin* (Oxford, 1987).

Appiah, Anthony, 'The Uncompleted Argument: Du Bois and the Illusion of Race', *Critical Inquiry*, 12 (1985), pp. 21–37.

Armitage, Andrew, *Comparing the Policy of Aboriginal Assimilation: Australia, Canada and New Zealand* (Vancouver, 1995).

Arnold, David, *The Problem of Nature: Environment, Culture and European Expansion* (Oxford, 1996).

Augstein, Hannah, *James Cowles Prichard's Anthropology: Remaking the Science of Man in Early Nineteeth-Century Britain* (Amsterdam, 1999).

Azjenstat, Janet, *The Political Thought of Lord Durham* (Kingston, 1987).

Ballara, Angela, *Proud to be White? A Survey of Pakeha Prejudice in New Zealand* (Auckland, 1986).

Ballara, Angela, *Iwi: the dynamics of Maori tribal organisation from c.1769 to c.1945* (Wellington, 1998).

Ballhatchet, Kenneth, *Race, Sex and Class Under the Raj: Imperial Attitudes and their Critics, 1793–1905* (London, 1980).

Banton, Michael, *Race Relations* (London, 1967).

——, *Racial Theories* (Cambridge, 1987).

Barrett, Te Rongotoa, *Ngati Te Maawe: the Barretts of Waiharakeke Kawhia, New Zealand* (Wellington, 1986).

Barrington, J.M. and T.H. Beaglehole, 'A Part of Pakeha Society': Europeanising the Maori Child', in (ed.) J.A. Mangan, *Making Imperial Mentalities: Socialisation and British Imperialism*, (Manchester, 1990), pp. 163–83.

Barth, Fredrik, (ed.), *Ethnic Groups and Boundaries: The Social Organization of Culture Difference* (Boston, 1969).

Barzun, Jacques, *Race: A Study in Superstition*, revised edn., (New York, 1965).

Bassett, Judith, Judith Binney and Erik Olssen, (eds.), *The People and the Land/te Tangata me te Whenua: an Illustrated History of New Zealand 1820–1920* (Wellington, 1990).

Bayly, C.A., *Imperial Meridian: The British Empire and the World 1780–1830* (London, 1989).

——, *Empire and Information: Intelligence Gathering and Social Communication in India, 1780–1870* (Cambridge, 1996).

Beaglehole, J.C., *Captain Hobson and the New Zealand Company* (Northampton, MA, 1928).

Beattie, J. Herries, *Traditional Lifeways of the Southern Maori: The Otago University Ethnological Project, 1920*, (ed.) Atholl Anderson, (Dunedin, 1994).

Beer, Gillian, 'Speaking for the Others: Relativism and Authority in Victorian Anthropological Literature', in Robert Fraser, (ed.), *Sir James Frazer and the Literary Imagination: Essays in Affinity and Influence* (Basingstoke, 1990).

Belich, James, *The New Zealand Wars and the Victorian Interpretation of Racial Conflict* (Auckland, 1986).

——, *I Shall Not Die: Titokowaru's War, New Zealand, 1868–9* (Wellington, 1989).

——, *Making Peoples: A History of the New Zealanders, From Polynesian Settlement to the End of the Nineteenth Century* (Auckland, 1996).

——, 'Myth, Race, and Identity in New Zealand', *NZJH*, 31 (1997), pp. 9–22.

Bell, Gerda, *Ernest Dieffenbach: Rebel and Humanist* (Palmerston North, 1976).

Bell, Leonard, *Colonial Constructs: European Images of the Maori 1840–1914* (Auckland, 1992).

Bentley, Trevor, *Påkeha Måori: The Extraordinary Story of the Europeans Who Lived as Måori in Early New Zealand* (Auckland, 1999).

——, *Captured by Maori: White Female Captives, Sex and Racism on the Nineteenth-century Frontier* (Auckland, 2004).

Betts, Raymond F., 'The Allusion to Rome in British Imperialist Thought of the Late Nineteenth Century and Early Twentieth Centuries', *Victorian Studies*, 15 (1971), pp. 149–59.

Bhabha, Homi K., *The Location of Culture* (London, 1994).

Biddiss, Michael, *Father of Racist Ideology: The Social and Political Thought of Count Gobineau* (London, 1970).

——, (ed.), *Images of Race* (Leicester, 1979).

Biggs, Bruce, *Maori Marriage: an Essay in Reconstruction* (Wellington, 1960).

Bilcliffe, John, *'Well Done the 68th': the Story of a Regiment, Told by the Men of the 68th Light Infantry, During the Crimea and New Zealand Wars, 1854 to 1866* (Chippenham, 1995).

Binney, Judith, *The Legacy of Guilt: A Life of Thomas Kendall* (Auckland, 1968).

——, 'Whatever Happened to Poor Mr Yate? An Exercise in Voyeurism', *NZJH*, 9 (1975), pp. 111–25.

——, *Redemption Songs: a Life of Te Kooti Arikirangi Te Turuki* (Auckland, 1995).

——, ' "In-Between" Lives: Studies from Within a Colonial Society', in Tony Ballantyne and Brian Moloughney, (eds.), *Disputed Histories: Imagining New Zealand's Pasts* (Dunedin, 2006), pp. 93–117.

Bloomfield, G.T., *New Zealand, a Handbook of Historical Statistics* (Boston, 1984).

Bodelson, C.A., *Studies in Mid-Victorian Imperialism* (London, 1960).

Bohan, Edmund, *To be a Hero: Sir George Grey, 1812–1898* (Auckland, 1998).

Bolt, Christine, *Victorian Attitudes to Race* (London, 1971).

——, 'Race and the Victorians', in C.C. Eldridge, (ed.), *British Imperialism in the Nineteenth Century* (London, 1984), pp. 126–47.

Boon, James A., *Other Tribes, Other Scribes: Symbolic Anthropology in the Comparative Study of Cultures, Histories, Religions, and Texts* (Cambridge, 1982).

——, *Affinities and Extremes: Crisscrossing the Bittersweet Ethnology of East Indies History, Hindu-Balinese Culture and Indo-European Allure* (Chicago, 1990).

Bowler, Peter, *The Invention of Progress: the Victorians and their Past* (London, 1989).

——, *Evolution: The History of an Idea*, revised edn., (Berkeley, 1989).

Bozic-Vrbancic, Senka, *Tarara: Croats and Maori in New Zealand* (Dunedin, 2008).

Bradbury, Bettina, 'From Civil Death to Separate Property: Changes in the Legal Rights of Married Women in Nineteenth-Century New Zealand', *NZJH*, 29 (1995), pp. 40–66.

Brah, Avtar, and Annie Coombes, (eds.), *Hybridity and its Discontents* (London, 2000).

Brantlinger, Patrick, 'Victorians and Africans: the Genealogy of the Myth of the Dark Continent', *Critical Inquiry*, 12 (1985), pp. 166–203.

Brent, Richard, *Liberal Anglican Politics: Whiggery, Religion, and Reform 1830–1841* (Oxford, 1987).

Briggs, Asa, *Saxons, Normans and Victorians* (Hastings, 1966).

Brodie, Fawn, *The Devil Drives: A Life of Sir Richard Burton* (London, 1986).

Brookes, Barbara, Charlotte Macdonald and Margaret Tennant, (eds.), *Women in History 2* (Wellington, 1992).

Browne, Janet, *The Secular Ark: Studies in the History of Biogeography* (New Haven, 1983).

——, 'Biogeography and Empire', in N. Jardine, J.A. Secord and E.C. Spary, (eds.), *Cultures of Natural History* (Cambridge, 1996), pp. 305–21.

Buck, Peter Henry, (Te Rangihiroa), *The Coming of the Maori*, 2nd edn., (Christchurch, 1950).

——, 'The Passing of the Maori', *TPNZI* 55 (1924), pp. 362–75.

Burns, Patricia, *Fatal Success: a History of the New Zealand Company* (Auckland, 1989);

Burroughs, Peter, *The Canadian Crisis and British Colonial Policy, 1828–1841* (London, 1972).

Burrow, J.W., *Evolution and Society: A Study in Victorian Social Theory* (London, 1966).

——, *A Liberal Descent: Victorian Historians and the English Past* (Cambridge, 1981).

Burrow, John, Stefan Collini and Donald Winch, *That Noble Science of Politics: A Study in Nineteenth-Century Intellectual History* (Cambridge, 1983).

Burton, Antoinette, *At the Heart of the Empire: Indians and the Colonial Empire in Late-Victorian Britain* (Berkeley, 1998).

Butterworth, Graham, *Maori/Pakeha Intermarriage: Five Talks by Graham Butterworth* ([Wellington?], 1988).

Calder, Alex, Jonathan Lamb and Bridget Orr, (eds.), *Voyages and Beaches: Pacific Encounters, 1769–1840* (Honolulu, 1999).

Cell, John W., *British Colonial Administration in the Mid-Nineteenth Century: the Policy-Making Process* (New Haven, 1970).

Chamberlin, J. Edward and Gilman, Sander L., *Degeneration: the Dark Side of Progress* (New York, 1985).

Chatterjee, Indrani, 'Colouring Subalternity: Slaves, Concubines and Social Orphans in Early Colonial India', *Subaltern Studies*, X (1999), pp. 49–97.

Chatterjee, Partha, *The Nation and its Fragments: Colonial and Post-colonial Histories* (Princeton, 1993).

Clifford, James, *The Predicament of Culture: Twentieth Century Ethnography, Literature, and Art* (Cambridge, 1988).

Colley, Linda, *Britons: Forging the Nation 1707–1837* (New Haven, 1992).

Collier, James, *Sir George Grey: Governor, High Commissioner, and Premier* (Christchurch, 1909).

Collini, Stefan, *English Pasts: Essays in History and Culture* (Oxford, 1999).

Collini, Stefan, Richard Whatmore and Brian Young, (eds.), *History, Religion, and Culture: British Intellectual History 1750–1950* (Cambridge, 2000).

Condliffe, J.B. and W.T. Airey, *Short History of New Zealand*, 6th edn revised and expanded (Auckland, 1938).

[Cook Whanau], *Cook Whanau Reunion Otaki: A Genealogical Account of the Family Cook 1816–1990* ([Otaki, 1990]).

Cooper, Frederick, *Colonialism in Question: Theory, Knowledge, History* (Berkeley, 2005).

—— and Ann Laura Stoler, (eds.), *Tensions of Empire: Colonial Cultures in a Bourgeois World* (Berkeley, 1997).

Cooper, Nigel, *Ngati Mahanga: A Pakeha Family Search For Their Maori Ancestry* (Christchurch, 1990).

Cowan, James, *The Adventures of Kimble Bent: A Story of Wild Life in the New Zealand Bush* (London, 1911).

——, *The New Zealand Wars: a History of the Maori Campaigns and the Pioneering Period*, 2 vols., (Wellington, 1922–23).

——, *A Trader in Cannibal Land: the Life and Adventures of Captain Tapsell* (Dunedin, 1935).

Cox, Lindsay, *Kotahitanga: The Search for Māori Political Unity* (Auckland, 1993).

Crosby, Alfred W., *Ecological Imperialism: the Biological Expansion of Europe, 900–1900* (Cambridge, 1986).

Crosby, Ron, *The Musket Wars: a History of Inter-iwi Conflict 1806–45* (Auckland, 1999).

Curtin, Philip, *The Two Jamaicas: The Role of Ideas in a Tropical Colony* (Cambridge, MA, 1955).

——, *The Image of Africa: British Ideas and Action, 1780–1850* (Madison, 1964).

——, *Death By Migration: Europe's Encounter with the Tropical World in the Nineteenth Century* (Cambridge, 1989).

Curtis, L.P., *Anglo-Saxons and Celts: A Study of Anti-Irish Prejudice in Victorian England* (Connecticut, 1968).

Dacker, Bill, *The Pain and the Love/Te Mamae me te Aroha: A History of Kai Tahu Whanui in Otago, 1844–1994* (Otago, 1994).

Dalton, Brian, *War and Politics in New Zealand: 1855–1870* (Sydney, 1967).

——, 'Sir George Grey and the Keppel Affair', *Historical Studies*, 16 (1974), pp. 192–215.

Dalziel, Raewyn, 'An Experiment in the Social Laboratory? Suffrage, National Identity, and Mythologies of Race in New Zealand in the 1890s', in Ian Fletcher, Laura Mayall and Philippa Levine, (eds.), *Women's Suffrage in the British Empire: Citizenship, Nation and Race* (London, 2000), pp. 87–102.

Darwin, John, 'Imperialism and the Victorians: the Dynamics of Territorial Expansion', *English Historical Review*, 112 (1997), pp. 614–42.

Davis, David Brion, *The Problem of Slavery in the Age of Revolution 1770–1823* (Ithaca, 1975).

Degler, Carl, *Neither White Nor Black: Slavery and Race Relations in Brazil and the United States* (New York, 1971).

Dempster, W.J., *Patrick Matthew and Natural Selection* (Edinburgh, 1983).

Dening, Greg, *Islands and Beaches: A Discourse on a Silent Land, Marquesas 1774–1880* (Honolulu, 1980).

——, *Mr Bligh's Bad Language: Passion, Power and Theatre on the Bounty* (Cambridge, 1992).

Desmond, Adrian, *The Politics of Evolution: Morphology, Medicine, and Reform in Radical London* (London, 1989).

——, *Huxley: The Devil's Disciple* (London, 1994).

Desmond, Adrian, *Huxley: Evolution's High Priest* (London, 1997).

—— and James Moore, *Darwin: The Life of a Tormented Evolutionist* (New York, 1991).

Diaz, Vicente, and J. Kehaulani Kauanui, 'Native Pacific Cultural Studies on the Edge', *Contemporary Pacific*, 13:2 (2001), pp. 315–341.

Dirks, Nicholas, (ed.), *Colonialism and Culture* (Ann Arbor, 1992).

Donaldson, R., 'Dr J.P. FitzGerald: Pioneer Colonial Surgeon, 1840–1854', *New Zealand Medical Journal*, 101 (1988), pp. 636–8.

Dover, Cedric, *Half-Caste* (London, 1937).

——, *Know This of Race* (London, 1939).

Dow, Derek, *Maori Health and Government Policy 1840–1940* (Wellington, 1999).

Drayton, Richard, *Nature's Government: Science, Imperial Britain, and the 'Improvement' of the World* (New Haven, 2000).

Dubois, Laurent, *Avengers of the New World: the Story of the Haitian Revolution* (Cambridge, MA, 2004).

Dunmore, John, (ed.), *The French and the Maori* (Waikanae, 1992).

Dutt, Kuntala Lahiri, *In Search of a Homeland: Anglo-Indians and McClukiegunge* (Calcutta, 1990).

Eastwood, David, 'Amplifying the Province of the Legislature', *Historical Research* (1989), pp. 276–294.

——, 'Men, Morals and the Machinery of Social Legislation', *Parliamentary History* (1994), pp. 190–205.

——, 'The Age of Uncertainty: Britain in the Early Nineteenth Century', *Transactions of the Royal Historical Society*, sixth series, VIII (1998), pp. 91–115.

Eccles, Alfred, and A.H. Reed, *John Jones of Otago: Whaler, Coloniser, Shipowner, Merchant* (Wellington, 1949).

Eiseley, Loren, *Darwin's Century: Evolution and the Men Who Discovered It* (New York, 1961).

Eldridge, C.C., (ed.), *British Imperialism in the Nineteenth Century* (London, 1984).

Ellinghaus, Katherine, *Taking Assimilation to Heart: Marriages of White Women and Indigenous Men in the United States and Australia, 1887–1937* (Lincoln, 2006).

Elsmore, Bronwyn, *Mana from Heaven: a Century of Maori Prophets in New Zealand* (Tauranga, 1989).

Epstein, James, *In Practice: Studies in the Language and Culture of Popular Politics in Modern Britain* (Stanford, 2003).

Evans, Rex D., (comp.), *Charles Marshall of the Waikato: Whanau (1830–1992)* (Auckland, 1992).

——, (comp.), *The Family of Charles and Sarah Williams of the Hokianga* (Auckland, 1993).

Evans, Rex and Adriene, (comp.), *The Whanau of Hoeroa Tahau* (Auckland, 1993).

————, (comp.), *The Whanau of Irihapeti Te Paea (Hahau): the McKay and Joy (Joyce) Families*, 2 vols., (Auckland, 1994).

————, (comp.), *A Haberfield Genealogy* (Auckland, 1996).

————, (comp.), *The Whanau of Te Paea and William King* (Auckland, 1997).

Eze, Emmanuel, (ed.), *Race and the Enlightenment: A Reader* (Cambridge, MA, 1997).

Fairchild, Hoxie, *The Noble Savage: a Study in Romantic Naturalism* (New York, 1928).

Caroline Fitzgerald, (ed.), *Letters from the Bay of Islands: The Story of Marianne Williams* (Auckland, 2004).

Flanagan, Thomas, *Riel and the Rebellion: 1885 Reconsidered* (Saskatoon, 1983).

Flashoff, Ruth, *Reremoana Hakiwai* (Napier, 1981).

Forbes, Archibald, *Chinese Gordon: A Succinct Record of His Life* (London, 1884).

Forbes, Duncan, *The Liberal Anglican Idea of History* (Cambridge, 1952).

Forbes, Jack D., *Black Africans and Native Americans: Color, Race, and Caste in the Evolution of Red-Black Peoples* (Oxford, 1988).

Fortescue, J.W., *A History of the British Army*, 13 vols., (London, 1930), vol. 13.

Foucault, Michel, *The History of Sexuality: An Introduction*, (trans.) Robert Hurley, (New York, 1990).

————, *Discipline and Punish: The Birth of the Prison*, (trans.) Alan Sheridan, (London, 1991).

Frame, Janet, *To the Is-land* (New York, 1982).

Francis, Mark, *Governors and Settlers: Images of Authority in the British Colonies, 1820–1860* (Houndmills, 1992).

Galbreath, Ross, 'Images of Colonisation: Native Rats and Dying Pillows', *The Turnbull Library Record*, xxv (1993), pp. 33–42.

Geertz, Clifford, 'Blurred Genres', *American Scholar*, 49 (1980), pp. 165–82.

Gibson, Tom, *The Maori Wars: The British Army in New Zealand 1840–1872* (London, 1974).

Gilman, Sander L., *Difference and Pathology: Stereotypes of Sexuality, Race, and Madness* (Ithaca, 1985).

Gilroy, Paul, *Against Race: Imagining Political Culture Beyond the Color Line* (Cambridge, MA, 2000).

Goldberg, David Theo, *Racist Culture: Philosophy and the Politics of Meaning* (Oxford, 1993).

Gordon, Lewis R., 'Critical "Mixed Race"?', *Social Identities*, 1 (1995), pp. 381–95.

Gould, Stephen Jay, *The Mismeasure of Man* (New York, 1981).

Greene, John, *The Death of Adam: Evolution and its Impact on Western Thought*, revised edn., (Ames, 1996).

Greenwood, William, 'The Upraised Hand', *JPS*, 51 (1942), pp. 1–81.

Grimshaw, Patricia, 'Interracial Marriages and Colonial Regimes in Victoria and Aotearoa/New Zealand', *Frontiers*, 23:3 (2002), pp. 12–28.

Grove, Richard, *Green Imperialism: Colonial Expansion, Tropical Island Edens and the Origins of Environmentalism, 1600–1860* (Cambridge, 1995).

Gruber, Jacob, 'The Moa and the Professionalising of New Zealand Science', *Turnbull Library Record*, 20 (1987), pp. 61–100.

Gunson, Niel, *Messengers of Grace: Evangelical Missionaries in the South Seas 1797–1860* (Melbourne, 1978).

Haami, Bradford, *Pūtea Whakairo: Maori and the Written Word* (Wellington, 2004).

Hall, Catherine, *White, Male and Middle Class: Explorations in Feminism and History* (Cambridge, 1992).

——, Keith McClelland, and Jane Rendall, *Defining the Victorian Nation* (Cambridge, 2000).

——, (ed.), *Cultures of Empire, Colonizers in Britain and the Empire in the Nineteenth and Twentieth Centuries: A Reader* (Manchester, 2000).

——, *Civilizing Subjects: Metropole and Colony in the English Imagination, 1830–1867* (Oxford, 2002).

Hall, Stuart, 'Race, Articulation, and Societies Structured in Dominance', in *Sociological Theories: Racism and Colonialism* (UNESCO, Paris), pp. 305–345.

Haller, John S., *Outcasts from Evolution: Scientific Attitudes of Racial Inferiority, 1859–1900* (Urbana, 1971).

Hall-Jones, F.G., *Historical Southland* (Invercargill, 1945).

Hardt, Michael, and Antonio Negri, *Multitude: War and Democracy in the Age of Empire* (New York, 2004).

Harris, Aroha, *Hikoi: Forty Years of Maori Protest* (Wellington, 2004).

Harrop, A.J., *England and the Maori Wars* (London, 1937).

Hawes, C.J., *Poor Relations: The Making of a Eurasian Community in British India 1773–1833* (Richmond, 1833).

Hawtrey, Florence Molesworth, *The History of the Hawtrey Family*, 2 vols., (London, 1903).

Healey, Mark Alan, 'Powers of Misrecognition: Bourdieu and Wacquant on Race in Brazil', *Nepantla: Views From the South*, 4:2 (2003), pp. 391–402.

Hechter, Michael, *Internal Colonialism: The Celtic Fringe in British National Development 1536–1966* (London, 1975).

Henderson, Philip, *Samuel Butler, the Incarnate Bachelor* (London, 1953).

Henriques, Louis Fernando M., *Children of Caliban: Miscegenation* (London, 1974).

Heuman, Gad J., *Between Black and White: Race, Politics, and the Free Coloureds in Jamaica, 1792–1865* (Westport, 1981).

——, '*The Killing Time': The Morant Bay Rebellion in Jamaica* (London, 1994).

Hill, Richard, *Policing the Colonial Frontier: the Theory and Practice of Coercive Social and Racial Control in New Zealand, 1767–1867*, 2 vols., (Wellington, 1986).

Hilliard, Chris, 'James Cowan and the Frontiers of New Zealand History', *NZJH*, 32 (1997), pp. 219–33.

——, *To Exercise Our Talents: The Democratization of Writing in Britain* (Cambridge, MA, 2006).

Hilton, Boyd, *The Age of Atonement: The Influence of Evangelicalism on Social and Economic Thought, 1795–1865* (Oxford, 1988).

——, 'Politics of Anatomy and an Anatomy of Politics, *c.* 1825–50', in Stefan Collini, Richard Whatmore, and Brian Young, (eds.), *History, Religion, and Culture: British Intellectual History 1750–1950* (Cambridge, 2000).

Hingley, Ronald, *Roman Officers and English Gentlemen: the Imperial Origins of Roman Archaeology* (London, 2000).

Hoare, Michael, and Leonard Bell, (eds.), *In Search of New Zealand's Scientific Heritage* (Wellington, 1984).

Hobsbawm, Eric and Terence Ranger, (eds.), *The Invention of Tradition*, paperback edn., (Cambridge, 1992).

Hocken, Thomas Morland, *Contributions to the Early History of New Zealand* (London, 1898).

Hodgen, Margaret T., *Early Anthropology in the Sixteenth and Seventeenth Centuries* (Philadelphia, 1964).

Holloway, Judith, *The Bryers Family: An Account of a Maori-Pakeha Family in New Zealand* ([Porirua], 1993).

Holt, Thomas, *The Problem of Freedom: Race, Labor and Politics in Jamaica and Britain, 1832–1938* (Baltimore, 1992).

Howard, Basil, *Rakiura: A History of Stewart Island, New Zealand* (Wellington, 1940).

Howe, K.R., *Race Relations, Australia and New Zealand: A Comparative Survey* (Wellington, 1977).

——, *Where the Waves Fall: a New South Seas Island History from First Settlement to Colonial Rule* (Sydney, 1984).

——, *The Quest for Origins: Who First Discovered and Settled the Pacific Islands* (Auckland, 2003).

Hulme, Peter, *Colonial Encounters: Europe and the Native Caribbean, 1492–1797* (London, 1986).

Hyam, Ronald, *Empire and Sexuality: The British Experience* (Manchester, 1990).

——, *Britain's Imperial Century, 1815–1914*, 2nd edn., (Basingstoke, 1993).

Ip, Manying, *Being Maori-Chinese: Mixed Identities* (Auckland, 2008).

Jacobson, Evelyn, *The Cape Coloured: A Bibliography* (Cape Town, 1945).

James, C.L.R., *The Black Jacobins: Toussaint L'Ouverture and the San Domingo Revolution*, new edn., (London, 1984).

Jardine, N., J.A. Secord and E.C. Spary, (eds.), *Cultures of Natural History* (Cambridge, 1996).

Jellicoe, Roland L., *The New Zealand Company's Native Reserves: Compiled from Parliamentary Papers, Departmental Documents, and Other Authentic Sources of Information* (Wellington, 1930).

Jones, Greta, *Social Darwinism and English Thought: the Interaction between Biological and Social Theory* (Brighton, 1980).

Jones, Pei Te Hurinui, *Nga Iwi o Tainui*, (ed.) Bruce Biggs, (Auckland, 1995).

Jordan, Winthrop D., 'American Chiaroscuro: the Status and Definition of Mulattoes in the British Colonies', *The William and Mary Quarterly*, 19 (1962), pp. 183–200.

——, *White over Black: American Attitudes Toward the Negro, 1550–1812* (Baltimore, 1969).

Kaplan, Sydney, 'The Miscegenation Issue in the Election of 1864', *Journal of Negro History*, 34 (1949), pp. 274–343.

Kawharu, I.H., *Maori Land Tenure: Studies of a Changing Institution* (Oxford, 1977).

Keegan, Timothy J., *Colonial South Africa and the Origins of the Racial Order* (London, 1996).

Kelly, Leslie G., *Tainui: The Story of Hoturoa and His Descendants* (Wellington, 1949).

Kenny, Robert W., 'Yankee Whalers at the Bay of Islands', *The American Neptune*, XII (1952), pp. 22–44.

Kiernan, V.G., *The Lords of Human Kind: European Attitudes Toward the Outside World in the Imperial Age* (London, 1969).

King, Michael, *Moriori: A People Rediscovered* (Auckland, 1989).

Knaplund, Paul, *James Stephen and the British Colonial System 1813–1847* (Madison, 1953).

Kociumbas, Jan, *The Oxford History of Australia: Volume 2, 1770–1860, Possessions* (Melbourne, 1992).

Kuper, Adam, *The Invention of Primitive Society: Transformations of an Illusion* (London, 1988).

LaCapra, Dominick, (ed.), *The Bounds of Race: Perspectives on Hegemony and Resistance* (Ithaca, 1991).

Lacquer, Thomas, and Catherine Gallagher, (eds.), *The Making of the Modern Body: Sexuality and Society in the Nineteenth Century* (Berkeley, 1987).

Laidlaw, Zoë, '"Aunt Anna's Report": The Buxton Women and the Aborigines Select Committee, 1835–37', *Journal of Commonwealth and Imperial History*, 32:2 (2004), pp. 1–28.

——, *Colonial Connections, 1815–45: Patronage, the Information Revolution and Colonial Government* (Manchester, 2005).

Lange, Raeburn, *May the People Live: A History of Maori Health 1900–1918* (Auckland, 1999).

Latour, Bruno, *Science in Action: How to Follow Scientists and Engineers Through Society* (Cambridge, MA, 1987).

Lee, Jack, *Hokianga* (Auckland, 1987).

——, *The Old Land Claims in New Zealand* (Kerikeri, 1993).

Lester, Alan, *Imperial Networks: Creating Identities in Nineteenth-Century South Africa and Britain* (London, 2001).

Lethbridge, Christopher, *The Wounded Lion: Octavius Hadfield 1814–1904. Pioneer Missionary, Friend of the Maori & Primate of New Zealand* (Christchurch, 1993).

Levine, Philippa, *Prostitution, Race, and Politics: Policing Venereal Disease in the British Empire* (London, 2003).

Lightman, Bernard, (ed.), *Victorian Science in Context* (Chicago, 1997).

Livingstone, David N., 'Human Acclimitization: Perspectives on a Contested Field of Inquiry in Science, Medicine, and Geography', *History of Science*, XXV (1987), pp. 359–94.

——, *The Geographical Tradition: Episodes in the History of a Contested Enterprise* (Oxford, 1992).

Lorimer, Douglas, *Colour, Class and the Victorians: English attitudes to the Negro in the mid-Nineteenth Century* (Leicester, 1978).

——, 'Theoretical Racism in Late-Victorian Anthropology, 1870–1900', *Victorian Studies*, 31 (1988), pp. 405–30.

Louis, Wm. Roger, (gen. ed.), *Oxford History of the British Empire*, 5 vols., (Oxford, 1998–1999).

Macdonald, Charlotte, and Merimeri Penfold, (eds.), *The Book of New Zealand Women/Ko Kui Ma te Kaupapa* (Wellington, 1991).

MacDougall, Hugh A., *Racial Myth in English History: Trojans, Teutons, and Anglo-Saxons* (Hanover, New England, 1982).

Macgregor, Miriam, *Petticoat Pioneers: North Island Women of the Colonial Era: Book Two* (Wellington, 1975).

Mackrell, Brian, *Hariru Wikitoria! An Illustrated History of the Maori Tour of England, 1863* (Auckland, 1985).

MacLeod, Roy and P. Collins, (eds.), *Parliament of Science: The British Association for the Advancement of Science, 1831–1981* (Northwood, 1981).

—— and Rehbock, Philip F., (eds.), *Nature in its Greatest Extent: Western Science in the Pacific* (Honolulu, 1988).

Macmillan, William M., *The Cape Colour Question: A Historical Survey* (London, 1927).

——, *Bantu, Boer, and Briton*, 2nd revised edn., (Oxford, 1963).

Malik, Kenan, *The Meaning of Race: Race, History and Culture in Western Society* (Houndmills, 1996).

Marais, J.S., *The Colonisation of New Zealand* (Oxford, 1927).

Marsden, Māori, 'God, Man and Universe: a Maori View', in Michael King, (ed.), *Te Ao Hurihuri: Aspects of Maoritanga*, (Auckland: Reed, 1992), pp. 118–138.

Martel, Gordon, (ed.), *Studies in British Imperial History: Essays in Honour of A.P. Thornton* (Houndmills, 1986).

Martin, Ged, *The Durham Report and British Policy: a Critical Essay* (Cambridge, 1972).

——, 'An Imperial Idea and its Friends: Canadian Confederation and the British', in Gordon Martel, (ed.), *Studies in British Imperial History* (Houndmills, 1986), pp. 49–94.

Mason, Barry, and John Hitchen, *One Hundred and Fifty Years of the Mason Family in New Zealand, 1837–1987*, 2nd edn., (Christchurch, 1988).

Maude, H.E., *Of Islands and Men: Essays in Pacific History* (Melbourne, 1968).

McClintock, Anne, *Imperial Leather: Race, Gender and Sexuality in the Colonial Contest* (New York, 1995).

McLintock, A.H., *Crown Colony Government in New Zealand* (Wellington, 1958).

McNab, Robert, *Murihiku: A History of the South Island of New Zealand and the Islands Adjacent and Lying to the South, from 1642 to 1835* (Wellington, 1909).

——, *The Old Whaling Days: A History of Southern New Zealand from 1830 to 1840* (Christchurch, 1913).

Mehta, Uday, *Liberalism and Empire: a Study in Nineteenth Century Liberal Thought* (Chicago, 1999).

Metge, Joan, *The Maoris of New Zealand* (London, 1967).

Miller, Harold, *Race Conflict in New Zealand 1814–1865* (Auckland, 1966).

Miller, John, *Early Victorian New Zealand: A Study of Racial Tension and Social Attitudes 1839–1852* (London, 1958).

Morrell, W.P., *British Colonial Policy in the Age of Peel and Russell* (London, 1966).

——, *British Colonial Policy in the Mid-Victorian Age: South Africa, New Zealand, West Indies* (Oxford, 1969).

——, *The Provincial System in New Zealand 1852–1876*, 2nd edn., (Christchurch, 1964).

Morton, Harry, *The Whale's Wake* (Honolulu, 1982).

Mosse, George L., *Toward the Final Solution: A History of European Racism* (London, 1978).

Mulvaney, D.J., *Encounters in Place: Outsiders and Aboriginal Australians 1606–1985* (St Lucia, 1989).

Natusch, Sheila, *Brother Wohlers: A Biography of J.F.H. Wohlers of Ruapuke* (Christchurch, 1969).

——, (ed.), *My Dear Friend Tuckett: Letters From a Fouveaux Strait Outpost in the 1850s* (Christchurch, 1998).

Newbould, Ian, *Whiggery and Reform, 1830–41: The Politics of Government* (Basingstoke, 1990).

Ngata, Mihi Keita, and Katerina Te Reikoko Mataira, *Taura Tangata: Te Whakapapa o Nga Kiore o Ohinewaiapu* (Raglan, 1988).

Nicholson, John, *White Chief: The Colourful Life and Times of Judge F.E. Maning of the Hokianga* (Auckland, 2006).

Nicolson, Malcolm, 'Alexander von Humboldt, Humboldtian Science and the Origins of the Study of Vegetation', *History of Science*, XXV (1987), pp. 166–94.

——, 'Medicine and racial politics: changing images of the New Zealand Maori in the nineteenth century', in David Arnold, (ed.), *Imperial Medicine and Indigenous Societies* (Manchester, 1988), pp. 66–104.

Obeyesekere, Gannanath, *The Apotheosis of Captain Cook: European Mythmaking in the Pacific* (Princeton, 1992).

O'Donnel, E., *Te Hekenga: Early Days in Horowhenua Being the Reminiscences of Mr Rod McDonald* (Palmerston North, [1934]).

Oliver, W.H., *The Story of New Zealand* (London, 1960).

——, (ed.), *The Oxford History of New Zealand* (Oxford, 1981).

Olssen, Erik, 'Mr Wakefield as an Experiment in Post-Enlightenment Experimental Practice', *NZJH*, 31 (1997), pp. 197–218.

Orange, Claudia, *The Treaty of Waitangi* (Wellington, 1987).

——, 'The Maori and the Crown (1769–1840)', in Keith Sinclair, (ed), *The Oxford Illustrated History of New Zealand* (Auckland, 1990).

Orchiston, D. Wayne, 'George Bruce and the Maoris (1806–8)', *JPS*, 81 (1972), pp. 248–52.

Osborne, Michael A., *Nature, the Exotic, and the Science of French Colonialism* (Bloomington, 1994).

Owens, J.M.R., 'Missionary Medicine and Maori Health: the Record of the Wesleyan Mission to New Zealand Before 1840', *JPS*, 81 (1972), pp. 418–36.

——, *Prophets in the Wilderness: The Wesleyan Mission to New Zealand 1819–27* (Auckland, 1974).

Pagden, Anthony, *Lords of All the World: Ideologies of Empire in Spain, Britain and France c.1500 –c.1800* (New Haven, 1995).

Parham, W.T., *James Francis Fulloon: A Man of Two Cultures* (Whakatane, 1985).

Parsons, Murray, *John and Te Aitu Jury: The Jurys of the Wairarapa* (Christchurch, 1986).

Pascoe, Peggy, 'Miscegenation Law, Court Cases, and Ideologies of "Race" in Twentieth-Century America', *Journal of American History*, 83 (1996), pp. 44–69.

Paterson, Lachy, '*Kiri Ma, Kiri Mangu*: The Terminology of Race and Civilisation in the Mid-Nineteenth-Century Maori-Language Newspapers', in Jenifer Curnow, Ngapare Hopa and Jane McRae, (eds.) *Rere Atu, Taku Manu* (Auckland, 2002), pp. 78–93.

——, *Colonial Discourses: Niupepa Māori, 1855–1863* (Dunedin, 2006),

Pearson, David, *A Dream Deferred: the Origins of Ethnic Conflict in New Zealand* (Wellington, 1990).

Peires, J.B., *The Dead Will Arise: Nongqawuse and the Great Xhosa Cattle-Killing movement of 1856–7* (Johannesburg, 1989).

Pere, Joseph, 'Hitori Maori', in Colin Davis and Peter Lineham, (eds.), *The Future of the Past: Themes in New Zealand History* (Palmerston North, 1991), pp. 29–48.

Perry, Adele, *On the Edge of Empire: Gender, Race, and the Making of British Columbia 1849–1871* (Toronto, 2001).

Petrie, Hazel, *Chiefs of Industry: Maori Tribal Enterprise in Early Colonial New Zealand* (Auckland, 2006).

Pick, Daniel, *Faces of Degeneration: A European Disorder, c.1848–c.1918* (Cambridge, 1989).

Piggott, Stuart, *Celts, Saxons and the Early Antiquaries* (Edinburgh, 1967).

Pocock, J.G.A., *The Discovery of Islands: Essays in British History* (Cambridge, 2005).

Polanyi, Karl, *The Great Transformation: the Political and Economic Origins of Our Time* (Boston, 1957).

Poliakov, Leon, *The Aryan Myth: A History of Racist and Nationalist Ideas in Europe*, (trans.) Edmund Howard, (London, 1971).

Pool, Ian, *The Maori Population of New Zealand 1769–1971* (Auckland, 1977).

——, *Te Iwi Maori: A New Zealand Population Past, Present and Projected* (Auckland, 1991).

Poovey, Mary, *Uneven Developments: The Ideological Work of Gender in Mid-Victorian England* (Chicago, 1988).

——, '"Scenes of an Indelicate Character": The Medical "Treatment" of Victorian Women', in Thomas Lacquer and Catherine Gallagher, (eds.), *The Making of the Modern Body: Sexuality and Society in the Nineteenth Century* (Berkeley, 1987), pp. 137–68.

Pratt, Mary Louis, *Imperial Eyes: Travel Writing and Transculturation* (London, 1992).

Prest, John M., *Lord John Russell* (London, 1972).

Rainger, Ronald, 'Race, Politics, and Science: The Anthropological Society of London in the 1860s', *Victorian Studies*, 22 (1978), pp. 51–70.

Ralston, Caroline, *Grass Huts and Warehouses: Pacific Beach Communities of the Nineteenth Century* (Canberra, 1977).

Reid, Stuart J., *The Life and Letters of the first Earl of Durham, 1792–1840*, 2 vols., (London, 1906).

Reilly, Michael, 'An Ambiguous Past: Representing Maori History', *NZJH*, 29 (1995), pp. 19–39.

Reynolds, Henry, *Nowhere People: How International Race Thinking Shaped Australia's Identity* (Camberwell, 2005).

Rice, Geoffrey W., (ed.), *The Oxford History of New Zealand*, 2nd edn., (Auckland, 1992).

Rich, Paul B., *Race and Empire in British Politics* (Cambridge, 1986).

Richards, Evelleen, 'The "Moral Anatomy" of Robert Knox: the Interplay between Biological and Social Thought in Victorian Scientific Naturalism', *Journal of the History of Biology*, 22 (1989), pp. 373–436.

Richardson, Ruth, *Death, Dissection and the Destitute* (London, 1988).

Riddell, Kate, '"Improving" the Maori: Counting the Ideology of Intermarriage', *New Zealand Journal of History*, 34 (2000), pp. 80–97.

Ritvo, Harriet, *The Animal Estate: the English and Other Creatures in the Victorian Age* (Cambridge, MA, 1987).

——, 'Barring the Cross: Miscegenation and Purity in Eighteenth and Nineteenth Century Britain', in Diana Fuss, (ed.), *Human, All Too Human* (New York, 1996).

——, *The Platypus and the Mermaid and Other Figments of the Classifying Imagination* (Cambridge, MA, 1997).

Robbins, Keith, *Nineteenth-Century Britain: England, Scotland, and Wales; the Making of a Nation* (Oxford, 1988).

Rodger, N.A.M., *The Wooden World: an Anatomy of the Georgian Navy* (London, 1986).

Rogers, Anna, Miria Simpson and Mira Szaszy, *Early Stories from the Maori Women's Welfare League/Te Timatanga Tātau Tātau: Te Rōpū Wāhine Māori Toko i te Ora* (Wellington, 1993).

Root, Maria P.P., (ed.), *Racially Mixed People in America* (Newbury Park, 1992).

Rosaldo, Renato, *Culture and Truth: The Remaking of Social Analysis* (Boston, 1989).

Rose, Michael, *Curator of the Dead: Thomas Hodgkin (1798–1866)* (London, 1981).

Ross, Robert, *Adam Kok's Griquas: A Study in the Development of Stratification in South Africa* (Cambridge, 1976).

———, (ed.), *Racism and Colonialism* (The Hague, 1982).

Ross, Ruth, *New Zealand's First Capital* (Wellington, 1949).

Royal, Te Ahukaramu Charles, *Te Haurapa: An Introduction to Researching Tribal Histories and Traditions* (Wellington, 1992).

Rupke, Nicolaas, *Richard Owen: Victorian Naturalist* (London, 1994).

Rusden, George, *History of New Zealand*, 3 vols., (London, 1883).

Rutherford, James, *Sir George Grey K.C.B., 1812–1898: a Study in Colonial Government* (London, 1961).

Sahlins, Marshall, *Islands of History*, (Chicago, 1985).

Said, Edward W., *Orientalism: Western Representations of the Orient* (London, 1895).

———, 'Representing the Colonized: Anthropology's Interlocutors', *Critical Inquiry*, 15:2 (1989), pp. 205–25.

———, *Culture and Imperialism* (London, 1993).

Salesa, T. Damon, 'Half-Castes Between the Wars: Colonial Categories in New Zealand and Samoa', *NZJH*, 34 (2000), pp. 98–116.

———, '"The Power of the Physician": Doctors and the Dying Maori in Early Colonial New Zealand', *Health and History*, 4 (2001 [in press]).

———, *'Troublesome Half-castes': a Study of a Samoan Borderland, 1830–1900* (in preparation).

Salmond, Anne, *Two Worlds: First Meetings Between Maori and European 1642–1772* (Auckland, 1991).

———, *Between Worlds: Early Exchanges Between Maori and Europeans 1773–1815* (Auckland, 1997).

Scott, James, *Seeing Like a State: How Certain Schemes to Improve the Human Condition Have Failed* (New Haven, 1998).

Scott, Joan Wallach, *Gender and the Politics of History* (New York, 1988).

Scott, Linda, and Finlay Bayne, *Nathaniel Bates of Riverton: His Families and Descendants* ([Christchurch], 1994).

Semmel, Bernard, *The Governor Eyre Controversy* (London, 1962).

Showalter, Elaine, *Sexual Anarchy: Gender and Culture at the Fin de Siecle* (London, 1997).

Simmons, D.R., *Great New Zealand Myth: a Study of the Discovery and Origin Traditions of the Maori* (Wellington, 1976).

Sinclair, Keith, *The Origins of the Maori Wars* (Wellington, 1957).

——, 'Why are Race Relations in New Zealand Better than in South Africa, South Australia or South Dakota?', *NZJH*, 2 (1971), pp. 121–7.

——, *A Destiny Apart: New Zealand's Search for National Identity* (Wellington, 1986).

——, *A History of New Zealand*, revised edn., (Harmondsworth, 1988).

——, *Kinds of Peace: Maori People After the Wars, 1870–85* (Auckland, 1991).

——, (ed.), *The Oxford Illustrated History of New Zealand*, 2nd edn., (Auckland, 1996).

Skidmore, Thomas, *Black Into White: Race and Nationality in Brazilian Thought* (New York, 1974).

——, *Black into White: Race and Nationality in Brazilian Thought*, 2nd edn., (Durham, 1993).

Slotkin, Richard, *Regeneration Through Violence: The Mythology of the American Frontier, 1600–1860* (New York, 1996).

Small, Stephen, 'Racial Group Boundaries and Identities: People of "Mixed Race" in Slavery Across the Americas', *Slavery and Abolition*, 15 (1994), pp. 17–37.

Smith, Bernard, *European Vision and the South Seas, 1768–1850: A Study in the History of Art and Ideas* (Oxford, 1960).

——, *European Vision and the South Pacific*, 2nd edn., (Oxford, 1989).

Smith, S. Percy, 'Wars of the Northern Against the Southern Tribes of New Zealand in the Nineteenth Century', *JPS*, 8 (1899), pp.

——, *Maori Wars of the Nineteenth Century*, 2nd edn., (Christchurch, 1910).

Sonnabend, H., and Cyril Sofer, *South Africa's Stepchildren: A Study of Miscegenation* (Johannesburg, 1948).

Sorrenson, M.P.K., 'The Politics of Land', in J.G.A. Pocock, (ed.), *The Maori and New Zealand Politics* (Wellington, 1965), pp. 21–45.

——, 'How to Civilize Savages: Some "Answers" From Nineteenth-Century New Zealand', *NZJH*, 9 (1975), pp. 97–110.

——, *Maori Origins and Migrations: the Genesis of some Pakeha Myths and Legends* (Auckland, 1979).

——, *Manifest Duty: the Polynesian Society over 100 Years* (Auckland, 1982).

——, 'Polynesian Corpuscles and Pacific Anthropology: the Home-Made Anthropology of Sir Apirana Ngata and Sir Peter Buck', *JPS*, 91 (1982), pp. 7–27.

——, (ed.), *Na To Hoa Aroha/From Your Dear Friend: The Correspondence Between Sir Apirana Ngata and Sir Peter Buck 1925–50*, 3 vols., (Auckland, 1986–1988).

Spoehr, Alexander, 'Port Town and Hinterland in the Pacific Islands', *American Anthropologist*, 62 (1960), pp. 586–92.

Sprague, D.N., *Canada and the Métis, 1869–1885* (Waterloo, 1988).

Stafford, Donald, *Te Arawa: A History of the Arawa People* (Wellington, 1967).

Stafford, Robert A., *Scientist of Empire: Sir Roderick Murchison, Scientific Exploration and Victorian Imperialism* (Cambridge, 1989).

Stannard, David E., *Before the Horror: the Population of Hawai'i on the Eve of Western Contact* (Honolulu, 1989).

Stanton, William, *The Leopard's Spots: Scientific Attitudes toward Race in America, 1815–59* (Chicago, 1960).

Stark, Herbert, *The Call of the Blood; or, Anglo-Indians and the Sepoy Mutiny* (Rangoon, 1932).

Stenhouse, John, '"A Disappearing Race Before We Came Here": Dr Alfred Kingcome Newman, the Dying Maori and Victorian Scientific Racism', *NZJH*, 30 (1996), pp. 123–140.

Stepan, Nancy Leys, *The Idea of Race in Science: Great Britain 1800–1960* (London, 1982).

——, 'Biological Degeneration: Races and Proper Places', in J. Edward Chamberlin and Sander L. Gilman, (eds.), *Degeneration: the Dark Side of Progress* (New York, 1985), pp. 97–120.

——, 'Race and Gender: The Role of Analogy in Science', in David Theo Goldberg, (ed.), *Anatomy of Racism* (Minneapolis, 1990), pp. 38–57.

——, *"The Hour of Eugenics": Race, Gender and Nation in Latin America* (Ithaca, 1991).

Stocking, George W., Jr, 'Review' [of Thomas F. Gossett, *Race: the History of an Idea in America*], *Journal of the History of the Behavioural Sciences*, 1 (1965), pp. 294–6.

——, *Race, Culture and Evolution: Essays in the History of Anthropology* (New York, 1968).

——, 'What's in a name? The Origins of the Royal Anthropological Institute (1837–71)', *Man*, 6 (1971), pp. 369–90.

——, 'From Chronology to Ethnology: James Cowles Prichard and British Anthropology, 1800–1850', in J.C. Prichard, *Researches into the Physical History of Man*, Stocking (ed.), (Chicago, 1973), pp. ix–cx.

——, *Victorian Anthropology* (New York, 1987).

——, *The Ethnographer's Magic and Other Essays in the History of Anthropology* (Madison, 1992).

Stoler, Ann Laura, 'Rethinking Colonial Categories: European Communities and the Boundaries of Rule', *Comparative Studies in Society and History*, 13 (1991), pp. 134–161.

——, 'Carnal Knowledge and Imperial Power: Gender, Race and Morality in Colonial Asia', in Micaela di Leonardo, (ed.), *Gender at the Crossroads of Knowledge: Feminist Anthropology in the Postmodern Era* (Berkeley, 1991), pp. 51–101.

——, 'Sexual Affronts and Racial Frontiers: European Identities and the Cultural Politics of Exclusion in Colonial Southeast Asia', *Comparative Studies in Society and History*, 34 (1992), pp. 514–551.

——, *Race and the Education of Desire: Foucault's History of Sexuality and the Colonial Order of Things* (Durham, 1995).

Stoler, Ann Laura, *Carnal Knowledge and Imperial Power: Racex and the Intimate in Colonial Rule* (Berkeley, 2002).

——, (ed.), *Haunted By Empire: Geographies of Intimacy in North American History* (Durham, 2006).

Stoler, Anne and Frederick Cooper, (eds.), *Tensions of Empire: Colonial Cultures in a Bourgeois World* (Berkeley, 1997).

Sturm, Terry, (ed.), *The Oxford History of New Zealand Literature in English* (Auckland, 1991).

Thomas, Nicholas, *Out of Time: History and Evolution in Anthropological Discourse* (Cambridge, 1989).

——, *Colonialism's Culture: Anthropology, Travel and Government* (Cambridge, 1994).

——, *In Oceania: Visions, Artifacts, Histories* (Durham, 1997).

Thomas, William, *Philosophic Radicals: Nine Studies in Theory and Practice, 1817–1841* (Oxford, 1979).

Tully, James, *Strange Multiplicity: Constitutionalism in an Age of Diversity* (Cambridge, 1995).

Turnbull, Michael, *The New Zealand Bubble: the Wakefield Theory in Practice* (Wellington, 1959).

Turner, Te Muri, *Hetet Reunion Held at Te Kuiti Marae: 31st December 1994 to 3rd January 1995* (Te Kuiti, 1995).

Van Kirk, Sylvia, *'Many Tender Ties': Women in Fur-Trade Society in Western Canada, 1670–1870* (Winnipeg, 1981);

Varma, Lal Bahadur, *Anglo-Indians* (New Delhi, 1979).

Vaughan, Megan, *Curing Their Ills: Colonial Power and African Illness* (Cambridge, 1991).

Vennell, C.W., and Alan Taylor, 'Louis Hetet: Government Agent in the King Country', *Historical Journal Auckland-Waikato*, 30 (1977), pp. 12–16.

Vercoe, Andrew, *Educating Jake: Pathways to Empowerment* (Auckland, 1998),

[Waitangi Tribunal], *Muriwhenua Land Report* (Wellington, 1997).

Walker, Ranginui, *Ka Whawhai Tonu Matou: Struggle Without End* (Auckland, 1990).

Walkowitz, Judxith R., *Prostitution and Victorian Society: Women, Class, and the State* (Cambridge, 1982).

Wanhalla, Angela, idem, 'Marrying "In": the Geography of Intermarriage on the Taieri, 1830s-1920s', in Tony Ballantyne and Judith A. Bennett, (eds) *Landscape/Community: Perspectives from New Zealand History* (Dunedin, 2005), pp. 72–94.

——, *In/Visible Sight: the Mixed Descent Families of Southern New Zealand* (Wellington, 2009).

Ward, Alan, 'The Origins of the Anglo-Maori Wars: A Reconsideration', *NZJH*, 1 (1967), pp. 148–70.

——, *A Show of Justice: Racial 'Amalgamation' in Nineteenth Century New Zealand* (Auckland, 1995 [1974]).

——, 'Review Article', *NZJH*, 21 (1987), pp. 270–4.

——, (ed.), *Rangahaua Whanui*, 3 vols., (Wellington, 1997).

——, *An Unsettled History: Treaty Claims in New Zealand Today* (Wellington, 1999).

Wards, Ian, *The Shadow of the Land: a Study of British Policy and Racial Conflict in New Zealand 1832–1852* (Wellington, 1968).

Wells, K.D., 'The Historical Context of Natural Selection: The Case of Patrick Matthew', *Journal of the History of Biology*, 6 (1973), pp. 225–58.

West, Shearer, (ed.), *The Victorians and Race* (Aldershot, 1996).

Whaanga-Schollum, Mere, *Bartlett: Mahia to Tawatapu* (Mahia, 1990).

Wheeler, Roxann, *The Complexion of Race: Categories of Difference in Eighteenth-Century British Culture* (Philadelphia, 2000).

White, Luise, *The Comforts of Home: Prostitution ixn Colonial Nairobi* (Chicago, 1990).

Williams, David, *'Te Kooti Tango Whenua' : The Native Land Court 1864–1909* (Wellington, 1999).

Williams, Elizabeth, 'Anthropological Institutions in Nineteenth-Century France', *Isis*, 76 (1985), pp. 331–48.

——, *The Physical and the Moral: Anthropology, Physiology, and Philosophical Medicine in France, 1750–1850* (Cambridge, 1994).

Williams, H.W., *Bibliography of Printed Maori to 1900* (Wellington, 1924).

Williamson, Joel, *New People: Miscegenation and Mulattoes in the United States* (Baton Rouge, 1995).

Wilson, Ormond, 'Maori and Pakeha', *Journal of the Polynesian Society*, 72 (1963), pp. 11–20.

Wolfe, Richard, *Hell-Hole of the Pacific* (Auckland, 2005).

Woodward, E.L., *The Age of Reform 1815–1870* (Oxford, 1938).

Wright, Harrison, *New Zealand, 1769–1840* (Cambridge, MA, 1967).

Wright-St Clair, Rex, 'Arthur S. Thomson, Army Medical Officer, Statistician and Epidemiologist', *New Zealand Health Review*, 4 (1984), pp. 17–18.

Young, Robert J.C., *Colonial Desire: Hybridity in Culture, Theory and Race* (London, 1995).

Zack, Naomi, *Race and Mixed Race* (Philadelphia, 1993).

——, (ed.), *American Mixed Race: the Culture of Microdiversity* (Lanham, 1995).

Unpublished theses and papers

Adams, Peter, 'British Intervention in New Zealand, 1830–1846', D.Phil. thesis, University of Oxford, 1974.

Ballara, Angela, 'The Origins of Ngati Kahungungu', Ph.D. thesis, Victoria University of Wellington, 1991.

Belich, James, 'The New Zealand Wars, 1845–1870: An Analysis of Their History and Interpretation', D.Phil. thesis, University of Oxford, 1981.

Booth, J.M., 'A History of New Zealand Anthropology During the Nineteenth Century', MA thesis, University of New Zealand, 1949.

Byrnes, Giselle, 'Inventing New Zealand: Surveying, Science, and the Construction of Cultural Space', Ph.D. thesis, University of Auckland, 1995.

Callister, Paul, Robert Didham and Deborah Potter, 'Ethnic Intermarriage in New Zealand', Statistics New Zealand Working Paper, 2005.

Campbell, I.C., 'European Transculturalists in Polynesia, 1789–ca.1840', Ph.D. dissertation, University of Adelaide, 1976.

Cleave, Peter, 'The Languages and Political Interests of Maori and Pakeha Communities in New Zealand During the Nineteenth Century', D.Phil. thesis, University of Oxford, 1979.

Donaldson, R., 'Dr John Patrick Fitzgerald: Pioneer Colonial Doctor 1840–1860', MPhil thesis, Waikato, 1988.

Fraser, Clementine, '"Incorrigible Rogues" and Other Female Felons: Women and Crime in Auckland 1870–1885', MA thesis, University of Auckland, 1998.

Hickford, Mark, 'Making "Territorial Rights of the Natives": Britain and New Zealand, 1830–1847', D.Phil. thesis, University of Oxford, 1999.

Howe, K.R., 'Missionaries, Maories, and "Civilization" in the Upper-Waikato, 1833–1863: A Study in Culture Contact with Special Reference to the Attitudes and Activities of the Reverend John Morgan', MA thesis, University of Auckland, 1970.

Laidlaw, Zoë, '"Aunt Anna's Report": the Buxton Women's Political and Intellectual Contribution to the Aborigines Select Committee, 1835–7', [forthcoming].

——, 'Networks of Patronage and Information, British Colonial Governance 1826–43', D.Phil. thesis, University of Oxford [in progress].

Petrie, Hazel, 'The "Lazy Maori": Pakeha Representations of a Maori Work Ethic, 1890–1940', MA thesis, University of Auckland, 1998.

Riddell, Kate, 'A "Marriage" of the Races? Aspects of Intermarriage, Ideology and Reproduction on the New Zealand Frontier', MA thesis, Victoria University of Wellington, 1996.

Sinclair, Keith, 'The Aborigines Protection Society and New Zealand: A Study in Nineteenth Century Opinion', MA thesis, University of New Zealand, 1946.

Smit, Grace, 'Mana Maori: Questions of Authority on the East Coast During the Nineteenth Century', MA thesis, University of Auckland, 1997.

Thomas, Caroline, 'Professional Amateurs and Colonial Academics: Steps Towards Academic Anthropology in New Zealand 1860–1920', MA thesis, University of Auckland, 1995.

Wanhalla, Angela C., 'Transgressing Boundaries: A History of the Mixed Descent Families of Maitapapa, Taieri, 1830–1940', Ph.D. Thesis, University of Canterbury, 2004.

Ward, Damen, 'An Exceptional Law: Governor FitzRoy, Humanitarianism and the Native Exemption Ordinance 1844', BA (Hons) dissertation, University of Otago, 1997.

Index

abandonment 111–12
abolition 1, 12–13, 41–2, 53, 80, 96, 150;
  see also slavery
aborigines
  Australian 65, 70, 83, 98, 134–6,
    148, 155
  British 136, 164
  general term 12, 14, 21–2, 94–6
Aborigines' Committee, 36, 96–7, 141
Aborigines Protection Society 96–7,
  141–7
Aborigines Report 96–8
Admiralty 92
adoption 111–12, 188–9, 203–4
adultery 61
African Americans 65, 151, 168
Africans 137, 217
alcohol 63, 119, 121, 134, 153, 237
aldermen 33
Allen, John 203
Anderson, Atholl 16, 167
Anderson, Benedict 12
Anderson, Rongi (Rebecca) 128–9
Anderson, William 128–9
Andrews, John 167
Anglo-Saxons 49–50, 162–3; see also
  mixed race people
Anthropological Society of London
  148–51, 168
anthropology 13, 148–51; see also
  ethnology
apartheid 1
Arabs 137
archives 11–12, 135–6, 152–3, 208–9,
  237–9
ariki, see rangatira
Arnold, Thomas 5, 136
aroha 187, 224–7, 250; see also
  whanaungatanga
Aryanism 16, 244–5
assimilation 15
Auckland 90, 100–2, 174, 181
aukati 200–2, 204
Australia 1, 12, 83, 90, 96, 98, 250–1
  aborigines 65, 70, 83, 98, 134–6,
    148, 155
  colonial discourses 83, 98, 134–6
  New South Wales 41, 54, 90
  South Australia 28–30, 108

Sydney 35, 54, 76
  Tasmania 249–50
Austria 216
Azjenstat, Janet 39

Ballantyne, Tony 8, 16, 215–16, 245
banks (savings) 110
Baring, Francis 28
Barrett, Nathaniel 203
Bartlett, Thomas 189
Bartlett, William 189
Bay of Islands 72–4, 123–4
Beecham, John 36
Bennett, Harry 223–4
Belich, James 99, 176
Bennett, Harry 223–4
Bent, Kimble 197
Beria, see Peria
Betts, Raymond 164
Bible 231–2
  Biblical history 3–4, 137, 147–8
Binney, Judith 19, 20, 99, 183, 193–4
Board of Trade 92
bodies 54–5, 60–1, 79, 89, 110, 191–2, 219
Boultbee, John 66
Bonaparte, Napoleon 159
Bonwick, James 165
Bounty mutineers 7
Bowen, George 227–30
Brace, Charles 165
British Army 109, 156, 187
  12th Regiment 197
  57th Regiment 197
  65th Regiment 197–8
British Association for the Advancement of
  Science 141, 145–6, 150–1,
  158, 226
British Empire 1–14, 27–9, 35–42, 52–5,
  80–1
  and abolition 41–2
  expansionism 90–3
  liberalism of 41–2, 239–43
  problems 6–14
  racial discourses 133–5, 141–70,
    237–43
  wars 172–4, 177–8
  see also Colonial Office, liberalism, racial
    amalgamation, systematic
    colonization

McLean, Edward Baker 194
Maketu 193
Malayans 166
Malthus, Thomas 96, 97
Maitapapa 19, 68–9
Mana 57, 200, 219, 227–8, 232
  see also sovereignty
Maniapoto, Rewi 235–6
Maning, Frederick 206–7, 249–50
Maning, Maria Aminta 5, 249–50
Māori *see* Tangata Whenua
  terminology 21–4, 109, 156, 212
marae 215, 226
Marists (Society of Mary) 81–2
market policies 40–1, 124–5
Markham, Edward 71
marriage 58–60, 78–81, 106, 112–14,
  185–213
  Christian marriage 79–82
  and slavery 80
  see also civilizing natives; family,
    illegitimacy, *whanau*;
    whanaungatanga
Married Women's Property Act (1884) 212
Marsden, Samuel 76–7, 80–1
Martin, Ged 38
Matawhero Killings 194–5
Matthew, Patrick 34–6
Mauaranui, Riria 87
Maxwell, Andrew (Anaru Makihara) 129,
  208
Maxwell, George 129
Maxwell, James 129
Maxwell, John 129
Maxwell, Ngeungeu 129–30
Maxwell, Patrick 129
Maxwell, Robert 129
Maxwell, Thomas 129–30
Mecca 227
mediators, 70, 72, 121, 220, 222, 225,
  231–5
medicine 110–11
Mehta, Uday 239–40
Melbourne, 2nd Viscount 29
Merivale, Herman 94–6, 98, 147, 157, 242
Meurant, Eliza (Kenehuru) 173
Mihinoa, Paeata 202
Mill, John Stuart 240–1
Milner's Church History 10
missionaries 36–7, 47–8, 61, 75–82,
  113–21, 144, 201, 216
Mitford, John Guise 124
Mixed race people 95–6, 133–41
  Britain 137, 162–6, 167, 240
  Eurasians 7

education of 114–21, 249–50
  French 195, 240
  Haitian 217–18
  Métis 2, 6, 7, 143
  Mulattoes 6, 80, 134, 137, 149, 166
  New Zealand 16–20, 32–3, 51–2, 64,
    67–9, 74–5, 82–9, 106–7, 110–121,
    126–31, 155–7, 183–230
  as objects of study 133–70
  terms for, 6, 21–4, 82, 84, 190–1;
    see also hybridity
moa 166–8
moa hunters 166–8
Moengaroa, Te Hikutu *see* Moengaroa
  Te Hikutu
Moffat, William 197
Molesworth, William 28
Mongolian (race) 166
monogenesis 3–4, 133–41, 145, 147–52
Moore, James 140
Morant Bay Uprising 108, 239, 240
Moriori (pre-Māori people)
  see Moa-hunters
Morgan, John 5, 115–21
Morgan, Maria 118
Motutapu 129–30
Müller, Frederich Max 155
Mulvaney, D.J. 135
Murchison, Roderick 141, 146, 155,
Murihiku 65–6, 118–20, 183
Muriwhenua 183
Murphy, Humphrey 197

Native Americans 95, 96, 172
Native Department 105
Native Exemption Ordinance 109
Native reserves 30–2, 43–6, 51
Native Land Act 205
Native Land Court 125, 189, 205–9,
  225, 228
Native Trust Ordinance 106, 111
nature 3, 34–6, 40, 98, 138–9, 150,
  159–62, *see also* climate, race, science
Negri, Antonio 9
negroes *see* Africans, African Americans
Nelson 46
Nene, Tamati Waka 207
networks 8–10, 13, 16, 135–6, 146–7,
  152, 154–5
'new system' *see* systematic colonization
New Zealand
  Colonial Office 36–7, 91–113
  colonial rule 99–132, 171–230
  early encounters 55–69, 82–9
  historiography 14–25, 171–2, 175

Printed in Great Britain
by Amazon